Forensic Firearm Examination

Forensic Firearm Examination

CHRIS MONTURO

Precision Forensic Testing, LLC, Centerville, Ohio, United States

Hamilton County Coroner's Office Crime Laboratory, Cincinnati, Ohio, United States

ACADEMIC PRESS

An imprint of Elsevier

Academic Press is an imprint of Elsevier
125 London Wall, London EC2Y 5AS, United Kingdom
525 B Street, Suite 1650, San Diego, CA 92101, United States
50 Hampshire Street, 5th Floor, Cambridge, MA 02139, United States
The Boulevard, Langford Lane, Kidlington, Oxford OX5 1GB, United Kingdom

Copyright © 2019 Elsevier Inc. All rights reserved.

No part of this publication may be reproduced or transmitted in any form or by any means, electronic or mechanical, including photocopying, recording, or any information storage and retrieval system, without permission in writing from the publisher. Details on how to seek permission, further information about the Publisher's permissions policies and our arrangements with organizations such as the Copyright Clearance Center and the Copyright Licensing Agency, can be found at our website: www.elsevier.com/permissions.

This book and the individual contributions contained in it are protected under copyright by the Publisher (other than as may be noted herein).

Notices
Knowledge and best practice in this field are constantly changing. As new research and experience broaden our understanding, changes in research methods, professional practices, or medical treatment may become necessary.

Practitioners and researchers must always rely on their own experience and knowledge in evaluating and using any information, methods, compounds, or experiments described herein. In using such information or methods they should be mindful of their own safety and the safety of others, including parties for whom they have a professional responsibility.

To the fullest extent of the law, neither the Publisher nor the authors, contributors, or editors, assume any liability for any injury and/or damage to persons or property as a matter of products liability, negligence or otherwise, or from any use or operation of any methods, products, instructions, or ideas contained in the material herein.

British Library Cataloguing-in-Publication Data
A catalogue record for this book is available from the British Library

Library of Congress Cataloging-in-Publication Data
A catalog record for this book is available from the Library of Congress

ISBN: 978-0-12-814539-5

For Information on all Academic Press publications
visit our website at https://www.elsevier.com/books-and-journals

Publisher: Stacy Masucci
Acquisition Editor: Elizabeth Brown
Editorial Project Manager: Megan Ashdown
Production Project Manager: Vijayaraj Purushothaman
Cover Designer: Matthew Limbert

Typeset by MPS Limited, Chennai, India

Contents

List of contributors   *xi*
Foreword   *xiii*
Acknowledgments   *xv*

1. History of forensic firearm examination   **1**

2. Firearm nomenclature   **3**
    Barrel   3
    Breech face   3
    Cartridge case head   3
    Chamber   3
    Cylinder   3
    Ejector   3
    Ejection port   5
    Extractor   5
    Firing pin   5
    Firing pin aperture   5
    Gas port   5
    Hammer   6
    Magazine   7
    Mandrel   7
    Muzzle   8
    Obturation   8
    Pistol   8
    Polygonal rifling   8
    Practical impossibility   8
    Primer   9
    Projectile   9
    Propellant   9
    Rifling marks   9
    Rifling twist   10
    Safety mechanism   10
    Sear   11
    Striker   11
    Trigger   11
    Firearm types   11
    Semiautomatic firearm   11

Gas-operated semiautomatic firearms	14
Revolvers	14
Lever action	16
Pump action	16
Bolt action	17
Break open	17
Derringers	18
Shotguns	20

3. Ammunition 21

Primers	21
Gunpowder	23
Bullets	25
Full metal jacket	27
Copper-plated bullet	29
Jacketed soft point	29
Jacketed hollow point	30
Solid copper hollow point	30
Wadcutter	31
Semiwadcutter	31
Lead round nose	33
Spitzer bullet	33
Boattail	33
Cannelure	34
Special purpose/premium ammunition	35
Federal ammunition	36
Speer	41
Remington	41
Hornady	42
Aguila	44
Starfire	45
Browning jacketed hollow point	46
Specialty ammunition by design	49
Glaser safety slugs	50
Solid copper bullets	51
Frangible ammunition	53
Subsonic ammunition	54
Manufacturer identifiers on bullets	55
Caliber	57
Cartridge case	58
Rifle ammunition	59

Belted base	60
Wildcat cartridges	60
Shotgun ammunition	61
Shotgun gauge	61
Wad	62
Shot	64
Alternative shot compositions	65
Shotgun slugs	66
Shotgun chokes	69
Types of chokes	69
Rimfire ammunition	69
Necked Down Rimfire Ammunition	70

4. Fundamentals of forensic firearm examination — 73

Types of marks for comparison purposes	73
Impressed toolmarks	73
Striated toolmarks	74
Class characteristics of cartridge cases	75
Cycle of operation	76
Class characteristics of the firing pin	79
Rectangular/elliptical firing pins	80
Flat-based firing pins	83
Class characteristics of the firing pin aperture	84
Class characteristics of a firearm barrel	88
Individual characteristics	93

5. Firearm manufacturing techniques — 95

Mechanics of machining	95
Surface roughness	96
Chip formation	98
Built-up edge	98
Plowing	100
Sideflow	101
Shearing	102
Chatter	103
Tool wear	105
Pressure weld	108
Types of machining	108
Grinding	108
Machining methods used in the manufacturing of firearm parts	114
Electrical discharge machining	129

Stamping	131
Metal injection molding	135
Powdered metal	136
Die casting	137
Investment casting	138
Finishing processes of firearm parts	138
Abrasive blasting	138
Tumbling	139
Chrome plating	140
Parkerization	141

6. Barrel manufacturing and rifling — 143

Barrel drilling and reaming	143
Hook rifling	145
Broach rifling	145
Hammer forging	148
Button rifling	150
Electrochemical rifling	152
Cast barrels	154
Honing and lapping	155

7. Equipment used for forensic firearm examination — 157

Comparison microscope	158
Stereo microscope	160
Balance	160
Calipers	160
Linear measuring device	160
Force gauge	162

8. Comparison of cartridge cases — 163

Primer flow back	168
Aperture shear	168
Firing pin drag	172
Firing pin drag as a result of incidental interaction	173
Firing pin	175
Firing pin bounce	176
Firing pin contact as a result of cycling	177
Ejector	178
Extractor	183
Chamber marks	187
Ejection port marks	187

Magazine marks	189
Slide drag	190
Bunter marks	191
Individual characteristic comparison	193

9. Comparison of bullets — 195
Individual characteristics resulting from alteration	202
Alternative comparisons involving bullets	203

10. Documentation, notes, and reports — 205
Documentation	205
Marking evidence	206
Report writing	209

11. The expert witness — 211
Bias	211
Contextual bias	211
Confirmation bias	213
Ethics and court testimony	214
Court testimony	215

12. Subclass characteristics in firearm examination — 219
Subclass characteristics	219
Subclass due to tool manufacture	219
Subclass due to tool use	220
Examples of tool use causing subclass characteristics	222
Subclass marks on breech faces	225
Subclass in barrels	227
Summary of subclass in rifled barrels	229
Subclass due to damage and wear	229
Subclass due to manufacturing method	231
Ways to avoid subclass misidentification	233

13. Pitfalls and challenging comparisons — 235
Preexisting marks	235
Reloading and associated marks	239
Marks from previous interaction	241
Differences in ammunition	242
Bullet seating marks	243
Incorrect ammunition usage	245
Aperture shear presence and absence	246

Ported barrels	247
Replacement barrels	247
Convex and blown out primer	248
Cartridges made from different calibers	249
Subcaliber devices	252
Sabot cartridges	253
Copper plated bullets	254
Multiple loads in a single cartridge	255
Frangible ammunition	259
Manufacturer coatings	260
Manufacturer primer sealant	262

14. Legal challenges to the science of forensic firearm examination — 265
Ronald Nichols

15. Emerging technology in comparisons — 275
T.V. Vorburger, J. Song, N. Petraco and R. Lilien

Introduction	275
Topography measurement	277
Analysis and parameters	283
Standards, traceability, and uncertainty for topography measurements	295
Ballistics identification systems in the crime lab	299
Ongoing issues and opportunities	302
Conclusions	304
Acknowledgments	304

References	*305*
Index	*313*

List of Contributors

R. Lilien
Cadre Research Labs, Chicago, IL, United States

Ronald Nichols
Nichols Forensic Science Consulting, Antioch CA, United States

N. Petraco
John Jay College and The Graduate Center, City University of New York, New York, NY, United States

J. Song
National Institute of Standards and Technology (NIST), Gaithersburg, MD, United States

T.V. Vorburger
National Institute of Standards and Technology (NIST), Gaithersburg, MD, United States

Foreword

I was flattered when Chris Monturo asked me to write the foreword for his book. Then I read his manuscript and realized I was being given the unique opportunity to reflect on the intersection of my professional life as a state judge for 30 years and my personal life as the daughter of the late Walter J. Howe.

My father authored his first book, *Professional Gunsmithing*, in 1946. The book remains in print today. Although only as technically precise as the knowledge base for gunsmithing at that time, my father's book shares many features with Chris Monturo's book.

In each instance, the reader is provided with a more-than-substantial "how to" treatise. Monturo's book, like my father's, contains numerous illustrations, diagrams, and cut-aways.

Most importantly, both books provide a step-by-step narrative for each topic, which readers must master to hold themselves out as professionals in their respective fields of study—gunsmithing and forensic firearm examination.

In Monturo's new book, however, the "student reader" is being challenged in a much more multifaceted and complex way than the aspiring gunsmith reading my father's 1946 book.

This brings me to the next intersection between Monturo's extraordinary book and my father's contributions to the field of firearm examination. As the reader learns early on in Monturo's book, the anecdotal use of firearm examination to "solve a crime" dates back at least as far as 1835. Professional presentations on specific aspects of firearm examination—such as rifling marks on fired bullets and the observation of individual extractor marks and firing pin impressions—appear in the early 1900s.

A review of early instances offering credible testimony about the likelihood that a subject projectile was fired from a particular firearm is important reading. It also illustrates how legal scrutiny of the work of firearm examiners has increased exponentially in each decade since the early 1900s.

This brings us to another milestone in the profession of forensic firearm examination—the founding of the Association of Firearm and Tool Mark Examiners (AFTE). AFTE was founded in Chicago, Illinois in 1969, essentially by a "spin off" group of fellows and associates of the American Academy of Forensic Sciences. My father was one of the founders and also the first president of the association and the first editor of the *AFTE Journal*. I remember from the association's inception in 1969 until my father's passing in 2011, his commitment was that AFTE would always be about developing, advancing, and promulgating scientific aspects of firearm and tool mark identification in an unbiased manner, and therefore participation in the association never would be limited to examiners who worked for a particular "side" on these issues.

I provide this backdrop about AFTE to commend Monturo's book to any examiner or potential expert in a related field. In my role as a judge, I observed expert witnesses struggle because they disregarded fundamentals laid out in this book's chapters on "the expert witness" and "legal challenges to the science of forensic firearm examination." The state of the law, with judges as gatekeepers as to what type of testimony can be offered by an expert in a particular field, is such that an examiner who has mastered the substantive materials in this treatise—starting with the firearm nomenclature from the AFTE Glossary and continuing to the "what to expect in court" materials—should be at the same time cautious and confident in any situation. For this, all of us should thank Chris Monturo.

Barbara Howe PhD, JD
NY State Supreme Court and Surrogate Court Judge (retired)

Acknowledgments

It goes without saying that I was anticipating my family to be supportive throughout my efforts to complete this work. However, it was not until I set forth and entrenched myself in research and typing that I realized how important my wife and kids support is in undertaking such a monumental task. There were countless missed practices and games with my boys, Connor and Gavin and date nights with my wife, Meredith. Without their silent understanding and support, I would not have continued with my efforts.

Looking back further, my career and love for firearms, mechanics, forensics, and science would not have entered my thoughts without the support and encouragement from three people essential in my earlier years. My dad taught me the sport of shooting early on and his love for learning how things work was passed on to me. As with my family, my mom encouraged hard work, my mom was one of my biggest supporters. My passion for science can be attributed to my high school science teacher, Dean Deerhake, who challenged me to succeed.

Along my professional career, there have been countless people who have been essential in helping me to work harder, learn more, and provide me with the information and tools to do so. To maintain an acknowledgment section of reasonable length, I will only mention a few. Tom Deeb, who was a great friend to me and friend of the Forensic Firearm community—a man who devoted his life to his family and firearms. Jim Hamby, a Forensic Firearm Examiner who throughout his career has welcomed new examiners into the field and encouraged research and publication.

Thank you all for your support, encouragement, and sharing of information.

CHAPTER 1

History of forensic firearm examination

One of the earliest documented cases where a bullet was compared to a firearm dates back to 1835 in London, England, where a homeowner was shot, and the suspect was a servant. In this case, the examination involved marks from the bullet mold. In the 1800s, bullets were made by pouring molten lead into a mold in the shape of the bullet. Any imperfections in the bullet mold will be transferred onto the bullet. While this was not a case involving comparison of rifling marks which firearm examiners use to identify a bullet to a barrel, it does utilize the imperfections caused by the manufacturing process of the bullet mold.

Throughout the mid to late 1800s, there were several other comparisons involving various characteristics of the bullets. In 1863, General Stonewall Jackson was killed on the battlefield during the Civil War. The bullet that was removed from his body was examined, and the caliber (bullet diameter) and design had the characteristics of those used by his army. During that time, they were issued firearms that used a .67 caliber ball, whereas the Union used .58 caliber minie ball projectiles (Hamby and Thorpe, 1999).

One of the earliest articles on the examination of rifling marks on fired bullets were presented at the 32nd annual meeting of the Medical Association of Central New York at Syracuse, New York, on October 17, 1899 by A.L. Hall. This presentation was later published in 1900 in the Buffalo Medical Journal in a work titled, "The Missile and the Weapon." In this article the author states, "I have known of an instance where bullet defacement resulted from the sight being driven through the rifling with the effect of invariably producing a noticeable tear upon the surface of a bullet when fired." This is a clear documentation of both class and individual characteristics. In addition, the author describes test firing the firearm into a bag of meal for the recovery of a test-fired bullet (Hall and Fairhaven, 1900).

The use of forensic firearm examination with respect to rifling characteristics in the United States dates back to 1902 in the case of Commonwealth versus Best where an expert was able to demonstrate comparisons of photographs of the bullets recovered from the victim to those of a bullet that was pushed through the barrel of the suspect firearm.

Another historic event in the evaluation of cartridge cases for evidentiary purposes occurred in 1907. In this case, a riot in Brownsville, Texas, resulted in 150–200 shots having been fired allegedly from soldiers from a nearby US Army Infantry Regiment.

Subsequently, 39 fired .30 caliber cartridge cases were found. The cartridge cases were sent to Frankfort Arsenal for examination. The staff there compared the test-fired cartridge cases from firearms belonging to members of the US Army. After their efforts to determine the source of the cartridges, it was determined that 33 of 39 cartridge cases were identified back to four rifles by the Frankfort Arsenal in Philadelphia. They did this by test firing the rifles and comparing the firing pin impressions on the test-fired cartridge cases to the cartridge cases recovered from the event (US War Department, 1907).

A presentation given by Victor Balthazard on May 20, 1912 at the Conference of Forensic Medicine, and later published in the Archives of the Anthology of Crime and Forensic Medicine on June 15, 1913, discussed firearm examination. In this presentation, the individualization of both fired bullets and cartridge cases to a specific firearm was discussed. At an even more in-depth examination of firearms, the observation of extractor marks and firing pin impressions was evaluated. The use of individual characteristics in these comparisons is the basis of modern forensic firearm examination.

CHAPTER 2

Firearm nomenclature

The following definitions of firearm components and associated terms are defined by the Association of Firearm and Toolmark Examiners Glossary (2013).

Barrel

That part of a firearm through which a projectile or shot charge travels under the impetus of powder gasses, compressed air, or other like means. A barrel may be rifled or smooth.

Breech face

That part of the breechblock or breech bolt which locks against the rear of the chamber and is against the head of the cartridge case or shotshell during firing (Fig. 2.1).

Cartridge case head

The base of the cartridge case which contains the primer.

Chamber

The rear part of the barrel bore that has been formed to accept a specific cartridge or shotshell. In a revolver the holes in the cylinder represent multiple chambers (Fig. 2.2).

Cylinder

The rotating component of a firearm, typically a revolver, that contains the chambers.

Ejector

A mechanical device that expels a cartridge, cartridge case, or shotshell from a firearm (Fig. 2.3).

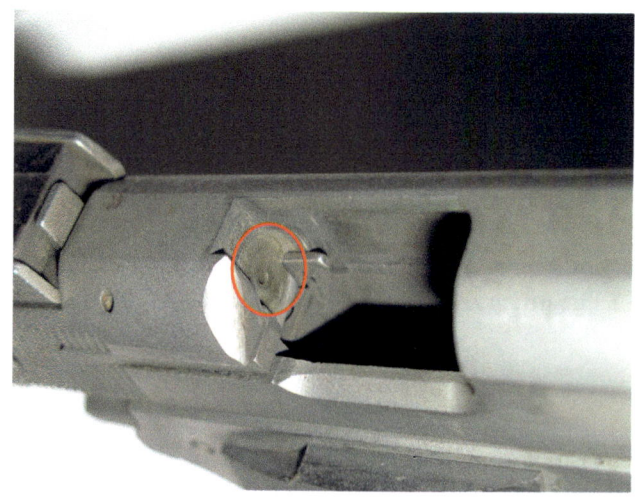

Figure 2.1 Breech face circled.

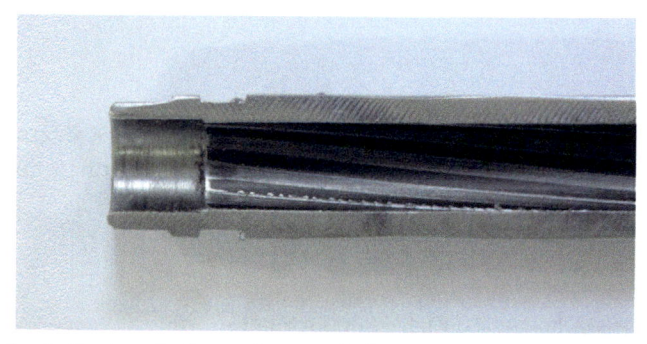

Figure 2.2 Chamber in the barrel of a semiautomatic firearm.

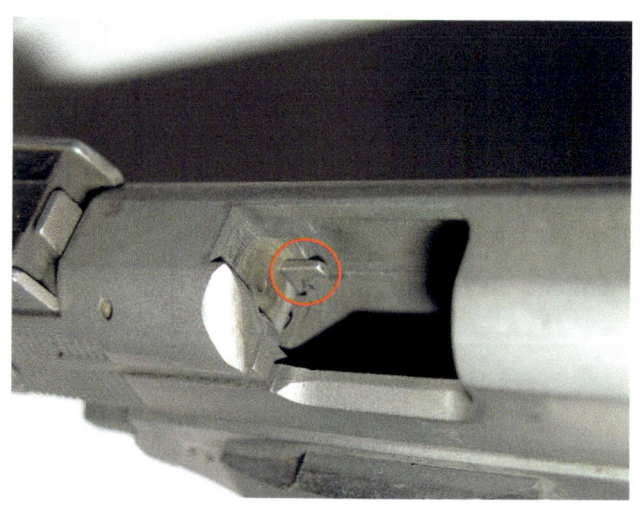

Figure 2.3 Ejector circled.

Figure 2.4 Extractor circled.

Ejection port

An opening in the receiver or slide to allow for ejection of a cartridge, cartridge case, or shotshell.

Extractor

The component of a firearm designed to remove the cartridge, cartridge case, or shotshell from the chamber of the firearm (Fig. 2.4).

Firing pin

The part of a firearm mechanism which strikes the primer or rim of a cartridge to initiate the firing sequence. In some revolvers, it is the nose of the hammer, or in some semiautomatic firearms, it is referred to as a striker (Figs. 2.5 and 2.6).

Firing pin aperture

The opening in the breech face of a firearm through which the firing pin protrudes (Fig. 2.7).

Gas port

An opening in the barrel or receiver of a firearm that serves several purposes: (1) to allow the vented gas to operate a mechanism, (2) to reduce recoil, and (3) to provide

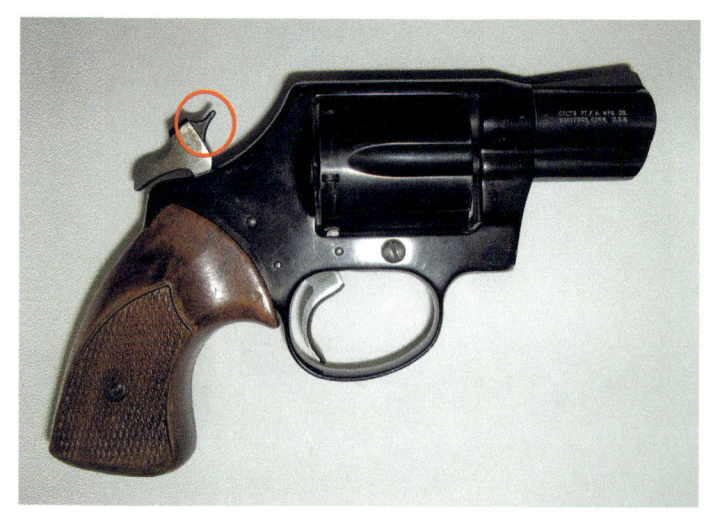

Figure 2.5 Firing pin incorporated with the hammer of a revolver.

Figure 2.6 Firing pin in a semiautomatic pistol.

an escape route for high-pressure gases should a case or primer rupture occurs upon firing, reducing the amount of gas that might be directed back through the action into the shooter's face (Fig. 2.8).

Hammer

A component of the firing mechanism which strikes the firing pin or primer.

Figure 2.7 Aperture circled.

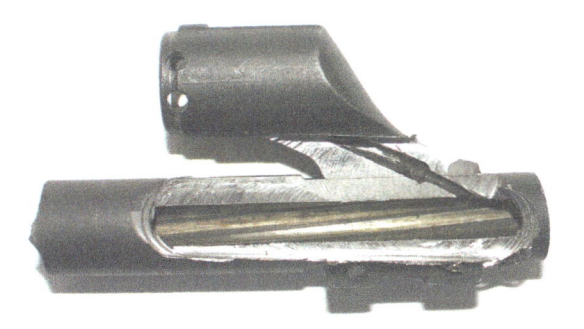

Figure 2.8 Gas port.

Magazine

A receptacle attached to or inserted into a firearm that holds cartridges stacked on top of one another ready for feeding into the chamber (see Fig. 2.9).

Mandrel

A metal rod or bar used as a core around which metal, wire, etc. is cast, molded, forged, or shaped.

Figure 2.9 Hammer on a semiautomatic pistol with magazine removed from the firearm.

Muzzle

The end of a firearm barrel from which the projectile emerges.

Obturation

The sealing of a bore and chamber by pressure. During the firing process, pressure swells the cartridge case against the chamber walls, which minimizes the rearward flow of gases between the case and the chamber wall. The same pressure, applied to the base of the projectile, causes it to swell or upset, filling and sealing the bore.

Pistol

A handgun in which the chamber is integral with the barrel.

Polygonal rifling

Lands and grooves having a rounded profile instead of the traditional rectangular profile. Polygonal rifling is often seen in hammer forged barrels (Fig. 2.10).

Practical impossibility

A phrase, which currently cannot be expressed in mathematical terms, that describes an event that has an extremely small probability of occurring in theory, but which empirical testing and experience has shown will not occur. In the context of firearm

Figure 2.10 Ploygonal rifled barrel.

and toolmark examination, "practical impossibility" means that based on (1) extensive empirical research and validation studies and (2) the cumulative results of training and casework examinations that have either been performed, peer-reviewed, or published in peer-reviewed forensic journals; no firearms or tools other than those identified in any particular case will be found that produce marks exhibiting sufficient agreement for identification.

Primer

The ignition component of a cartridge (Fig. 2.11).

Projectile

An object propelled by an external force and continuing in motion by its own inertia (for example, a bullet propelled from a firearm by the force of rapidly burning gases or other means).

Propellant

In a firearm the chemical composition that generates gas when ignited by the primer. The gas propels the projectile(s) down the barrel. Also known as gunpowder.

Rifling marks

Rifling impressions on the surface of a fired bullet. Also known as bullet engraving.

Figure 2.11 Primer circled.

Rifling twist

The direction (right or left) and rate at which the rifling of the firearm turns within the bore. This is normally expressed as the distance required for the rifling (and projectile) to make one complete revolution. Depending on the origin of the firearm, this may be written in inches or in millimeters (e.g., 1 turn in 12 in. or 1 turn in 305 mm).

Safety mechanism

A device on a firearm intended to help in providing protection against unintentional discharge under normal usage when properly engaged, or "on". Such a mechanism is considered "off" when it is set to allow the firearm to be discharged by a normal pull of the trigger. A manual safety is one that must be manually engaged and subsequently disengaged to permit normal firing. An automatic safety is one that goes to the "on" position when the action of the gun is opened. A passive safety is in place (or "on") until the trigger is pulled. An example would be the transfer bar system in some revolvers.

Figure 2.12 Striker from a semiautomatic pistol.

Sear

A part which retains the hammer or striker in the cocked position until the trigger is pulled.

Striker

A rod-like firing pin or a separate component which impinges on the firing pin (Fig. 2.12).

Trigger

The part of a firearm mechanism that is moved manually to cause the firearm to discharge.

Firearm types

Firearms are designed with different operating mechanisms depending on the end use of the firearm and desire of the customer. The types of firearms range from those which will fire all ammunition from the feeding device with the single pull of a trigger to those which only have the capacity and ability to fire one. In addition, there are those which extract the cartridge case for the next one to fire and those that retain the cartridge case within the firearm.

Semiautomatic firearm

Currently, the most commonly sold firearm is the semiautomatic pistol. These handguns are designed to fire a cartridge with each pull of the trigger. The firearm will use the energy of the discharge of the cartridge to drive the slide rearward. In doing so the extractor will pull the fired cartridge case from the chamber, and the ejector will assist in kicking the fired cartridge case out of the ejection port. As the slide, which has already extracted and ejected the fired cartridge, completes its rearward travel, it also recocks the hammer or striker; it will then return forward under spring tension. During its forward travel, the slide will strip a cartridge from the magazine and feed into the chamber of the barrel. The magazine is the ammunition source for semiautomatic pistols. Generally, the magazine is a rectangular spring-loaded box that contains the cartridges. At this point, the firearm is ready to be fired again and repeat the cycle. It is important to note that each of these cycles will result in a cartridge case being ejected from the firearm.

There are several ways that semiautomatics contain the pressure prior to extracting and ejecting the cartridge case. They range from simple designs that have minimally integrated components to complex designs that require the interaction of multiple parts to complete the cycling.

The most basic of the designs is blowback. In these types of firearms, the slide is not locked by any physical means, and the cartridge is held in the chamber by a spring pushing the slide forward. The mass of the slide is the force used to contain the cartridge at the time of discharge. As the cartridge size and pressure increases, the required weight of the slide increases to assist in containing the energy from the discharged cartridge. The most commonly encountered firearms in forensic laboratories that are of this design include Hi-Point, Davis, Lorcin, and Raven semiautomatic pistols. In addition, due to the relatively low pressure of the cartridge, most .22 caliber semiautomatic pistols are blowbacks.

Another common design utilized in semiautomatic firearms is the recoil operated. In these types of firearms, the breechblock (slide when discussing semiautomatic pistols) is not physically locked against the cartridge; however, there is a mechanism to hold the cartridge in place until the initial pressure peak has subsided. When this occurs, the mechanism releases the action to allow for ejection and extraction of the cartridge. Semiautomatic pistols of this design typically demonstrate this action by incorporating a tilting barrel that will drop slightly by a mechanical action and allow the slide to travel rearward (Figs. 2.13 and 2.14).

The method to engage the barrel to the slide can be done either with a physical linkage such as that used in the 1911 design by John Browning or by means of an angled ledge machined into the barrel to engage the slide such as that used by Glock pistols. These designs allow for the use of a lighter slide because the firearm does not rely on the mass of the slide to absorb the entire amount of energy created during the discharge of a firearm.

While the typical design of recoil operation incorporates a tilting barrel, there are exceptions to this. One of the most prolific examples of this is the Beretta/Taurus 92 models. These firearms have a detachable barrel that moves linearly to the slide. Therefore, it does not produce an aperture shear on the resulting fired cartridge case.

Figure 2.13 Firearm with the barrel locked into position.

Figure 2.14 Barrel tilting downward as part of the cycling operation.

This is accomplished with the use of a separate pivoting lug underneath the barrel, which acts as the linking mechanism like that used in 1911 style designs.

Another example of recoil operation is found on the Beretta Storm full-sized semi-automatic pistols series. These are designed to absorb the initial recoil through rotation of the barrel on lugs within recessed areas machined in the slide. This type of recoil operation was patented by John Browning in 1897 (US Patent number US580925).

A different design that is used to retain the barrel in position until the pressures have subsided is the delayed blowback design. In this type of action the firearm accommodates the delay of the system by manufacturing flutes in the chamber for the passage of gas between the cartridge case and chamber. When the initial pressure has subsided, the bolt can move rearward. An example of this is the Heckler & Koch MP-5 series of firearms. The barrel in these firearms is in a fixed position, and the bolt moves directly to the rear.

In addition to pistols, some long guns utilize the semiautomatic platform. Rifles work in the same fashion in that they extract and eject cartridges during the firing cycle. They may use the same mechanisms as previously discussed with semiautomatic pistols. However, rifles are more versatile due to the larger platform allowing for more options. These actions include gas operated, lever, bolt, pump, and slide action.

Gas-operated semiautomatic firearms

Some semiautomatic rifles that are centerfire are chambered for bottleneck cartridges that use a larger amount of gunpowder resulting in higher pressures. One method rifles overcome these pressures in the locking system is to use the gas produced from the discharge of the cartridge to cycle the action of the firearm. In these types of firearms the bolt remains locked and holds the cartridge in the chamber until the gas of the discharged cartridge passes by the gas port. Once the bullet passes the gas port, the gas enters a tube and forces the bolt rearward. The delay between the time of the discharge and the bullet passing the gas port allows the initial pressure to drop to a safe level for the cycling of the cartridge. In addition to centerfire rifles using this system, there are a few semiautomatic pistols that also use a gas-operated system. One of the most common is the Desert Eagle .357 Magnum and larger caliber pistols. Due to the limited space of the handgun platform, a gas tube is not used. Instead, the gas directly encounters the action via a plug below the gas port.

Revolvers

Revolvers are similar to semiautomatic pistols in that they are designed to be fired with one hand. As the name implies, the firearm functions by revolving the cartridges into a firing position. Revolvers have a cylinder which contains chambers that hold the cartridges (Figs. 2.15 and 2.16).

Revolvers can hold anywhere from 5 to 12 cartridges depending on the caliber. These firearms are different than semiautomatic firearms in that they do not eject the cartridge when fired. Instead, the cartridge case remains in the cylinder when fired and is not released from the firearm until the cylinder is manually opened and the cartridge cases are removed by the extractor. In addition, reloading these firearms require the separate insertion of each cartridge into the respective chamber.

Figure 2.15 Revolver with an empty cylinder opened.

Figure 2.16 Revolver with cylinder opened and loaded with cartridges.

Revolvers can be fired by two methods: single action and double action. In single action revolvers the trigger performs one action only; release the hammer. In these types of firearms, the hammer must be manually pulled back, or cocked. At this point, the hammer is under spring tension. When the trigger is pulled, it releases the hammer allowing it to fall on the cartridge in the cylinder. After the cartridge has been ignited, the firearm has completed its' cycle. To fire the next shot with a single action revolver, the hammer must be manually retracted. These types of revolvers are among the oldest design and were common in the late 1800s.

In contrast to the single-action revolvers, there are double-action revolvers. In these types of firearms, the trigger can perform two actions. It can both retract the hammer and release it. The double-action revolver does not require manual manipulation of the hammer to fire; instead, the operator can rapidly fire the firearm with each pull of the trigger. And like the single-action revolver, the cartridge remains in the cylinder until it is physically removed.

Some revolvers are designed to be both single and double action. These revolvers function by giving the shooter the option of how the hammer is manipulated (prior to or in conjunction with the pull of the trigger). This is the most commonly manufactured type of revolver currently. The benefit to the double/single-action revolver is that in single action the trigger pull is lighter and is typically more accurate due to less interaction with the firearm. However, it can also be fired in a double-action fashion. This type of firearm is used by both target and action shooters.

Lever action

The lever action is suitable for any cartridge from .22 rimfire through centerfire rifle cartridges. In this type of action the cartridge is locked into position by the bolt which is actuated by a lever forward of the trigger. These types of firearms can only fire one cartridge per pull of the trigger without further actuation by the operator. When the firearm discharges, the cartridge is locked into position, and to facilitate the next shot, the cartridge must be physically removed by lowering the lever, which retracts the bolt. When the bolt moves rearward, as with semiautomatic firearms, the cartridge encounters an extractor and ejector and is removed from the firearm. When the operator lifts the lever back toward the firearm in the firing position, a cartridge from the magazine is lifted and placed into the chamber. In addition, the hammer is cocked rearward. This prepares the firearm to fire a subsequent shot.

Pump action

Pump-action rifles function similar to lever action rifles in that they require a deliberate movement by the operator to facilitate the firing of the next cartridge. However, with this type of firearm, the foregrip is attached to a bar or pair of bars which ride along the length of the firearm from the foregrip to the bolt. The foregrip must be retracted and returned to the foremost position to actuate the ejection, extraction, and rechambering of the next cartridge (Fig. 2.17).

Figure 2.17 Pump action rifle.

Figure 2.18 Bolt action rifle.

Bolt action

As with the lever action and pump action, the bolt action requires operator manipulation to facilitate the chambering of the next cartridge into the chamber. However, with this type of firearm, the bolt is directly actuated by the operator to open and close the action (Fig. 2.18).

Upon retracting the bolt, the cartridge is extracted from the chamber and ejected through the ejection port. On the forward movement of the bolt, the bolt will pick up a cartridge from the magazine (if the firearm has an ammunition source) and insert it into the chamber in preparation to fire the subsequent shot.

Break open

Another type of action that is encountered occasionally in forensic crime laboratories is the break-open action. These rifles or shotguns are typically single shot with no provisions for a magazine or ammunition source. These firearms are loaded by manually opening the rifle by depressing a release button or lever which allows the action to pivot open on a hinge below the barrel/breech interface. In these types of firearms, the expended cartridge case is removed solely by an extractor. The extractor will grasp the cartridge case by the base and under spring tension, expel the cartridge case. In some circumstances the cartridge may require physical removal by the user. When loading the firearm, the cartridge must be manually inserted (Fig. 2.19).

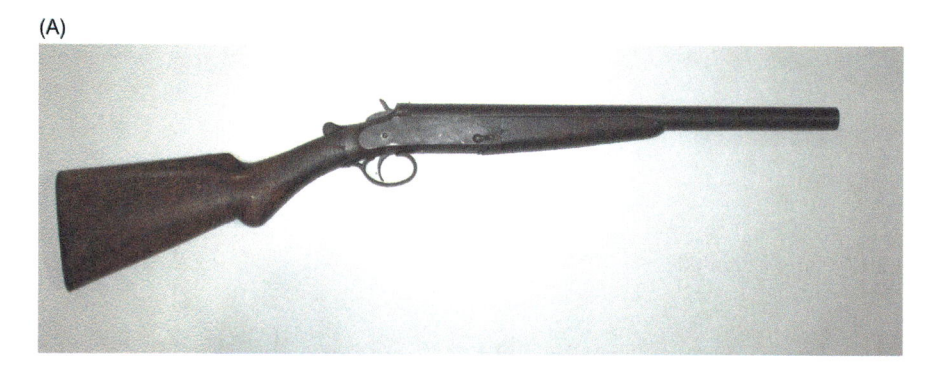

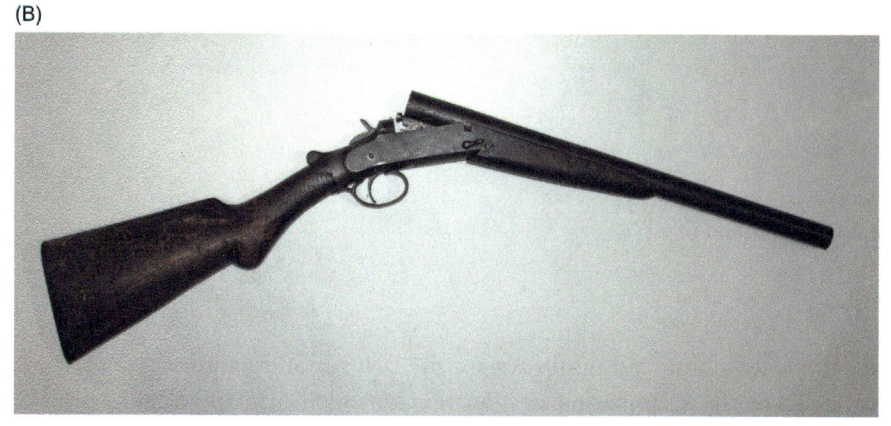

Figure 2.19 (A) Break-open shotgun in the closed, locked position; (B) break-open shotgun in the open position.

Derringers

Derringers are a type of firearm similar to a revolver in that they both require the operator to manually open the breech to load and remove the cartridges. These firearms are most commonly designed with two barrels positioned one on top of the other. Much like the break-open action, the barrels on these firearms are hinged and manually locked into place by a lever. This lever is rotated into the locked and unlocked position. When unlocked, the barrels can be pivoted up for loading and unloading. When locked, the barrels are secure for firing. These firearms fire with a single-action design. The hammer on these guns must manually be retracted to fire the firearm. The hammers on most derringer designs do not actually contact the firing pin. Instead, there is a pivoting cam that alternates locations of contact with the firing pin within the breech of the firearm (Figs. 2.20−2.22).

Figure 2.20 Derringer in the closed/locked position.

Figure 2.21 Derringer in the open position.

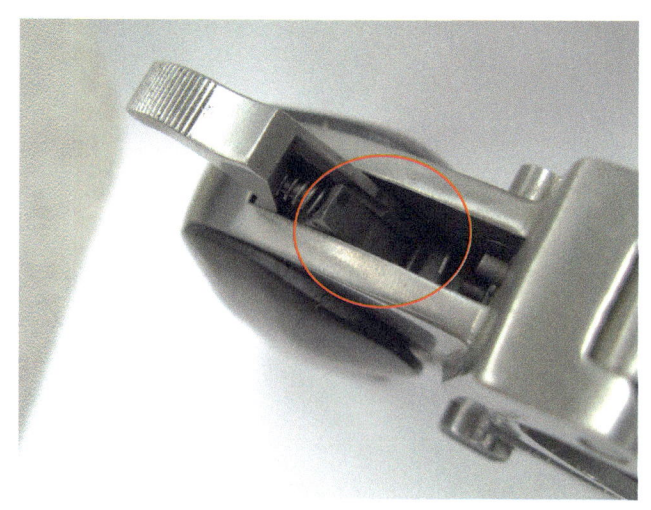

Figure 2.22 Derringer cam circled.

Shotguns

Shotguns function similarly to rifles in that they share similar designs with respect to profile. They are both traditionally designed to be fired from the shoulder. Some modern shotguns feature a pistol grip allowing it to be fired from a lower position. Shotguns utilize different ammunition than rifles or handguns. The most common type of ammunition used in shotguns contains multiple pellets in various sizes depending on the intended type of shooting. The shotgun is primarily used for hunting and sport shooting. In hunting, they can be utilized for hunting game varying in size from squirrels to deer.

Shotguns are manufactured in pump, semiautomatic gas operated, delayed locking, bolt, and break-open actions. Shotgun ammunition is naturally larger in size, which results in a general diminished magazine capacity of cartridges relative to rifles. However, fired shotgun ammunition may be exposed to the same components with respect to extractor, ejector, chamber, and magazine marks as rifles.

CHAPTER 3

Ammunition

Ammunition, also referred to as cartridges, consists of a priming system, gunpowder, a bullet, and a cartridge case which contains all the components. Historically, there have been a variety of designs to achieve the ignition of a cartridge. However, for the purpose of this book, the focus will be on modern ammunition that is currently encountered in forensic laboratories. The types of ammunition that are typically evaluated include pistol, rifle, and shotgun. The priming systems include rimfire and centerfire.

Primers

There are two priming systems used in modern ammunition, centerfire primers and rimfire primers. The centerfire primer system uses separate components placed in the rear of the cartridge in an area called the primer pocket. Centerfire primers contain a shock-sensitive explosive that will ignite or detonate when crushed between the rear of the primer cup and its internal anvil by the impact of the firing pin or striker (Fig. 3.1). The sparks created by the priming compound travel through a hole in the base of the cartridge case called the flash hole. The flash hole allows the sparks to ignite the gunpowder in the cartridge. The gunpowder then burns rapidly and produces gas, which causes obturation and propels the bullet down the barrel.

When discussing centerfire cartridge primers, there are two different types. The most common centerfire primer used in the United States is the Boxer primer design. The Boxer primer consists of all the parts to facilitate ignition, the primer cup, explosive mixture, and anvil. Therefore when the cartridge has been fired, the cartridge case can be reloaded (reused) by removing the fired primer and inserting a new primer.

The second type of centerfire primer is the Berdan primer. This is like the Boxer primer in that it has the primer cup and explosive compound; however, the anvil component is incorporated in the cartridge. Berdan primers can be distinguished from boxer primers by observing the interior of the cartridge case. Boxer primed cartridges will have one flash hole, whereas Berdan primed cartridges will have two flash holes (Fig. 3.2). Berdan primers are used widely throughout the world with the exception of the United States.

Figure 3.1 Rear image of a cartridge with the primer in the center.

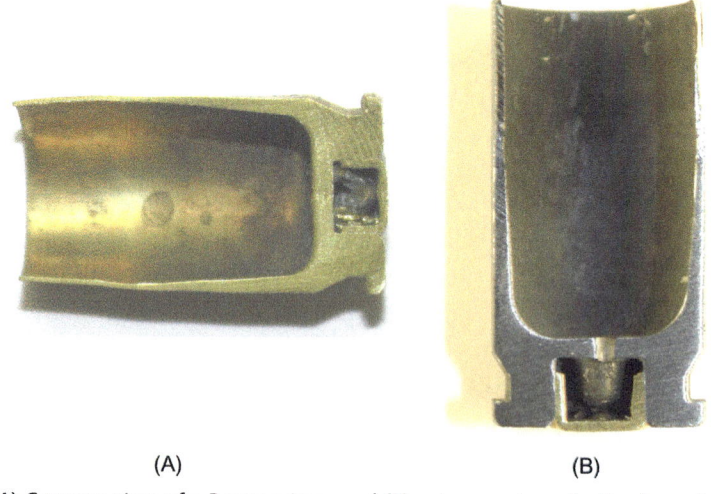

(A)　　　　　　　　　　　(B)

Figure 3.2 (A) Cutaway view of a Boxer primer and (B) cutaway view of a Berdan primer.

Rimfire primers constitute the second main priming system. In these cartridges, the priming compound is inserted along the entire rim of the base of the cartridge case. When the firing pin or striker is released, it will crush the rim resulting in ignition of the priming compound. This will in turn ignite the gunpowder. Modern rimfire cartridges are currently limited in size of .22 caliber base cartridges, but historical rimfire designs included larger caliber cartridges (Fig. 3.3).

An alternate priming system that has been developed is an electric primer. Instead of a firing pin or striker impacting the cartridge, an electrical discharge from the

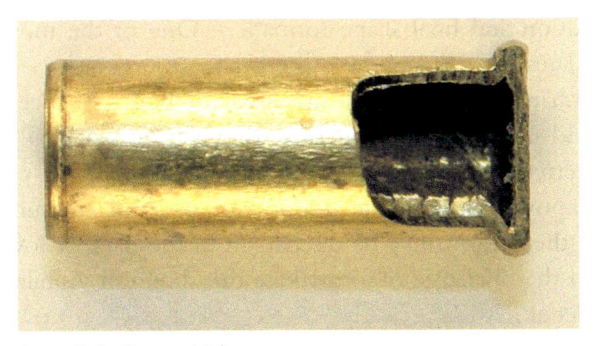

Figure 3.3 Cutaway view of rimfire cartridge.

firearm ignites the primer. The Remington 700 ETRONX is an example of this design. These are rare firearms, and the likelihood of encountering one in a forensically involved case would be extremely uncommon.

Gunpowder

Gunpowder is the propellant used to drive projectiles down the barrel of a firearm. There are a variety of gunpowder types that differ depending upon the intended purpose of the firearm and the ammunition. Gunpowders may be designed to be fast burning, slow burning, or controlled burning based on the chemical composition, shape, and coating.

Gunpowder has a long history, but for the purpose of this book, the focus will be on modern smokeless gunpowder. However, the fundamental aspects of gunpowder, the manufacturing process, and the design of gunpowder do warrant discussion.

Modern smokeless gunpowder is manufactured by combining cellulose with nitric and sulfuric acid in a controlled environment with optimized temperature, pressure, and concentration level. The absorption of nitrogen and oxygen by the cellulose results in nitrocellulose. The nitrocellulose now has the potential to explode and act as the basis for gunpowder. After production of the nitrocellulose, further steps are performed to purify the product (Dillon, 1991).

The next step involves the addition of compounds that will improve the performance of the powder. Manufacturers use a variety of additives to provide an increased shelf-life, improve forming characteristics, and control the performance aspects of the gunpowder. Stabilizers are added to gunpowder to improve the shelf-life. The decomposition of nitrocellulose produces nitric and nitrous acids which are stabilized by the diphenylamine. Without the stabilizer, the decomposition of the powder will increase the decomposition rate. Another addition to the production of gunpowder is plasticizers. Plasticizers help the nitrocellulose compound take on a consistency more conducive to extrusion and final shape formation. One of the most commonly used plasticizers is phthalates.

Performance enhancing compounds are used for both enhancements that can be observed by the end user and those integrated for performance to benefit the manufacturer. Flash deterrents are used to minimize the bright flash produced from the burning of the gunpowder. This is an important aspect for ammunition designed for self-defense where the firearm may be discharged in the dark or low-light conditions. A bright flash from the discharge of a cartridge can diminish visibility by causing brief blindness (Bussard et al., 2017a).

If the cartridge is primarily intended to be used in a handgun, such as a 9 mm or .38 Special with a relatively short barrel, the cartridge will be loaded with a faster burning powder that will maximize the use of the powder while the bullet is still in the barrel. Ammunition intended to be fired from a rifle, such as a .223 Remington or .30-06, will use powder that has been designed to burn slower, so there is a consistent push to the bullet as it travels through the longer barrel of a rifle.

To assist in controlling the intensity and rate of burn of the powder, manufacturers form the powder in different shapes. The shape of the powder determines the surface area of the gunpowder, which is a factor in the speed at which it will burn. Rifle caliber gunpowders are typically rod shaped. Other powder shapes include rod, tube, disk, ball, flattened ball, lamel, and flake (Figs. 3.4–3.10). In addition, manufacturers may apply a coating to the gunpowder. The coating can help control the burning rate, improve flow of the powder for the purposes of loading, and act as a flash suppressant to minimize flash with the firearm is fired. Gunpowder without a graphite or additional coating is naturally amber in color (Fig. 3.11).

Figure 3.4 Rod powder.

Figure 3.5 Tube powder.

Figure 3.6 Disk powder.

Bullets

A bullet is the projectile that is forced through the firearm barrel by the rapid expansion of gas produced by the burning gunpowder. Bullets are classified by their design, composition, diameter, and weight. The weight of a bullet is provided in the unit of

Figure 3.7 Ball powder.

Figure 3.8 Flattened ball powder.

grains. Grains have been traditionally used to define both the bullet and powder weight. As a means of conversion, there are 7000 grains in a pound. The intended use of the bullet will determine the shape, design, and composition of the bullet. The different designs and uses will be discussed next.

Figure 3.9 Lamel powder.

Figure 3.10 Flake powder.

Full metal jacket

The most common bullet type sold is the full metal jacket. This design has a metal jacket that encompasses a lead alloy core. The lead in all lead bullets or bullet cores has added alloys to harden them. The most common way this is achieved is through

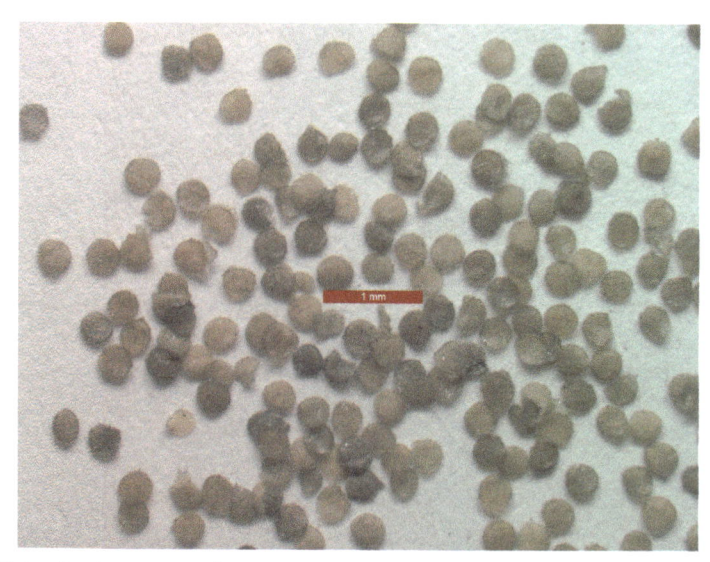

Figure 3.11 Natural color gunpowder.

Figure 3.12 Full metal jacket bullet.

the addition of antimony. The metal jacket is typically copper but can also be made from brass or copper. The main function of the metal jacket is to minimize fouling of the barrel grooves. Lead is very soft relative to copper. When bullets are only made from lead, the heat from the burning gunpowder and friction from the bullet will foul the barrel and reduce accuracy. Because of this, many shooters prefer jacketed bullets. Full metal jacketed ammunition is primarily used for target shooting (Fig. 3.12).

Figure 3.13 Copper-plated bullet on top, copper-jacketed bullet on bottom.

Copper-plated bullet

An alternative to encapsulating a lead core in a separate copper jacket is the use of electrochemical plating of the lead core with a thin layer of copper. This plating of copper that aids in reducing the fouling of the barrel, however, is not as thick as a traditionally formed copper-jacketed bullet (Fig. 3.13). Because the copper plating is electronically applied, it is not as thick as a separate copper jacket which is swaged around the lead core. The thin, electrically applied copper plating on lead cores is susceptible to being stripped off by the rifling. When this occurs, the markings from the barrel rifling can be lost with only the general land and groove widths remaining. This occurrence is discussed in greater detail in Chapter 11, The expert witness.

Jacketed soft point

The jacketed soft point bullet has a metal jacket surrounding the base and area that engages the rifling; however, the top portion is exposed lead. As discussed earlier, lead

Figure 3.14 Jacketed soft point bullet.

is soft, thus the name soft point. The bullet will have the benefit of a jacket that will minimize fouling, but the soft nose will retain the benefit of lead in that it will expand on impact. The expansion of the nose is a desirable feature for ammunition that is used for hunting or self-defense. By having an expanded bullet, there is a greater surface area; therefore the bullet is more likely to slow down quicker, stay in the target, and not overpenetrate and potentially hit an unintended target (Fig. 3.14).

Jacketed hollow point

The jacketed hollow point is similar in function to the jacketed soft point in that the bullet is designed to expand on impact with the target. However, to aid in a more reliable expansion, these bullets have a hollow cavity in the nose. The thinner the material, the area between the hollow center and outside of the bullet jacket should readily expand. One aspect of such a thin-walled, lead nose is the potential of bullet fragmenting. To control the expansion and prevent fragmentation, manufacturers score the bullet jacket so that it will give in a more predictable manner when the bullet expands (Fig. 3.15). This type of bullet design is primarily used for hunting and self-defense, again to prevent overpenetration and maximize surface area contact with the target.

Solid copper hollow point

One of the more expensive methods of manufacturing bullets is by making them from solid copper. Solid copper has the benefits of the minimizing or eliminating lead exposure (if lead-free primers are used in conjunction with the bullet) and providing improved expansion potential. The solid copper petals of the hollow

Figure 3.15 Jacketed hollow point bullet.

point design can be more precisely engineered for the desired expansion due to the thickness of the copper. Achieving this type of precision can be more problematic when designing a bullet using two types of metals, such as the traditional lead core with a copper jacket.

Due to the expense of this manufacturing process, these bullets are reserved for higher end ammunition loadings, such as those for self-defense. Many companies have produced solid copper bullets for use in their performance lines, including Colt, Taurus, Magtech SCHP (solid copper hollow point), and Corbon (Fig. 3.16).

Wadcutter

Wadcutter bullets are cylindrical in design and have a very limited, if any, profile to the nose. The edges are at a 90 degrees angle to the nose area to produce a sharp edge. This will result in a clean cutting edge when the bullet is fired through a paper target. This assists in easier scoring in target shooting. Due to the lack of a curved nose profile, these bullets will not function reliably in semiautomatic pistols which rely on bullets feeding into an angled feed ramp. Wadcutter bullets are primarily used in revolvers where the bullet aligns with the barrel through the cylinder, which is in a fixed position when firing (Fig. 3.17).

Semiwadcutter

The semiwadcutter is similar in design to the wadcutter in that it has the 90 degrees edge around the periphery; however, there is nose incorporated into the design.

Figure 3.16 Solid copper hollow point bullet.

Figure 3.17 Wadcutter bullet.

Figure 3.18 Semiwadcutter bullet.

The nose in semiwadcutters is truncated and inset from the edge of the bullet. This will result in the same effect when fired through the paper, a clean hole for easier scoring in target shooting. The benefit of the truncated nose is reliable feeding of the cartridge in semiautomatic firearms (Fig. 3.18).

Lead round nose

These projectiles are made entirely of lead (with antimony) and have a round nose as the name suggests. The benefit of the round nose is reliable feeding in semiautomatic firearms. The bullet being made entirely of lead results in a lower cost of production. The extended use of lead can result in substantially more barrel fouling due to the residual lead in the barrel grooves and lengthen any cleaning processes. Lead round nose bullets are primarily used for target and recreational shooting (Fig. 3.19).

Spitzer bullet

A projectile design having a sharp pointed nose, a long ogive, and sometimes a boattail base.

Boattail

A boattail bullet is a bullet designed with a tapered or truncated conical base. The boattail design is typically found in rifle bullets. Rifles are used to shoot longer distances than handguns, so boattail bullets are used to help maximize the flight of the bullet by minimizing the air drag.

Figure 3.19 Lead round nose bullet.

Figure 3.20 Boattail bullet.

Cannelure

A circumferential groove generally of a knurled or plain appearance on a bullet or cartridge case used to assist in crimping, lubrication, and examination (AFTE Glossary, 2013) (see Fig. 3.20). Cannelures are typically found on revolver and rifle bullets. Revolvers rely on the rotation of the cylinder to facilitate subsequent shots to be fired. If the recoil of the firearm were to dislodge the bullets in the unfired cartridges, the bullet could potentially extend past the cylinder. This would prevent rotation of the cylinder and render the firearm unusable. The added grip of the cannelure aids in keeping the bullet in place in the unfired cartridge. The additional securing of the bullet to the cartridge case is also prominent in rifle ammunition due to the increased recoil. This occurrence is typically not an issue with semiautomatic firearms; therefore, they do not generally utilize cannelures. That is not to say some manufacturers of traditionally semiautomatic ammunition do not incorporate cannelures in their ammunition (Fig. 3.21). Manufacturers including Hornady, Winchester, and Federal

Figure 3.21 Nine millimeter Federal bullet with a cannelure.

are among the major manufacturers who utilize cannelures in their pistol caliber ammunition bullets.

Special purpose/premium ammunition

Most brands of ammunition have a premium line or special line designed for a specific purpose. These bullet designs differ from the traditional generic designs listed earlier and are specified to a particular use. Typically, a uniquely designed bullet will be reserved for the premium line of defense ammunition intended for home defense or police use. The forensic benefit of specialized ammunition is that the firearm examiner can typically identify the bullet type with a cursory view and provide investigators with an immediate lead with respect to which brand of ammunition to look for during the course of their investigation.

The globalization of industry has not eluded the firearm and ammunition community. In efforts to keep production costs down or to meet volume demands that exceed their capabilities, manufacturers may seek out other manufacturers to produce a component of the cartridge. This integration of components from various manufacturers can add to some confusion when discussing specific components and specifying the manufacturer. This is because the cartridge can be manufactured with respect to assembly of components and be considered the manufacturer. Whereas if only the component is recovered from a crime scene and referring to that component, the manufacturer of that component may be different than the manufacturer of the entire cartridge. Other instances occur where the entire cartridge is manufactured by an entirely different company that is branding and marketing it.

In the realm of forensic firearm examination, the origin of the component has little bearing on the comparison and examination to a firearm. Therefore without extensive research into the specific item and documentation from the manufacturer/marketer and knowledge of the lot number, any definitive assertion to the origin may be questioned. Simply referring to the item as "Winchester" brand or "Remington" brand would be technically correct as the components fall within their brand line. It could also be argued that the industry standard is to use the term manufacturer when referring to the cartridge and all parts of it. This concept carries through to other industries, such as the automobile industry. For example, not all the components of a Ford are made by Ford. They subcontract out many parts to other companies who specialize in those components. However, when legally titling a vehicle, the manufacturer is listed as Ford.

As with most areas of Forensic Firearm Examination, there are exceptions to the earlier statements. In the United States, the state of origin is critical in federal charges of Interstate Nexus. The basis of these charges includes the use of components from a state other than where the crime occurred. In these instances, knowledge of the actual manufacturer of the component is critical in progressing with charges.

Federal ammunition

Federal ammunition has a long history of producing proprietary lines of ammunition. One of the earliest ventures by Federal Ammunition was the NYCLAD bullet (Fig. 3.22). The NYCLAD projectile was initially designed and marketed by Smith & Wesson, but the rights were later sold to Federal. The earliest forensic observations of the forensic aspects of NYCLAD bullets were reported in 1979 (Conrad, 1979).

Figure 3.22 Federal NYCLAD cartridge.

These projectiles were made with a lead bullet encapsulated in a nylon coating to minimize lead exposure along with fouling in the barrel. While the use of a nylon polymer did accomplish the minimization of vaporous lead from the bullet and reduced barrel fouling, the jacketing material presented a challenge to forensic firearm examiners conducting bullet comparisons. This occurrence will be discussed in further detail in Chapter 11, The expert witness.

The next evolution in notable bullet designs produced by Federal was the Hydra-Shok bullet introduced in 1989 (Federal Ammunition, 2018) (Fig. 3.23). One of the challenges in the performance of jacketed hollow point bullets is reliable expansion regardless of the medium encountered. The basic design on the hollow point bullet lends itself to both rapid expansion when encountering a soft medium or acting as a cookie cutter and filling the cavity with a denser medium, such as a leather jacket. The result of a plugged jacketed hollow point is performance similar to a non-expanding full metal jacket (EFMJ). Therefore Federal incorporated a center post in the hollow point cavity to provide expansion in instances where the bullet first impacts denser objects. They named this bullet design the Federal Hydra-Shok (Fig. 3.24).

A follow-up to the Federal line that again is designed to negate any influence of the medium encountered to the hollow point is the EFMJ which was introduced in 2001. This bullet was designed to provide a projectile that would have a soft nose area

Figure 3.23 Federal Hydra-Shok cartridge.

Figure 3.24 Expanded Hydra-Shok bullet.

to accomplish reliable expansion on impact yet retain reliable feeding in semiautomatic firearms. The resulting projectile utilized a design with the plastic plug forward of the lead core. The relatively soft plastic in the nose of the bullet is intended to be crushed yet held in place by the copper jacket creating a large frontal area, such as that seen in expanded jacketed hollow points. The combination of plastic and lead in the bullet jacket creates substantially lighter than traditional bullets of the same caliber. For example, the most common weight of a full metal jacketed .45 Auto Colt Pistol (ACP) bullet is 230 grains, whereas the Federal EFMJ weighs in at 165 grains. This substantial reduction in weight will result in a cartridge with a higher velocity.

The EFMJ bullet was discontinued, and in 2011 introduced the Federal Guard Dog line of ammunition. It featured very similar characteristics with respect to being a total jacketed bullet with a plastic plug in the nose portion of the bullet. One of the most noticeable differences is the color of the plastic insert. Instead of white as with the EFMJ, the Guard Dog uses a blue plastic insert (Carter, 2013) (Fig. 3.25).

In 2016, Federal returned to the concept of producing a projectile with a lead bullet encapsulated in polymer (Fig. 3.26). As with the NYCLAD bullets, these touted less barrel fouling, less friction, and eliminated the contribution of lead from the bullet. This ammunition is currently marketed under the American Eagle line by Federal as the Syntech cartridge. The coating process of this projectile results in two distinct small voids in the coating as a result of the coating process.

Figure 3.25 Cutaway Guard Dog bullet.

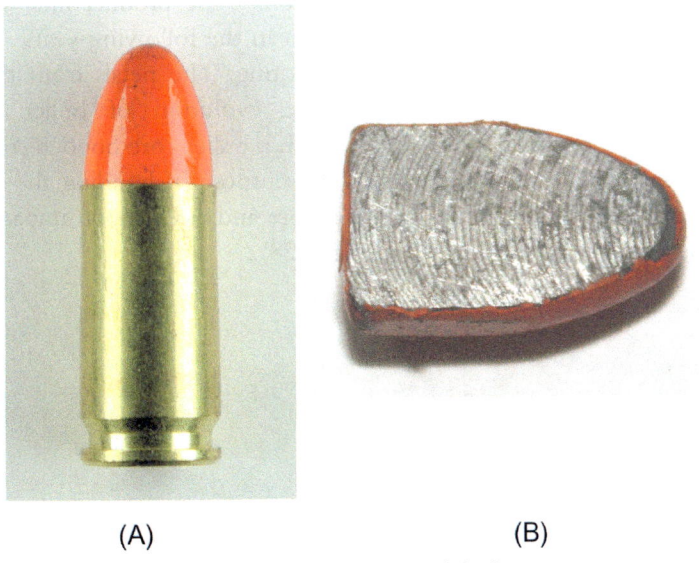

(A)   (B)

Figure 3.26 (A) Syntech cartridge and (B) cutaway Syntech bullet.

Winchester ammunition also has a colorful history of producing ammunition exclusive to its product line. One of the first was the Silvertip Hollow Point. The first Silvertip was an aluminum jacketed 115 grain 9 mm bullet that was introduced in 1979. When initially offered, aluminum was also used to produce the jackets for the .32 Auto, .380 Auto, .38 Special, .38 Special +P, .44 S&W Special, .45 Colt, and .45 Auto. In 2003, the jacket composition was changed from aluminum to nickel-plated brass. Older bullets with the aluminum jacket can be distinguished from the more modern nickel visually by the differentiating appearance of the amount of shine.

Aluminum jackets have a duller, oxidized finish, whereas the nickel will be much shinier (Fig. 3.27). The nickel plating, along with the previously mentioned aluminum jacket, provides the distinguishing silver color for which the cartridge is named (Szabo, 2010). The Silvertip line of ammunition has since been discontinued by Winchester, however, still presents itself in casework and should be known by forensic firearm examiners.

At one time, Winchester sold the individual bullets as reloading components for some of their calibers, including .357 Magnum, 9 mm, .40 S&W, 10 mm, and .44 Remington Magnum. Therefore the source of a Silvertip cannot exclusively be attributed to having come from a factory-loaded cartridge.

The next major introduction to the Winchester premium line was the Black Talon line of ammunition. These cartridges were designed with a copper jacket that had a black coating and the hollow point petals which when exposed after opening result in sharp exposed edges, thus the name "Black Talon." The product line was replaced with the (Supreme Expansion Talon) SXT design in the following years. The SXT is essentially the same bullet without the black coating. The petals from the resulting expansion have the same characteristics. The evolution of bullet designs by Winchester eventually brought about a bullet with a bullet core bonded to the copper jacket. This series is called the PDX1 line. The purpose of bonding the core to the jacket is to prevent the separation of the bullet core and jacket upon impact with hard objects, such as windshields and car doors (Fig. 3.28).

Figure 3.27 Winchester Silvertip cartridges, nickel plated on top, aluminum jacket on the bottom.

Figure 3.28 Expanded Winchester STX on the left, expanded Winchester Black Talon on the right.

Speer

Speer is a manufacturer with a long history of special purpose ammunition for hunting and law enforcement. They began by creating a line of jacketed hollow point bullets in the early 1970s called the Lawman and was nicknamed "The Flying Ashtray" due to the large diameter hollow point cavity. Speer has developed other lines of premium ammunition which have characteristics which are unique to their company. Among the most popular is the Gold Dot bullet. This bullet features a bullet core that is electrochemically bonded to the jacket. The production of the hollow point cavity creates a dot in the center of the cavity, thus the name Gold Dot (Fig. 3.29).

Remington

Remington is a manufacturer of both firearms and ammunition. As with most ammunition manufacturers, they produce performance ammunition that is marketed toward law enforcement and defense-minded consumers. The design is specific to Remington

Figure 3.29 Expanded Speer Gold Dot bullet.

and can easily be identified as a component from their product line. The performance ammunition manufactured by Remington is called Golden Saber, due in part to the golden color of the brass jacket. The core of the projectile is lead and the jacket is composed of brass. In addition to the traditional Golden Saber line, Remington produces a version where the jacket is bonded to the core. This line is called Golden Saber Bonded. The purpose of bonding the jacket to the core is to maintain the maximum weight of the bullet after it passes through an object. Unbonded bullets, when encountering a hard surface tend to separate the jacket from the core (Fig. 3.30).

Remington has also developed a bullet design that utilized a mechanical method to reduce the potential of separation of the bullet jacket from the bullet core in their Golden Saber Black Belt line of centerfire ammunition (Fig. 3.31). This bullet design retains the traditional bullet composition of a brass jacket hollow point with a lead core. However, Remington added a separate component of what they have termed a MechaniLokt belt. This is essentially a metal band that encompasses the circumference of the bullet. The intent is that the jacket is secured to the core and reduces the potential of separation (Fig. 3.32).

Hornady

Hornady produces a variety of performance ammunition that is made both for the defense market and as a novelty. The Hornady line of premium ammunition takes a

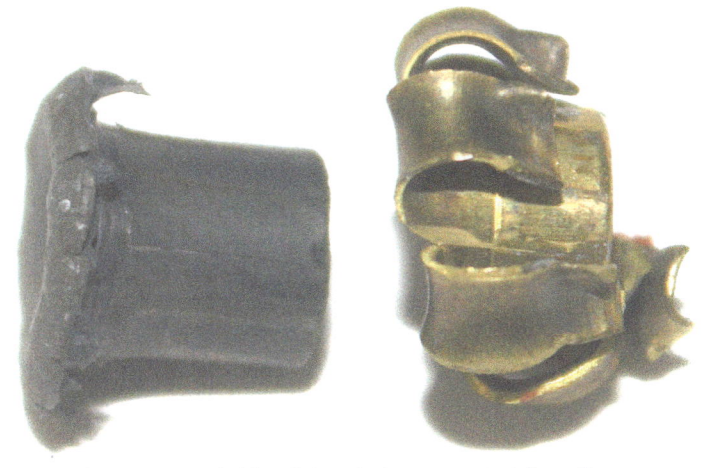

Figure 3.30 Expanded Remington Golden Saber, jacket separated from the core.

Figure 3.31 Remington Black Belt cartridge.

Figure 3.32 Remington Black Belt cutaway.

Figure 3.33 Hornady cutaway.

different approach to the production of ammunition than the traditional hollow point design. An obstacle of hollow point ammunition with respect to performance is the potential of the hollow point cavity to be plugged with intermediate material, such as leather from a coat or metal from a car door. To reduce the potential of this occurring, Hornady preemptively inserts a soft rubber-like post in the cavity that is designed to push into the bullet and expand the jacket (Fig. 3.33). The color of the post is dependent on the line of ammunition produced by Hornady. Their most popular line, Critical Defense, utilizes a red rubber post. However, they also offer other products, such as the Critical Defense Lite which contains a lighter bullet (100 grains) and is promoted as producing reduced recoil. The rubber post in this version is pink on color.

Another offering from Hornady that incorporates a rubber post is the Zombie Max line of ammunition. This ammunition is similar in design to other projectiles offered by Hornady; however, the rubber post is light green in color. Due to Hornady's marketing history, other colored rubber posts may be introduced, and research should be performed if a rubber cylindrical piece is found associated with a shooting to determine if Hornady is a candidate (Fig. 3.34).

Aguila

Although discontinued, Aguila previously manufactured specialty centerfire handgun ammo designed for self-defense. This was marketed under the name of Aguila IQ, with the IQ referring to the bullet as an intelligent bullet. The bullet was composed

Figure 3.34 Hornady bullets with various colored posts.

of a zinc alloy rather than the traditional lead core. This alternative material is lighter than lead, therefore results in a higher velocity. In addition to a higher velocity, the bullet has characteristics to enhance performance. The sides of the bullet have deep scores to easily and reliably fragment on impact. This controlled fragmentation increases the number of projectiles within the wound track (Wallace and Becker, 2000) (Fig. 3.35).

Aguila produces a specialty rimfire cartridge with subsonic characteristics. This is an important feature for shooters who use a suppressor while shooting. In addition to the sound of the discharge of the cartridge, the bullet passing the sound barrier creates a crack, adding to the sound during shooting. Designing a cartridge that will not exceed the speed of sound requires modification from traditionally designed cartridges. In the case of the Aguila .22 SSS (Sniper Subsonic), the cartridge is based on a .22 Short cartridge case with a long (60 grain) bullet. The overall length of the cartridge, despite using a .22 Short cartridge case, is the same as traditional .22 Long Rifle (LR) cartridges.

Starfire

The performance line of ammunition made by Precision Made Cartridges is designated as Starfire. As with other performance bullet designs, these are jacketed with a lead

Figure 3.35 Aquila IQ bullet.

core. However, the profile of the interior of the hollow point leads to a profile that is distinct and easily recognizable. The interior of the hollow point cavity of the bullet has raised ridges which are designed to strengthen the sides and control expansion (Figs. 3.36 and 3.37).

Browning jacketed hollow point

The product line marketed by Browning takes a slightly different approach to the hollow point design. These bullets have a cross-sectional support in the center of the hollow point cavity to ensure expansion. While the design is easily recognizable in an unfired condition, the cross-sectional design may not endure impact. Testing this ammunition in a water tank revealed that the cross-sectional lead is no longer present (Figs. 3.38 and 3.39).

Figure 3.36 Starfire bullet.

Figure 3.37 Expanded Starfire bullet.

The specialty cartridges marketed by their respective manufacturers are not intended to be an inclusive list of all the cartridge types and designs produced by that manufacturer. Rather it is provided to assist Forensic Firearm Examiners in a fundamental awareness of the variety of the vast types of bullets that have been and

Figure 3.38 Browning jacketed hollow point.

Figure 3.39 Expanded Browning jacketed hollow point.

continue to be marketed to the shooting community. In addition, there are many more that have been introduced that are specific for certain hunting or target shooting applications. The focus of the cartridges mentioned earlier is more likely to be encountered in typical forensic laboratories. As with any bullet or cartridge case that the examiner is not familiar with, additional research is encouraged.

Specialty ammunition by design
Shot cartridges

As with any business, ammunition manufacturers make an effort to address the needs of their clients. One such design is the production of cartridges that perform a specific purpose as seen with the CCI shot cartridge. The parent cartridge for this is a standard centerfire or rimfire cartridge with the projectile utilizing a plastic case encapsulating very small birdshot. The plastic case merely contains the shot until the time of discharge. The result is a handgun that is capable of shooting a small load of birdshot. The intent of this is for discouraging or dispatching snakes while hiking or hunting.

There are two varieties of loadings for the CCI shot cartridge chambered in 9 mm Luger. The first offering utilizes a transparent blue plastic bullet capsule filled with 12 lead shot. The other option from this company has a transparent red bullet filled with 4 shot (Fig. 3.40). The larger shot diminishes the number of pellets in the shot cartridge but will have a further effective range. Other calibers of shot cartridges manufactured by CCI incorporate 9 shot or 4 depending on the intended use. In addition, shot cartridges have also been designed that use a lengthened, tapered cartridge case rather than a plastic bullet. All of these components can be of forensic value if

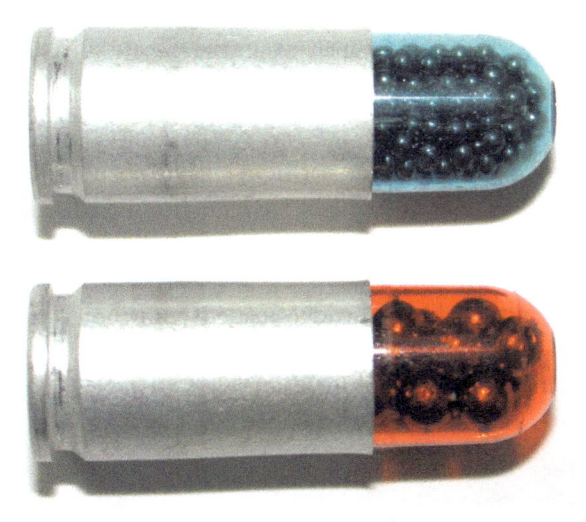

Figure 3.40 CCI shot cartridges. 12 shot on top, 4 shot on bottom.

Figure 3.41 US military .45 caliber shot cartridge.

recovered at a crime scene or from a victim and assist in determining the manufacturer of the components.

Other commercially available shot cartridges have been produced for the same purpose, however, with a different design. Older styles used modified cartridge cases to encapsulate the lead shot. This design will result in a distinctly shaped fired cartridge case that should be easily identifiable.

The concept of a pistol caliber cartridge loaded with shot is not a new one. The US military adopted a cartridge with 7.5 shot in October of 1943 (Molans, 2018). This design was specifically created for inclusion with aircrew survival kits (Fig. 3.41).

Glaser safety slugs

Glaser Safety Slugs were the first bullet design that diverged from the traditional solid lead bullet core and replaced it with small shot pellets placed in a traditional copper jacket and a plastic nose piece to contain the shot. The intent behind the design was to prevent overpenetration through walls when fired in an indoor environment, thus preventing accidental injury to people in adjacent rooms. Because the small shot does not contain the mass of an entire bullet core, it rapidly disperses its energy into the wall.

Other companies have followed in designing bullets like the Glaser design, such as Mag Safe, which is now out of business. As with the Glaser, the Mag Safe had a bullet jacket that contained shot. The Mag Safe, however, used an epoxy to contain the shot within the bullet jacket (Wallace, 2000). While the company is out of business, ammunition has an indefinite shelf-life if properly stored; therefore there is still a potential it could be encountered.

Solid copper bullets

In an effort to eliminate shooters to lead exposure, manufacturers have pursued various bullet compositions. One type of bullet production that uses no lead is bullets made entirely of copper. These bullets are most commonly manufactured using a computer numerically controlled lathe which automatically feeds the barstock through the lathe and turns the bullet to the predetermined design. Due to the difference in weight of copper and lead, copper bullets will be lighter than their similarly sized lead counterparts (Fig. 3.42).

Figure 3.42 Solid copper bullet.

In addition to being lead free, copper bullets, being uniform in composition, do not have the potential to separate upon impact. Traditional copper-jacketed lead bullets may separate when they encounter a target, thus diminishing their effectiveness.

The concept of prefragmented ammunition has also been adopted by other manufacturers. An example of this is an offering by G2 Research (Fig. 3.43). This bullet is composed of a solid copper projectile with petals that are prescored to allow for the disbursement of the petals upon impact. In situations with prefragmented bullets, it is not uncommon to have the resulting evidence composed of the solid base and recovered fragments. While these fragments will not contain the entire circumference of the rifling, there may be sufficient individual characteristics to conclude an identification. As with any identification based on individual

Figure 3.43 G2 Research cartridge.

Figure 3.44 Solid copper hollow point bullet.

characteristics, the quality of the characteristics will determine the potential of identification.

Another bullet design made entirely of copper is the hollow point which has been made by a variety of manufacturers. As with the solid copper bullets, these are made from a solid copper rod and cut to the desired dimensions (Fig. 3.44).

Frangible ammunition

Frangible ammunition is produced with a projectile that is designed to disintegrate when it impacts a hard surface. This is a desirable feature especially when training and target shooting in close proximity to steel targets. Traditional ammunition can ricochet, sending the bullet or fragments back at the shooter causing injury. The increase in large-scale production and marketing to the mainstream firearms community of frangible ammunition has increased its appearance in the forensic setting.

Another benefit to the use of compressed metal bullets made from copper and binders is the elimination of lead from the projectile (Fig. 3.45). Lead, while an

Figure 3.45 Frangible bullet.

inexpensive way to add mass to the projectile, carries with it negative health implications. Exposure to vaporous lead from the ignition of the primer and bullet can be absorbed through the skin and breathed in by shooters. The use of powdered metal bullets primarily made from copper and binders in combination with lead-free primers ensures the shooter is not exposed to the effects of lead exposure.

Frangible ammunition is typically manufactured using a powdered metal process. During this manufacturing method, powdered copper along with a variety of binders are pressed into the shape of the bullet (Ainsworth, 2017). The bullet is then sintered (heated) to fuse the binders and powdered copper into a solid projectile. While the bullet is hardened and solid, it is relatively brittle. The brittle nature of the sintered compressed bullet makes it ideal to perform as a frangible bullet. The forensic aspects of these projectiles will be discussed in Chapter 11, The expert witness.

Earlier attempts to produce frangible ammunition have taken alternative approaches to ensure the projectile will fragment upon impact. One of these includes a cartridge made by Federal BallistiClean called "Close Quarters Training" frangible ammunition. This bullet was produced by utilizing thin zinc cables wrapped in a spiral and encapsulated in a copper jacket. When the bullet impacts a hard surface, the zinc cables separate and will not ricochet (McConaghy, 1999).

Subsonic ammunition

Subsonic ammunition is specifically designed to have a velocity below the speed of sound. This is especially important for individuals who are using suppressors on their

Figure 3.46 115 grain full metal jacket bullet left, 147 grain full metal jacket bullets center and right.

firearms and want to minimize the sound produced by discharging the firearm. Suppressors, sometimes incorrectly called silencers, are accessories that attach to the end of a firearm barrel designed to diminish the report of a firearm. The majority of sound from a firearm is a result of the rapid release of hot gas from the muzzle. To counter this, suppressors are designed with internal baffles to disrupt and cool the gases as they exit the barrel.

In addition to the sound produced by the exiting gases, the bullet itself will create a considerable amount of sound when it crosses the sound barrier entering supersonic flight. As a means to eliminate this secondary sound source, manufacturers will design ammunition that is subsonic. The obvious solution to creating subsonic ammunition is to reduce the amount of gunpowder which controls the velocity of the bullet. However, to maximize the potential of the ammunition, manufacturers will also utilize a heavier bullet. A heavy bullet will provide the best exterior ballistic performance with respect to energy attributed to the impact of the bullet. The diameter of the barrel (caliber) will determine the maximum diameter of the bullet. Therefore to increase the weight of the bullet, manufacturers will increase the length of the bullet. The most common heavy weight bullet for 9 mm cartridges is 147 grains. The difference in length of a 115 grain 9 mm bullet versus a 147 grain bullet is readily apparent (Fig. 3.46).

Manufacturer identifiers on bullets

Manufacturers may also make their ammunition stand out from the competitors by impressing numbers, letters, or symbols on the bullet nose or base. Federal uses this

Figure 3.47 "F" stamp on the nose of the Federal Guard Dog bullet.

method in their production of the Guard Dog branded bullet. To further distinguish it from other manufacturers, the bullet contained an "F" stamped on the nose of the bullet. This may also have been to distinguish the bullet from traditional Full Metal Jacket bullets due to the design (Fig. 3.47).

Other manufacturers mark the base of their bullet to signify that it is their product. Due to the limited space on the base of a bullet, marks are typically limited to one letter or symbol. The letter or symbol generally signifies a specially designed bullet from a manufacturer. Examples of this include bullets made by Barnes for their magnum line which have an "M" on the base (Fig. 3.48). They also have produced a product line of high-velocity bullets with an "X" on the base. Another manufacturer who marks the base of their bullets is Federal. Federal used a "T" on some of their tactical and performance ammunition (Fig. 3.49).

There are instances where manufacturers mark their components for the purpose of tracking the production process. The Aguila IQ which was previously discussed incorporates a number molded in the base of the hollow point. In the example demonstrated in Fig. 3.50, the number "2" is present.

Figure 3.48 "M" stamp on the base of Barnes Magnum bullet.

Figure 3.49 "T" stamp on the base of Federal Tactical bullets.

Caliber

The caliber of the projectile has been designated by a variety of names with respect to the bullet. The caliber most commonly referred to as "nominal caliber." Nominal caliber is not the exact diameter of a bullet. The exact diameter of the bearing surface of

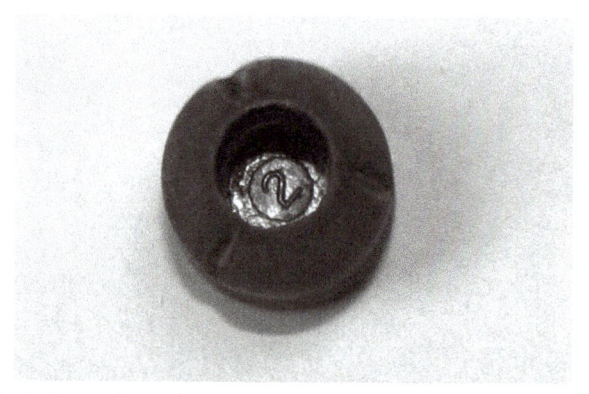

Figure 3.50 Aguila IQ bullet with production identifier in the cavity.

a bullet is called the true caliber of the bullet. Nominal caliber refers to an approximate bullet diameter shared by a group or family of ammunition. For example, 9 mm Luger, .38 Special, and .357 Magnum are all nominal .38 caliber ammunition, meaning that they have an approximate bullet diameter near 0.38 in. In the application of forensic firearm examination, bullets that have been recovered after having been fired may encounter hard objects and become deformed, making exact measurement difficult. Therefore the nominal caliber is typically recorded.

Cartridge case

The cartridge case houses the components of a cartridge. Cartridge cases are commonly made from brass; however, there are cartridge cases made from steel, aluminum, and polymer. The latter cartridge cases are most commonly loaded with Berdan primers not intended for reloading purposes.

Brass cartridge cases are made from a drawing process. They begin as solid brass and are progressively pressed into their final shape through a progression of dies. Some cartridge cases have extractor grooves, which are machined into the cartridge cases with a lathe. Some cartridge cases, such as bottleneck rifle-type cartridge cases, require annealing to soften the brass to allow for forming. The annealing process can be evident by discoloration of the brass.

Cartridge cases bear information with respect to the manufacturer and caliber designation on their base. This information can be beneficial in a forensic investigation. In addition to the manufacturer and caliber, there are microscopic marks on the cartridge cases that can be examined by forensic firearm examiners. These stampings of information are made by die stamps called bunters. The significance of bunter marks will be discussed in greater detail in Chapter 8, Comparison of cartridge cases.

The caliber designations of cartridges have changed throughout the design and development of firearms. Some of the earliest cartridges were named by their caliber and the amount of black powder used for loading the cartridge. An example of this is the .45-70. The .45 designator refers to the caliber of the bullet, while 70 refers to the amount of black powder in the cartridge.

The caliber of the cartridge is generally, at a minimum, an indication of the diameter of the bullet. Alternate naming methods incorporate other information about the cartridge. The .30-06 cartridge indicates the caliber size with the first number of the name and the year of introduction, 1906, as the remainder. The designers of cartridges also use characteristics of the cartridge in the naming process. The .250-3000 is an example of this. The .250 in the name references the caliber of the cartridge, and the second half of the name indicates the velocity of the cartridge, 3000 ft/s.

The additional name of the cartridge may indicate the designer, intended use, or distinguishing feature. For example, the .25 ACP has a bullet diameter of .25 in. and was introduced by Colt for their pistol (Barnes and Woodard, 2016a). However, the cartridge name may not always indicate the exact diameter. A good example of this is the .38 Special. The bullet diameter is actually .357 in. Designed as an improvement to the .38 Special, the .357 Magnum was developed. The term "Magnum" refers to a longer cartridge case capable of holding more gunpowder and is loaded to higher pressures resulting in an increase in velocity of the bullet.

Some cartridge designations include the length of the cartridge. This is common in European and cartridges designed for the military. The cartridge used by the US military for their infantry rifle is the 5.56×45 mm. The Soviet Union utilizes the 5.45×39 mm and 7.62×39 mm cartridges. In these cartridges, the bullet diameter is the first number and the cartridge case length is the second number.

Some cartridges may have multiple accepted names for the same cartridge. The 9 mm Luger was originally designed in 1902 for the German Luger pistol. It is also referred to as the 9 mm Parabellum, 9×19 mm, and 9 mm NATO. These are all the same cartridge.

Rifle ammunition

Centerfire rifle ammunition is typically designed differently than pistol ammunition in that it has a cartridge case that has a wider body and the top portion tapers to a smaller diameter where the bullet is seated. Because of the resemblance to a bottle, cartridge cases with this design are called bottleneck cartridges. The wide base allows for a larger amount of gunpowder relative to the bullet diameter. This increased amount of gunpowder will serve to increase the velocity of the bullet as it is driven down the longer barrel utilized by rifles (Fig. 3.51).

Figure 3.51 Bottleneck cartridge.

There are pistols designed around bottleneck rifle ammunition. Pistols utilizing rifle ammunition do not benefit from the longer barrel which assists in increasing the velocity due to the longer burn time resulting in the exiting bullet having a maximized velocity. However, they typically have an increased velocity above that of an equal bullet weight loaded in a straight wall pistol caliber cartridge. This is a result of the initial increase in burned gunpowder.

As with most statements, there are exceptions to what is traditionally encountered. There are pistol cartridges which use a dedicated bottleneck design to increase velocity. An example of this is the .357 Sig. This cartridge was designed by Sig Sauer to provide a bullet in the area of the velocity of the .357 Magnum in a semiautomatic platform. The .357 Sig is a 10 mm, which is traditionally a straight-walled pistol cartridge that has been necked down (formed to a different size) to .355 in. in diameter. This will allow for a smaller caliber bullet to be encased in a cartridge that has an ability to hold a large amount of gunpowder relative to the size of the bullet. This in turn allows for more powder to burn behind the bullet producing a higher velocity. An additional benefit to this design is that the firearm can retain the profile and design as a traditional handgun with respect to the grip size.

Belted base

Some larger rifle cartridges are loaded to particularly high pressures. In these instances, the cartridge case requires reinforcement to contain the increased pressure created in the chamber of the firearm. Manufacturers address this by increasing the thickness of the cartridge case with additional brass. This type of cartridge case design is reserved for larger cartridges that are not commonly encountered in forensic laboratories. However, awareness of this type of cartridge is important as part of a general knowledge of ammunition and components of ammunition (Fig. 3.52).

Wildcat cartridges

Wildcat cartridges are cartridges developed by both commercial loaders and hobbyists and gunsmiths. Wildcat cartridges begin as factory cartridge cases. The purpose of

Figure 3.52 Belted base cartridge.

using factory cases is because the production of brass cartridge cases requires expensive specialized equipment. Wildcat designers typically have a specific purpose in mind when developing a cartridge. They may desire a larger caliber bullet than offered by factory ammunition in that particular cartridge case. Another goal may be to downsize the designated caliber to a smaller one resulting in higher velocities. To facilitate the altering of cartridges, wildcat designers use specially made dies to form the cartridge to the desired profile. Additional processing may be performed to trim the newly formed cartridge case to the desired length (Shem, 1993).

Wildcat cartridges are not frequently encountered in forensic laboratories due to the relatively small number of wildcat firearms in existence. In addition, developers of wildcat cartridges utilize these firearms for target shooting and hunting and these types of firearms are not typically used in crimes. That being said, it is valuable to be aware of the potential for these types of cartridges as a source of recovered evidence.

Wildcat cartridges that gain wide acceptance in the shooting community can evolve into commercially manufactured ammunition. Prior to manufacturers investing in the production of a new caliber, sufficient interest from customers must be established. An example of a cartridge that began its' existence as a wildcat is discussed in Chapter 11, The expert witness, in the section titled Cartridges made from different calibers.

Shotgun ammunition

Shotgun ammunition is like centerfire ammunition in that it has a primer in the center of the shotshell and there is gunpowder located past the primer. However, after the gunpowder, shotshells have what is called a wad. The most common load for shotshells is lead pellets. Shotshells can also be loaded with a single solid projectile called a slug (Fig. 3.53).

Shotgun gauge

Shotguns are chambered in various calibers which, when discussing shotguns, are defined as gauges. The gauge size is determined by dividing 1 lb of lead into equal

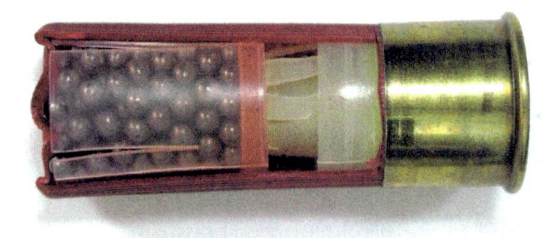

Figure 3.53 Cutaway shotshell exposing the lead shot.

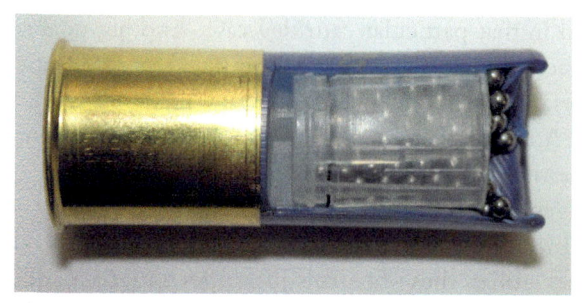

Figure 3.54 Cutaway shotshell exposing plastic wad.

spherical portions. For example, a 1 lb lead piece divided into 12 spherical portions is equal to 0.729 in. in diameter, which is the diameter of a 12 gauge shotgun. The following holds true for other commonly encountered gauges including 10 (0.775 in. in diameter), 16 (0.662 in. in diameter), 20 (0.615 in. in diameter), and 28 (0.550 in. in diameter). The exception to the rule is the .410 gauge shotgun. In this instance, the shotgun bore is .410 gauge.

Wad

The wad in a shotshell serves a multitude of purposes in the function of a shotshell. Current shotshell designs incorporate a wad that multiple duties (Fig. 3.54). Modern wads are made from plastic as that is the most cost-effective and efficient way to produce them. The wad contacts the gunpowder and keeps it in place close to the flash hole and primer. Along with contacting the gunpowder, it seals the gas produced by ignition of the powder to maximize the velocity of the shot charge. It also serves as a spacer to account for the difference in amount of shot relative to the space consumed by the gunpowder. In addition, the wad acts as what is termed a shot cup which contains the shot until the shot exits the barrel and protects the barrel from contact direct contact with the shot. The shot cup also gives an even push of the shot down the barrel. Lastly, it serves as a gas check for semiautomatic shotguns which rely on gas from the combustion of gunpowder to cycle the action of the firearm.

Depending on the design of the shotshell, the wad may or may not encapsulate the shot. Typically, shotshells loaded with smaller shot utilize a wad that surrounds the shot as it travels down the barrel. Larger shot, such as buckshot, will have a wad at the base of the shot load, but the plastic sleeves may be absent or only partially encompass the shot. In these cases, the shot will contact the barrel directly (Fig. 3.55).

Older designs of shotshells used multiple components to accomplish the task of the one-piece plastic piece of current wads. The older shotshells used a separate overpowder wad. The overpowder wad in older shotshells is traditionally made of wax-coated cardboard and separately placed over the gunpowder to hold it in place. Next, there are spacers for the area between the overpowder wad and the shot. In the older shotshells, the spacers were made from waxed felt. The thickness of the spacers was determined by the amount of space necessary to accommodate the shot pellets. The use of waxed paper overpowder wads was eventually replaced with plastic overpowder wads which performed better at sealing the gases from the ignited gunpowder. The cost of feeling of the production of spacers leads to the use of pressed paper wads. The evolution of modern plastic manufacturing processes has made the currently used all-in-one design the standard in shotshell production (Bussard et al., 2017b) (Fig. 3.56).

Figure 3.55 Cutaway shotshell exposing 00 Buckshot.

Figure 3.56 Cutaway older shotshell with waxed paper and cardboard wads.

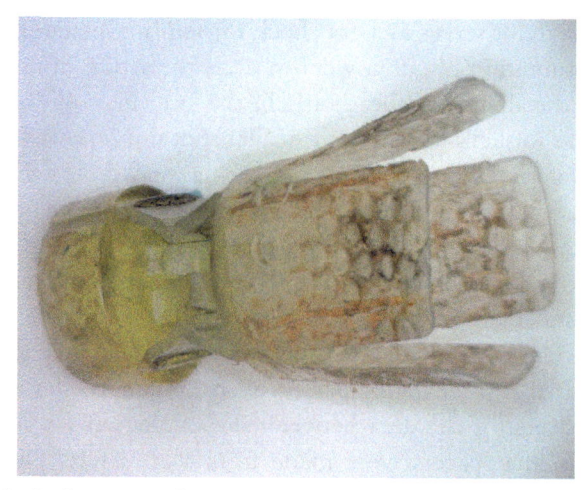

Figure 3.57 Fired plastic shotgun wad.

Shotshells differ from traditional cartridges in that they typically contain multiple projectiles rather than a singular projectile. Shotshells are appreciably larger in diameter than handgun and rifle cartridges. The increased volume is to allow for the loading of shot. Shots are spherical pellets that range in size and composition depending on the intended use.

From a forensic aspect, wads can provide valuable information to investigators. The diameter of the wad can be measured to determine the gauge of the shotgun used. In addition, when the wad, along with the shot is propelled down the barrel of the shotgun, the shot impresses a profile into the wad. The profile can be measured to approximate the size of the shot that was loaded in the wad and correspondingly the shotshell. Lastly, the design of the wad can be examined to possibly determine the manufacturer of the shotshell (Fig. 3.57).

Shot

Shotguns are primarily used for hunting, sport, and self-defense. When used in the application of hunting, the size shot utilized will depend on the type of game being hunted. The size of shot used in shotgun ammunition is designated by numbers and letters. The larger the number, the smaller the size of the shot. Popular sizes of shot range from size 9 to BB. The smallest, 9 shot, is 0.080 in. (2.03 mm) in diameter, whereas the largest, BB, is 0.180 in. (4.57 mm) in diameter. The size of the shot will determine the number of pellets that will fit in a shotshell. Typical 12 gauge shotshells contain 1 ounce of shot. Based on 1 ounce, 579 pellets of 9 size shot will be loaded in a shotshell. The smaller shot is typically reserved for hunting of small game, such as

Figure 3.58 Cutaway shotshell with 4 Buck and granular filler.

squirrels. As the shot size increases (and the shot designation decreases), the type of game or application will change.

Another class of shotgun shot is categorized as buckshot. Pellets in the buckshot category are defined with the use of numbers. Shot sizes range in size from Number 4 to 000. Buckshot, as the name implies, is designed for deer and other larger game. As with the other shot sizes, as the buckshot number decreases, the diameter of the individual pellets increases. The larger buckshot pellets benefit from cushioning when rapidly accelerated from the shotgun. To assist in cushioning, manufacturers use a plastic granulated filler (Fig. 3.58).

Alternative shot compositions

The hunting of waterfowl is exclusively done with shotguns. Because waterfowl are hunted over wetlands and bodies of water, there are environmental concerns of introducing lead into water which may be used for drinking. Lead was traditionally used for both shotgun shot and other ammunition due to the low cost and high density. A dense, heavy projectile can travel further with more energy than a lighter projectile. To find an environment-friendly alternative to lead, manufacturers have utilized various materials. Commonly used alternates include steel, bismuth alloy, tungsten matrix, and tungsten iron. While these types of materials minimize impact on the environment, they are not as dense as their lead counterparts and will alter the amount of shot in a 1 ounce load. The flight characteristics of these will also change due to their density.

Along with alternative compositions, the shape of the shot may be altered to provide improved performance as advertised by the manufacturer. An example of this is the Winchesters Blind Side shot pellets (Fig. 3.59). The pellets in this load are square in shape rather than the traditional spherical-shaped pellets. The purpose of the shape of these pellets according to the manufacturer is to improve penetration and allow for a greater number of pellets to be loaded in the same volume as spherical pellets. Another example of this is pellets loaded in Federal shotshells.

Figure 3.59 Winchester Blind Side shotshell.

Figure 3.60 Shotshell loaded with rubber 00 Buckshot.

The composition of the shot may also be determined by its purpose. Fiocchi produces a shotshell loaded with rubber 00 Buck pellets. They are marketed toward law enforcement for a less lethal method for controlling a situation. While they are designed to be less lethal, any projectile has the potential to cause fatal injuries (Fig. 3.60).

Shotgun slugs

Shotguns can also be used to hunt larger game, such as deer. When used for deer hunting, shotshells are most commonly loaded with slugs. Slugs are large singular projectiles that are made from lead or copper. The singular projectile will offer greater accuracy at further distances than shotshells loaded with multiple projectiles. The slugs loaded in 12 gauge shotshells are generally 1 ounce in weight and can encompass the diameter of the barrel. An alternate design is where the slug is encapsulated in a sabot. Sabots are made from plastic and can either be formed in two halves or one piece (Fig. 3.61). If the sabot is used, the projectile is smaller in diameter than the barrel and to accommodate a tight seal with the barrel and engagement with the rifling, if present. Sabots are intended to separate from the slug upon exit from the barrel, allowing only the projectile to carry on toward the target.

Shotgun barrels are traditionally smooth bore. That is, there is no rifling within the barrel. The purpose of rifling is to impart a spin on the projectile. Because shot is designed to spread upon exiting the barrel, there is no need for rifling. However, there

Figure 3.61 12 gauge saboted slug.

are shotgun barrels that are rifled for the same purpose as other barrels, to impart a spin on the projectile. These shotgun barrels are intended to fire slugs or saboted slugs.

Forensically, sabots are a valuable component because they can assist in identifying both the gauge of shotgun used and the manufacturer of the ammunition. In addition, if the shotgun barrel was rifled, the rifling from the barrel may be imparted to the sabot and potentially identified to the shotgun.

Manufacturers produce specialty slugs which are proprietary to their company. Examples of this include those produced by Winchester, Federal, Remington, and Hornady (Fig. 3.62). When these slugs are encountered, the manufacturer can be quickly determined by direct comparison to known reference slugs.

As with other centerfire cartridges, shotgun ammunition can be loaded with nontraditional projectiles. Among these are sintered slugs, which are designed to disintegrate upon impact with a solid object (Figs. 3.63 and 3.64). Another example of a specialized slug design that is unconventional is a solid rubber slug, such as that produced by Fiocchi. As with the rubber buckshot produced by the same company, the rubber slug is designed to be less lethal than a lead projectile (Fig. 3.65).

Figure 3.62 Hornady 12 gauge slug.

Figure 3.63 12 gauge cartridge loaded with a sintered slug.

Figure 3.64 Sintered 12 ga slug with cardboard sleeve.

Figure 3.65 12 gauge rubber slug.

Shotgun chokes

Chokes are additions to shotguns that restrict or open up the end of the shotgun to affect the shot distribution as it exits the barrel by tapering the exiting point of the muzzle. Some shotguns have the choke manufactured permanently into the barrel with the designated taper integrally formed in the barrel. In these cases, the choke will be stamped on the side of the barrel. Other manufactures thread the interior of the barrel to allow the user to alternate chokes depending on the purpose of shooting. The purpose of changing the pattern is to increase the effective range of the shotgun. As the pattern is restricted, the effective range increases. The restricted pattern provides a larger number of pellets to impact the target.

Types of chokes

Chokes are designated by name and the type of choke will be determined by the intended purpose. A cylinder choke has no constriction at the end of the muzzle and is typically used for slugs and buckshot. A skeet choke provides a 0.005 in. restriction at the muzzle and as the name implies is commonly used for skeet shooting. The next type of choke in order of amount of reduction in muzzle size is improved cylinder. This has a difference of 0.011 in. and is used for hunting at closer ranges. A modified choke restricts the muzzle by 0.020 in. and is useful for all-around hunting with shot. The improved modified choke has a constriction of 0.027 in. and again is useful for all-around hunting and birds which require longer range patterns. A full choke is more restrictive and yields a 0.036 in. reduction in muzzle diameter and is beneficial in long range hunting and trap shooting. The final type of choke is the extra full choke. This is the most restrictive choke constricts the muzzle by 0.040 in. and is used when hunting geese and turkey where the maximum number of pellets is required to impact the target.

Rimfire ammunition

Rimfire ammunition is a category of ammunition that is different than larger centerfire ammunition in that the priming compound is incorporated within the rim of the cartridge rather than as a separate component as with centerfire cartridges. Rimfire cartridges have a gap in the rim of the cartridge that is filled with priming compound. If the rim is pinched anywhere along the circumference of the rim, the priming compound is ignited and, in turn, the gunpowder is ignited (Fig. 3.66). The most prominent caliber of rimfires encountered in a forensic laboratory is the .22 LR. Other cartridges in the .22 rimfire family include the .22 Short, .22 Long, and .22 Magnum.

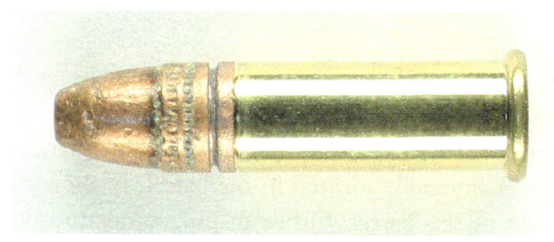

Figure 3.66 .22 Long Rifle .22 cartridge.

The .22 Short is much as the name implies in that it is a shortened version of the other .22 rimfire cartridges with a diminished capacity of gunpowder resulting in a lower velocity. It was introduced in 1857 and is currently manufactured making it the oldest American self-contained metallic cartridge commercially produced.

The .22 Long cartridge followed development chronologically having been listed as revolver offered by the Great Western Gun Works in 1871. The .22 Long cartridge utilizes a cartridge case that is the same diameter as the .22 Short, however, is longer. The additional volume in the case allows for increased gunpowder, therefore an increased velocity.

Following in development was the .22 LR. This cartridge was introduced in 1887 by the J.Stevens Arms & Tool Company (Barnes and Woodard, 2016b). The .22 LR cartridge case is indistinguishable from the .22 Long cartridge case; therefore examiners must exercise caution in empirically stating that a cartridge case is one caliber or the other. The .22 Long is typically loaded with a 29 grain bullet, whereas the .22 LR cartridge is typically loaded with projectiles weighing 36, 38, or 40 grains.

Necked Down Rimfire Ammunition

Traditional rimfire cartridges are straight walled. This is ideal for inexpensive mass production which lends to the primary use of rimfire cartridges, hunting, and recreational target shooting. However, because the .22 rimfire is a popular platform, firearm and ammunition designers have used the parent .22 rimfire as foundation for other caliber creations.

To offer the shooting community options for both target shooting and hunting, manufacturers explore changes to the cartridge design. One change is to increase the velocity of the bullet. There is very little room for safely increasing the amount of gunpowder to achieve this, therefore other options were explored. The most effective way to increase the velocity while keeping all other parameters equal is to decrease the bullet weight, thus the bullet diameter. The result is a bottlenecked .22 rimfire. Various options have been developed as seen in the .17 HM2 and .17 HMR.

Figure 3.67 From left to right, .22 Long Rifle, .17 HM2, .22 Magnum, and .17 HMR.

The noticeable difference between these two bottlenecked cartridges being the length and associated amount of powder capable of being used in the cartridge. There is, however, a constant between the cartridges which is the .17 caliber bullet. Because multiple cartridges use this bullet, without a fired cartridge case to attribute the bullet to, a definitive cartridge prediction should be approached cautiously (Fig. 3.67).

CHAPTER 4

Fundamentals of forensic firearm examination

Toolmark examination is the examination of marks left by the contact between two objects; the harder object acts as a tool and leaves marks on the softer object, which acts as the work piece. Forensic firearm examination is a subdiscipline that uses the firearm as the tool and the ammunition components as the work piece. Forensic firearm examination is a subdiscipline that uses the firearm as the tool and the ammunition components as the work piece. The components of the firearm are made of hardened steel. Ammunition components are significantly softer than the firearm counterparts they come in contact with; therefore, the marks from the firearm are transferred onto the ammunition components.

Types of marks for comparison purposes

When discussing toolmarks whether in the traditional sense of a pry bar and door jam or evaluating firearm-related evidence, there are two types of marks that result from contact: impressed, and striated. The direct impact of a hard object to a softer object will result in an impressed toolmark. An interaction of a harder object with a softer object while in motion results in a striated toolmark.

Impressed toolmarks

According to the Association of Firearm and Tool Mark Examiners (AFTE) Glossary (2013), impressed toolmarks are defined as "contour variations on the surface of an object caused by a combination of force and motion where the motion of the tool is approximately perpendicular to the plane being marked. The class characteristics (shape) can indicate the type of tool used to produce the mark. These marks may contain class, subclass, and/or individual characteristics of the tool producing the marks. Also known as compression marks."

Another way to think of an impressed toolmark is to consider a harder object producing a reverse image on a softer object when the two come into contact with direct force. The most common areas where impressed marks are observed when comparing firearm-related evidence are breech face marks produced on the primer and cartridge case and the firing pin impression.

Striated toolmarks

Based on the definition in the AFTE Glossary (2013), striated toolmarks are defined as "contour variations, generally microscopic, on the surface of an object caused by a combination of force and motion where the motion of the tool is approximately parallel to the plane being marked. Friction marks, abrasion marks, and scratch marks are terms commonly used when referring to striated marks. These marks may contain class, subclass, and/or individual characteristics of the tool producing the marks."

In simpler terms, striated marks can be thought of as scratch marks where a hard object comes in contact with a softer item while in motion. The resulting mark is a striated or scratched mark which will have parallel marks caused by the movement of the raised and lowered portions of the harder object moving against the softer object. This motion displaces the metal of the softer metal. When evaluating firearm-related evidence, these marks can be seen on the bullet, ejector, extractor marks, among others. Breech face marks may also exhibit striated marks. This can occur with the firearm designed with a tilting barrel which holds the cartridge case during the course of firing. After the firearm was discharged, the barrel tilts downward and the cartridge case head rubs against raised areas of the firearm breech face creating striated marks (Fig. 4.1).

The appearance of striated marks is parallel in nature due to the motion of the tool across the surface of the workpiece. However, it is important to note that striated marks can be imparted through an impressed action. This is most often demonstrated on cartridge cases with breech face marks which have been manufactured using a method where the tool scrapes across the surface such as

Figure 4.1 Aperture shear.

Figure 4.2 Parallel breech face marks on a fired cartridge case.

broaching (see Chapter 5: Manufacturing techniques used in the manufacturing of firearms). In these instances, the parallel marks from the breech face are imparted on the cartridge case and primer and will appear as striated marks (Fig. 4.2).

The influence of these types of marks on bullets and cartridge cases relative to their interaction with the firearm are discussed in detail in Chapter 8, Comparison of cartridge cases. However, defining these two types of marks is essential in understanding the further discussion of the comparison of evidence.

Cartridge cases are typically made from brass, aluminum, or mild steel. All of these materials are softer than the hardened steel of the firearm. The primers of centerfire cartridges are also made from these softer metals while the breech face, firing pin, and other parts designed to withstand intense pressure from firing, are all made from hardened steel.

Class characteristics of cartridge cases

When a firearm fires a cartridge, the force exerted on the cartridge case drives it to the rear and the cartridge case impacts the breech of the firearm. This impact produces an impression of the breech face (being the harder of the two) onto the cartridge case head and primer which is the softer of the two materials. In the case of forensic firearm identification, the marks left by the firearm are essential in determining if the cartridge case came from that particular firearm. The interaction of the firearm with the cartridge resulting in these marks can be attributed to the cycle of operation.

Cycle of operation

The vast majority of firearms follow a similar set of steps during firing. This is referred to as the cycle of fire, or cycle of operation. Each type of firearm will have unique aspects to each step, such as method of extraction or ejection. Additionally, some steps may be combined with another, such as feeding and chambering. With training and experience, the steps of the cycle of operation will be easy to recognize and describe. Each step has the potential to leave class and individual characteristics that can be found on the ammunition. By discussing the cycle of operation, the different tool marks associated with the firing and cycling of a firearm will be better understood.

The cycle of operation can generally be reduced to the following steps: feeding, chambering, locking, firing, obturation, unlocking, extraction, ejection, and cocking. When each stage is analyzed individually, the associated tool marks can easily be distinguished. The creation of these tool marks will be discussed later in the book.

Feeding – This is generally the first step in the cycle of fire because it provides the source of ammunition. Feeding can be done manually with single cartridges or automatically with a magazine. Regardless of the type of feeding, each cartridge ultimately ends up in the chamber.

Chambering – Chambering involves securing the proper cartridge into the chamber after feeding. Only cartridges with specific dimensions are able to successfully fit into a chamber. If the wrong cartridge is chambered, a malfunction may occur.

Locking – This is the final step that must be achieved prior to firing. Locking is also referred to as battery, and firearms can be in- or out-of-battery. Locking is generally a fixed and secured status of a bolt or breechblock with the chamber. Locking can also affect the timing of firearms; improper timing can result in a misfire or failure to fire. Locking the action of the firearm is critical in order to resist the pressures of firing.

Firing – Simply put, this is the shooting or discharging of a firearm. In the cycle of operation, this step includes the pulling of the trigger, which releases the hammer or firing pin and allows it to fall forward striking the primer of the cartridge.

Obturation – This step involves the sealing of the bore and chamber due to pressure. This allows the gasses and pressure to force the projectile down the barrel. The pressure on the projectile, which is larger than the bore diameter, causes it to form into the rifling and improve the seal.

Unlocking – This is the opening of the bolt or breechblock. Many firearms perform extraction in combination with unlocking.

Extraction – This step is the removal of the fired cartridge case from the chamber. Because of obturation, the cartridge case may need the assistance of an extractor. Cartridge cases are designed with rims or grooves to facilitate the removal from the chamber by the extractor.

Ejection – At the end of extraction, the cartridge case will contact an ejector located opposite of the ejection port or opening. Many firearms combine the steps of extraction and ejection into one smooth step. Additionally, firearms such as revolvers require manual extraction and ejection after opening the cylinder.

Cocking — Depending on the action, cocking may be automatically accomplished during unlocking and extraction, or it may need to be done manually. For a semiautomatic pistol, the movement of the slide rearward cocks the hammer. Cocking allows a semiautomatic firearm to repeat the cycle until ammunition is exhausted.

The marks left by the firearm have two types of characteristics that are evaluated by the forensic firearm examiner. They are class and individual characteristics. Class characteristics are defined by the AFTE Glossary (2013) as "Measurable features of a specimen which indicate a restricted group source. They result from design factors and are determined prior to manufacture." These are caused by the manufacturing method, tooling, and how the tooling is used. These parameters will be discussed in detail in Chapter 5, Firearm manufacturing techniques. The result of these methods will leave gross marks which can easily include a cartridge case as having come from a particular type of firearm. They can also include the shape of a part that came in contact with the cartridge case, such as the firing pin and its aperture.

The machining process will determine both the individual and class characteristics. There are five general types of class characteristics observed in cartridge cases (Figs. 4.3–4.7). They include: parallel, concentric, arched, crosshatched, and smooth.

An example of using class characteristics in the examination process is given in Fig. 4.8. In this example, the cartridge case on the left has arched breech face marks, whereas the cartridge case on the right has parallel breech face marks. Likewise, a firearm that has parallel breech face marks will not leave circular marks; therefore two

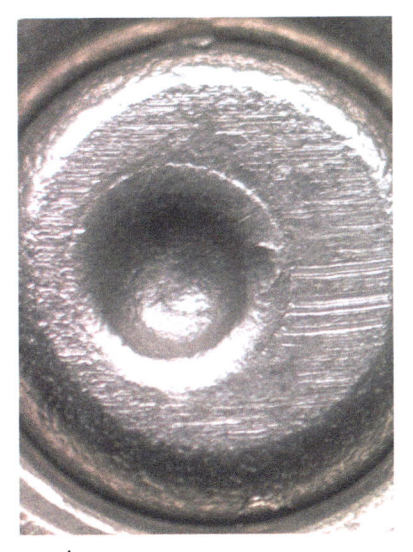

Figure 4.3 Parallel breech face marks.

Figure 4.4 Concentric breech face marks.

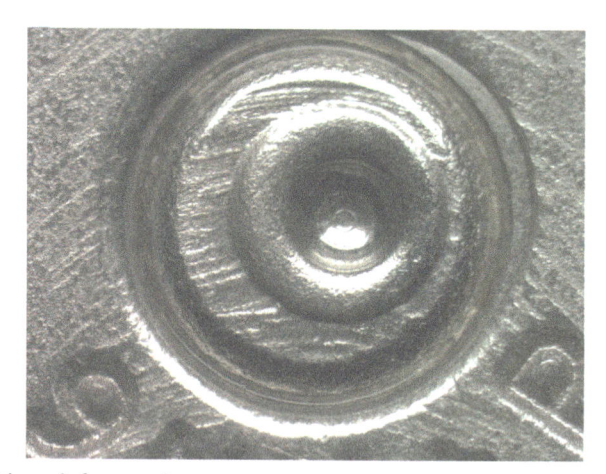

Figure 4.5 Arched breech face marks.

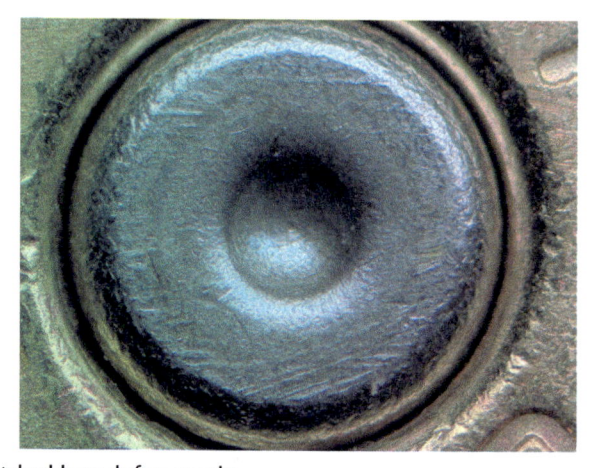

Figure 4.6 Crosshatched breech face marks.

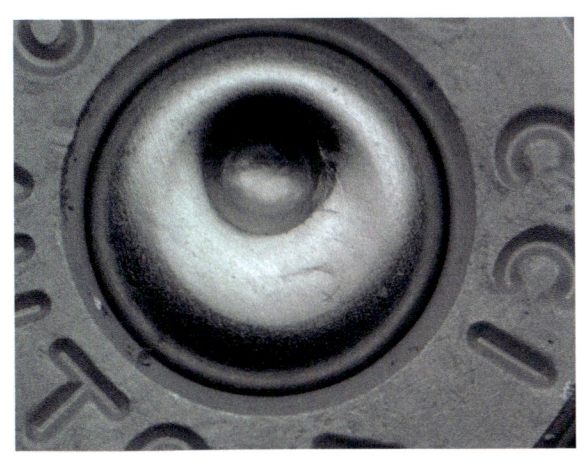

Figure 4.7 Smooth breech face marks.

Figure 4.8 Arched breech face marks on the left, parallel breech face marks on the right.

different firearms would have fired the cartridge cases and they can be excluded as having come from the same firearm.

Class characteristics of the firing pin

As with other components of firearms, the firing pin can display characteristics which are specific to a particular manufacturer. These are demonstrated by the size, shape, and other distinguishing characteristics that are unintentionally produced by the manufacturer. The primary design of the firing pin by the manufacturer is based on quality, production cost, and performance. They do not intentionally design a firing pin for

Figure 4.9 Hemispherical firing pin impression.

the purpose of distinguishing it from other designs; rather, it is a result of the manufacturing specifications to meet the aforementioned criteria.

Most firearm designs have a cylindrical channel for passage of the firing pin. This is due in part to the ease in manufacturing by using a drill to produce the channel. Due to the cylindrical nature of the channel, most firing pins are produced with a round profile and have a hemispherical nose. However, based on additional manufacturing techniques available, alternative firing pin profiles can be observed on specific make and models (Fig. 4.9).

Some manufacturers produce their firing pins in a shape or style that will lead a firearm examiner to be able to distinguish it from other potential contributors. This information can be helpful to investigators when searching for a firearm that may be associated with a crime. Since the most prevalent type of firing pin face is hemispherical with concentric marks, due to the popular use of the Swiss-type machine (see Chapter 5: Manufacturing techniques used in the manufacturing of firearms), the firing pins exhibiting characteristics other than that will be discussed along with the associated make and model.

Rectangular/elliptical firing pins

There are various manufacturers that produce firing pins with either rectangular or elliptical shapes depending on the manufacturing process. For example, earlier generation Glock semiautomatic pistols exhibit an elliptical firing pin shape which is almost exclusive to these firearms. The exception to this is early Smith & Wesson Sigma polymer framed pistols which shared many of the same characteristics. The Smith & Wesson Sigma subsequently modified their design to a hemispherical round shape. Another firearm that has adopted the elliptical firing pin along with the rectangular aperture is the Springfield XD-S series semiautomatic pistols. The elliptical shape of this type of firing pin is readily apparent and easy to distinguish from other firearms (Fig. 4.10). The resulting impression produced by firing pins with this shape will be easily distinguishable from hemispherical firing pins (Fig. 4.11). A more recent firearm to enter the market that shares similar firing pin characteristics with the earlier Glock pistols is the SAR9 semiautomatic pistol. As with all the information in this publication, manufacturers are subject to modifying the design of their firearm and future designs may incorporate different styles of firing pins and firing pin designs.

Another firing pin shape that lends itself to class characteristic identification is that produced by the Cobray (M-11) style firearms (Fig. 4.12). These also exhibit a rectangular firing pin. However, because the firing pin aperture hole and blowback design, they are easily distinguishable from Glock or other firing pins with rectangular or elliptical firing pins. The firing pin aperture on the Cobray style firearms is round, resulting in a rectangular firing pin inside a raised rounded primer flow back as discussed in Chapter 8, Comparison of cartridge cases (Fig. 4.13).

A different approach to the elliptical firing pin/rectangular aperture is observed on the Springfield model XD-S .45 caliber semiautomatic pistol. The use of an elliptical firing pin by some manufacturers is an intentional design for the purpose of minimizing the stress on the part at the time of impact. This is the case with the firing pin used in the Springfield

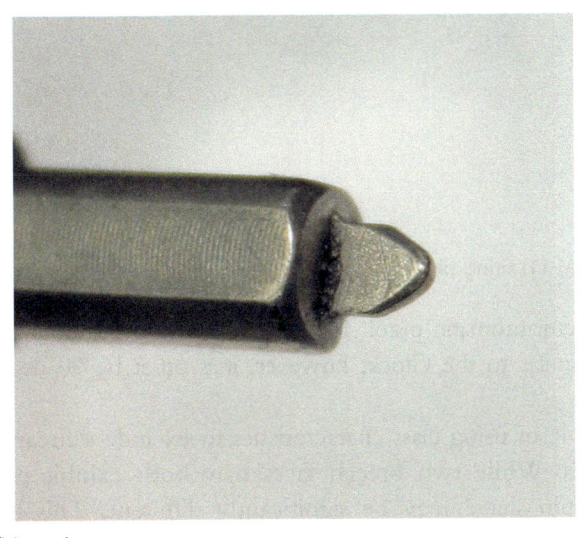

Figure 4.10 Glock firing pin.

Figure 4.11 Elliptical firing pin impression.

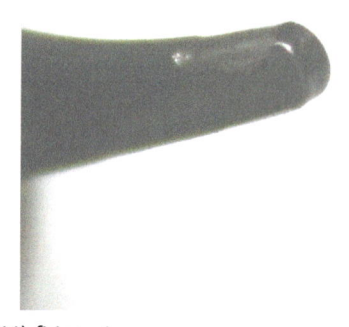

Figure 4.12 Cobray (M-11) firing pin.

XD-S .45 caliber semiautomatic pistol. In these firearms, at the time of this printing, the firing pin appears similar to the Glock; however, it is offset by 90 degrees relative to the aperture (Fig. 4.14).

Another example of using class characteristics to exclude a firearm would be based on differing shapes. While two breech faces may both exhibit parallel breech face marks, the firing pin shape may be significantly different. This is demonstrated in Fig. 4.15 where the firearm on the left has an elliptical firing pin and the firearm on

Figure 4.13 Cobray (M-11) firing pin impression.

Figure 4.14 Springfield XD-S .45 firing pin impression.

the right left a circular firing pin impression. This is another instance where the cartridge cases could be excluded as having come from the same firearm.

Flat-based firing pins

While a majority of firing pins demonstrate hemispherical, concentric characteristics, some may forgo the hemispherical profile and opt to utilize a flat nose. In these cases,

Figure 4.15 Elliptical firing pin impression on left and hemispherical firing pin on right.

Figure 4.16 Flat-based firing pin.

the resulting impression will be easily distinguishable from hemispherical firing pin impressions under magnification (Fig. 4.16). Firing pins manufactured with this profile are most commonly made on a Swiss-type machine; however, the tool cuts the tip at a 90-degree angle versus a hemispherical profile.

Class characteristics of the firing pin aperture

As described in Chapter 2, Firearm nomenclature and firearm types, the firing pin aperture is the opening through which the firing pin passes to contact the primer of the cartridge. During the production process, firearm manufacturers will use the most efficient, cost-effective method for producing this feature. The design of the aperture

Figure 4.17 Round firing pin hole (aperture).

will be based on what the manufacturer deems the most reliable and effective for their design. The shape can vary among manufacturers and will be a class characteristic of that make/model.

Round

The most common and easiest shape of aperture to produce is round. This is because a round hole easily lends itself to being produced by a drill. Therefore when attempting to narrow down a possible firearm by the aperture alone, the presence of a round aperture will have minimal value, except of course, to eliminate a suspected firearm that exhibits anything but round (Fig. 4.17).

Some manufacturers incorporate additional characteristics to the aperture hole for improved performance. An example of this is most commonly seen on the Springfield Armory model military and police semiautomatic pistols. These firearms have a relief machined into the lower area of the hole which produces a teardrop shape on the fired cartridge case (Fig. 4.18). The purpose of the relief is to reduce the amount of stress on the firing pin. This feature has also been utilized by other manufacturers, such as Glock in their model 42 and 43 semiautomatic pistols.

In addition, as part of the finishing process, some manufacturers perform an additional step to remove any burrs from the drilling process. One of the best examples of this is apparent in Beretta 92/96 series of firearms which have an aggressively counter-drilled aperture hole.

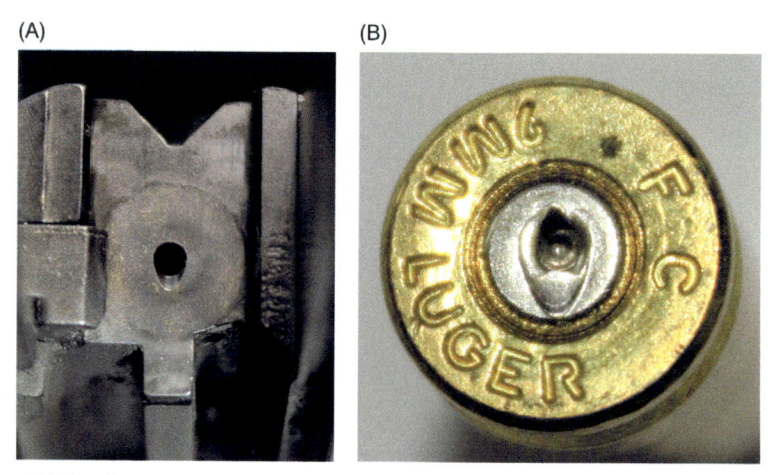

Figure 4.18 (A) Smith & Wesson M&P firing pin aperture; (B) firing pin impression from the Smith & Wesson M&P. *M&P*, Military and police.

Rectangular

Rectangular firing pin apertures are most commonly observed on Glock firearms. The double stack full size, compact, and subcompact models up to at least the Generation 5 models incorporate a rectangular firing pin aperture. The sheer volume of Glocks on market in addition to the Glocks that are sold by distributors as trade-ins from police departments makes them a popular firearm in the United States. A rectangular aperture is not limited to Glock firearms. Another firearm that was made for a brief period with a rectangular firing pin aperture was the Smith & Wesson Sigma semiautomatic pistol. Smith & Wesson eventually changed their design to a round aperture. In addition, in 2018, Sarsilmaz introduced the model SAR9 with a rectangular aperture and an elliptical firing pin (Quereau, 2018) (Fig. 4.19).

Glock produces the aperture hole by means of a punch press. The slide fits into a fixture on the press and a hardened punch in the shape of the aperture hole pierces the breech face. The punch is in the shape of a rectangle; however, after repeated usage and wear, the punch will eventually demonstrate rounded edges. The overall profile will still resemble a rectangle, but with some ovoid features (Fig. 4.20).

Other types of aperture holes that fall within the rectangular profile are those produced by the Springfield XD-S Series of firearms. These have rectangular apertures; however, the corners are rounded on every example observed. The rounded corners appear to be incorporated in the design rather than as a result of wear on the tool (Fig. 4.21).

Figure 4.19 Sarsilmaz model SAR9 firing pin impression.

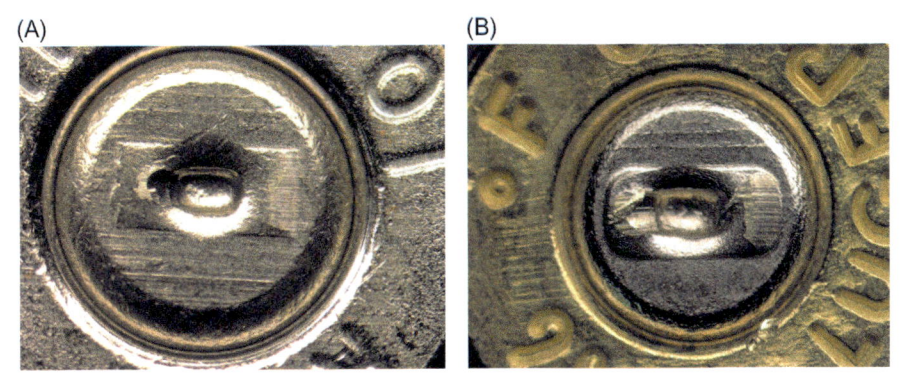

Figure 4.20 (A) Glock aperture with squared edges. (B) Glock aperture with rounded corners from punch wear.

Figure 4.21 Springfield model XD-S 9 mm aperture.

Figure 4.22 Phoenix Arms HP25 with rectangular firing pin.

Square

The square firing pin aperture hole is not as common as the rounded or rectangular; therefore, it is not seen as frequently. However, because it is more uncommon, the potential firearms that could have produced it is limited and provides more value in use for inclusion or exclusion as having come from a particular firearm.

The most commonly encountered firearm in the forensic laboratory that exhibits a square aperture hole is the Phoenix Arms model HP25 .25 ACP caliber semiautomatic pistol. The aperture hole on these firearms ranges from a perfect square to a square with a circular relief cut in the top. Either profile is very uncommon and can be strongly associated with the Phoenix Arms semiautomatic pistol and can be useful in the examination process, especially when a suspect firearm has not been associated with the case. Earlier versions of this firearm utilize a round firing pin; however in 2018, the firing pin had been changed to a rectangular shape (Fig. 4.22).

Class characteristics of a firearm barrel

Class characteristics are also present in the barrel of a firearm. These are in turn imparted onto the bullet as it passes down the barrel when the firearm discharges.

Firearm barrels have four class characteristics that forensic firearm examiners will use when evaluating evidence.

The four class characteristics of a barrel are as follows:
1. caliber;
2. direction of twist;
3. number of lands and grooves;
4. width of the lands and grooves.

Caliber

The caliber of the firearm is the bore diameter and may be expressed in inches or millimeters. Typically, cartridges designed in the United States use the Imperial System. These include the .357 Magnum, where the bore diameter is .357 in. Likewise, the .40 Smith & Wesson has a diameter of .40 in. Naturally, there are exceptions to the rule. The .38 Special cartridge has a bullet diameter of .357 in. The name, in this case, refers to the diameter of the cartridge case. However, overall, the caliber designation is generally true to the diameter of the bullet loaded in the cartridge.

When evaluating cartridges from European countries, the designation is typically given using the metric system. One of the most commonly encountered types of these is the 9 × 19 mm, also called 9 mm Luger or 9 mm Parabellum. In this case, the bullet is 9 mm in diameter. The inch equivalent is .355 in. in diameter. Because the diameter of the 9 mm is .355 in., it would fall into the class characteristics with the .38 Special and .357 Magnum, both being .357 in. That being said, there are instances where a 9 mm bullet could be distinguished from a .38 Special or .357 Magnum if the bullet had a unique design exclusive to 9 mm bullets or other distinguishing features.

Because of the sheer number of calibers and bullet designs, this section will not go into great detail of which calibers are typical of which bullet designs. When evaluating evidence, it is essential to have access to a large variety of ammunition to evaluate and observe the design, profile, and characteristics. These features may help in narrowing down the particular bullet submitted for evaluation.

There are many cartridges that share the same or very similar diameter bullets. The difference between the cartridges lies within the design and shape of the cartridge case. The optimum design as determined by the manufacturer is determined by the resulting characteristics of the ammunition. An example of a cartridge designed with specific parameters is the .300 Blackout, which is discussed in further detail in Chapter 12, Subclass characteristics. Essentially, the .300 Blackout is a cartridge that is designed to utilize a larger caliber bullet (.30 in. diameter) in a cartridge that has a similar profile and length as its smaller diameter cousin, the

Figure 4.23 5.56 × 45 mm on top, .300 Blackout on bottom.

5.56 × 45 mm cartridge. Utilizing similar cartridge characteristics allows for the integration of an additional cartridge in a firearm platform without the necessity of requiring additional components (Fig. 4.23).

Another example of a cartridge that developed as a means for firearm compatibility is the .300 Winchester Short Magnum (.300 WSM). The .300 WSM shares many of the same ballistic capabilities of the longer .300 Winchester Magnum; however, due to its shortened design, it is able to be used in short action rifles. Short action rifles incorporate a shorter bolt to cycle the action and prepare for the next shot.

There have been numerous examples of .30 caliber cartridges mentioned with respect to multiple cartridges sharing the same bullet diameter. The nominal caliber of .30 includes those ranging from a true .30 in. diameter to the metric designation of 7.62 mm in diameter (.308 in.). Because these diameters overlap, caution should be exercised when attempting to provide investigators with an assessment of potential firearm calibers. The .30 caliber class of firearm includes one of the most, if not the most, variants of cartridges which includes scores of different cartridges.

There are instances where the caliber can empirically exclude a bullet from having come from a particular firearm. In a case where a .45 caliber bullet was recovered from a crime scene and the analyst was presented with a 9 mm pistol, the 9 mm could easily be ruled out as having fired the .45 caliber bullet since a bullet with a diameter of .45 in. could not physically fit down the barrel of a 9 mm firearm having a diameter of .355 in.

Direction of twist

The barrel of the firearm is manufactured with what is called rifling. Rifling is raised and lowered areas travelling in a spiral pattern down the barrel. The purpose of rifling is to impart a spin on the bullet so that it is gyroscopically stable as it exits the barrel and flies through the air. Much like a football which is thrown in a spiral

Figure 4.24 Bullet with left-hand twist on the left and bullet with right-hand twist on the right.

fashion for accuracy, bullets will fly further and more accurately if they are stabilized and travel nose first. The methods of rifling will be discussed later in the book; however, it is important to elaborate on the importance of rifling as it relates to class characteristics.

Because rifling is machined in the barrel by the manufacturer, they determine what type of rifling best suits the firearm they are producing. They can choose either a clockwise or counter-clockwise twist. A clockwise twist is also called a right twist, while a counter-clockwise twist is a left twist. Rifling twist is as equally important as the other class characteristics when it comes to evidence examination. A bullet with a left twist, even if from the same caliber of firearm, could not have come from a firearm with a right twist barrel (Fig. 4.24).

Number of lands and grooves

The number of lands and grooves (raised and lowered portions) is the third class characteristic of a firearm barrel. Once again, this will be determined by the firearm manufacturer and varies from manufacturer to manufacturer. However, like the direction of twist, there are a finite number of lands and grooves that can be imparted into a barrel and can be overlapped between manufacturers. Some firearms have as few as 2 lands and grooves, and some up to 18 (Fig. 4.25). Those are the extremes, and most modern firearms exhibit between four and eight lands and grooves.

Width of lands and grooves

The width of the lands and grooves is the final class characteristic that firearm examiners routinely examine in order to either include or exclude a firearm as a potential

Figure 4.25 Bullet with 18 lands and grooves.

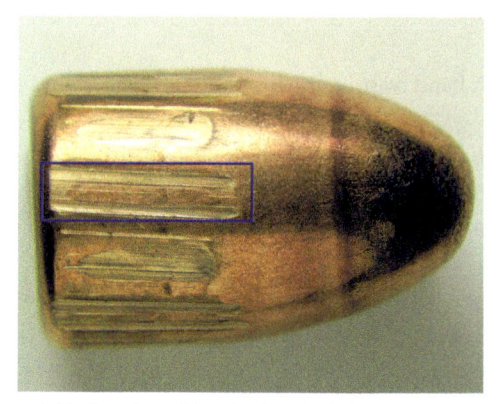

Figure 4.26 Bullet groove width (produced by the land of the barrel).

candidate for further examination. As the lands and grooves are formed in the barrel, the widths of those lands and grooves are determined by the tool used to impart them. Those widths are specified by the manufacturer based on testing on what will provide the best stability and accuracy for that caliber. The manufacturer may use the same rifling configuration on multiple models and multiple manufacturers may use the same rifling parameters in their rifling. Therefore a class of rifling with the same direction of twist, number of lands and grooves, and width of lands and grooves may not be exclusive to one particular manufacturer and may overlap (Figs. 4.26 and 4.27).

Class characteristics are design features that the manufacturer intentionally incorporates in the production process. Because of this, the manufacturer may change the process at any time. The change may be small or a complete redesign of the model. Most commonly, the change is small due to the amount and cost of tooling to totally redesign a model. In addition, if a model is redesigned, manufacturers will denote the model change with a new model number. However, smaller changes may come about as a means to lower production costs or to shorten production time. The class

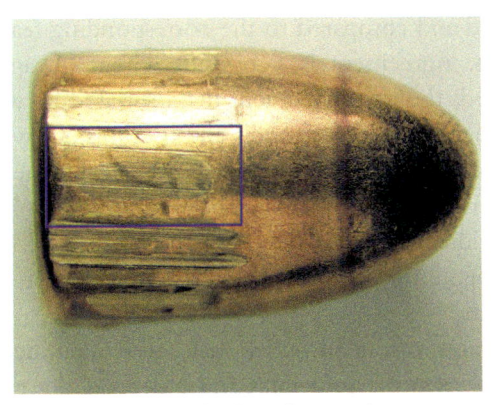

Figure 4.27 Bullet land width (produced by the barrel groove).

characteristics mentioned above with respect to particular makes and models of firearms may change and if class characteristics are used to include or exclude a particular model, research should be performed to ensure that current manufacturing techniques are taken into account.

Individual characteristics

Individual characteristics are defined by the AFTE Glossary (2013) as "marks produced by the random imperfections or irregularities of tool surfaces. These random imperfections or irregularities are produced incidental to manufacture and/or caused by use, corrosion, or damage. They are unique to that tool to the practical exclusion of all other tools." These marks are not intended by the manufacturer to be present and are a result of the interaction of the tool and the working surface of the workpiece. The source of these marks will be discussed in more detail in the next chapter. Ultimately, these random imperfections create unique marks which can be identified as having come from one source.

The theory of identification has been defined by the AFTE in the 2013 Glossary based on the following criteria:

1. The theory of identification as it pertains to the comparison of toolmarks enables opinions of common origin to be made when the unique surface contours of two toolmarks are in "sufficient agreement."
2. This "sufficient agreement" is related to the significant duplication of random toolmarks as evidenced by the correspondence of a pattern or combination of patterns of surface contours. Significance is determined by the comparative examination of two or more sets of surface contour patterns comprising individual peaks, ridges, and furrows. Specifically, the relative height or depth, width, curvature, and spatial relationship of the individual peaks, ridges, and furrows within one set of surface

contours are defined and compared to the corresponding features in the second set of surface contours. Agreement is significant when the agreement in individual characteristics exceeds the best agreement demonstrated between toolmarks known to have been produced by different tools and is consistent with agreement demonstrated by toolmarks known to have been produced by the same tool. The statement that "sufficient agreement" exists between two toolmarks means that the agreement of individual characteristics is of a quantity and quality that the likelihood another tool could have made the mark is so remote as to be considered a practical impossibility.

3. Currently, the interpretation of individualization/identification is subjective in nature, founded on scientific principles and based on the examiner's training and experience.

The understanding of class and individual characteristics will play a vital role in Chapter 8, Comparison of cartridge cases, and Chapter 9, Comparison of bullets, when the comparison of cartridge cases and bullets will be discussed in detail. However, introducing the concept of class and individual characteristics prior to the discussion of manufacturing techniques is important because the various manufacturing processes will induce these different characteristics.

CHAPTER 5

Firearm manufacturing techniques

The fundamental basis of forensic firearm identification involves evaluating the toolmarks generated during the manufacturing processes. To fully understand the toolmarks being evaluated on the fired bullet or cartridge case, it is important to understand the source of these marks. The foundation of the machining process is the basis of forensic firearm identification.

The machining process used on the firearm is dependent on multiple factors. One of the biggest factors is the type of machinery already in use by the manufacturer. Firearm companies are businesses, and they are in business to make a profit. If they have equipment which is already paid for and capable of making a part to their specifications, and they can manufacture it for less than outsourcing or purchasing new equipment, they will make it on that machine. In addition, manufacturers may have multiple methods for producing parts. If a machine goes out of commission, the alternate method will be employed. The next factor in the machining process in producing a firearm is the location and orientation of the area on the part being machined. Because of the restricted internal clearances inside a firearm slide or frame, a specific tool or fixture may best accomplish the final dimensional specifications. The last major determining factor is the final shape of the area being cut. Different tools will produce different shapes. The clearest example of this is a drill producing a round hole. In this type of operation, a drill bit will be the tool utilized to produce the desired shape.

Mechanics of machining

Regardless of the tool utilized in machining metal, the same action is occurring: the removal of metal from its source by a shearing action of a harder, sharpened tool. In the traditional sense, shearing is thought of as a clean cut, such as when cloth is sheared or paper is cut. However, on a microscopic level, the fabric and paper are being separated and pulled from the fibers from which they are attached. The same phenomenon occurs when metal is sheared from the surface of the workpiece.

During metal cutting, there are multiple events occurring that contribute to the removal process. In an ideal situation, a tool would come directly in contact with the workpiece, there would be no erosion of the tool, no heat buildup, and the metal would shear directly from the surface with no adhesion to itself. However, in practical application, all these events occur and more.

When there is interaction between a tool and workpiece, regardless of the tool being used, there are multiple contributors to the surface produced on the workpiece. The major contributors to the workpiece surface are built-up edge, shearing, plowing, sideflow, and tool wear. These factors are essential in evaluating the microscopic result of the machining process.

Surface roughness

In the machining industry, the irregularity of the surface is termed surface roughness. In the area of forensic firearm examination, the irregular surface consists of individual characteristics. The occurrence of surface roughness, to some degree, is unavoidable and eliminating it has been an issue for machinists since machines have been used to cut metal. The use of specialized lubricants, coolants, tool compositions, and tool coatings can decrease the amount of surface roughness; however, it cannot be eliminated.

Studies have been performed to evaluate methods to minimize the surface roughness of a workpiece under controlled environments, which still resulted in measurable variations of surface topography (Waikar and Guo, 2008). During this research, ASI 52100 steel was subjected to both "gentle" and "abusive" machining. The gentle machining was designed to impart a minimal amount of stress on the workpiece from the tool by controlling the tool (use of a new, sharp tool) and lower cutting speed. The abusive parameters included a worn tool with a higher cutting rate. In addition, the study included the effect of gentle and abusive grinding using an abrasive wheel. These are both machining methods employed in the manufacturing of firearm components.

The results as reported by Waikar and Guo state, "The 3D topographies of the turned and ground surfaces clearly show the difference in spacing between the peaks, the sharpness of the peaks, and the randomness of the profile. It can also be observed that the abusive turned surfaces show much sharper and random peaks, and surface cracks than those of the gently turned ones."

The statement regarding the abusive turned surfaces is an especially important one to note because the parts manufactured for firearms are subjected to what would be considered an abusive environment in that the tooling is used for multiple workpieces and is worn to some degree.

Research into the relationship between cutting speed and the surface finish of turned steel was conducted to determine a mathematical model that could be used to minimize surface roughness (Munoz-Escalona and Cassier, 1998). This study incorporated four different grades of steel (AISI 1020, AISI 1045, AISI 4140, and AISI D2) and four different types of tungsten carbide tools (TN35, DNMG 150604, DNMG 150608, and DNMG 150612). In using different cutting speeds, feed rates, depths of cuts, and tool nose radii, the resulting test encompassed 1584 samples. Compilation of the data demonstrated a surface roughness greater than 0.25 mm for any of the given samples. As shown in Fig. 5.1, this is a difference easily observable under the comparison microscope when evaluating firearm-related evidence.

Surface roughness varies depending on the type of machining that is being performed. In the earlier example, the method was turning, which is done using a lathe-type machine. Research has been conducted evaluating the resulting surface roughness of metal machined using face milling where the end of the endmill is drawn across a surface to produce a removed area (typically to form a slot). In this research, the surface roughness was significantly lower with an average roughness of 0.5 μm (Begic-hajdarevic et al., 2014). This can be attributed to the tool design having essentially four cutting surfaces (one from each flute of the endmill) and the high speed of 1000−2250 m/min. This type of machining is not commonly encountered in areas that come in contact with fired components from firearms; however, this demonstrates the differences in the surface roughness from different manufacturing methods.

Figure 5.1 Machined surface with a 0.20-mm scale for reference.

One factor encountered in the cutting tool world is the difference between the United States and European/Japanese machining philosophy. Traditionally, US manufacturers tended to practice "grip it and rip it": big depths of cut, lower RPM, heavy feed rates on a large workpiece. However, the more competitive machine shops or large manufacturers have already changed their mentality. Tooling today is being designed to fit more of the European model which includes faster RPM with lighter depths of cut, high-efficiency machining, or high-feed machining on workpieces which are cast or molded in nearly the final dimensions (Mackintosh, 2018).

Chip formation

The machining process is a cutting process which ultimately produces chips of removed material, or swarf (Kibbe et al., 1999a). There are three general classifications of how chips are formed during this process: continuous chip, discontinuous chip, and chip with built-up edge. Continuous and discontinuous chips have very little effect on the surface of the workpiece because they are the result of a clean separation of the workpiece from the tool. The exception to this would occur when the chip falls back into the interaction of the tool and workpiece. In those instances, a portion of the chip may be plowed into the surface of the workpiece. The most influential classification of chip formation in the forensic identification of both bullets and cartridge cases is the occurrence of built-up edge.

Built-up edge

Built-up edge is the result of an accumulation of material on the surface of the cutting tool. As the friction of the contact between the tool and workpiece increases, the ductile nature of the material causes a plastic flow of the metal. The heat and pressure cause the metal from the workpiece to weld to the surface of the tool (Shaw, 2005a). This in turn hardens the metal on the edge of the tool to further gain adherence. The accumulation of metal on the tool is a dynamic process, which results in multiple layers of workpiece material building up. In addition to growing forward of the tool edge, the built-up edge grows downward. This will create a variation in the depth of the surface being machined (Shaw, 2005b). The constant changes to the surface due to the evolution of the built-up edge is an obstacle in the process of machining firearms; however, it is a contributing factor to the fundamental principle of the individuality of firearm identification (Figs. 5.2 and 5.3).

There are countless research articles in the area of built-up edge and its effect on both tooling and the workpiece (Fang and Dewhurst, 2005). This plethora of research is largely due to the financial implications of the occurrence of built-up edge; that is,

Firearm manufacturing techniques 99

Figure 5.2 Built-up edge on endmill cutting surface.

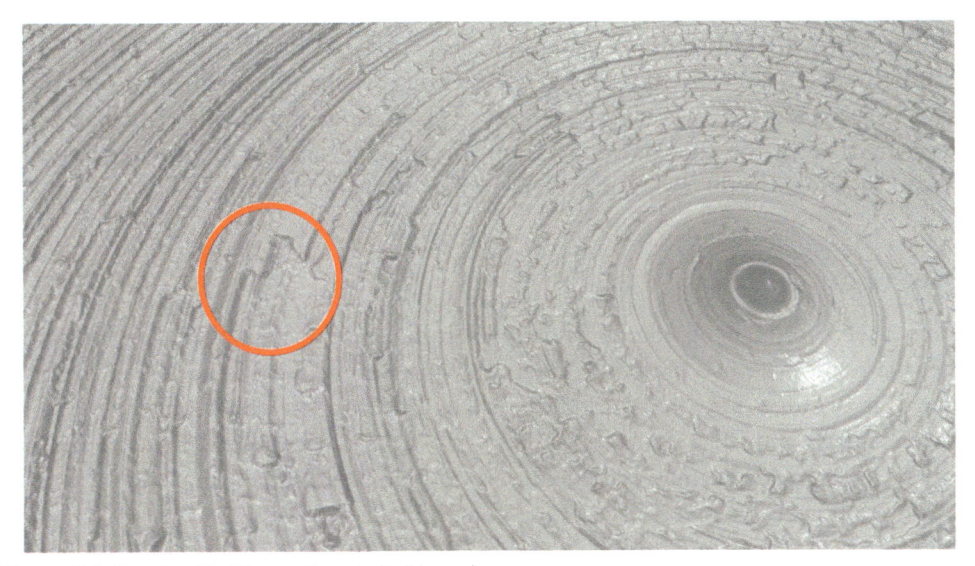

Figure 5.3 Result of built-up edge circled in red.

the cost of tooling and the downtime in manufacturing to replace tooling. In an article examining the source of and an attempt to predict built-up edge, Fang and Dewhurst provide the following statement:

The built-up edge (BUE) in machining is an irregular and unstable structure, being constructed of successive layers greatly hardened under extreme strain conditions at the tool–chip interface. It is formed on the tool rake face when cutting ductile metals and alloys, such as steels and aluminum alloys, under a certain range of low-to-moderate cutting speeds. Because the BUE alters tool angles, it has profound effects on cutting forces, cutting temperatures, tool-wear, tool-life, surface roughness, and geometric dimensions of machined products.

The earlier statement is valuable in the area of forensic firearm identification and warrants rereading and a thorough understanding. This is because it and other citations which echo the same principal are at the core of what provides the unique features on machined components of firearms. The statements are from the academic community working in conjunction with mechanical engineers and machinists to demonstrate the underlying principles of forensic firearm identification.

The occurrence of built-up edge is most prevalent in harder metals, including medium carbon steels, tool steels, and alloys. These are also the most commonly used metals in the production of firearm parts that interact with the cartridge case and bullet (McCarthy and Smith, 1968).

As with the initial adhering material, the additional material is what contacts the surface being machined. Eventually, the built-up edge will become too stressed due to its size and the accumulated piece will break off. When the piece breaks off, it can either break off and free itself from the work entirely, slip under the tool, and gouge into the workpiece or be pushed to the side in the form of sideflow.

Built-up edge not only has a negative effect on the surface roughness of the workpiece, it also has a negative effect on the tool. The constant welding and breakage of the material from the tool causes wear and subsequent change to the tool's cutting surface. This wear to the tool is discussed further along in this chapter.

Plowing

When a piece of built-up edge is displaced into the workpiece rather than forming a chip, the result is termed plowing. When plowing occurs, there is no loss of material. Instead, it is forced into the workpiece (Shaw, 2005c). The result of plowing is an uneven surface with depressions due to the gap from the deposited material and the item being cut. An example where this is commonly observed in forensic firearm identification is on the breech face of the Glock (Fig. 5.4).

Plowing has been found to be caused by a combination of both the feed velocity and the tool edge geometry (Laakso et al., 2018). In the broaching of breech faces, the broach may have a less than ideal tool edge for making a clean cut. However, if

Figure 5.4 Glock breech face with material plowed into the surface.

the dimensions stay within specifications of the manufacturer, the broach will continue to be used. Manufacturers of firearms are primarily concerned with dimensional specifications rather than surface finish when interior parts of the firearm are concerned.

Sideflow

Sideflow is the plastic deformation of workpiece material displaced to the side of the area being cut by the tool. This is a form of built-up material to the side of the surface being cut. "In machining process [sic], the produced sideflow deteriorates the machined surface quality to increase the surface roughness" (Liu et al., 2017). This again demonstrates the randomness of the resulting surface and subsequent surface roughness, which is observed when evaluating marks produced by firearms (Fig. 5.5).

Figure 5.5 Side produced by a single point cutting tool.

The occurrence of sideflow was found to increase as tool wear increased. A large contributor to this is the increase of the radius of the toolface, which has a direct effect on sideflow. The likelihood of squeezing the workpiece material between the tool flank and machined surface also rises. As the radius changes, the ability to efficiently cut is reduced and the resulting friction from contact escalates the conditions for sideflow to occur (Fang and Jawahir, 1992).

During his study of sideflow and the most common influences contributing to it, Shaw (2005d) found that sideflow was most prevalent when alloy steel was machined. Firearms are most commonly manufactured from alloy steel, thus it is expected to see sideflow as a contributing characteristic to the workpiece surface.

Shearing

The ideal method for machining a workpiece is shearing. Shearing involves the complete removal of the metal being cut and extracted from the surface. However, even in the perfect situation, the result is not a perfectly smooth surface. The granular structure of the metal will be separated with an inconsistent result. During the occurrence of shearing with no displacement of metal, there are still irregularities in the surface of the workpiece.

The speed and relative precision at which modern firearms are produced do not put them on par with precision items machined for use by the aerospace industry. The acceptable tolerances expected by firearm manufacturers allow tools to be used longer before replacement. This leads to an increased chance of built-up edge, sideflow, and plowing.

Chatter

As with all occurrences of interrupted machining of metal, chatter has long been recognized and there have been many attempts to minimize or eliminate it. In 1907, Fredrick Taylor wrote an article titled, "On the Art of Cutting Metals." In the article, he states, "Chatter is the most obscure and delicate of all problems facing the machinist, and in the case of castings and forgings of miscellaneous shapes probably no rules or formulas can be devised which will accurately guide the machinist" (Taylor, 1907).

The effect of chatter and how to minimize it has been the topic of many research articles. In an article authored by Siddhpura and Paurobally, they state, "Chatter vibrations are present in almost all cutting operations and they are major obstacles in achieving desired productivity. Regenerative chatter is the most detrimental to any process as it creates excessive vibration between the tool and the workpiece, resulting in a poor surface finish, high-pitch noise and accelerated tool wear which in turn reduces machine tool life, reliability and safety of the machining operation" (Siddhpura and Paurobally, 2012).

Chatter occurs when there is vibration either in the workpiece, tool, or both, during machining. In addition to just the workpiece or tool, any component of the system attributing to the machining can play a role in inducing chatter. Some of these components include the spindle, tool holder, machine tool structure, and any fixturing system used to hold the workpiece. The vibration in any of these components will lead to a surface with disrupted contact resulting in irregular but patterned contact. In the machining community, chatter has been attributed to disrupted work surfaces, reduction in life of the machine, and tool life (Munoa et al., 2016) (Fig. 5.6).

A source of chatter, as evaluated by Altintas and Chan, is the result of deflection of the tool while contacting the workpiece. Based on the research performed, there were several factors contributing to deflection. The depth of cut, angle of cut, rotational speed of the cutting tool, and feed rate were variables used to evaluate changes in deflection. The result of their experiments displayed a deflection of up to 0.8 mm, which is considerable in terms of surface finish (Altintas and Chan, 1991).

There have been two types of chatter identified with respect to the machining process. The main source of chatter, as previously mentioned, includes the friction

Figure 5.6 Chatter demonstrated on workpiece.

between the tool and workpiece and the resulting thermodynamics from this interaction. In addition to primary chatter, secondary chatter can occur. Secondary chatter is caused by the regeneration of waviness of the workpiece surface. These types of chatter produce the pattern discussed earlier (Lamraoui et al., 2014).

Once chatter initiates, it will not stop until it departs from the workpiece. An example of this is the use of an endmill to produce a slot, where the slot can create a tuning fork effect. When an endmill is used in a face milling operation, the endmill will resonate in the same fashion that a finger on the rim of a glass will create harmonics (Mackintosh, 2018). The effect of chatter on the product finish, that is, the surface roughness consisting of an irregular surface, is such a common occurrence that researchers continue to formulate methods to minimize its effect (Altintas and Chan, 1992).

Tool wear

Tool wear also plays an important role in a forensic firearm examiner's ability to differentiate bullets and cartridge cases fired from different firearms, even those consecutively manufactured (Fadul et al., 2013). Tribology is a science dedicated to the study of the occurrence of friction, wear, and lubrication. According to the Martini Research Group (Martini Research Group, 2018), while the term was only designated in 1964, the concept of utilizing lubricant to minimize wear and friction dates to Egyptian times when oil was used to lubricate stone statues during transportation. The word tribology comes from the Greek word for rub.

This science is essential in the manufacturing industry as minimizing tool wear minimizes the downtime associated with changing tooling and machine setup. However, the effect of tool wear cannot be overcome. As tools interact with workpieces, the combination of heat, friction, abrasion, and welding of material to the tool and subsequent deposition of that material causes erosion to the tool. This erosion results in an ever-changing surface of the cutting edge. Thus, the scientific study of surface interaction in relative motion, or tribology, is an intensely studied area.

There are three major contributors that diminish the tolerances of the tool during the machining process: abrasive, adhesive, and diffusive wear (Tay et al., 2002). When the tolerances of the cutting tool change, the tool may remain in service or be pulled from production. The determining factor will rely on the expectations of the manufacturer.

Abrasive wear involves material loss due to rubbing and friction when a harder material contacts a softer one. This is commonly observed in the grinding of metal. A grinding wheel is composed of oxides, which are harder than the steels they grind. However, in the case of machining, the wear debris of the workpiece can oxidize and form hardened particles. These hardened particles then effectively grind or cause abrasive wear on the cutting tool. In addition to hardened particles from the workpiece, the compromised condition of the tool, which has been softened due to the heat generated from machining, can contribute to the likelihood of the tool becoming abraded by a hardened particle (Binder et al., 2017).

Adhesive wear occurs when the substrate being cut bonds to the cutting tool with enough strength to supersede the adherence of the cutting tool material to itself. Then, when the accumulated particle breaks off, a portion of the cutting tool is also removed (Shaw, 2005e). According to research, adhesive wear is a major contributor to part of tribology-related differences in terms of surface damage, including transition from mild-to-severe adhesive wear (Fukuda and Morita, 2017). Adhesion of metal to metal is facilitated by heat, pressure, and friction. All these events occur during the interaction of a tool with a workpiece, thus the prevalence of this type of wear.

Diffusive wear is the result of progressive loss of material from one surface to another. This process is different than adhesive wear. Adhesive wear is the buildup of material on one surface until the point where the entire piece of built-up material breaks free from the surface, resulting in both loss of the built-up material and the adhesive portion of the other surface, in this case, the tool. In the situation of diffusive wear, particles of the tool are passed directly to the workpiece (D'Acunto, 2003).

The analysis of tool wear plays such an important role in the manufacturing industry that researchers have developed formulas for predicting the wear profiles on tools. This not only demonstrates the occurrence that the tool is constantly changing, as proposed by the forensic firearm examiner community but also incorporates the effect of the contributing factors (Ko and Kim, 2000). The formula is expressed as:

$$D_w = \frac{kPL}{3h}$$

D_w is the wear depth, k is the constant which is dependent on material combination and contact condition, P is the normal pressure, L is the sliding length, and h is the hardness of the tool.

Tool wear changes the tool surface as the effects of abrasive, adhesive, and diffusive wear occur. During single point cutting (lathe), an indexable carbide tool with multiple cutting edges may be used. These offer an optimal use of the carbide since the same piece of carbide can be used multiple times by being rotated to the next sharp edge. A new insert will exhibit no wear and a sharpened edge. As the tool wears, the edge will diminish, and the resulting cutting edge will change. The resulting marks will be unique to that tool during the contact at that point of wear (Figs. 5.7 and 5.8).

The minimization and calculation of tool wear are very important to the manufacturing industry; therefore, studies to understand the factors affecting wear are continuously being researched. To further understand the effect of tool wear, a study was performed by Fang and Jawahir. This study incorporated variables in both the tool material and the workpiece material to evaluate the differences in the amount and locations of the tool wear. The hardness of the bit and the hardness of the material being machined were both varied to provide a wider range of results. The measured tool wear was found to be between 0.8 mm during 15 minutes of use and 0.73 mm during 34 minutes of use. The difference in the amount of tool wear versus time can be attributed to the combination of the tool and workpiece hardness (Fang and Jawahir, 1992).

One factor that remains constant in the abovementioned example is that there is indeed change in the tool surface as a result of use. The change in tool profile is among the contributors to individual characteristics, which is the foundation to individualizing a mark from a firearm as having produced the mark on the ammunition component.

Figure 5.7 New lathe insert.

Figure 5.8 Worn lathe insert.

Pressure weld

The contact of two metals may be susceptible to establishing metallic bonds between the two. The friction caused by the machining process is the main contributing source to this type of deposit on the cutting tool. This can occur at room temperature. The pressure alone can be sufficient in providing the energy to complete the welding process. In these instances, the two largest contributing factors are the magnitude of the load and the cleanness of the surfaces (Shaw, 2005f). These are factors that are typically controllable by the manufacturer; however, if the end result of the production piece is not significantly affected by pressure welds, adjustments may not be made to the manufacturing process.

Types of machining

The aforementioned mechanics of machining contribute significant effects to the machining processes to follow. All of the processes in the various types of machining contain surfaces of removed metal which will demonstrate characteristics of chip formation, built-up edge, plowing, sideflow, shearing, chatter, tool wear, and pressure welds. These characteristics will in turn be imparted on the surfaces of the items in contact with a cutting tool.

Grinding

The process of grinding is an important aspect to forensic firearm identification because this process is used to make nearly every tool that comes in contact with the firearm. The result of the grinding process creates toolmarks on the tools, which in turn create toolmarks on the final product used in the examination process. Endmills, drill bits, lathe tools, and broaches all have the final edge finished with the grinding process.

Grinding wheels are made by embedding grit or abrasive in a bonding matrix. Common size grit used to make the abrasive wheel can range from size 8 to 600. The smaller the number, the larger the grit, with size 8 being very coarse and 600 being very fine. An easy way to remember this is to view it as a fraction: 1/8 is larger than 1/600. The finer the grit, the smoother finish that will be achieved on the final product and very little material will be removed. In contrast, a coarser grit will give a rougher finish but remove more material. The choice of grinding wheel is dependent on the amount of material to be removed and the final surface finish of the product. With items where tolerances are expected to be held to the thousandth of an inch, such as endmills, a finer grit grinding wheel would be used (Figs. 5.9 and 5.10).

The interaction of the grit will cause chip formation in the form of plastic deformation of the workpiece grain. During the metal shearing process, oxidized chips are formed by

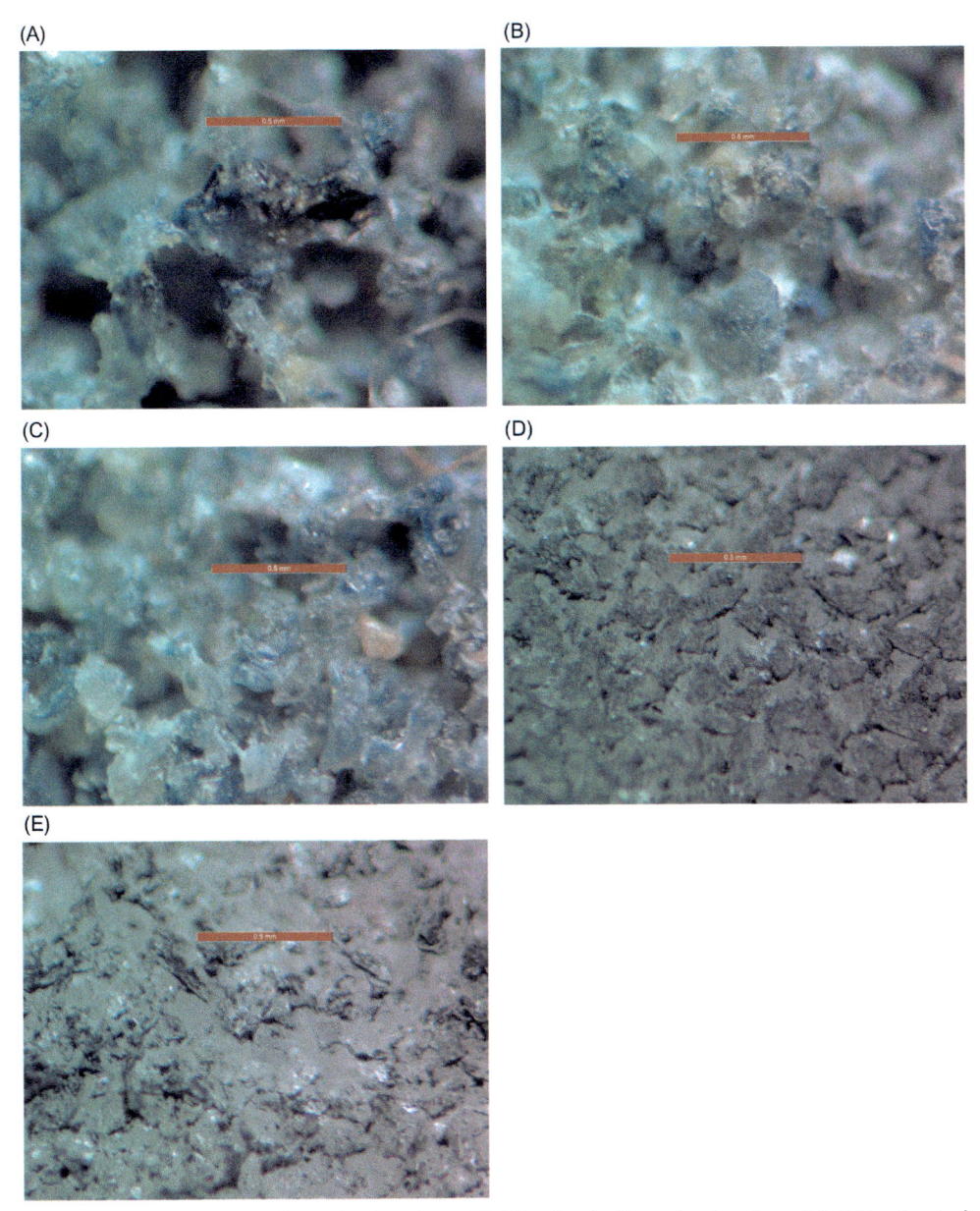

Figure 5.9 (A) 36 grit grinding wheel surface, (B) 60 grit grinding wheel surface, (C) 100 grit grinding wheel surface, (D) 120 grit grinding wheel surface, and (E) 150 grit grinding wheel surface.

adiabatic and surface tension (Malkin, 2008a). Plowing is a type of plastic deformation where the metal remains in contact with the workpiece. This causes chip formation when the buildup of metal from the plowing action contacts the workpiece. The built-up edge is an ever-changing surface of material that is acting as the cutting tool.

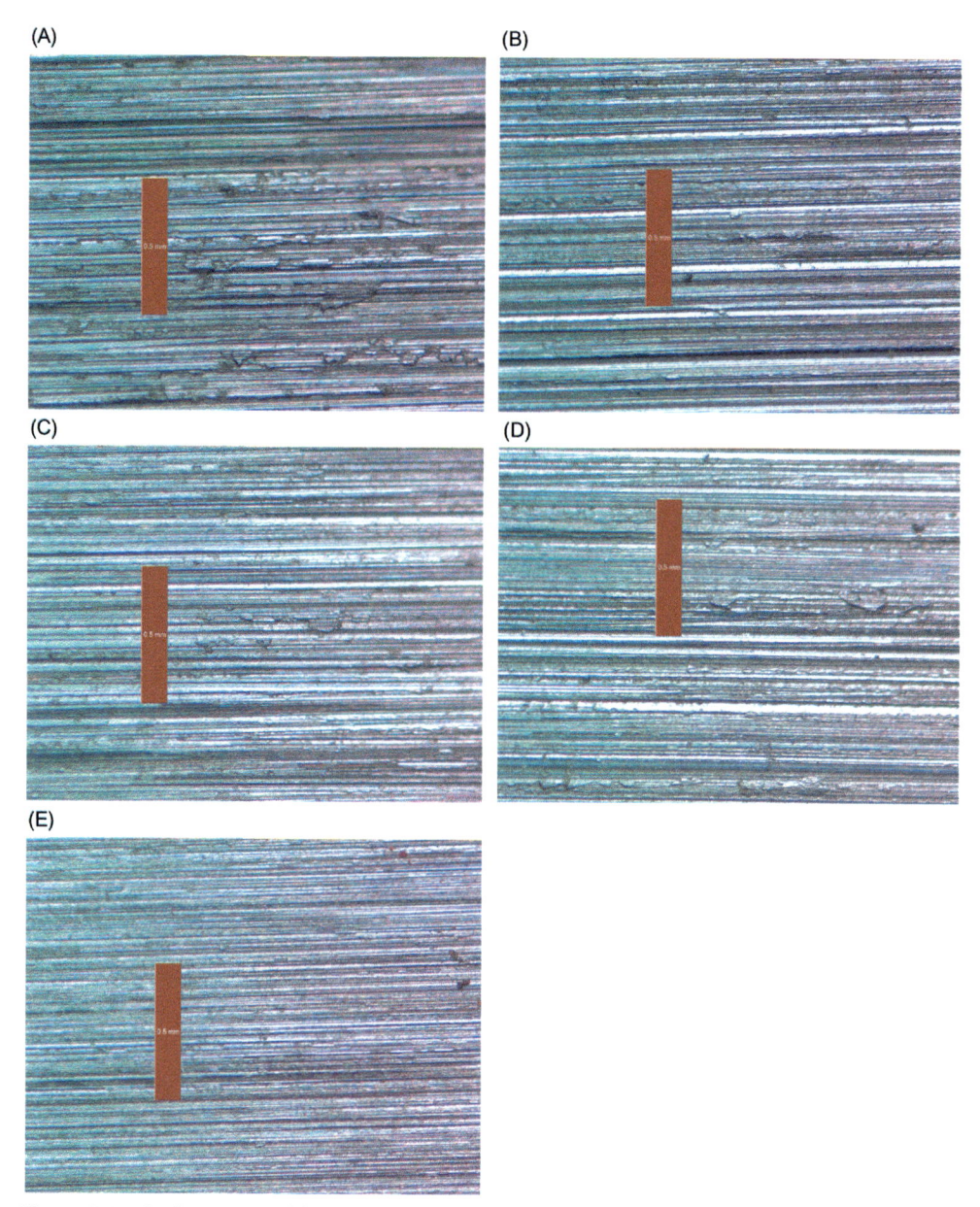

Figure 5.10 Surfaces ground by (A) 36 grit grinding wheel, (B) 60 grit grinding wheel, (C) 100 grit grinding wheel, (D) 120 grit grinding wheel, and (E) 150 grit grinding wheel.

Another force that affects the interaction of the grinding wheel and the workpiece is vibration. There are two sources of this vibration: self-excited chatter and forced vibration. Self-excited chatter is caused by instability of the grinding condition, which includes wheel speed, workpiece speed, metal type, etc. Forced vibration includes those caused by the dynamic grinding force and an unbalanced wheel condition (Chang and Wang, 2008). An important observation by Chang and Wang is described when they state, "The random distribution of the grits on the wheel surface, however, makes the grinding process stochastic in nature." They go on to state, "Since the distribution of grits is irregular and nondeterministic over the entire wheel and varies with time due to some unique phenomena during grinding such as loading, pulling out, wear, and self-sharpening of grits, the distribution of engaging grits is a random function of time and space." These two statements are again important to note in that they emphasize the randomness of tool/workpiece interaction.

When using a grinding wheel to remove material, the grit is the tool that removes metal from the workpiece. A grinding wheel is designed to be consumed during the cutting process. This occurs when the grit breaks during the interaction with the metal. In addition, the grit pieces break completely away from the matrix exposing a new piece of grit. The occurrence of chipped and removed grit results in randomly arranged, ever-changing cutting tools (grit). The final contribution to the surface of the grinding wheel is the transfer metal from the workpiece being embedded into the grinding wheel. The combination of grit breakage, grit removal, and metal embedded into the grinding wheel produces an evolving profile of tools (grit).

The random and fluctuating shape of the grain is further described in a paper researched by Hou and Komanduri from the School of Mechanical and Aerospace Engineering at Oklahoma State University titled, "On the mechanics of the grinding process—Part I. Stochastic nature of the grinding process" published in the *International Journal of Machine Tools and Manufacture*. In this article, they state, "Grinding of metals is a complex material removal operation involving cutting, plowing, and rubbing depending on the extent of interaction between the abrasive grains and the work material under the conditions of grinding. It is also a stochastic process in that a large number of abrasive grains of unknown geometry, whose geometry varies with time, participate in the process and remove material from the workpiece. Also, the number of grains passing through the grinding zone per unit time is extremely large.... The analysis is applied to some typical cases of fine grinding and cutoff operations reported in the literature. It is found that out of a large number of grains on the surface of the wheel passing over the workpiece per second (∼million or more per second)" (Hou and Komanduri, 2003).

In efforts to predict the effects of the grinding process for the purpose of maximizing tool use and improving the desired results, research has been conducted in modeling and simulating the grinding process through computer programs. However, during this research, the occurrence of what are considered individual characteristics by firearm examiners is also discussed by the researchers. In a paper titled, "Modeling and simulation of grinding processes with mounted points: Part I of II—Grinding tool surface characterization" presented at the 7th Annual High Performance Cutting Conference, the following description of grinding was discussed:

"The grinding process is a complex process which involves the interaction of multiple cutting edges, without a specific geometrical form, with a specific workpiece. Therefore several difficulties can arise during the modeling of the process, for example, issues concerning the random size, shape and distribution of the cutting edges along the grinding tool, its removal mechanisms along the material removal process of a workpiece and its surface structure" (Uhlmann et al., 2016).

The use of a grinding wheel in removing material has three distinct processes: rubbing, plowing, and cutting. These occur when the grain of the grit traverses through the grinding zone (Qi et al., 1997). However, when exploring the aspect of grinding and the irregular shape of the grit, it was demonstrated that only a small percentage (5%—10%) of the grit actually participates in the cutting process. The remaining contact of the grit rubs or plows the surface of the workpiece (Hou and Komanduri, 2004).

The removal of metal, regardless of the cutting tool, has the same interaction. When discussing the grinding process, the individual grit acts as single point cutting tools similar to a lathe, which will be discussed later in this chapter. The microscopic study of surfaces, as a result of grinding and the grinding process with respect to chip formation, is discussed in the *Mechanical Engineers' Handbook* First Edition published in 1916. In this treatise, grinding is described as "…a true cutting process. Under the microscope, the particles of metal removed by an abrasive wheel are seen to have the shape and character of chips cut by a lathe tool from the same material." (Marks, 1916). The documented examination of microscopic imperfections specifically attributed to the cutting process from the machining process by machinists predates documented sources of these toolmarks as described by firearm examiners. While the theory of individuality is understood and utilized by firearm examiners, it is important to note that separate, unaffiliated fields of study also recognized these differences.

In research performed by Hou and Komanduri, the focus was to determine the thermal analysis of the grinding process. The thermal aspects of the interaction between the grinding wheel and the workpiece are important in the field of machining because they contribute to premature wear of the grinding wheel and reduced productivity. The sole source of thermal contribution to the system is the friction caused by the interaction of the grinding wheel grit with the workpiece. Therefore, the research into this interaction is valuable to the machining industry. It is also valuable to the field of forensic firearm examination because the grit of the grinding wheel is the source of the individual characteristics of the tools used to produce firearm components.

The application of the formula used to calculate contact of grit provided by Hou and Komanduri can be applied to calculate the number of grit in contact with a workpiece. In the next example, the width of the area being ground is 3/16 in. wide (4.7625 mm). The parameters of the grinding wheel, speed, and feed are outlined next and provide an example of the interaction of a grinding wheel and workpiece during the grinding operation. The minimum and maximum diameters for a given grit size are industry standards provided by the manufacturer.

Grinding wheel: 120 grit (nominal grain of the wheel), resin bond structure 6—volumetric fraction 52%

Velocity of wheel (V_{wheel}): 3500 cm/s

Down feed: 60 inches per minute (ipm)

Width of contact (b): 0.47625 cm (3/16 in.)

Contact time (t): 3 seconds

The nominal grain of the wheel is 120. Based on that information, the mean grain abrasive size (d_{mean}) can be calculated.

$$d_{mean} = \frac{(d_{max} + d_{min})}{2}$$

$$d_{mean} = \frac{(0.165 + 0.051)}{2}$$

$$d_{mean} = 0.108 \text{ mm}$$

First, the number of grains per unit of length (N_l) must be calculated and converted to cm:

$$N_l = \frac{10}{d_{mean}} \times (\text{volumetric fraction of abrasives in wheel})^{1/3}$$

$$N_l = \frac{10}{0.108} \times (0.52)^{1/3}$$

$$N_l = 74.5 \text{ grains/cm}$$

Then, the number of grains per unit area (N_a) can be calculated as:

$$N_a = N_l^2$$
$$N_a = 74.5^2$$
$$N_a = 5550 \text{ grains/cm}^2$$

The total number of grains passing through the grinding area per second (N_{Total}) is then calculated as:

$$N_{Total} = v_{wheel} \times b \times N_a$$
$$N_{Total} = 3500 \text{ cm/s} \times 0.47625 \text{ cm} \times 5550 \text{ grains/cm}^2$$
$$N_{Total} = 9.2 \times 10^6 \text{ grains/s}$$

The total number of grains in contact ($N_{contact}$) with the 3/16 inch path can be calculated as:

$$N_{contact} = N_{Total} \times \text{time}$$
$$N_{contact} = 9.2 \times 10^6 \text{grains/s} \times 3 \text{ s}$$
$$N_{contact} = 2.7 \times 10^7 \text{ grains}$$

Therefore, 27,000,000 abrasive grains interact with a 3/16-in. surface during the grinding process (Hou and Komanduri, 2003).

Additional citation for the occurrence of striated marks caused by the grinding process is mentioned in a book dedicated to the mechanics of grinding titled *Grinding Technology* by Stephen Mailkin. He states, "The presence of wear-flat areas, with their characteristic striated markings in the grinding direction, indicates that part of the energy expended in grinding is due to their sliding against the workpiece" (Malkin, 2008b).

While it is important to discuss the potential for change of the grinding wheel during the grinding process, it is also important to note that the changes are not immediate and do not change on a large scale with each contact. This is evident in the use of a grinding wheel. If the grinding wheel were to change in an equal amount by way of loss of grit with each encounter of a piece of metal, it would degrade in such an aggressive manner as not to be utilized for an extended period. If this were the case, a grinding wheel would only perform effective grinding on a very limited number of items without having to be replaced. Simple observation of grinding demonstrates that this is not the situation.

The relatively slow change of the grinding wheel has the potential to impart subclass characteristics on the workpiece. If the grinding wheel were to have a large exposed piece of grit or series of grit that was not easily displaced, the resulting gross abrasions may carry over onto subsequent parts. Another potential source of subclass marking that can occur during the grinding process is self-excited chatter vibrations. Self-excited chatter vibrations are indicated by the observation of waviness on the surface of the workpiece (Altintas and Weck, 2004). This is important to recognize in preventing the use of subclass characteristics for identification purposes. The observation of plowing, sideflow, and built-up edge within these gross marks is an essential element in discerning subclass from individual characteristics.

Machining methods used in the manufacturing of firearm parts
Milling

One of the most important pieces of equipment used in the manufacturing of firearms and firearm parts is the milling machine. There are two types of milling machines: vertical and horizontal mills. The application of the machine and type of cut will determine the type of machine to be used. The most commonly used milling machine is the vertical milling machine. This type of machine typically encounters the workpiece at a 90-degree angle. The first vertical milling machine appeared in the 1860s. The first type of milling machine was very similar to a drill press. Eventually, the design evolved into a sturdier configuration, which increased the rigidity and improved the capacity of material removal (Kibbe et al., 1999b).

The process of milling and its associated tools has not changed since its inception. However, there have been significant improvements in both the design and functionality of milling machines and the related tooling design. One of the first improvements in the milling machine was the addition of an automated table in 1920. This type of automation was a leap in the production output and efficiency. As technology advanced, milling machines were paired with computer technology, allowing for full automation of the machining process. The modern machining process typically used by manufacturers is automated and produces exact replicas with little to no operator interaction. This is called computer numerically controlled (CNC) machining and is applicable to any machine, such as a mill, lathe, or drill press.

The second type of mill is the horizontal mill. As the name indicates, this type of mill is designed to machine objects in the same plane (horizontally) as the workpiece. Horizontal milling is generally reserved for removing material from flat surfaces. The use of this type of milling has been virtually eliminated from the firearm manufacturing process with the development of advances in preliminary casting and forging of the initial workpieces. However, the result of the machining of the workpiece by a horizontal mill has the same effect on the workpiece as the vertical mill with respect to the production of both class and individual characteristics.

Along with improvements in the machines used to perform the milling operation, the tooling used to cut metal has also advanced with technology. The materials used to produce these tools have evolved from steel to hardened materials, such as carbide. In addition, the coatings used on the tooling provide lubricity and an additional layer of protection from wear.

The tooling used in the milling process is an endmill. As described by the name, endmills primarily remove material with the end of the tool. As the endmill is rotating and the workpiece is moving, the machine marks will appear as overlapping concentric marks. The side of the endmill may also be used for machining. When the endmill is used in this type of application, the resulting marks are parallel or wavy in nature depending on the angle of the endmill relative to the workpiece. Endmills are manufactured with features according to the application for which they are being used. One of the most noticeable differences in the design of endmills is the number of flutes. The number of cutting edges is proportional to the number of flutes. For example, an endmill with two cutting edges will have two flutes. The most common endmill has four cutting edges. However, they can range from two to six cutting edges (and flutes). When softer metals, such as aluminum, are machined, the cutting process is run at a faster rate. The faster rate results in large pieces of metal being removed

Figure 5.11 Endmill.

Figure 5.12 Concentric marks made from the face milling operation.

during the machining process. The most efficient method of chip removal is with a large flute to clear out the metal chip. The maximum flute volume in an endmill is provided in two flute endmills (Figs. 5.11–5.13).

To further assist in increased life of the tool and efficient cutting, endmills may be processed with a coating that is designed to provide an additional hardness to the surface protection. These coatings are applied using a chemical vapor deposition process. This is an ultrathin coating resulting in a thickness of approximately 2–4 μm on the surface of the tool. The coatings include titanium nitride (TiN), titanium aluminum nitride (TiAlN), titanium carbonitride (TiCN), and aluminum titanium nitride

Figure 5.13 Three, four, and five flute endmills.

(AlTiN), which have a Rockwell Hardness of 81, 85, 87, and 90 Rc, respectively. This coating is beneficial in increasing the life of the tool. Manufacturers strive to improve tool life because it results in less downtime and lower overall costs in tooling.

Endmills, as with all tooling, are created from steel, steel alloys, or carbide and have the initial profile of the finished product. However, the final dimension of the endmill can only be produced using a cutting technique with a hardness greater than the item being machined. When dealing with materials designed to be hard enough to cut metal, there are few options. The most efficient and effective method of accomplishing this task is utilizing a grinding wheel, which, essentially, has an infinite number of carbide (silica carbide) edges to perform this function. The grinding process involved in producing the sharpened edge of the endmill is the same grinding process utilized in machining other metal components. Therefore, the same random imperfections are imparted onto the cutting surface of the endmill. In addition to the random microscopic imperfections produced in the surface of the endmill, use of the endmill will create imperfections in the form of built-up edge, plowing, sideflow, shearing, chatter, and tool wear (Fig. 5.14).

The most common type of endmill used in the production of tools and firearms is a traditional endmill, as discussed previously. These are easily recognized by the 90-degree edges of the end. However, alternate profiles of endmills may be required based on the necessities of the final surface to be produced. An example of this is when a concave surface is required. In these situations, the endmill is designed with rounded edges to produce a concave path. The radius of that concave is based on the desired final profile of the endmill.

To minimize the cost of tooling and maximize production, endmills have been designed to incorporate the use of inserts in place of the cutting surfaces. The inserts

Figure 5.14 Cutting edge of endmill.

are typically made from carbide with the host tool made from steel. This allows for the benefit of carbide cutting surfaces without having to make the entire endmill from carbide. The inserts also provide a quick and efficient method for maintaining a sharp surface. The carbide inserts are secured by placing them in a form-fitted recessed area designed to fit the insert. The insert is further held in place by a screw. However, due to the limited contact surface of the inserts, the type of machining these types of endmills can perform is limited (Fig. 5.15).

There are many areas on a firearm that are milled during the manufacturing process. However, the areas that are most important to be aware of in the area of firearm examination are those that contact the bullet or cartridge case. The most prevalent area observed is the breech face of some firearms. One common firearm type that exhibits breech face marks produced by an endmill is the Beretta 92 series and Taurus 92 series of firearms. These firearms have arched marks cause by the movement of the slide into the rotating endmill. In general, any breech face that demonstrates arched toolmarks will have been produced by an endmill in lateral motion (Fig. 5.16).

Figure 5.15 Endmill with replaceable inserts.

Figure 5.16 Beretta breech face with concentric marks from the milling process.

Another commonly encountered breech face design that is made with an endmill is one in which the cartridge head is seated in the bolt. This is accomplished by creating a flat-based circular pocket in the bolt using the endmill in a plunging action. In this application, the endmill will create concentric marks. The most commonly encountered types of firearms that are manufactured in this method include the Cobray M-11, Intratec Tec-9, Uzi, AK, and AR style rifles (Fig. 5.17).

An endmill may also be used in a face milling operation in conjunction with lateral movement. This occurs when the endmill is smaller than the desired area of metal removal. A smaller endmill requires the movement to accomplish the material removal, which results in toolmarks that differ from one that directly plunges and cuts the precise shape. A face milling operation with movement of the mill results in overlapping toolmarks which exhibit distinct marks. The overlapped arched and diamond pattern in a breech face is typical of this type of endmill use. An example of these types of marks can be observed on the Ruger model AR-556 semiautomatic rifle (Fig. 5.18).

Figure 5.17 Breech face plunge cut by an endmill demonstrating concentric marks.

Figure 5.18 Ruger AR-556 breech face.

Lathe

The second most common method of machining where material is removed to produce a final shape is by use of a lathe. A lathe is a machine designed to hold the workpiece perpendicular to the cutting tool. The technical term for the metal cutting process when employing a lathe is turning. In opposition to the mill, the lathe rotates the workpiece and holds the cutting tool in a fixed position. Another difference in the lathe is that the cutting tool is a single point tool with only the tip contacting the workpiece. The use of single point contact to machine the metal diminishes the amount of metal that the operation is capable of removing in a pass. Therefore multiple passes by the cutting tool are typically required to achieve the final profile. By way of contrast, the milling machine tool has an entire blade in contact with the workpiece. As with milling machines, the tool is made of a harder material than the metal it is cutting (Fig. 5.19).

There are many aspects to the lathe tool design to maximize performance and minimize wear. Machinists consider the approach and departure angle of the tool when encountering the workpiece. These specific angles are based on the application of the

Figure 5.19 Lathe tool in relation to workpiece.

tool and the type of metal being turned. The angle on top of the tool edge relative to the workpiece is termed the back rake angle. The angle perpendicular to the workpiece below the tool is the end relief angle. When discussing the tool angles with respect to the sides of the tool, the left side is the side rake angle and the right side is the side relief angle (Shaw, 2005g). In order to maximize cost savings and the usefulness of a tool bit in lathe production, modern lathe tools are designed to hold inserts, which are small multisided cutting tools that can be rotated to a new cutting edge when the cutting tip has been dulled. In addition, when using lathe bits, the tool holder itself can be made from a less expensive material, such as steel, while the end that contacts the workpiece can be made from carbide or other hardened material (Fig. 5.20).

Figure 5.20 Various lathe tool bits.

Modern lathes are equipped with computer numerically controlled (CNC) controls to allow for automated manufacturing. Along with the automated profiling of the workpiece, some CNC lathes are equipped with bar feeders that automatically load the bar stock. This automation greatly improves the rate of production and minimizes the contribution of the operator (Fig. 5.21).

The computer-controlled actuation of the lateral movement of the tool and incorporation of rotation of the tool has diversified the functionality of a lathe. Through CNC movement and timing of the interaction of the workpiece and tool, lathes are capable of more than simple round shapes. The contact can be timed to allow for square, rectangular, and other irregular shapes.

The design of the lathe lends itself to profiling larger rod-shaped pieces into their final dimensions, which are cylindrical in nature. One of the most prolific items machined on a lathe that is found on a firearm is the exterior profile of the barrel. The exterior of the barrel does not commonly contact any component the firearm examiner will analyze. However, a frequently encountered item that encounters an ammunition component is a firing pin.

Many firing pins are designed to function within a round channel. This is because round channels are easiest to machine by simply drilling a hole. As with any

Figure 5.21 CNC lathe. *CNC,* Computer numerically controlled.

machining process, businesses will choose the least expensive route to achieve the desired result. The easiest way to produce firing pins in these designs is by using a lathe. However, when dealing with smaller diameter metals, a different type of lathe is utilized. In this application, the machine is commonly called a Swiss-type machine or screw machine. These machines share the same fundamental design as the lathe; however, it is made to accommodate smaller pieces with more precise tolerances. Like CNC lathes, the Swiss-type machine is capable of automatic feeding and contouring of metal bar stock into the final product.

The result of machining performed on a lathe (or Swiss-type machine) with the use of a single point cutting tool is concentric marks on the surface of the workpiece. As with other machining processes, lathe cutting is subjected to built-up edge, sideflow, plowing, chatter, tool wear, and shearing. All the aforementioned effects of the machining process lend to individual characteristics. However, the basic function of the CNC or Swiss-type lathe is automated, so the prescribed rate of feed, speed of the tool, and speed of the workpiece will result in evenly spaced gross marks of the tool bit's interaction with the workpiece (Fig. 5.22).

Drilling

Another method of metal removal that is very prevalent in the manufacturing of firearms is the drilling process. Drilling in firearm manufacturing is typically reserved for

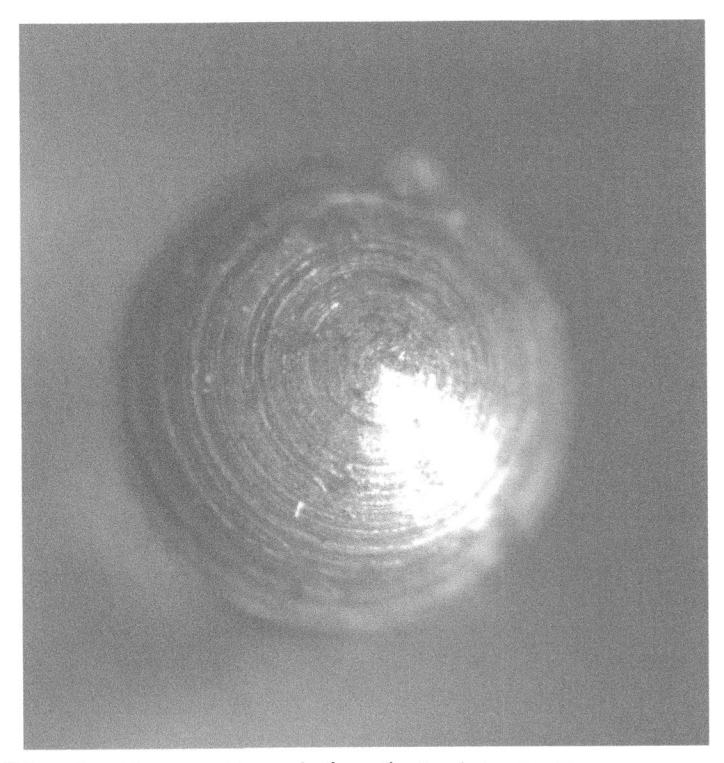

Figure 5.22 Firing pin with concentric marks from the turning process.

holes for pins and screws. The areas where pins and screws are present do not touch unfired or fired cartridges. There are two areas in a firearm that are typically made by drilling which commonly encounter ammunition components, the firing pin aperture and the barrel. The cartridge case impacts the aperture or firing pin hole. Most manufacturers form the firing pin aperture by drilling and then finish the hole by removing burrs with countersinking. Countersinking is a form of drilling; however, in these instances, the tool is angled to produce an increasingly larger hole instead of a producing a uniform hole. Material removal by countersinking on the breech face will cause the primer to flow back into the resulting void (Fig. 5.23).

However, individual characteristics from countersinking the aperture are not typically transferred onto the fired cartridge case. With regards to blowback firearms, the cartridge case remains in a fixed position during the time of discharge. The flow back of the primer metal will not generally impact the aperture with sufficient force to transfer the concentric marks from within the aperture. Delayed blowback firearms that incorporate a tilting barrel will produce noticeably different marks from the contact of the cartridge case in motion with the edges of the countersinked area. Due to the machining process and the burrs produced by the countersink/drilling

Figure 5.23 Countersink.

action, these marks will be individual in nature (see Chapter 8: Comparison of cartridge cases).

As previously mentioned, the other area of a firearm that is commonly drilled to produce the initial shape is the interior of the barrel. Most barrels begin as a solid rod of steel with the initial hole for the passage of the bullet drilled with a specialized type of drill designed for long straight holes. The drill bit for this operation is called a gun drill.

The drill bit has six main elements that contribute to the cutting process (Smith, 2010). These elements include the land, flute, lip, margin, web, and chisel edge. There are two main cutting edges on a drill bit when it contacts the workpiece. The first edge that comes into contact is the chisel edge. The chisel edge is the sharpened edge between the lands of the drill bit. The length of the chisel edge is dependent on the diameter of the drill bit. The larger the diameter, the longer the chisel edge (Fig. 5.24).

After the chisel edge initiates contact and the cutting process, the lips of the land engage the workpiece. The lips run the length of the margin and are responsible for a majority of the metal removal. The land is the helical metal portion of the drill bit that runs the length of the drill and is sharpened to cut along the sides of the hole.

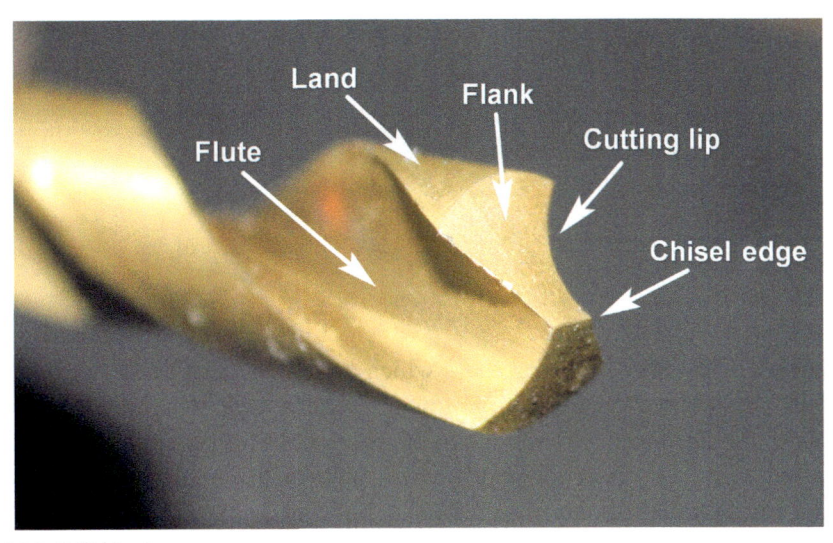

Figure 5.24 Drill bit diagram.

In conjunction with the land of the drill, there are flutes. Flutes are helical voids in the drill bit that allow for the flow of cut material to exit the hole. During the flow of metal chips from the hole, metal may become lodged between the land and the workpiece. This interaction of chips with the workpiece is random in nature and contributes to individuality in characteristics observed on the surface of the item being drilled.

As described earlier, a specialized drill bit called a gun drill is utilized when drilling firearm barrels. The specialized bit design typically has only two flutes and two holes that run the length of the drill bit. The holes carry a large volume of coolant and lubricant to the tip of the drill bit. In addition to cooling and lubricating, the flow of the fluid pushes the metal chips to the rear of the drill bit. The two large flutes allow clearance for the removal of metal chips from the front of the drilling operation. Due to the large length-to-diameter ratio of up to 100:1, gun drills are prone to vibration. When conducting deep-hole drilling, torsional vibration can occur and contribute to chatter marks (Altintas and Weck, 2004).

Reaming

Reaming is an industrial process used to produce an accurate and precise hole. While the traditional drilling method will provide a general hole, the hole produced by a drill bit is fairly inaccurate when specifications call for the actual diameter to be accurate within thousandths of an inch. The barrel diameter, which is the true caliber of the firearm, is measured to the thousandths of an inch. An example of this is the .223 caliber, which refers to the .223 inch diameter.

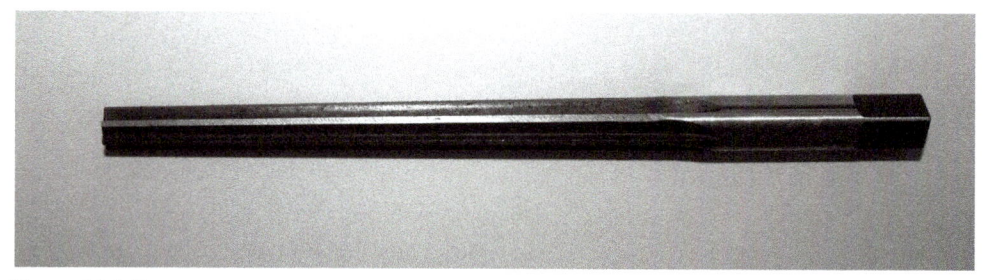

Figure 5.25 Reamer.

Reamers are dedicated cutting tools which can be accurately ground to precise dimensions. In contrast to drill bits, reamers typically have straight flutes in lieu of helictical flutes. Reamers are not designed to remove large amounts of material. Instead, they remove a few thousandths of an inch of material where the pilot hole deviated from the true diameter (Fig. 5.25).

Reamers are used not only in barrel drilling operations but also in creating the final tolerances of the chamber. As with barrels, the chamber of the firearm must be cut within thousandths of an inch, which is accomplished by the reamer. In the same fashion that metal chips can interfere with the contact of a drill land, metal chips from the reaming process can lodge between the reamer and workpiece surface. This interaction is random and will, in turn, result in random imperfections within the barrel and chamber.

Broaching

Broaching involves a tool with separate cutting edges (teeth) that gradually increase in size. The tool is pushed or pulled through the workpiece and increasing amounts of metal are removed as the teeth make contact. Broaches are used in many industries, not just firearm production. Broaches are commonly used to produce gears and square- or flat-edged holes (Fig. 5.26).

During the manufacturing of slides, the broach is drawn across the workpiece to cut it to the specified dimensions. While the broach moves in a much slower action relative to an endmill, the interaction of the cutting edges of the broach is the same as an endmill with respect to plowing, shearing, built-up edge, and sideflow. The relatively slow speed of the broach does not preclude it from accumulating a built-up edge. The friction from the massive pressure required to broach can cause sufficient heat to microweld metal to the surface of the teeth. During the course of this action, longitudinal marks are imparted from the contact of the broaching teeth onto the surface of the breech face.

Additional sources of surface roughness during the broaching process are produced by the tool and how the tool is used. The thickness of the part being broached affects

Figure 5.26 Broach.

the surface roughness (Zanger et al., 2014). The length of the broach can also induce vibration within the interaction between the broach and workpiece. Lastly, the speed at which the broach is used in the machining process can affect the surface roughness.

There are two commonly broached areas on a firearm that firearm examiners will encounter. One of the most common areas on firearms that are broached is the breech face. The slide of a firearm is typically cast in a raw shape or rough machined. Either of these methods results in a workpiece that requires further machining to reach the final dimensions. Firearms that have an open breech face, which is one that is unobstructed from the base of the slide to the top of the slide, are commonly machined with a broach to achieve the final tolerances. Broaching is the quickest and most efficient way to produce a squared off area. The most commonly encountered types of firearms with these profiles are Glock, Kel-Tec centerfire pistol calibers, and most 1911 designs. The other commonly broached area is the barrel rifling, which will be discussed in detail in the rifling methods chapter of this book.

Electrical discharge machining

Traditional machining physically removes material by a harder, sharpened surface coming into contact with a softer one resulting in the softer yielding and being removed. In contrast, electrical discharge machining (EDM) uses electricity to remove material. The tool in this situation is a wire or piece of graphite that acts as the cathode to remove material from the workpiece (Ramasawmy and Blunt, 2004). During the

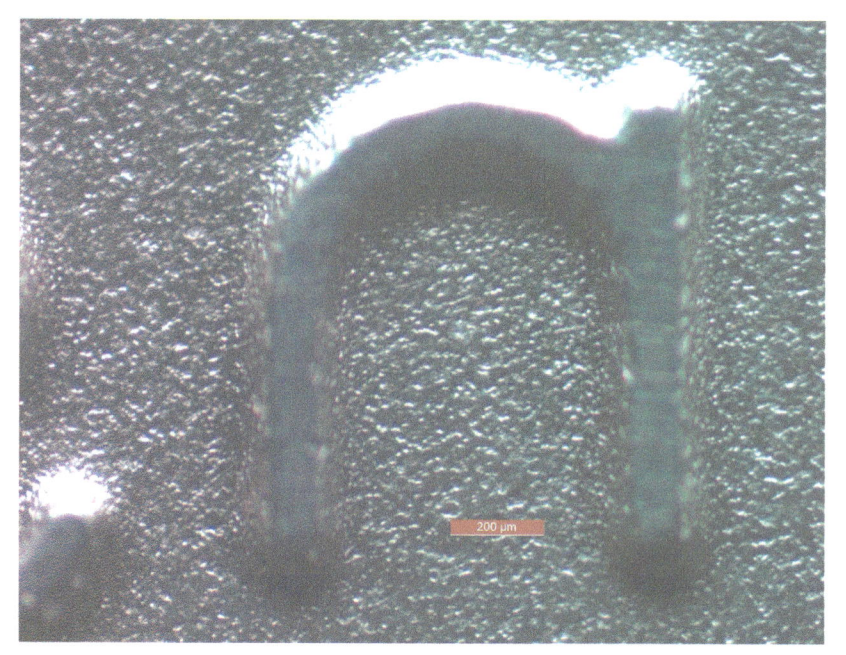

Figure 5.27 Granular marks on a bunter from the EDM process. *EDM*, Electrical discharge machining.

cutting process, an electrical discharge is generated thousands of times per second. These electrical pulses cause craters by melting and vaporizing the workpiece (Izwan et al., 2016). This operation is performed in the environment of a dielectric fluid that cools and flushes the removed material. The result on the surface of the workpiece is a granular surface with an appearance of cratering and blobs of metal (Fig. 5.27).

An easy to understand comparison of the resulting erosion caused by electrical spark is the spark plug in an engine. While the materials in the spark plug are designed to minimize wear and maximize the life of the spark plug, there is still erosion of the metal.

One of the most common tools made by EDM is a bunter used to produce cartridge cases. Bunters are made from tool steel, which is hard. The small lettering requires precise machining. The cathode is a graphite form with a negative contour of the final desired shape of the bunter. This method of metal removal is referred to as die sinking EDM. The bunter is effectively burned with the negative impression of the graphite. The most accurate and cost-efficient method to make these quickly and to the required dimensional specifications is EDM. The final finishing of bunters is accomplished by grinding the surface to the final dimensions. The result of the EDM and grinding can be seen on fired cartridge cases. The EDMed base of the bunter will have a granular appearance while the letters and numbers on the cartridge case will have striated marks from the grinder (Fig. 5.28).

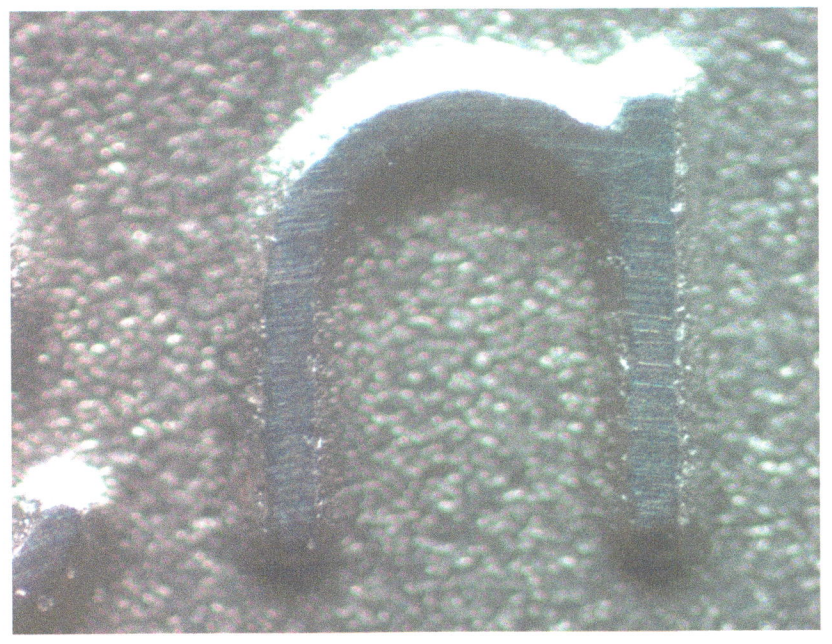

Figure 5.28 Grinding marks from the finishing process of characters on a bunter.

Manufacturers of firearms will use the most cost-effective method to produce their parts to their required specifications. Due to the dimensions, specifications, and availability of machinery, a company may dedicate a machine to perform this machining method. One example is STI Firearms who used EDM as a method to cut the breech faces for their firearms until 2013 (Maddox, 2017). In addition, Ruger has used the EDM process to cut the breech face to the final dimensions.

In this application, the type of EDM used is what is called wire EDM. Instead of a graphite cathode, a wire is used to carry the electrical current. This wire is constantly being eroded while it burns through the workpiece; therefore, the thin wire is being fed from a spool and constantly providing a new surface for metal removal. However, the most cost-effective method for cutting breech faces on firearms that have the proper access for metal removal is broaching.

Stamping

Stamping (also called blanking) is an economical method used in the production of flat, relatively thin parts of firearms. Stamping involves placing a flat piece of metal between a set of dies. The dies consist of two parts. One is a hollowed-out area in the shape of the desired part. The other is a positive shape of the item being stamped. A large amount of force is imparted to the positive shape, which drives

Figure 5.29 Punch and die set.

the metal flat into the negative hollowed-out area. The resulting piece of metal removed from the initial metal strip will be in the desired shape of the firearm part (Fig. 5.29).

As with other mechanical machining processes, marks will be transferred from the harder tool to the softer workpiece. In this case, the machine marks produced during the production of the dies set are transferred onto the stamped piece. In addition, because of the great amount of stress imparted during the stamping process, there is a shear zone created where the metal breaks free from itself. As part of this action, there is plastic deformation of the metal until a crack develops (Hernandez et al., 2006). The shearing of stamped metal parts is much more dramatic than shearing from machining when considering the use of sharp, relatively precise tools such as an endmill or broach. The sheared edge on a stamped item will be much rougher and more defined. In addition, it can show much grosser characteristics (Figs. 5.30 and 5.31).

As the workpiece shears from the host material, a burr may occur. The burr is a result of the release of the workpiece from the host material and is dependent on the clearance of the dies. As the clearance between the two dies increase, the burr will

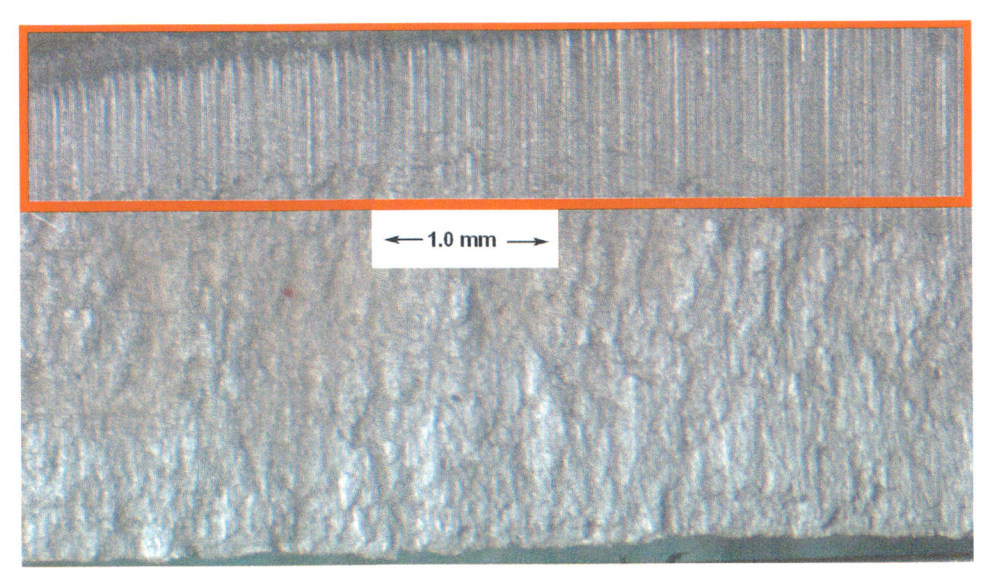

Figure 5.30 Toolmarks imparted by the die onto the workpiece.

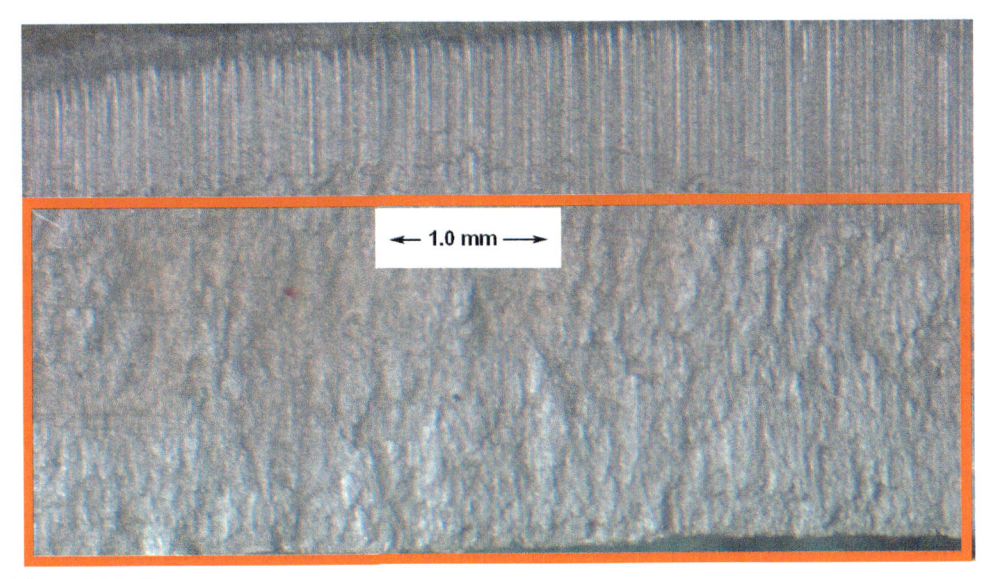

Figure 5.31 Shear zone.

increase in size. The clearance between the dies is affected by the wear on the dies as they are used and will increase throughout use (Fig. 5.32).

The cutting tool edge is the most greatly affected area during the stamping operation. This is also referred to as flank wear (Hambli, 2001). The flank of the tool is the

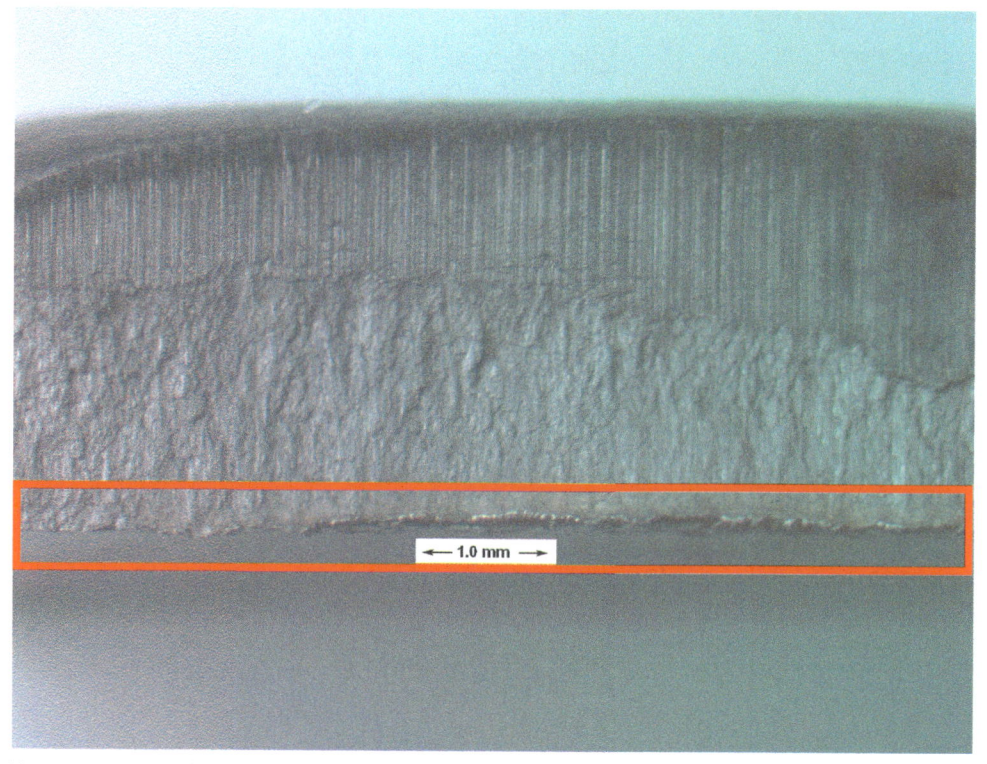

Figure 5.32 Burred area of stamped workpiece.

portion of the tool that contacts the workpiece. Because the process of stamping imparts a sudden impact to the host material and workpiece, flank wear may occur more rapidly than other machining methods. The amount of wear and change in the tool will depend on tool hardness, clearances between the dies, composition, and thickness of the material being stamped.

There are two common methods for the stamping process. Blank stamping occurs when the workpiece is produced in one single action resulting in one part produced by every hit of the die. The second type of stamping is progressive stamping. During this operation, the workpiece is moved through stages of dies which deform the metal progressively until the final shape is produced. While progressive dies involve more steps and expense, the result is a more precise workpiece.

Thicker, less precise pieces, such as extractors and firing pins, can be produced by blank stamping (Fig. 5.33). Items that are manufactured from thinner materials with deformation to the metal rather than cutting a flat shape require the use of an extensive series of dies to reach the final desired shape. Another example of the use of progressive dies is in the production of bullet jackets.

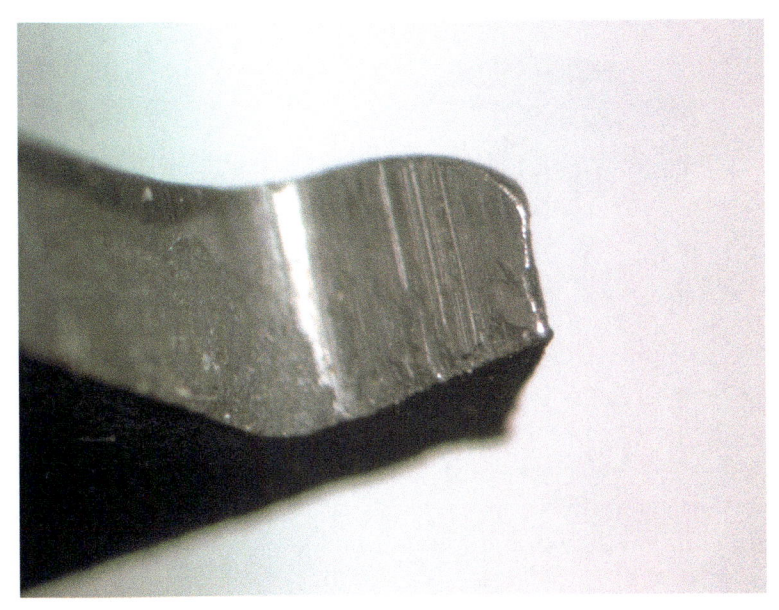

Figure 5.33 Hi-Point extractor.

Metal injection molding

The use of metal injection molding (MIM) in the industry for the production of metal parts is fairly new relative to traditional methods of making parts such as casting or milling from solid pieces of metal. The components manufactured by MIM are essentially in a finished state when they have completed the MIM process.

The MIM process begins by combining a fine powdered metal or alloys thereof with a binder. The binders are typically plastics and assist in holding the metal together during the injection sequence. The combination of metal and binder is then heated and ground into the material that will be used later in the manufacturing process. The result of heating and combining the binder and metal produces a feedstock that can be stored or used immediately. When ready for use, the feedstock is heated until it has the consistency of toothpaste. In that condition, it can be forced into a mold. While injecting the metal components into the mold, the pathway, called the runner or sprue, is heated. This ensures the metal/binders remain fluid and completely fill the mold.

The mold consists of two halves that are pressed together when the metal is being injected. After cooling sufficiently, the halves separate, and the part can be removed. A part that has been manufactured by MIM will have a seam along the sides where the die halves met. The seam line may not always be present if the part had additional finishing which removed the line (Fig. 5.34).

Figure 5.34 Seam line on a firing pin from the metal injection molding process.

After the part has been removed from the mold, there are further steps in completing the part. The binder must be removed to ensure the workpiece only contains the powdered metal. The removal of the binder will cause some shrinkage and that is taken into account when designing the mold. The binders are removed through a thermal and chemical process.

After the binders have been removed, the workpiece is ready to be hardened. This is done through a process called sintering. Sintering involves heating the metal at a point just below its melting point, at which time the metal will fill in any voids left by the loss of the binder. This will cause additional shrinkage between 10% and 25%. After the part has been cooled in a controlled manner, it will be complete and can be used in that condition or further machined or finished (Hunsinger, 2013).

Powdered metal

The powdered metal process is in the same family as the MIM process in that they both use fine metal particles along with binders. However, powdered metal is pressed in a mold and not injected in a softened state as with MIM. The powdered metal is also sintered to remove the binders and harden the final part. And as with MIM parts, the powdered metal part is in a state which requires little to no machining to be used. The use of this process will depend on the amount of stress encountered by the part. The lower the stress, the more applicable this process is in the manufacturing process. An example of this is the Phoenix Arms model HP-25 slide which, due to the nature of the .25 caliber cartridge, is exposed to fairly low pressures. The slide in this firearm is powder metal cast and no further finishing steps are performed on the product.

Die casting

Larger items may be manufactured to rough dimensions and the critical tolerances machined using a mill, lathe, or other machining operation. This is a common method in firearm production, particularly those which utilize a blowback action, such as Hi-Point, Jimenez Arms, Raven, and Bryco firearms, among others. The blowback design relies on the mass of the slide to retard the energy of the discharged cartridge. To easily and inexpensively provide the mass for the slide, these manufacturers use a zinc alloy for production. The zinc alloy has a much lower melting point than steel and is much easier to use in the casting process.

Casting involves the use of molds. Molds are cavities machined into two steel plates that are the reverse image of the desired final product. The plates are halves that when pressed together create a void in the shape of the product. As a means to supply the zinc alloy into the mold, there are holes connected to a hydraulic injection source. In the manufacturing industry, the term for the source of the substrate in a mold is the gate. After the metal alloy has been injected into the mold, which is pressed together, the alloy is allowed to cool for a few seconds. When the metal has solidified, the mold halves are hydraulically retracted revealing the product. The product will have additional areas of material where the metal hardened as it ran through the gate. These additional pieces of excess metal are called runners and are cutoff and recycled.

The hardness of the zinc alloy used for manufacturing firearm slides is significantly lower than steel used in producing slides by other manufacturers. Due to the high pressures imparted into the slide upon discharge, slides made using zinc alloy must be reinforced in the breech area with a steel insert. The steel insert can withstand the force of the impact and prevent damage to the zinc alloy slide. The die casting method allows for the addition of components to be placed within the mold prior to the injection of the zinc alloy. The zinc alloy forms and hardens around the steel insert and it essentially becomes one with the slide.

A part that is die cast requires additional machining to produce the final product. The machining process is used to remove the marks from the runner, final tolerances, and removal of the parting line. The parting line is the excess metal that forms where the two molds come together. The zinc alloy used in these parts is typically milled to the final dimensions.

Investment casting

Investment casting is a metal forming process that dates back prior to the Egyptian times and is still used today. Investment casting is also called the lost wax process. The reason it is appropriately called the lost wax process is because traditionally, the component to be cast is made from wax and placed in packed sand. Modern investment casting has been improved to provide a higher precision in part tolerances. The current method of investment casting utilizes a wax mold of the part to be cast. The wax molds are dipped in a silica slurry multiple times to encompass the wax in a thick layer. Multiple slurry-covered wax molds are then placed in a row, called a tree. Like the die casting method, a hole is placed in the sand mold and that is the entrance point for molten metal. As the molten metal encounters the wax, the wax melts and exits through a gate. The void produced by the melted wax is filled with molten metal. Once the metal has solidified, the silica slurry cast is broken away to expose the resulting part. The final part produced by the investment casting process is very close to the final tolerances and requires minimal machining.

Unlike die casting, the type of metal used in this process is open to a larger variety and type of steel. One company that has mastered and maximized the use of investment casting is Sturm Ruger. One of the major components that Ruger manufactures using investment casting is the slides for most of their firearms. While the slides are in a semifinished condition directly from the casting process, there are areas which require finish machining to bring the part within the manufacturer's specifications. The area of most importance to firearm examiners is the breech face, which is broached as mentioned earlier.

Finishing processes of firearm parts

Firearm parts may or may not require additional processing after machining to provide the finish desired by the manufacturer. The purpose of additional finishing is cosmetic, functional, and/or intentional. All of these methods will have an effect on and may alter the appearance of the machining method. They will also modify observable individual characteristics to the workpiece.

Abrasive blasting

One of the most cost-effective and efficient ways of removing machine marks is abrasive blasting. The generic term for abrasive blasting is "sand blasting." However, the use of actual sand is generally not an accepted practice. Sand, or silica, produces silica dust which, when inhaled, causes silicosis. This is a serious medical condition affecting the respiratory system. The advent of various types of media available has provided more options for manufacturers. Abrasive blasting involves using compressed air to force particles into the surface of a workpiece to abrade or deform (dent) it. The desired final result will dictate the type of abrasive to be used. If the surface has a rough, uneven surface, the manufacturer may choose an aggressive abrasive that will cut the surface and remove the raised portions of the workpiece. In the process of removing any course marks, the fine stria will be affected first and removed before coarse marks are leveled to the flat surface. If the workpiece is fairly smooth after the machining process, the manufacturer may use a fairly gentle method of abrasive blasting consisting of glass beads, which are relatively soft and result in mild deformation and evening of the surface of the workpiece. Abrasive blasting also allows the applicator to observe the resulting surface to ensure a thorough job has been done to achieve the desired result. This involves using abrasive materials, such as glass beads or oxide grit.

Abrasive grit is available in various sizes and compositions. Each has a specific quality to meet a precise requirement. As the size of the grit increases, so does its ability to cut and remove material. In addition, the hardness and sharpness of the grit will improve the ability to cut and remove workpiece material. Hard, sharp media, such as silicon carbide, will aggressively cut the surface, whereas, glass beads, which are relatively soft and rounded, will change the surface and will not effectively remove material.

An article in the *Association of Firearm and Toolmark Examiners Journal* by Evan Thompson describes correspondence with Taurus Manufacturing and their use of abrasive materials to finish the breech face of their revolver (Thompson, 2015). While the firearm in the article had a breech face that was produced by MIM, which is prone to carry over of the mold, the final product is machined for tolerances and then glass beaded. The glass beads, as documented in the article, produce a granular surface with individual characteristics.

Tumbling

Another method for smoothing and cleaning off the surface of a firearm part is performed by tumbling. Tumbling is done in a large bowl filled with media. In tumbling, the media is much larger than abrasive media. Tumbling media comes in sizes up to 3/4 inch in length while abrasive media is generally the size of a grain of sand. Media used for tumbling is generally made from ceramic. This allows for control over the size, shape, and abrasive quality of the media during the manufacture. The use of tumbling is a slower process than abrasive blasting in that it can take anywhere from 30 minutes to hours to tumble the workpiece. In contrast, individual blasting of a product can take less than a minute. However, a vibrating tumbling bowl, depending on the size of the bowl and workpiece, can handle hundreds or even thousands of

Figure 5.35 Tumbling media.

workpieces. Therefore, the average time per workpiece can actually be lower (Fig. 5.35).

Tumbling is not an area-specific method of finishing due to the random contact of the media on the workpiece. Conversely, abrasive blasting can be directed to only specific locations on a part where finishing is required. The decision on which method to use will depend on the equipment already in use by the manufacturer and the desired result.

Chrome plating

Chrome plating is a cosmetic finishing technique used by some manufacturers to enhance the appearance and provide a protective surface of their firearms. In addition, the chrome finish is easier to clean due to the smooth characteristic of chrome plating. This process does not remove material, such as tumbling or abrasive blasting. Rather, it adds a layer to the finished product. Chrome plating is done by placing the workpiece into an electrolytic bath that binds the chrome to the surface of the workpiece. The binding of chrome metal adds material to the surface and fills in the voids left by the previous machining methods. Because of this, the appearance of chrome-plated firearms may appear smooth. A commonly encountered firearm that exhibits this type of finish is the breech face of Lorcin pistols (Fig. 5.36).

Figure 5.36 Chromed breech face.

Chrome plating is used for a variety of reasons, such as ease of cleaning, protection, and added surface hardness. However, because chrome plating involves a metal electrically bound to another metal, there is a potential for the chrome to be dislodged from the host metal. The removal of chrome will result in the exposure of the original surface and additional individual characteristics.

Another part of a firearm that may be chrome plated in a firearm that contacts a cartridge case is the firing pin. Firing pins are prone to impact and debris from the combustion of a cartridge. Because of this, additional hardness and ease of cleaning are desirable. As with the breech face, manufacturing marks made during the production of the firing pin may be obscured by the chrome filling in the voids within the surface and related machining marks (Fig. 5.37).

Parkerization

A protective process that is commonly applied to firearms is parkerization. The term parkerizing has become a generic term for any treatment where the iron on the surface of the metal is converted using a phosphoric acid solution. The result is a dark gray to

Figure 5.37 Chrome-plated firing pin.

black colored part that is more resistant to rust. There is a chemical reaction occurring during the bath in the phosphoric acid solution and the surface of the workpiece changes; however, these changes are not large enough to affect the marks produced during the machining process.

CHAPTER 6

Barrel manufacturing and rifling

There are several methods employed to impart rifling into a barrel. These methods utilize: the cutting process, cold working which is displacing the metal by force, electrically removing the metal, and casting of the rifling as part of barrel cast. Each of these methods has its advantages and disadvantages and has different forensic aspects.

Barrel drilling and reaming

Barrels start out as solid rods of steel. The most common materials used to manufacture barrels are 4140, 4150 carbon steel, or 416 stainless steel. Other materials may be used, but those listed are the most common due to the machinability and heat treatability of the metal.

The solid rod of steel is first drilled through the center to produce the bore. Drilling such a long hole and ensuring it is true and straight requires a specialized drill bit. This type of drilling is called deep-hole drilling in the manufacturing community and uses what is appropriately called a gun drill (Fig. 6.1). This type of drill bit does not look like the traditional wood or metal-cutting bit. The drill travels deeply into the steel rod based on the length of the gun barrel. This length can exceed 30 in; therefore a design that allows for the rapid removal of chips is essential. The most efficient way to accomplish this is the use of a large open flute and coolant to flush the chips away from the cutting surface. Gun drill bits will have holes in the tips to allow for flow of coolant through the inside of the drill bit from the machine.

After the initial hole has been bored through the entire length of the bar stock, which will become the barrel, the rough opening for the bore has been completed. There is a second operation that must be performed to bring the barrel into the desired tolerances. The drilling of the initial hole is considered a roughing operation, in that it brings the barrel roughly into tolerance. The next step is the finishing process. This is typically done using a barrel reamer. Unlike a single-fluted gun drill that only cuts at the point of engagement, reamers typically have six longitudinal flutes with a sharp edge running the entire length (Fig. 6.2). The reamer is designed to remove a minimal amount of material and bring the barrel to the final tolerance prior

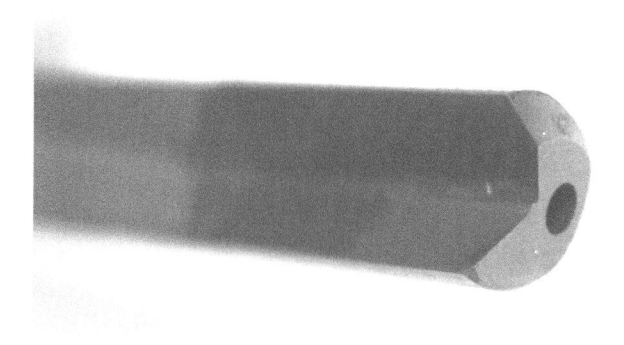

Figure 6.1 Gun drill.

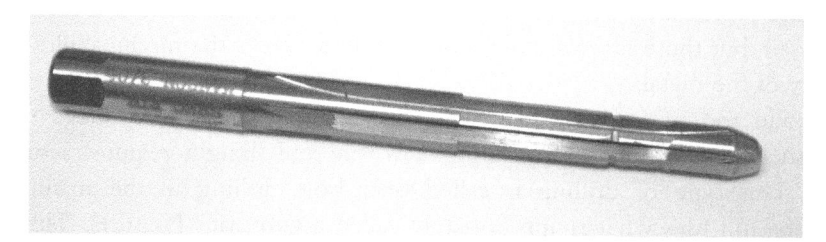

Figure 6.2 Chamber reamer.

to the rifling. However, because this is a machining operation and metal is being cut, the barrel will exhibit evidence of this operation in the form of concentric marks on the barrel surface (Fig. 6.3).

Depending on the condition of the gun drill, some artifact marks may remain even after the reaming process. A burr, or raised area, on the surface of the drill flute may impart concentric marks in excessive depth beyond the contact of the reamer. That situation would induce further individual characteristics within the barrel. These marks would be concentric in nature due to the rotation of the gun drill.

While reaming is the most common method to bring the bore into the final desired dimension, it is not the only process to accomplish this task. For example, Ruger has used a round broach to produce the final bore diameter prior to broach rifling the barrel grooves. In contrast to reaming, which leaves concentric marks within the barrel, broach sizing will produce parallel marks on the barrel lands which will, in turn, produce marks from the barrel-sizing broach on the grooves of the bullet.

Figure 6.3 Chamber reamer marks.

Hook rifling

The oldest method of rifling is hook rifling. Hook rifling uses a single cutter to remove metal in a spiral fashion. Because the hook is a single point-cutting tool, it can only cut one barrel groove at a time. It is then repositioned to cut the next groove. This is a metal-removing process and the same machining principles apply as discussed in Chapter 4, Fundamentals of Forensic Firearm Examination. The occurrence of built-up edge, plowing, and sideflow will occur. Any defects in the cutting edge of the hook cutter could potentially carry over to the subsequent barrel grooves. Relative to other modern methods, this method is a time-consuming and labor-intensive process. Hook cutting is all but obsolete in the modern manufacturing of firearms. Some specialized manufacturers may use this process to manufacture custom barrels. However, with respect to firearms encountered in a forensic crime laboratory, these would be rare occurrences.

Broach rifling

The second type of rifling technique that removes metal is broach cutting. Broach rifling uses the same metal-removal process as the broaching of breech faces in that the cutting tools have progressively larger teeth interacting with the barrel (Fig. 6.4). The final surface of the workpiece will be affected most by the final teeth as they are nearest to the final-sizing dimensions. Because this is a metal-cutting process, the same phenomena of built-up edge, plowing, and sideflow will contribute to the individual characteristics within the cut area. Any defects or damage to the teeth on the broach

Figure 6.4 Rifling broach.

can contribute to subsequent barrels produced with the broach. In these instances we see what are called subclass characteristics. This topic will be discussed more thoroughly in Chapter 10, Documentation, Notes, and Reports. This method is an improvement over single hook cutting in that if the firearm has six lands and grooves, all six grooves can be cut in one pass of the broaching tool.

While the development of cutting all barrel grooves at one time is a considerable improvement to the efficiency of machining rifled barrels, there are drawbacks to this method. The first, and possibly one of the largest, is the cost of the tooling. Rifling broaches are a custom-made product and not mass-produced by tooling manufacturers, such as keyway broaches, which can be found in any tooling catalog. Specialized tooling made to the specifications of the firearm manufacturer will cost considerably more. The nature of broaching means that the teeth will be subject to excessive wear. This will result in relatively few barrels produced per broach before having to sharpen the broach compared to other manufacturing methods. One firearm manufacturer has divulged that it produces approximately 300 pistol barrels before the broach needs to be replaced.

Broaches can be resharpened to maximize the productive lifespan of the tool. When broaches dull throughout use when cutting breech faces, they are resharpened for continued use. However, the process of resharpening will remove material from the teeth to produce a new sharp edge. Removing material will change the overall dimensions of the broach making the depth of cut shorter. This will change the dimensions of the workpiece being cut by the newly sharpened broach. To overcome this, manufacturers will place a thin piece of metal called a shim behind the broach to account for metal removed during the sharpening process. The shim will push the broach out to make the stroke of the broach remove the same amount of material as the initial cut specifications.

In the case of a rifling broach, all sides are contacting the barrel. This is advantageous since multiple surfaces are being machined in one action. However, if one were to sharpen a rifling broach and remove material from the teeth on the entire bearing surface, the depth of the cuts into the barrel grooves would be diminished from the few thousandths of an inch that are in the specifications of the rifling by the manufacturer. Unlike traditional single-sided broaching, these broaches cannot be shimmed into place to account for the loss of material from the sharpening process, and therefore have a limited lifespan and limited resharpening uses.

Firearms that have been broach rifled can be examined to determine if that was the method used to produce the rifling. When microscopically examining the barrel, there will be clear signs indicating it was broach rifled. This will be demonstrated by gross parallel marks within the grooves (lower portions) of the barrel and concentric marks on the lands (raised portions) of the barrel from the reaming process on the barrel (Fig. 6.5).

Figure 6.5 Broached barrel.

It is important to note that manufacturers can and do change their manufacturing method based on equipment availability, cost, and efficiency. The only way to be sure of the barrel manufacturing method of a particular firearm is to evaluate the actual barrel or its casting.

Hammer forging

Hammer forging was developed in Germany by GFM (Gesellschaft für Fertigungstechnik und Maschinenbau). The machines used to produce this type of rifling are called radial forgers. This is because the hammers move in a linear, radial motion. Around 1950 GFM produced its first dedicated barrel-forging machine (Higley and Briggs, 2007).

The hammer-forging process utilizes large hammers that surround the workpiece. There are four hammers which move approximately 2–5 mm and strike the barrel between 1000 and 1600 times per minute. The force of these hammers depends on the design of the hammer face and ranges from 100,000 to 200,000 lb of force. While this is happening, the barrel is moved through the hammers to form the barrel around the mandrel (Fig. 6.6). The mandrel is made from tungsten carbide with a reversed impression of the rifling cut into it. Tungsten carbide is an extremely hard metal and can only be profiled by one method, grinding with an abrasive grinding wheel. The mandrel is moved in concurrence with the hammers as they are striking the barrel, thus forming the rifling as the barrel is forced into the voids of the mandrel. The filled voids of the mandrel become the lands (or raised areas) of the firearm barrel. This is referred to as cold working in the machining community because no metal is removed during the process. Rather, it is formed around the tool.

The hammer-forging process can produce two different rifling profiles. The first is polygonal that exhibits rounded edges of the land and grooves. Because there is no clear edge in these types of hammer-forged barrels, the land and groove widths cannot

Figure 6.6 Mandrel.

be accurately measured (Fig. 6.7). The hammer-forging process can also produce rifling with what appears to be traditional rifling from the cutting process with squared edges of the barrel grooves. The shape of the mandrel will determine the profile of the rifling produced (Fig. 6.8).

Figure 6.7 Polygonal hammer-forged barrel.

Figure 6.8 Bullet from hammer-forged barrel with squared edges top, bullet from hammer-forged barrel with polygonal shape on bottom.

The equipment used to hammer-forge barrels is large, expensive, and specialized. Therefore, many manufacturers choose to use rifling methods that are faster, more cost-effective with respect to equipment cost, and easier to maintain. As new manufacturers of barrels emerge, the number choosing to use hammer forging is among the vast minority. Hammer forging is, and has been, prevalent in firearms manufactured by Glock, Heckler and Koch, Ruger, and manufacturers of several AR-15 barrels.

Button rifling

Button rifling is one of the most common methods of imparting rifling into a barrel. Like hammer forging, this is a cold working process. However, there is a cutting component involved in the button-rifling process. A rifling button is a carbide tool that is cut to have a reverse contour of the rifling designed by the manufacturer (Fig. 6.9). The button is either pushed or pulled through the barrel using a hydraulic press. Some manufacturers connect the rifling button to the hydraulic ram. As the button is moved, the hydraulic ram rotates with the same twist rate of the button. This will improve the life of the button since the edges of the button are not as aggressively encountering the interior of the barrel. Other manufacturers will simply force the button down the barrel and the angled edges of the button will impart the spin to the button. This method will prematurely wear the button; however, it is relative to the entire process. A tour of a major manufacturer of AR-15 barrels who utilizes a hydraulic rotating ram reported production of approximately 1000 barrels before having to replace the rifling button. Use of a hydraulic ram without a rotating ram to produce pistol barrels by a major manufacturer was reported to also be approximately 1000 barrels. The difference, in these instances, is that the AR-15 is a rifle-length barrel of 16 in, whereas the pistol barrel is only 4 in.

The cutting process that occurs when a button engages the barrel is not nearly as aggressive as broach rifling where metal is intentionally removed to produce the rifling. Instead, the groove area of the barrel is displaced by the protruding area of the button. However, the edges of the rifling button are sharp ledges which contact

Figure 6.9 Rifling button.

Figure 6.10 Sideflow in rifling from button rifling.

the barrel in a different manner than the flat, blunt surface of the raised portion which produces the barrel groove. The sharp edges cut into the barrel and displace the metal in the form of chips and sideflow. This, by definition, is both a machining and metal-forming process. Most of the rifling processes wherein the barrel grooves are produced with a rifling button are forming processes. An example of this type of chip formation can be observed in a cutaway of a button rifled Hi-Point barrel. The persistence of these chips and sideflow will be dependent on the adhesion of the material to the barrel (Fig. 6.10).

The button-rifling process is a very fast operation with a barrel only taking seconds for the button to pass through and create the rifling. In addition, the rifling button is relatively inexpensive compared to broaches. The hydraulic press used for this process is a common tool and can be purchased relatively inexpensively in a used condition versus a hammer-forging machine that costs up to 50 times as much. The minimal machine and tool cost, in conjunction with the rapid speed at which barrels can be produced, explains why this method is the most commonly used. Firearms manufacturers whom have traditionally button rifled their barrels include Hi-Point, Kel-Tec, and many AR-15 barrel manufacturers.

Barrels that have been button rifled will commonly demonstrate reaming marks in the barrel grooves. This is a result of the button pressing the rifling rather than cutting it. In Fig. 6.11A and B, the reaming marks can be observed running perpendicular to the rifling. Any marks from reaming will remain in the barrel.

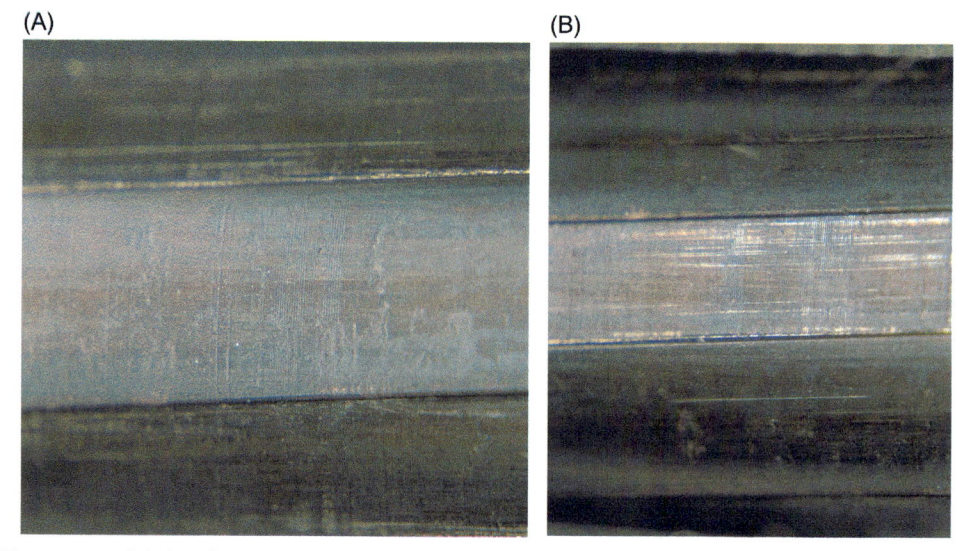

Figure 6.11 (A) Barrel groove reamer marks in a button rifled barrel; (B) barrel land reamer marks in a button rifled barrel.

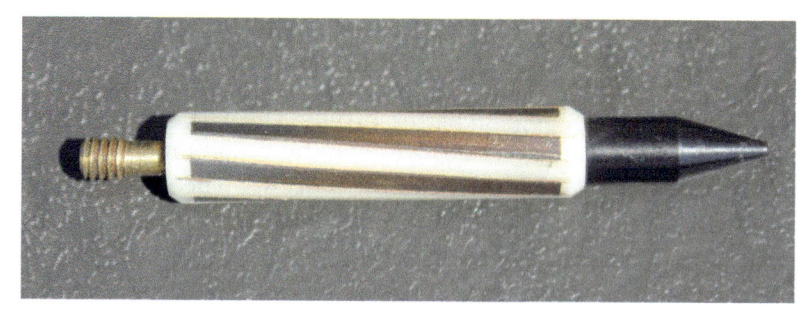

Figure 6.12 Electrochemical machining mandrel.

Electrochemical rifling

Electrochemical rifling is a newer process with respect to use in firearm manufacturing relative to hook cutting, broaching, hammer forging, and button rifling. As practices improve and evolve in the manufacturing industry, they may be utilized by firearm manufacturers to improve their process for maximum production.

Electrochemical machining is a process where metal is removed by electrolysis rather than by mechanical means. This is done by using a plastic cylinder in the shape of the barrel interior embedded with metal strips that spiral in the orientation of the desired rifling (Fig. 6.12). The metal strips of the tool act as the negatively charged cathode. The entire process takes place in an electrolytic bath composed of sodium nitrate. In this environment, the barrel is the anode and positively charged.

Figure 6.13 Barrel produced by electrochemical machining.

The solution of sodium nitrate flows through the barrel to remove the products produced by the electrolytic action (DeFrance and Van Arsdale, 2003).

The electrochemical method will leave different marks in the rifled grooves of the barrel than barrels rifled by traditional methods. Most noticeably, the areas affected by the electrolytic process will display random pockmarks where the metal will appear to have been dissolved from the surface (Fig. 6.13). This contrasts with the broaching process, which will produce parallel striations and hammer forged and button rifling, which will predominantly exhibit marks from the reaming process as no metal was removed.

Several major manufacturers have and continue to use electrochemical rifling. They include Smith & Wesson and Sig Sauer (Bolton-King, 2017). It is important to note that while these manufacturers may use or have used these methods to produce their rifling, that does not preclude the use of other techniques to produce rifling for the same make and model. Firearm manufacturers are businesses and, like any other for-profit business, maintain a contingency plan in order for production to continue in the event of an equipment failure. If the machine that is used to produce rifling goes down due to maintenance and cannot be repaired quickly, an alternate method may be employed. If that company has another method at its disposal that they may have previously used, they may switch to the previous method. It is not uncommon for a company to use electrochemical machining (ECM) one day, then 6 months later use button rifling. This applies not just to ECM, but any manufacturing process. So, while Sig Sauer used ECM as a rifling method in 2002–12 in their model P226 and SP2022 (Bolton-King, 2017), one should not assume that all barrels will be made like that in the future or were not supplemented by hammer-forged barrels if the supply required it.

Cast barrels

In the past, some manufacturers have used the casting process to produce their barrels and incorporated the rifling in the casting of the barrel. This is a less common method for imparting rifling for several reasons. The relatively high pressure produced during the discharge of a cartridge precludes many calibers from being a candidate for this method. The calibers that this method has been successfully used on include .45 Colt, .410 gauge, .32 ACP (Auto Colt Pistol), and .22 LR (Long Rifle). The most prolific firearm to incorporate cast rifling is the Thunder Five manufactured by Munitions International Laboratories, Inc. (MILI) from 1991 to at least 2004 (Fig. 6.14). The Thunder Five was the first revolver chambered for both .45 Colt and .410 gauge shotshells. In addition to the firearms made by MILI for themselves, they produced cast frames and barrels for North American Arms .22 revolver and .32 ACP Autauga model, approximately 4000 and 5000, respectively (Price et al., 2008). However, since this time, no other firearm manufacturers have reported investment casting as a method for incorporating rifling.

Examination of test-fired bullets from the Thunder Five revealed poorly marked rifling. This could indicate a result of poor accuracy during machining of the barrel, which would preclude manufacturers from using this method even if their intent was the production of a barrel for a low-pressure cartridge. Utilizing the casting process for barrel production may seem like a cost-effective method for manufacturing barrels; however, the tolerances required for accurate barrel rifling cannot be effectively produced by this process.

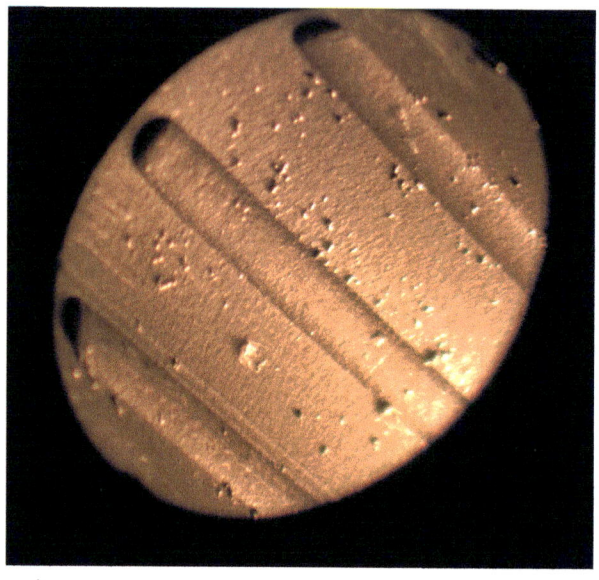

Figure 6.14 Cast barrel.

Honing and lapping

The process of both honing and lapping is performed to minimize inclusions and defects from the drilling and rifling processes. This is primarily done on higher end barrels due to the added expense and time in the manufacturing process.

Barrel honing and/or lapping is most likely to be done with hammer-forged barrels. Any imperfections from the barrel-drilling process, the initial step, will be emphasized because the hammer-forging method essentially forms the imperfections into the final profile of the barrel. If the final step for hammer-forged barrels that are not honed or lapped is to be chrome lined, the chrome lining also enhances any inclusions.

The honing process performs many functions in the barrel. It provides for a more uniform bore diameter and uniformity which increases accuracy. This also improves the accuracy and overall finish of the interior of the barrel throughout the length of the barrel.

Lapping is the final finish applied to some rifle barrels. This process involves the use of a very fine abrasive pushed down the barrel in conjunction with an object that is the same diameter as the barrel. The most common way to accomplish this is with a lead slug that has been cast into the barrel to record the exact diameter of the barrel. The fine abrasive is then placed between the lead slug and the barrel to provide constant contact which results in a smoothing of the surface of the barrel.

The main difference between a lapped and a honed bore is the direction of the finish lines in the bore. The honing process leaves fine spiraling crosshatch lines because the honing tool is rotated as it passes through the barrel. The lapping process leaves longitudinal lines in the bore due to the abrasive moving in conjunction with the longitudinally moving lead slug passing through the rifling of the barrel.

Honing is typically fast, accurate, and can be automated. Its surface quality and geometry can duplicate lapping, except for the longitudinal lines of the lapped finish.

CHAPTER 7

Equipment used for forensic firearm examination

Forensic firearm examination is one of the few disciplines in the field of forensic science where the core equipment currently used has not changed from the beginning of the practice. The essential equipment utilized in a crime laboratory include a bullet recovery method and a comparison microscope. There are other items used during the analysis of evidence such as calipers, balances, and stereo microscopes. However, for the purpose of this book, the focus will be on comparison of fired bullets and cartridge cases.

The first step in performing a comparison involving bullets is the recovery of a test-fired bullet, which will retain the marks imparted onto it from passage through the barrel. The most common method currently used for this task in crime laboratories is the use of a water tank. Water tanks are constructed of stainless steel to inhibit rust and are approximately 4-ft tall, 3-ft wide, and 10-ft long. This volume of water will sufficiently stop any handgun or rifle cartridge encountered in the crime laboratory. When a bullet enters the water, the gyroscopic stability is disrupted causing it to tumble and slow. The increased surface area of a tumbling bullet in combination with the resistance provided by water will result in the bullet coming to rest within a short distance.

Water is non-abrasive, inexpensive, and readily available. Therefore, it is the ideal medium for recovering bullets. The only downfalls to this method are portability and weight. However, in a laboratory setting, these issues would not prohibit use.

Other methods that have also been employed are cotton boxes and Kevlar traps. Cotton boxes have long been used as a bullet recovery method. The design is either a long rectangular box or a cylindrical tube that is filled with loose cotton fiber batting. The cotton will disrupt and bring the bullet to rest in a similar manner as water. The advantage of cotton boxes is lighter weight and lower cost to manufacture due to the use of steel versus stainless steel. However, bullet recovery from a cotton box takes longer as the analyst will need to search through the cotton batting to locate the fired bullet. Also, when the cotton needs to be replaced, it is not as inexpensive as water.

Generally, laboratories will choose water tanks if given the option; however, there are instances where a water tank is not an option due to weight or cost constraints. In those cases, a cotton box would be a suitable alternative.

Another option to a box recovery system is the use of Kevlar fabric as a medium for stopping the bullet. Kevlar is a much stronger synthetic fiber that will not yield as easily as cotton. Therefore the bullet will stop in a shorter distance when fired into a Kevlar trap. This brings the footprint of the recovery system down considerably, but at the expense of damage to the bullet. The Kevlar fibers can impart damage and imprints on the fired bullet from impact which may hinder the identification process. Multiple test firings may be necessary to obtain a bullet without damage to the area where a comparison is desired.

Comparison microscope

Regardless of the method used for bullet recovery, the result is a bullet with characteristics from the barrel imparted on the sample bullet. These bullets will be used in the next-stage of the examination process, which is the comparison of the test-fired bullets to those recovered from a crime scene. This involves the use of a comparison microscope.

The comparison microscope that was dedicated to the examination of firearm components was first designed by Philip O. Gravelle in 1925. The earliest models had one ocular as shown in Fig. 7.1. The first commercially produced comparison microscopes were manufactured by the Spencer Lens Company in 1934 (Dutton, 2002). The comparison microscope is comprised of two microscopes that are bridged optically and allow the examiner to view both samples simultaneously. By viewing both the samples at the same time, observations of the marks on the sample from contact with the firearm can be performed. The comparison process involves many factors and will be discussed more thoroughly in the following chapter.

The modern comparison microscopes manufactured almost 100 years later still use the same underlying design and concepts, that is, they consist of two stages under magnification, which are bridged optically (Fig. 7.2). Modern comparison microscopes incorporate luxuries such as electronically controlled stages, built-in digital cameras, and variable lighting options; however, the base of the unit design remains unchanged. In contrast to every other area of forensics, except for fingerprint analysis, forensic firearm examination has remained unchanged with respect to the equipment used to perform the analysis.

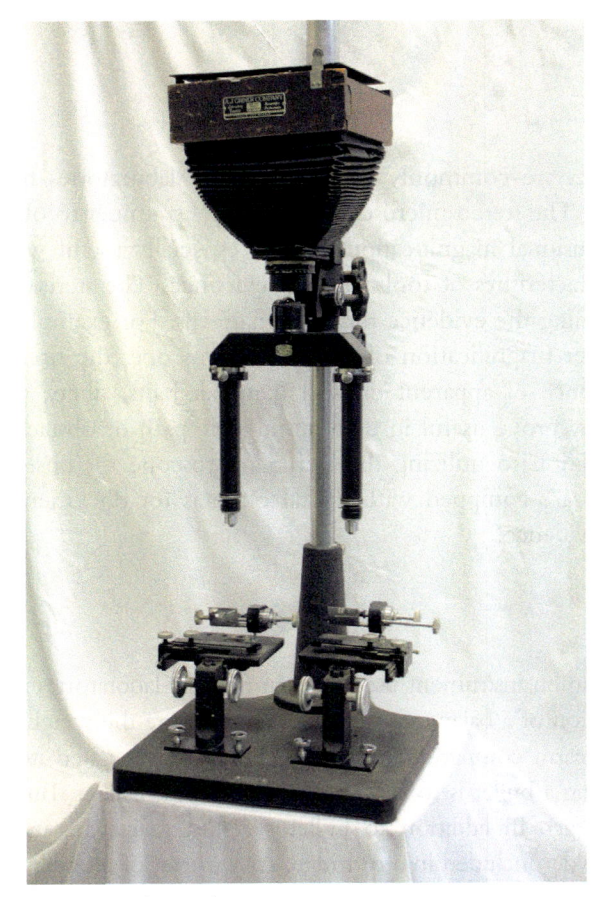

Figure 7.1 1934 Spencer comparison microscope.

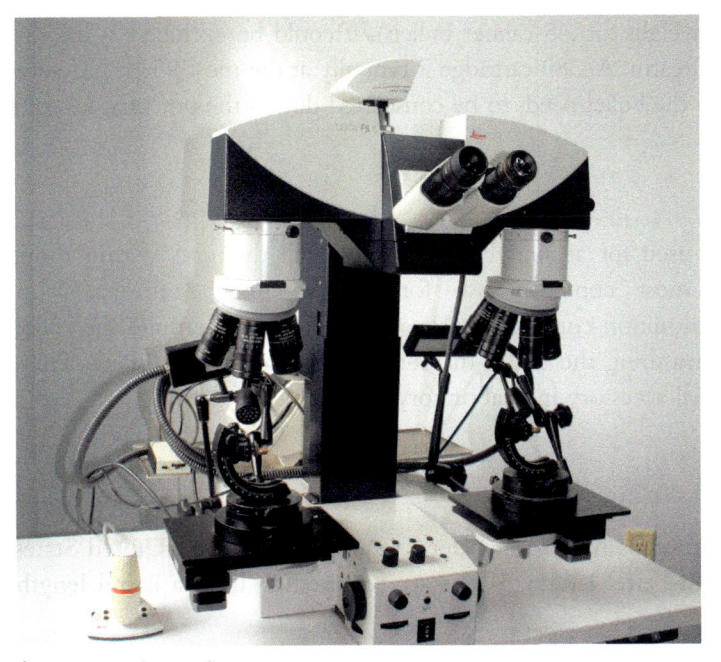

Figure 7.2 Modern comparison microscope.

Stereo microscope

Stereo microscopes are commonly used in forensic laboratories both to screen and evaluate evidence. The stereo microscope allows the examiner to observe the evidence under three-dimensional magnification. This is especially useful when evaluating the topographical characteristics of toolmarks on evidence. The stereo microscope is also valuable in examining the evidence for trace materials. For example, when examining a fired bullet under magnification of a stereo microscope, the firearm examiner may discover the presence of apparent drywall material, hairs, fibers, or other biological materials. This may prove useful in determining the path or obstacles encountered by the bullet. In addition to utilizing the stereo microscope for observational purposes, some microscopes are equipped with digital cameras for documentation of the trace materials on the evidence.

Balance

A balance is a common instrument used both in forensic laboratories and chemistry laboratories. The function of a balance is to accurately measure the weight of an item. In the area of forensic firearm comparison the most commonly weighed item is a bullet. The purpose of weighing a bullet is to assist in determining its caliber. Bullets are classified in weight by grains (gr). In addition to bullet weights, grains are used to measure the amount of gunpowder included in a cartridge. As a matter of reference, there are 7000 gr in a pound. When assessing a fired bullet, a caliber can be eliminated or included as a potential candidate based on the weight. For example, if a bullet was to weigh 230 gr (a common weight for .45 caliber bullets), it could be excluded as having come from a .380 caliber firearm. A .380 cartridge is typically at the most 95 gr. However, the amount of damage to the bullet needs to be considered due to the potential loss of weight.

Calipers

Calipers are used for accurately measuring small distances within thousandths of an inch. The most common use for calipers in the firearm laboratory is to measure ammunition components. In attempting to determine the caliber of a bullet, accurately measuring the bullet diameter at the base is important. Therefore, calipers are an essential accessory in a laboratory (Fig. 7.3).

Linear measuring device

Rifles and shotguns have legal federal requirements in the United States with respect to overall and barrel length. Rifles are required to have a barrel length of 16 inches

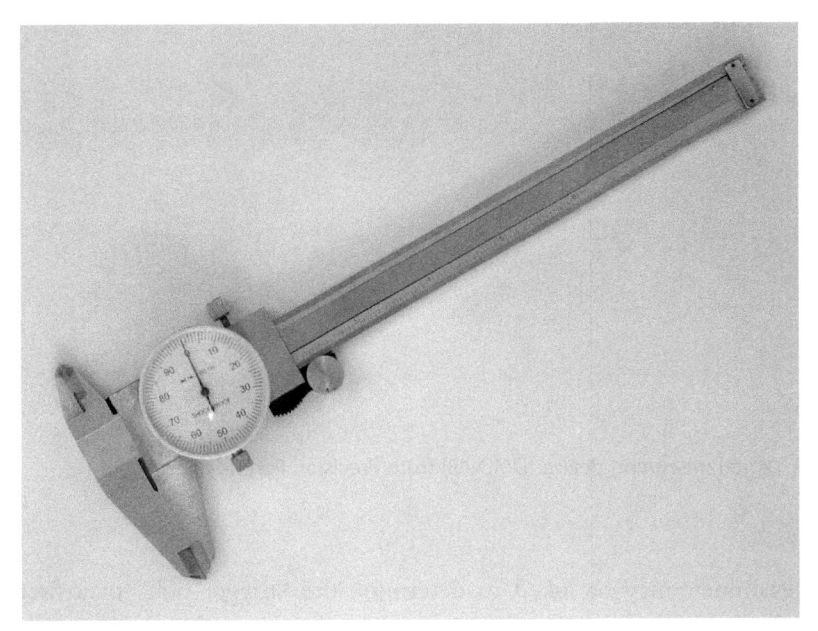

Figure 7.3 Dial calipers.

and an overall length of 26 inches. When measuring the length of the barrel, any item that is permanently affixed to the muzzle is included in the measurement. The most common attachment to a muzzle on a rifle is a flash hider or a muzzle break. Shotguns in the United States are required to have a barrel length of 18 inches and an overall length of 26 inches.

The correct method of measuring the overall length of a firearm is to measure the firearm with the barrel parallel to the scale by which it is being measured. The barrel is measured at the longest point. If the barrel had been modified by being cut with an unconventional tool such as a hacksaw, the barrel may be cut at an angle. In this instance the longest portion of the barrel constitutes the point of measurement. Measuring the firearm correctly is essential in reporting the overall and barrel length. Factors that could affect the correct reading of an overall length include not measuring perpendicular to the bore or misreading the scale if a ruler with fine readings is used.

One instrument designed to accomplish this is the digital measuring device (DMD-48), a digital measuring device manufactured by Precision Forensic Testing, LLC. This measuring device is designed to measure firearms repeatedly and reliably regardless of the operator due to the alignment rails. Reproducibility is an essential aspect when accurately measuring firearm lengths (Fig. 7.4).

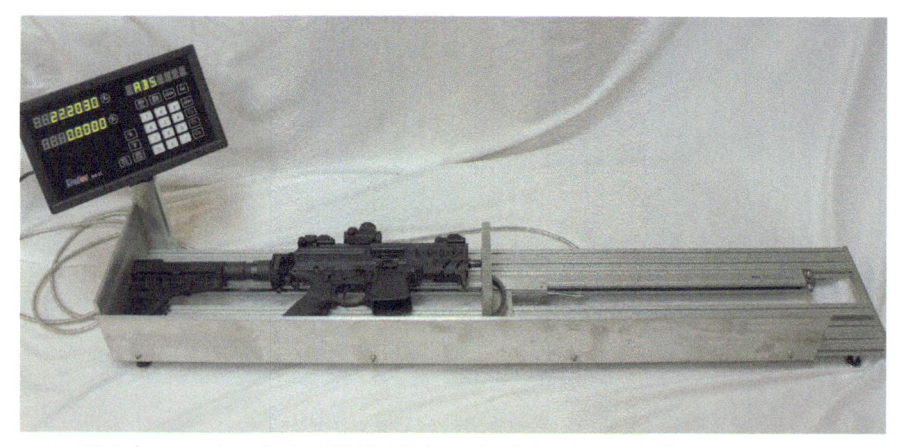

Figure 7.4 Digital measuring device (DMD-48) from Precision Forensic Testing.

Force gauge

Firearm examiners may be asked to determine the "trigger pull" of a firearm. The trigger pull is the amount of force required to disengage the sear from the striker, firing pin, or hammer. Trigger pull is frequently measured in pounds. The most accurate way to perform this test is with the use of a digital force gauge. There are many factors that can affect the force recorded by the digital force gauge, including the position of the gauge on the length of the trigger. The trigger is a fulcrum actuating a release of a spring-loaded component. Depending on where the force acts on the trigger, the amount of weight or pull necessary to disengage the sear will vary. The trigger pull of a firearm may be of particular interest to a forensic firearm examiner in cases where the unintentional discharge of a firearm is involved.

CHAPTER 8

Comparison of cartridge cases

Cartridge case comparison is a task frequently requested to forensic firearm examiners. Relative to bullets that can travel for over a mile if unimpeded, cartridge cases are cast out of a semiautomatic firearm by the action of the firearm. During the extraction and ejection of the fired cartridge case, there are a multitude of firearm parts interacting with the cartridge case. All of the parts in the firearm are machined and finished in some method and contain individual characteristics; therefore marks made by these parts may be considered by the firearm examiner to determine if they came from the same source.

The proper setup of the comparison microscope must first be established prior to use for any comparison. The appearance of the fired bullet or cartridge case under the microscope is dependent on the lighting of the specimen. The surface of the fired cartridge case or bullet is composed of raised and lowered areas resulting from contact with the surfaces of the firearm. Therefore the appearance of those surfaces will be affected by the angle of the lighting used to illuminate the samples. A cartridge case with a raised area caused by the brass flowing outward into a recess of the breech face of the firearm will result in a shadowed area from the angled light not illuminating the valley of the recessed area. The misalignment of lighting will result in an alteration of the appearance of the raised and lowered topography of the cartridge case or bullet. Fig. 8.1 is an example of the identification in Fig. 8.2 with the lighting rotated 180 degrees.

As discussed in Chapter 7, Equipment used for forensic firearm examination, the comparison microscope is the tool utilized for the comparison of firearm-related evidence. Prior to discharging, the primer of the cartridge case is smooth and void of the impact of the firing pin (Fig. 8.3). When comparing cartridge cases, the first step in the evaluation process is to examine test-fired cartridge cases from the suspect firearm. The class characteristics of the test fires from the suspect firearm must agree with those of the evidence cartridge cases. If, for example, the suspect firearm has arched breech face marks and the evidence cartridge cases exhibit parallel breech face marks, the evidence cartridge cases can easily be excluded as having come from the firearm (Fig. 8.4).

If the class characteristics on the test-fired cartridge cases from the firearm agree with the evidence, the comparison process can continue. The next step in comparing

Figure 8.1 Comparison of breech face marks with lighting in opposite directions.

Figure 8.2 Comparison of breech face marks with lighting in the same orientation.

Figure 8.3 Fired versus unfired cartridge case.

Figure 8.4 Arched versus parallel breech face impressions.

evidence is to evaluate the cartridge cases from the known source, the firearm. In evaluating the fired cartridge cases from the firearm, examiners are looking for repeating marks caused by the interaction of the firearm with the cartridge case. The photograph in Fig. 8.5 demonstrates two test-fired cartridge cases as observed under a

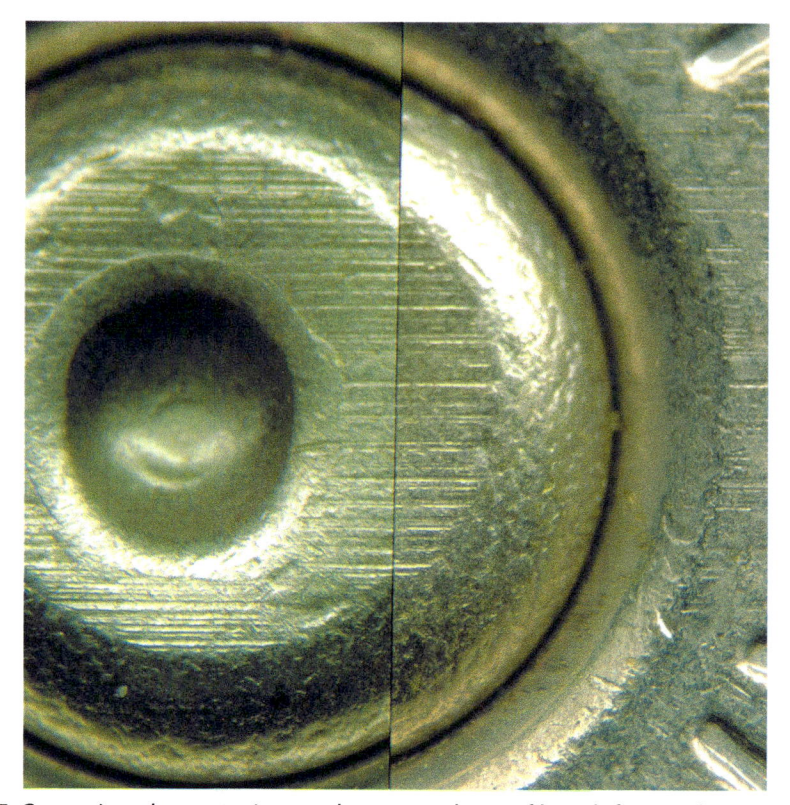

Figure 8.5 Comparison demonstrating good correspondence of breech face marks.

comparison microscope. The breech face of the firearm is the area of the slide supporting the back of the cartridge case and takes the brunt of the impact when a firearm is fired. In turn the impact of the cartridge case into the breech face of the slide will result in the transference of any machine marks from the manufacturing process of the slide, which is made from a hard steel onto the relatively soft surface of the brass cartridge case. The ideal location to find these marks is on the primer area of the cartridge case. Because these marks repeat on subsequent test-fired cartridge cases as demonstrated in the comparison of the test-fired cartridge cases to each other, these marks can be expected to have been imparted to the evidence cartridge cases if they were fired in the same firearm.

If no suspect firearm is present, the examiner may be tasked with determining if one firearm contributed to all the cartridge cases at the scene or if multiple firearms were used. At times, the fired cartridge cases can be easily separated into different groups based on the class characteristics as mentioned above. However, if the differences in class characteristics are not abundantly clear, examination under the magnification of the comparison microscope should be pursued.

Figure 8.6 Comparison exhibiting both gross and fine breech face characteristics.

When there is correspondence in the class characteristics of the cartridge cases, the next step is the evaluation of individual characteristics. As discussed in Chapter 4, Fundamentals of forensic firearm examination, individual characteristics are the fundamental basis for firearm identification and the ability to determine if a cartridge case was fired from a specific firearm. In addition, in Chapter 5, Manufacturing techniques used in the manufacturing of firearms, the various methods utilized in manufacturing breech faces were discussed in detail. All these manufacturing techniques will leave some degree of individualism due to the random nature of the machining and finishing processes. These differences can be very small in nature and should be carefully evaluated. Large, gross marks are valuable as a starting point to index the cartridge cases; however, within those gross marks, there will be fine, individual marks. Both are essential in performing a comparison (Fig. 8.6).

The primer area of a cartridge case can be a wealth of information regarding the firearm that fired it. In addition to the breech face marks, there will be a firing pin impression and the possibility of primer flow back, aperture shear, firing pin drag, and an ejector mark. All these marks will be unique to the firearm firing it. However, due to the dynamic interaction of these parts and the composition of the cartridge case, there may or may not always be carryover of markings.

Figure 8.7 Aperture with countersink relief.

Primer flow back

In addition to breech face marks, another characteristic that may be present is referred to as primer flow back. The 2013 Association of Firearm and Toolmark Examiners (AFTE) Glossary defines primer flow back as, "the extrusion of the primer into the firing pin aperture. This phenomenon can produce identifiable marks" (AFTE Glossary, 2013). This is a result of the pressure of the expulsion of the cartridge forcing the primer rearward into the firing pin aperture. When this occurs, the primer will flow back into the aperture (opening) of the firing pin hole. This commonly happens when there is a size difference of the firing pin aperture relative to the firing pin to provide a large, unsupported area. The result of the ignition is the appearance of the primer with a firing pin impression in the center and a raised portion around the firing pin that flows back into the aperture (Fig. 8.7).

Some instances of primer flow back can be very extreme, due to the lack of primer support at the time of discharge. In these instances, the firing pin impression may no longer exhibit a recessed impression. In fact, the firing pin can appear as convex rather than concave. Individual and class characteristics may still be present regardless of the shape of the firing pin impression and may still be used for identification purposes (Fig. 8.8).

Aperture shear

The next type of primer mark that can be present is aperture shear. This commonly appears in some firearms that exhibit primer flow back prior to the movement of the

Figure 8.8 Heavy primer flowback.

barrel. The act of a barrel tilting as part of the cycling action is defined as recoil operated. Most current firearms employ the recoil-type operation. This is defined by the 2013 AFTE glossary as "a firearm mechanism (action) in which the breechblock remains locked to the barrel only while the pressure is high. This involves a barrel travel of only about ½ inch. The device locking the breechblock to the barrel is then released and the two components separate. The barrel may remain stationary and await the return of the breechblock, but in most modern designs, the barrel has its own spring and goes forward into battery" (AFTE Glossary, 2013). Anytime a recoil-operated firearm with a tilting barrel is fired, there is a potential for aperture shear.

Aperture shear is a valuable occurrence for use in performing cartridge case comparisons. This is because the machining methods involved with producing the aperture are not conducive to subclass influences. The apertures are most commonly drilled, punched, or electrical discharge machined. The type of interaction these tools have with the breech face will produce random marks and, when present, is generally very pronounced.

During the operation of a recoil-operated firearm with a canting barrel, the barrel moves downward to partially retard the recoil prior to full encounter with the recoil spring. This method of deterring recoil is the most common method for delaying the recoil and containing the recoil of larger calibers. As the protruding primer is still positioned in the aperture of the breech face, the tilting action of the barrel downward results in marking or shearing the protruding primer area against the aperture with the machined surface of the aperture hole (Figs. 8.9 and 8.10).

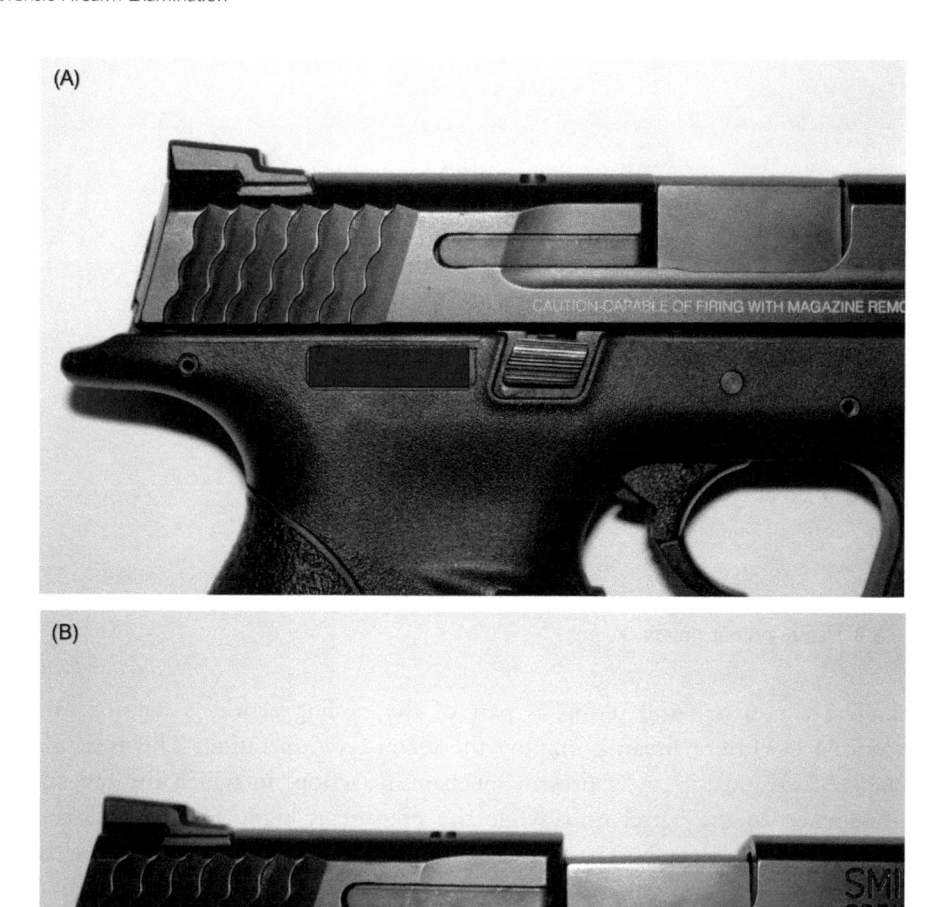

Figure 8.9 (A) Firearm with the barrel in the position prior to discharging a cartridge; (B) Firearm with the barrel canted downward during the recoiling action during discharge.

Aperture shear should not be expected to happen in every instance of interaction of the firearm and cartridge case. Because of this, cartridge cases cannot be eliminated based on the lack of aperture shear. Fig. 8.11 demonstrates the same firearm and the same ammunition with both aperture shear and lack of aperture shear. The dynamics of the interaction of the cartridge case with the firearm in the firing process involves,

Comparison of cartridge cases 171

Figure 8.10 Aperture shear.

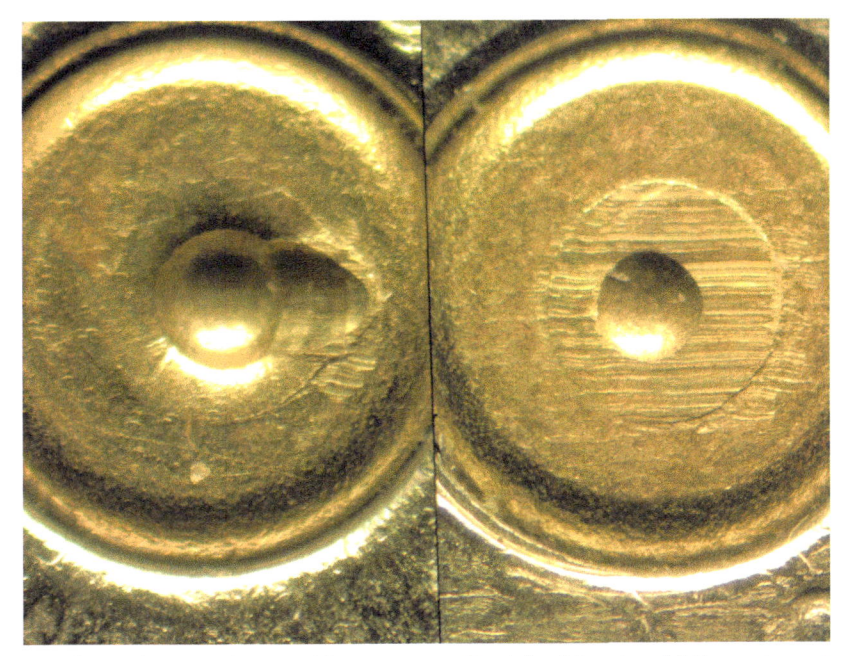

Figure 8.11 Same firearm, the cartridge case on the left did not exhibit aperture shear, the cartridge case on the right exhibited aperture shear.

at a minimum, the amount of pressure imparted to the cartridge case, hardness of the primer, thickness of the primer, contact of the cartridge case relative to the breech face of the firearm, and type of firearm. All these components play a critical role in the impartation of aperture shear.

In addition to firearms that utilize a tilting barrel to delay the recoiling action, there are firearms that use other mechanics to achieve the same desired result without affecting the movement of the barrel. An example of this is the Beretta 92/96 series and the Taurus series with a similar design. This design uses a cam beneath the barrel to accomplish the delayed pivoting action, traditionally accomplished by downward movement of the barrel in other firearm designs. This prevention of downward movement of the barrel inhibits the potential for aperture shear.

However, tilting barrels are not the sole source of aperture shear and firing pin drag. An example of this is the Beretta Storm 9 mm semiautomatic pistol. This firearm is designed with a rotating barrel to facilitate the delay in the locking action. Because the barrel rotates, it stays in alignment with the frame of the firearm and therefore does not tilt. The cartridge case is still subject to movement as it is extracted and ejected from the firearm. In the case of the Beretta Storm, the firing pin and primer flow back are still in contact with the breech face at the time of extraction and ejection. This contact in conjunction with the movement caused by the extractor and ejector results in lateral movement against the breech face. In this case even though the barrel does not tilt during firing, the fired cartridge cases can demonstrate both aperture shear and firing pin drag. Another example of a rotating action firearm which can cause aperture shear is the AK-style rifle system. In the AK rifle design, the bolt rotates compared to the barrel which rotates in the case of the Beretta Storm (Fig. 8.12).

Some firearms do not utilize a recoil-operated system to facilitate functioning. These types of firearms have a fixed barrel that does not move during the firing sequence. This type of action is called a blowback design. To counter the energy of the discharge of the cartridge, firearms of this design use a heavier slide and rely on the mass of the slide in conjunction with the recoil spring to accommodate the pressure of the discharge of the cartridge. The lack of downward movement of the barrel and delay of movement of the cartridge case prior to extraction precludes the occurrence of aperture shear in these designs.

Firing pin drag

Another component of the dropping of the delayed recoil barrel is the presence of a firing pin drag. Firing pin drag is defined by AFTE as "the toolmark produced when a projecting firing pin comes into contact with a cartridge case or shotshell during the extraction/ejection cycle" (AFTE Glossary, 2013). In simple terms, this occurs when

Figure 8.12 Aperture shear from a Beretta Storm with a rotating barrel action.

the firing pin remains protruding outward while the barrel cants downward during the cycling process, resulting in the firing pin leaving a drag mark across the surface of the primer of the cartridge case (Fig. 8.13).

The firing pin drag can be a useful element when comparing cartridge cases to determine if they originated from the same firearm (Fig. 8.14). This is due to the random imperfections imparted to the firing pin during the manufacturing process. These imperfections, or individual characteristics, will be transferred onto the firing pin drag on fired cartridge cases. However, caution should be used when using firing pin drag marks for inclusion or exclusion as a possible source. This is because some firearms have rotating firing pins, in that they are not supported and rotate as the firearm fires. Therefore the orientation of the firing pin can change from shot to shot as the firing pin freely rotates during the firing process.

Firing pin drag as a result of incidental interaction

Firing pin drag may not always be attributed to the dropping of a barrel during the cycling of the action. Because blowback firearms typically utilize the firing pin as the ejector, the action of the cartridge being removed from the chamber may cause the firing pin to encounter the primer while the cartridge case is in an upward motion. An example of this occurrence can be seen on some cartridge cases fired from a

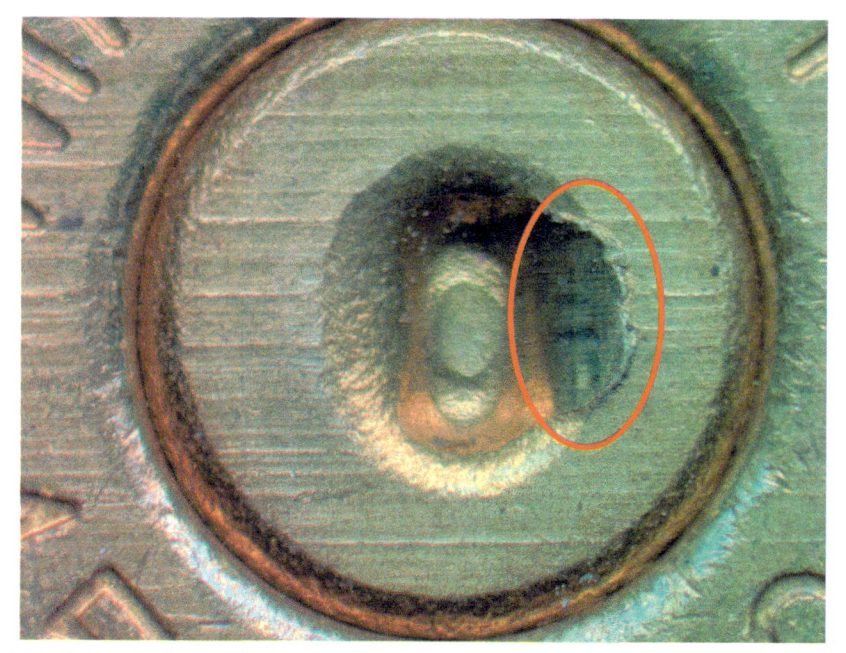

Figure 8.13 Firing pin drag circled.

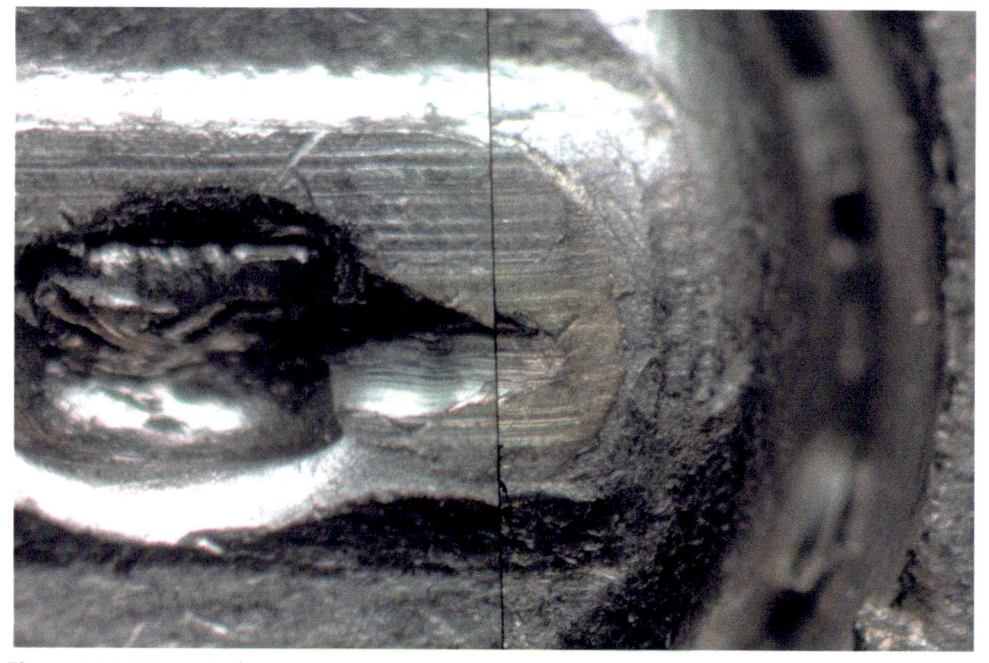

Figure 8.14 Firing pin drag comparison.

Figure 8.15 Firing pin drag exhibited on a cartridge case fired from a blowback design firearm (Hi-Point C9).

Hi-Point 9 mm semiautomatic pistol. The typical interaction consists of the cartridge case contacting the firing pin without upward movement, thus the general absence of the appearance of firing pin drag. While it is indeed a drag mark caused by the firing pin, most instances of firing pin drag are directly attributed to the movement of the barrel during the firing process. In the case of the appearance of firing pin drag on blowback firearms, the observed mark is technically an ejector mark, because it was caused as the result of the firing pin acting in the function of an ejector. However, since it was caused by a drag of the firing pin, a classification of firing pin drag would not be inaccurate either (Fig. 8.15).

Firing pin

In addition to the potential for identification based on marks within the firing pin drag, the impression of the firing pin can be a basis for assessment of an identification. Firing pins are machined by a variety of methods. One of the most common methods is the use of a screw machine. These are machines that are conventionally used to make small round items such as screws from round bar stock. A screw machine is essentially a lathe that has been designed to automatically feed a predetermined length of round bar stock into the machine. The mechanism used to cut metal on a screw

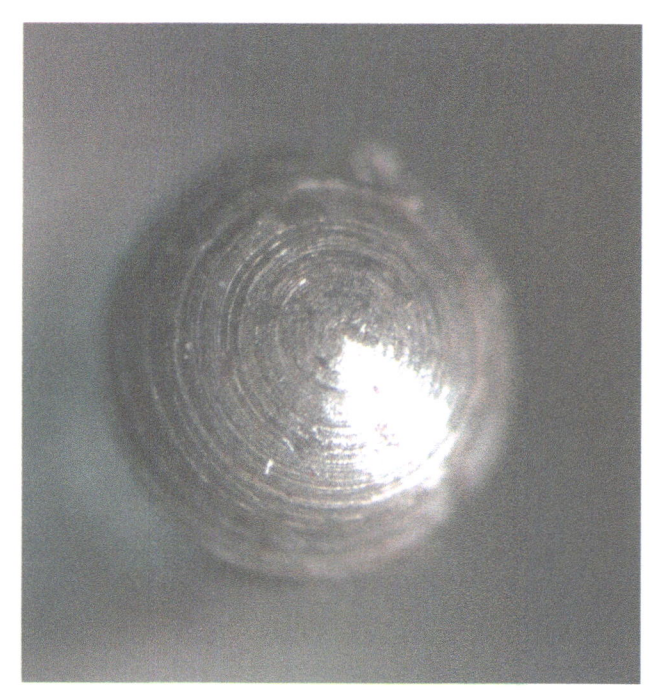

Figure 8.16 Concentric marks on the tip of a firing pin.

machine is a single-point cutting tool like that used on a lathe. This results in concentric marks on the finished product. That bar stock is turned to the specified dimensions and cutoff. The bar stock is then again fed to the correct length and the process begins again. The result is a pile of completed firing pins. The use of modern machining methods and computer numerically controlled equipment will result in very similar gross patterns with respect to spacing and orientation of concentric marks. However, since this is a machining process, sideflow, built-up edge, and plowing will occur. These will be the individual characteristics essential in identifying the firing-pin impression back to the firearm. These occurrences were previously discussed in Chapter 5, Manufacturing techniques used in the manufacturing of firearms (Fig. 8.16).

Along with individual marks produced by the manufacturing process, individual characteristics can be the result of the finishing process or incidental contact with a harder item. In these cases random marks can appear on the firing pin and, in turn, be imparted to the cartridge case it contacts.

Firing pin bounce

In addition to the initial contact of the firing pin to ignite the primer, there are instances of the firing pin making a second impact on the primer. The second

Figure 8.17 Firing pin bounce.

impact of firing pin bounce will appear as a lighter indentation offset from the initial impact. Firing pins are typically retained in a retracted position by spring tension. However, during the movement of the slide during the firing process, the slide velocity can exceed the spring tension of the firing pin. At that time, the firing pin protrudes through the firing pin hole a second time contacting the primer (Fig. 8.17).

Firing pin contact as a result of cycling

Firearms utilizing the blowback design, such as the Hi-Point C9 9 mm, use the firing pin as an ejector. When the slide of this firearm is retracted to the rear, the firing pin protrudes through the firing pin hole and works in conjunction with the extractor to remove the cartridge or cartridge case. If the cartridge has been cycled through the firearm manually by physically pulling the slide to the rear rather than by firing, the firing pin will impact the cartridge and may leave an indentation not associated with the firing of the cartridge. These marks may or may not have sufficient impact to leave identifiable marks (Fig. 8.18).

Figure 8.18 Primer with dents from contact with the firing pin during the extraction process.

Ejector

One component of the firing sequence that can leave an identifying mark on the outer edge of the primer or cartridge case is the ejector. The ejector is a metal piece inside the firearm that acts to assist in removing the cartridge case after the cartridge case has been fired or a cartridge in the case of removing an unfired cartridge (Fig. 8.19).

Another type of ejector system utilizes the firing pin to aid in the ejection process. As discussed earlier, this is commonly used in firearms that are blowback design. These types of firearms include Hi-Point, Bryco, Davis, Cobra Enterprises, and Jennings centerfire semiautomatic pistols to name a few. During the cycling action of these firearms, when the slide moves fully rearward, the firing pin protrudes through the breech face and contacts the primer, thus acting as an ejector (Fig. 8.20).

In lieu of a fixed ejector in the firearm, some designs incorporate the ejector as part of the bolt or breech face such as the AR-15–style firearms. The AR-15–type firearms combine the ejector with the bolt. In these types of firearms, the ejector is spring loaded from behind and aids in the ejection/extraction; however, the interaction is not as aggressive as other designs where the cartridge gains significant momentum prior to coming in contact with the ejector (Fig. 8.21).

Comparison of cartridge cases 179

Figure 8.19 Ejector circled.

Figure 8.20 Firing pin being used as an ejector in a blowback design.

Figure 8.21 AR-15 ejector.

Another type of firearm encountered in forensic laboratories is the SWD/Cobray/M-11 design. This design has been marketed by a variety of manufacturers, yet they all share the same components and design features. The fundamental design of the firearm has remained unchanged. This includes a rod-shaped ejector that rides through the bolt and is exposed when the bolt is retracted to the rear. The rod is manufactured by cutting it to an appropriate length with a parting tool. A parting tool is a tool used on a lathe designed to cut a part to length with a surface perpendicular to the rod. During the parting operation, the resulting marks on the workpiece are concentric circles. These concentric marks may be observed in the circular mark left by the ejector. Caution should be used in relying heavily on these marks to affect an identification due to the automated parting process. The parting tool leaves concentric marks where the spacing is very consistent from ejector rod to ejector rod due to the automated feed and speed rate of the parting tool (Figs. 8.22–8.24).

The ejector will contact the cartridge case head, typically toward the outer perimeter. The contact of the ejector with the cartridge case will generally leave a noticeable and comparable mark. As with any interaction of the firearm and cartridge case, there may not always be a mark present from the interaction. The pressure from the cartridge discharge, composition of the cartridge case, and nature of the ejector may all contribute to a lack of reproducibility. In addition, cartridges may be marked by the ejector from the action of manually cycling (retracting the slide fully rearward by hand) the cartridge through the firearm. At times, the manual cycling may leave

Figure 8.22 Cobray-style semiautomatic pistol.

Figure 8.23 Ejector with concentric marks.

ejector marks, which does not indicate that the cartridge case was *fired* through the firearm, only that the cartridge was *cycled* through the firearm. Therefore, caution should be used in assessing the value of the ejector mark relative to the condition of having been a result of firing rather than cycling.

Figure 8.24 Ejector mark on fired cartridge cases with concentric marks from impact with the ejector.

One pitfall to cartridge case examination is that cartridge cases could potentially be reloaded. Reloading cartridges involves removing the fired primer, replacing it with a new one, adding the correct amount and type of gunpowder for that particular cartridge, and inserting a new bullet. Once a cartridge has those new components, it can be fired again. However, any marks on the cartridge case from previous firings may be present (e.g., ejector and extractor marks). Therefore marks on the cartridge case must be evaluated to determine if they are from the current event or a past one.

The primer on a cartridge case must always be new for the cartridge to ignite. Therefore any breech face and firing pin impression marks transferred onto the primer will be new marks from the most recent firing. The marks on the primer can be valuable in orienting the cartridge cases relative to the other marks present on the cartridge case. For example, if the firing pin drag is oriented in the 3:00 position, and the ejector mark is pronounced from having come in solid contact with the ejector, it can be reasonably deduced that the ejector strike was a result of the most recent firing sequence rather than a previous occurrence. Therefore there is a value to ejector marks with respect to contributing to the identification of a cartridge case to a specific

Figure 8.25 Ejector mark circled.

firearm; however, due caution should be practiced ensuring that the other components are in agreement (Fig. 8.25).

Extractor

The extractor of the firearm is a metal piece in the shape of a hook under spring tension designed to remove the cartridge case or cartridge in the case of unfired ammunition from the chamber of the firearm. This metal hook is a machined and finished item and will, as a result, have individual characteristics from those processes. The hook of the extractor mechanically removes the unfired cartridge or fired cartridge case, which can result in marks transferring from the extractor to the rim of the cartridge case (Fig. 8.26).

The spring-loaded extractor, in conjunction with the ejector, is most commonly seen on modern semiautomatic pistols and some rifles. However, there are firearm designs that use only extractors as a means for the removal of fired cartridge cases or shotshells. The single-shot break-open shotgun is an example of this type of design. These shotguns use a spring-loaded extractor typically located at the bottom of the chamber to engage the rim of the shotshell. When the shotgun is fully opened, the

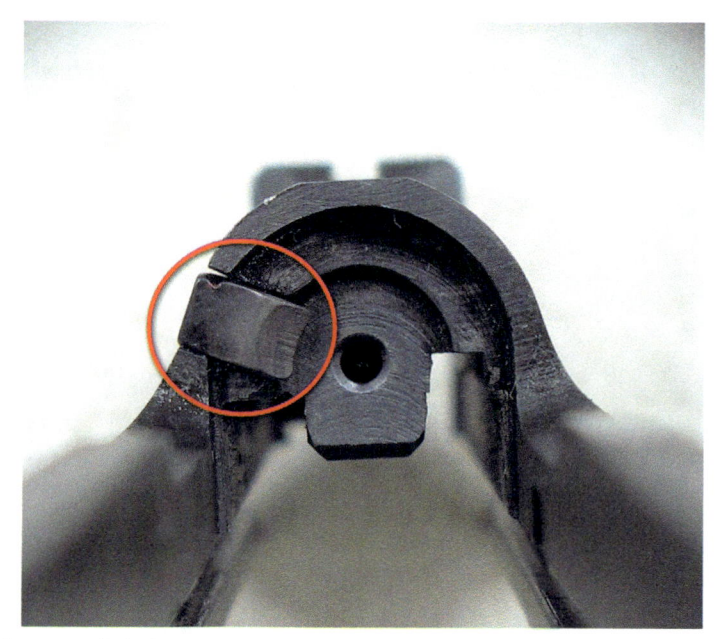

Figure 8.26 Extractor circled.

extractor is released from the spring tension and the shotshell is removed from the shotgun via that spring tension (Fig. 8.27).

Another firearm design that utilizes only an extractor for the removal of expended cartridge cases is revolvers. Most revolvers use cartridges with rimmed cases. The extractor on revolvers engages the rim partially along the circumference. Modern revolvers require manual unloading by the actuation of the extractor rod. Pressing the extractor rod moves the extractor rearward, thus pushing the cartridges from the cylinder chambers. In most situations the cartridge cases from revolvers are not found at crime scenes due to the extra time required to manually reload (Fig. 8.28).

Double-barrel derringer-designed firearms are another type of firearm that utilizes an extractor as the only means for removing fired cartridge cases. Much like revolvers, these firearms have an extractor that engages the rim of the cartridge and must be physically manipulated to pull the cartridges from the chambers (Fig. 8.29).

As with the ejector, this occurrence is not exclusive to the firing sequence. The marks on the rim of the cartridge from the extractor can be caused by manual cycling of the firearm and thus be present without having fired the cartridge through the firearm. There is a potential for this to happen at the same time that the ejector marks

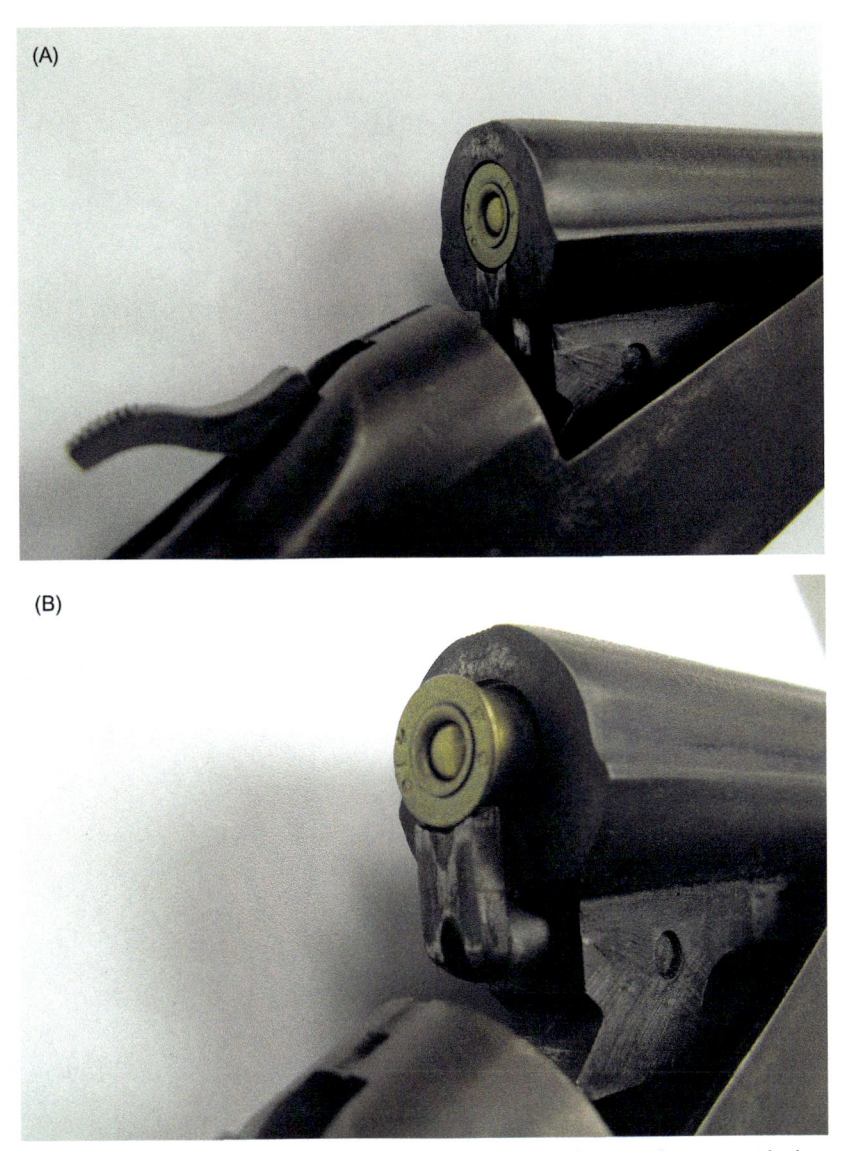

Figure 8.27 (A) Break-open shotgun prior to extraction; (B) Break-open shotgun with the extractor engaging the cartridge.

the cartridge. Therefore the agreement of only the ejector and extractor should not be the sole basis for an identification of firing. Other marks that are independent of the extractor and ejector must be in alignment to be of value when considering the value for identification purposes.

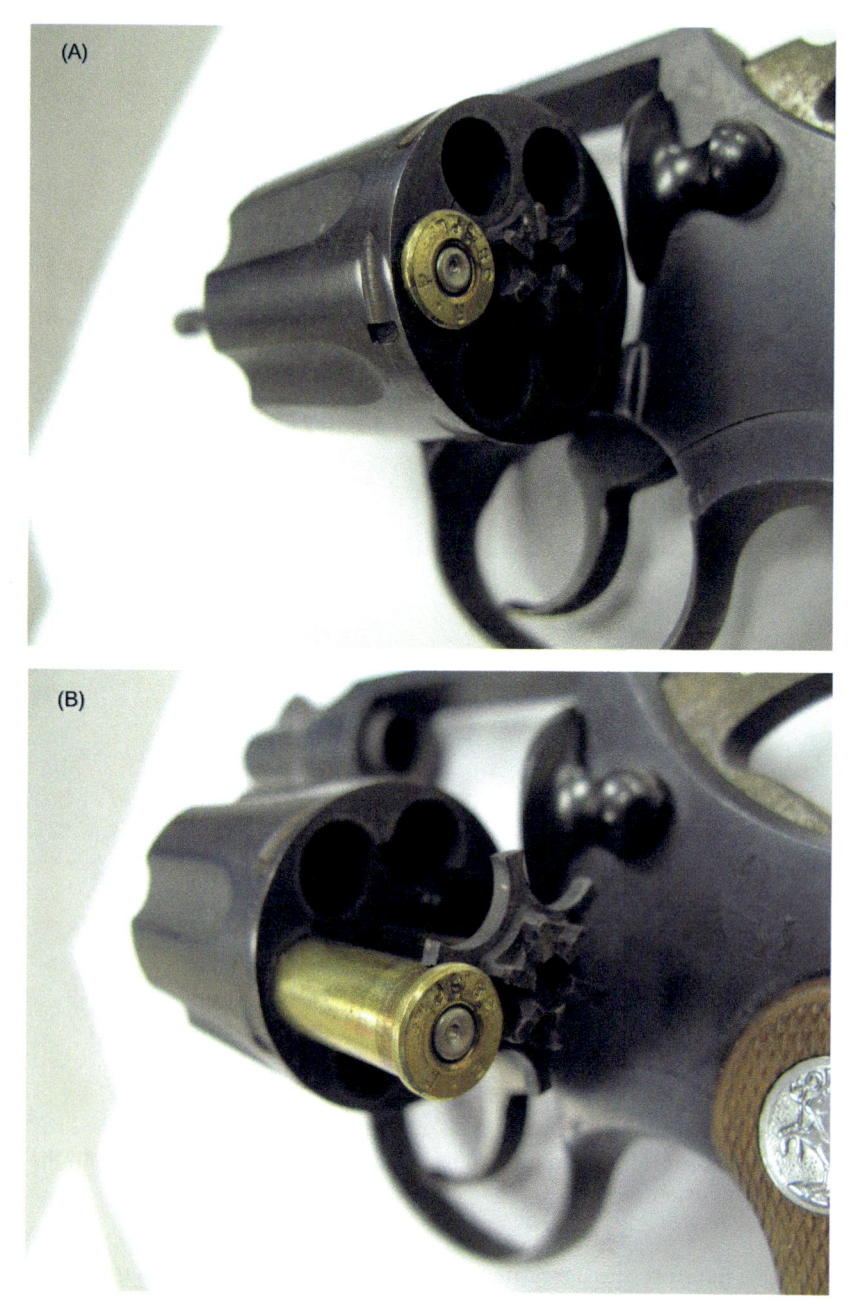

Figure 8.28 (A) Revolver with a fired cartridge case in the cylinder; (B) revolver with a cartridge case being removed by the extractor.

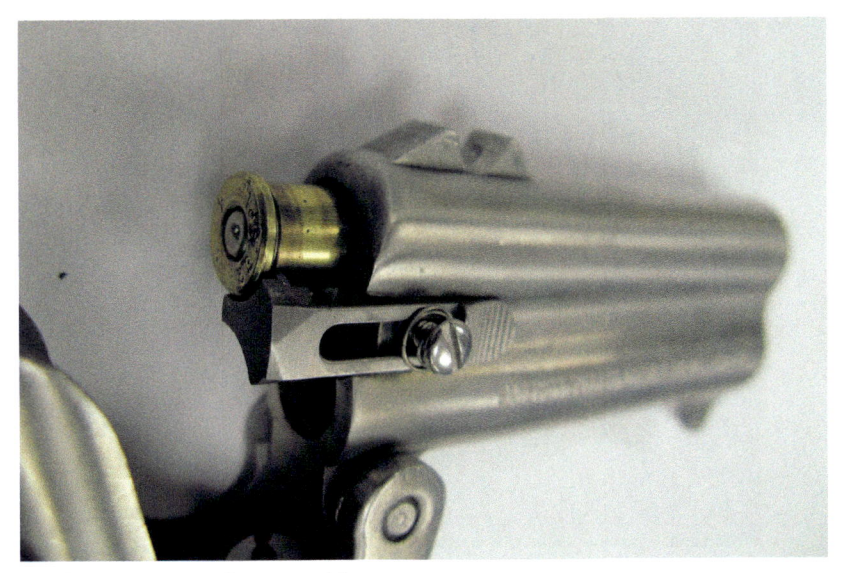

Figure 8.29 Derringer extracting a cartridge.

Chamber marks

Chamber marks are defined by AFTE as "Individual microscopic marks placed upon a cartridge case by the chamber wall as a result of any or all of the following: (1) chambering, (2) expansion during firing, and/or (3) extraction" (AFTE Glossary, 2013). They are a result of the finishing process of the firearm chamber. The chamber is rough cut with a chamber reamer and then followed up with a finishing reamer. The finishing reamer cuts the chamber to the final dimensions specified by the manufacturer and results in concentric marks in the chamber of the firearm (Fig. 8.30).

When a cartridge is discharged in a firearm, the pressure from the expanding gas can result in the swelling of the cartridge case in the chamber of the firearm. When the cartridge case swells, it is in tight contact with the wall of the chamber, thus engaging any toolmarks from the reaming process. The marks on the outside of the cartridge case will be individual in nature and valuable in determining if the cartridge case was fired from a specific firearm. As with any mark examined for the purpose of comparison, caution must be exercised to verify that the marks being examined are indeed from the firing process rather than an encounter from manually cycling the firearm (Fig. 8.31).

Ejection port marks

When a cartridge case is extracted from a firearm, it can encounter various areas of the firearm. One of these areas is the ejection port. This is the area of the firearm that is open to allow for the removal of the cartridge case. During this action, some

Figure 8.30 Chamber marks from the reaming process.

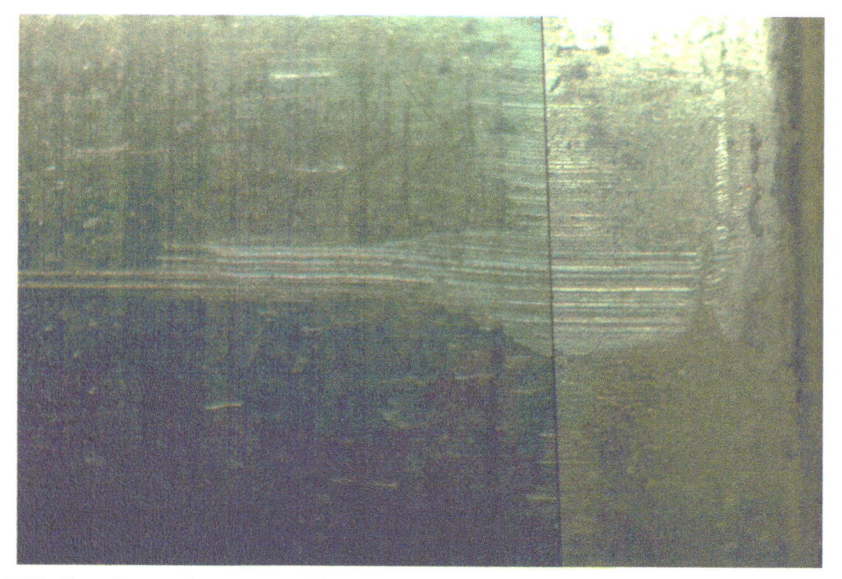

Figure 8.31 Chamber marks on a cartridge case.

semiautomatic pistols produce ejection port marks on the expended cartridge cases when the cartridge case contacts the ejection port during the ejection process. Glock firearms have been shown to demonstrate these marks fairly consistently in the ejection of cartridge cases from their firearms (Finklestein et al., 2005). These marks are called ejection port marks. They typically resemble tornado-shaped marks (Fig. 8.32).

Figure 8.32 Ejection port marks circled.

Another example of a firearm that traditionally leaves ejection port marks is various models manufactured by Berettas. In a study by McCombs of 91 different models and calibers of firearms manufactured by Beretta, she found that except for .22 caliber firearms, ejection port marks were present over 50% of the time. Included in the study were 16 different .40 caliber model 96 firearms. Interestingly, all the firearms of that model produced ejection port marks (McCombs, 2001).

The ejection port marks are a result of contact of the fired cartridge case with a surface of the firearm. As with the other machined areas of the firearm, the marks produced by contact are individual in nature and can be used for assisting in identification. As with all interactions between firearms and ammunition components, there is no guarantee that reproduction will occur 100% of the time. The presence of ejection port marks on test-fired cartridge cases from a suspect firearm and the absence of ejection port marks on evidence cartridge cases should not dismiss the potential of the firearm as having fired the cartridge cases.

Magazine marks

The magazine contains the ammunition to be fired in the firearm. Most magazines are made from stamped metal that is bent and welded into shape. They can also be polymer and typically have metal inserts at the top to maintain rigidity. The feed lips of the magazine come in direct contact with the ammunition. This area is the uppermost portion of the magazine that holds the cartridge in position prior to being pushed into the chamber.

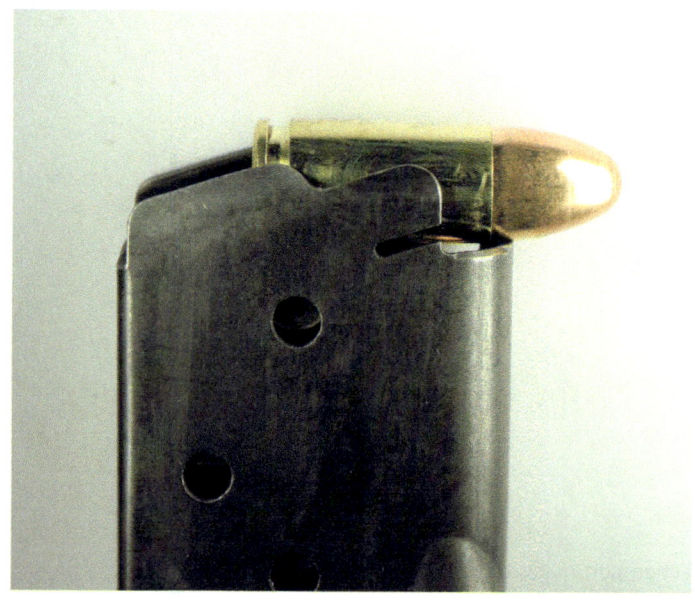

Figure 8.33 Cartridge engaging the lips of the magazine.

As the cartridge is pushed out of the magazine, the cartridge case is scraped against these feed lips, which can create magazine marks. These marks can be of assistance in the identification process. However, identification of these marks can only demonstrate that the cartridge was, at a minimum, cycled through that magazine. This identification could also indicate that the cartridge case was both cycled and fired from that firearm and magazine combination. The extent of the identification and inclusivity is dependent on other areas of identification on the cartridge case with respect to the firearm. This is because magazines are not exclusive to a firearm and can be interchanged (Fig. 8.33).

An example of the presence of magazine marks for use in assisting with an identification, and furthermore, associating a bullet with a cartridge case, is described in an article by Clow. In this instance, the magazine contacted not only the cartridge case but also the bullet. While comparing the test-fired bullets during the comparison process, Clow observed longitudinal marks along the bullet. Having previously observed similar marks on the test-fired cartridge cases, the marks on the test-fired bullet were then compared to the bullets recovered from the scene. Based on the agreement of the markings on the bullet and cartridge case, it was determined that both the bullet and cartridge case contacted the same magazine (Clow, 2008a).

Slide drag

During the operation of a semiautomatic firearm, upon forward movement of the slide after the fired cartridge case has been extracted and ejected from the firearm, the slide

Figure 8.34 Slide drag on a cartridge case.

encounters an unfired cartridge from the magazine and pushes it into the chamber of the firearm. During this interaction, the bottom of the slide will come in forceful contact with the cartridge case resulting in the deposition of impressed tool marks from the slide onto the cartridge case. This will predominantly be observed along the outer edge of the cartridge case (Fig. 8.34).

Bunter marks

As discussed in Chapter 3, Ammunition, cartridge cases contain information with respect to caliber and manufacturer. Bunters are made from hardened steel and are designed to stamp the information on up to 120,000 cartridge cases before being changed (Rosati, 2000). These marks can provide additional information other than the brand and caliber. The bunter is a tool and, as such, leaves toolmarks on the cartridge case. As a tool that is constantly contacting a surface, the tool surface changes throughout the process. Therefore, bunter marks are a valuable asset with respect to determining if the cartridge cases were produced by the same bunter in the same state of wear.

Bunter marks can be an invaluable investigative lead. They can associate a fired cartridge case to an unfired cartridge case in that they came from the same bunter that was in the same condition of wear. The importance of this type of evidence must be properly evaluated and considered when conveyed in a court of law. The likelihood of tens of thousands of cartridge cases with the same bunter marks is very high. However, when the type of cartridge case produced by the manufacturer is in the millions of that caliber for that year alone, in addition to the previous years, the value of that evidence increases.

The actual number of cartridge cases with a specific headstamp produced by a manufacturer annually is considered proprietary information and closely guarded. The author had a case where fired cartridge cases were recovered from a remote crime scene of a homicide. The cartridge cases were microscopically compared to each other and found to have been fired from the same firearm. The police developed a suspect and served a search warrant. During the search, no firearm was recovered; however, one unfired cartridge was recovered. The unfired cartridge was microscopically compared to the fired cartridge cases from the crime scene. The bunter marks were found to have sufficient individual characteristics to identify that the cartridge cases from the crime scene and the cartridge recovered from the suspect's house were made by the same bunter. Because the unfired cartridge from the suspect's house had no firing pin impression or other signs of having been in the firearm, limited analysis could be performed.

The bunter is made from carbide and acts as the tool (a harder object) which leaves a mark on the brass cartridge case (the softer object). However, after thousands, tens of thousands, even hundreds of thousands of stampings, regardless of the relative hardness of the tool, constant encounter with another material will change the surface of the harder object. Therefore the bunter will change over time. The increment of this change has been studied (Rosati, 2000). Because there is not a comprehensive study of all manufacturers and all associated factors, no exact number of cartridges made can be given for the average bunter.

In the abovementioned case the bunter marks were the primary firearm-related evidence. Unlike typical forensic firearm examination cases where a suspect firearm is recovered, and test-fired, cartridge cases can be compared to evidence cartridge cases, there were no breech face or firing pin marks to compare. The entirety of the comparison relied on bunter marks. Because there were no studies performed on this particular manufacturer with respect to the duration of identifiable marks, the prosecution in the case brought in a representative from the company to testify about the number of cartridges typically produced by their bunters. To protect the confidentiality of the company, the court records were sealed, and no further information regarding the production volume could be established. This is an example of the lengths firearm and ammunition manufacturers will go to in protecting proprietary information. In addition, this is an example of the difficulty encountered in establishing the importance of bunter marks (Fig. 8.35).

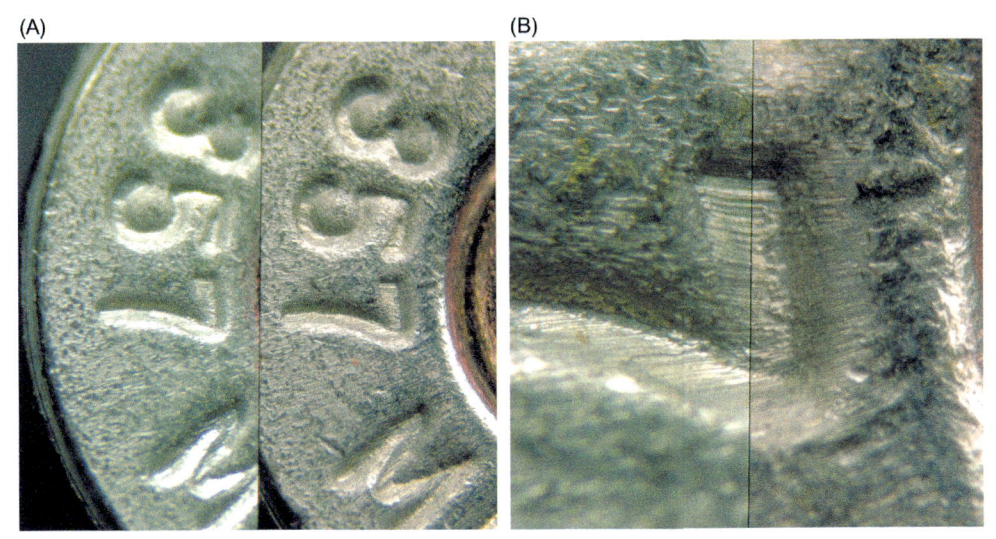

Figure 8.35 (A) Numbers produced by the same bunter; (B) comparison of the bunter marks.

Figure 8.36 Individual characteristics within the arched gross marks.

Individual characteristic comparison

Once the class characteristics of the firearm have been determined to agree with the fired cartridge cases, or in the event no suspect firearm was provided, the forensic firearm examiner must determine if the cartridge case was indeed fired from that firearm or one similar to it. To accomplish this, the individual characteristics imparted during the machining process are evaluated. As discussed in Chapter 5, Manufacturing techniques used in the manufacturing of firearms, during the machining process, anytime metal is removed from the surface of the base material, there will be microscopic inclusions in the workpiece that are unintended. These are the basis for the marks that will be evaluated to determine if the marks are specific to the encounter with one specific firearm.

Individual characteristics are best observed by evaluating the starting and stopping of the machine marks. These are a result of the plowing, built-up edge, and shearing of the metal as it departs from the host surface. Also, these are random in occurrence and will not duplicate during the manufacturing process (Fig. 8.36).

CHAPTER 9

Comparison of bullets

Bullet comparison is based on the same fundamental principles as the previously discussed areas of firearms that are subjected to the machining process and removal of metal. Firearm barrels typically start out as solid bars of metal, which are drilled through the center with the basic diameter of the intended caliber. The barrel is then reamed to more exacting tolerances. The barrel is then rifled by one of the methods described in Chapter 6. The barrel drilling and reaming processes will leave individual characteristics due to the machining process. Additional individual characteristics are imparted during the rifling process where the metal inside the barrel is either removed, as is the case with broach rifling, or disrupted and cut as occurs during button rifling. These unique marks will be the basis for the examination of evidence bullets to test-fired bullets from a specific firearm.

During the comparison process of bullets, the first thing to consider is the class characteristics of the bullet as described in Chapter 4. There must be agreement of the class characteristics to continue with the comparison process. For example, if given an evidence bullet that is .38 class (.38 Special, .357 Magnum, 9 mm, etc.) and asked to compare to a .45 Auto firearm, the evidence bullet can quickly be dismissed as not having been fired through the barrel of that firearm in its current configuration. As with most of the situations in the firearm world, there are exceptions where a firearm can be altered by the addition of different parts to accept different calibers.

With respect to using class characteristics to include or exclude a firearm as a potential contributor as a source, if the direction of rifling twist, the number of lands and grooves, or width of lands and grooves differ, the firearm can be excluded as a candidate of having fired that bullet. Caution should be exercised when using the width of the lands and grooves as a determining factor to exclude a bullet; the clarity of the edges, bullet composition, and condition of the evidence bullet should be considered. A bullet that has been damaged to where it has been flattened can alter the resulting widths of the lands and grooves (Fig. 9.1).

If it has been demonstrated that the class characteristics of the evidence bullet and the test-fired bullets are in agreement, the next step is to evaluate the agreement of individual characteristics. One of the first things to consider when performing bullet

Figure 9.1 Same firearm, flattened bullet groove on the left, pristine bullet on the right.

comparisons is the type of bullet. While it is not essential to use the exact same brand and lot of ammunition when making test-fired samples to be compared to the evidence, it is ideal to use ammunition with similar compositions. For example, if tasked with comparing lead bullets from a .38 Special revolver, the test-fired bullets to be compared should both be composed of lead. This will aid in most reliably reproducing the marks from the barrel.

When evaluating bullets, using the correct terminology is essential to allow for a common understanding of the characteristics being discussed. The land impression of the bullet is produced by the grooved area of the barrel (recessed area). When referring the bullet land, the barrel groove is also being referenced (Fig. 9.2). The groove of the bullet is produced by the impression of the land of the barrel (raised area of the barrel rifling). When referencing the bullet groove, the barrel land is also being referenced (Fig. 9.3). As defined by the 2013 Association of Firearm and Tool Mark Examiners Glossary, "The driving edge of a bullet fired from a gun with a right twist is the right edge of the land impression, or the left edge of the groove impression. The driving edge of a bullet fired from a gun with left twist is the left edge of the land impression or the right edge of the groove impression. Also known as leading edge when used in conjunction with the term following edge." The opposite edge of the land impression (bullet groove) is referred to as the trailing edge. The trailing edge of the bullet is defined in the 2013 Association of Firearm and Tool Mark Examiners Glossary as, "The edge of a bullet fired from a gun with a right twist is the left edge of the land impression, or the right edge of the groove

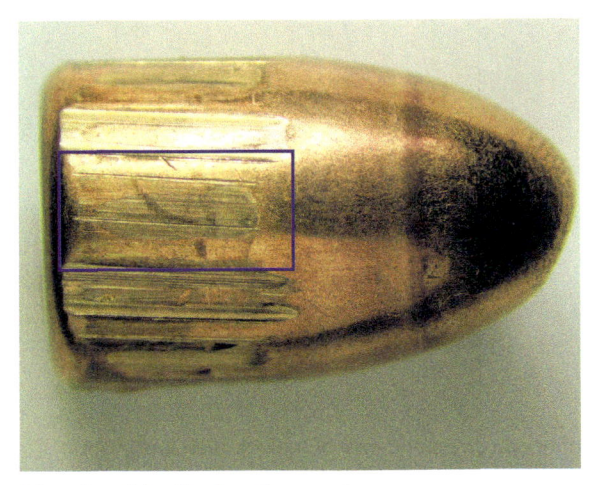

Figure 9.2 Bullet land (produced by the barrel groove).

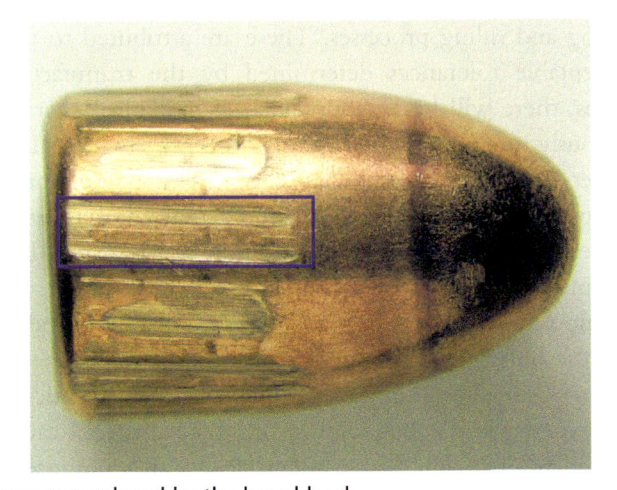

Figure 9.3 Bullet groove produced by the barrel land.

impression. The trailing edge of a bullet fired from a gun with left twist is the right edge of the land impression or the left edge of the groove impression."

Unlike cartridge cases, which have many different areas of the firearm contacting the cartridge case during the firing process, bullets primarily encounter only the barrel. Because of this, the majority of the marks used in performing bullet comparisons are based on the individual characteristics produced during the barrel manufacturing process. These microscopic imperfections, as with those produced when machining other parts of the firearm, result in marks that are random and specific to the barrel of the firearm.

Figure 9.4 Example of good correspondence of individual characteristics.

Firearm barrels can have a wide range of individual characteristics present from the initial barrel drilling and rifling processes. These are attributed to tool wear, machine stability, and acceptable tolerances determined by the manufacturer. In the most extreme conditions, there will be an abundance of individual characteristics from any or all of the previously mentioned contributors. In these situations the identification of the evidence bullet to the test-fired bullet will be fairly simple and easy to observe (Fig. 9.4). The quality and quantity of the individual characteristics exhibited on a bullet can vary greatly depending on the condition of the barrel, bullet composition, and surfaces encountered by the bullet on impact.

The bullet composition can also play a role in the quality of individual characteristics transferred to the bullet from passage through the barrel. Some bullet coatings are not conducive to the deposition of individual characteristics as discussed in Chapter 11, The expert witness. In addition, the jacket material can have an effect on the marks deposited on a bullet. Some bullet jackets are comprised of mild steel or copper-plated mild steel, both of which are harder than traditional copper jackets and may mark less aggressively.

Another cause of poor-quality individual characteristics occurs in firearms where the specifications are of lower standards than other manufacturers. During the production of these firearms, the quality of the steel barrel is lower, resulting in a softer barrel that is more prone to wear. Even though barrels are made of steel, and they are being contacted by a softer material (e.g., a copper jacket), the high velocity, heat, and friction can alter and erode the barrel. When this occurs, the bullet does not have as secure of engagement with the rifling as seen in a newer barrel. The lack of engagement with the barrel results in poor, sporadic individual characteristics within the observable lands and grooves. An extreme example of this may result in the absence of any visible lands and grooves. However, even in these instances, the bullet is making

Figure 9.5 Bullet exhibiting poor rifling.

contact with the barrel, albeit without the benefit of gyroscopic stability. When this occurs, the striations have a perpendicular orientation to the base of the bullet and are still useful for the evaluation of individual characteristics (Fig. 9.5).

There are instances where the manufacturing method is less conducive to the introduction of a large number of individual characteristics. The hammer forging process is an example of a rifling process that leaves few individual characteristics from the actual rifling process. As described previously, hammer forging is a cold working process where the barrel is essentially pressed around a reverse image of the desired barrel profile. No metal is being removed or cut, rather it is displaced. However, the mandrel is forcibly removed after the barrel has been completed, and the hard carbide mandrel can produce scratches in this process, which would be individual in nature (Fig. 9.6).

The condition of the barrel can play a factor in the observation of individual characteristics. While traditional barrel fouling, such as that which occurs from shooting a large number of jacketed bullets, may have a small influence, that generally is not the case, in situations where large numbers of lead bullets have been fired without cleaning, the lead can accumulate in the barrel. When this happens, the thin layer of lead in the barrel can mask the microscopic individual characteristics hindering the examination process.

Another contributor to diminished individual characteristics is not a factor of the firearm, rather the interaction of the bullet after it exits the barrel. Handgun bullets travel in the range of 800 to over 2000 ft/s and when a bullet comprised of lead with a copper jacket strikes an item at that velocity, damage can occur to the bullet. The impact can result in scuff marks from glancing off a hard object, flattening, fragmentation into multiple pieces, or any combination of those. The areas of the

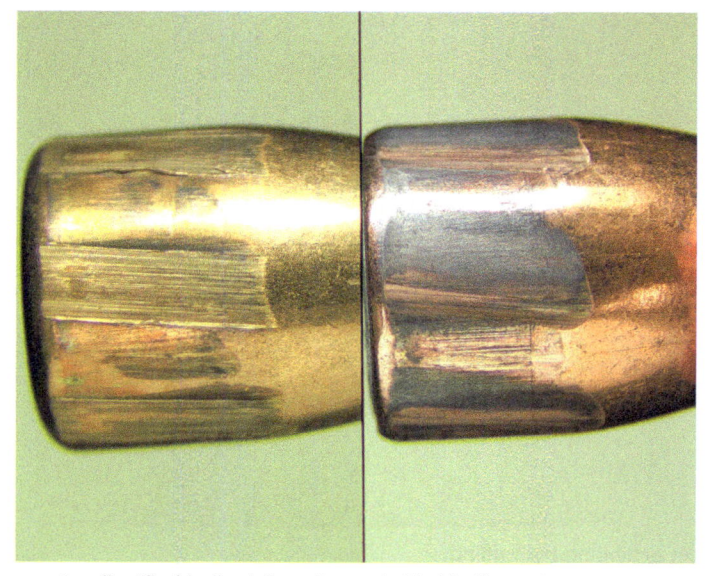

Figure 9.6 Conventionally rifled bullet left, polygonal rifled bullet right.

Figure 9.7 Flattened bullet jacket.

bullet that contacted hard areas are likely to have, at a minimum, the individual characteristics obscured, and at times, the class characteristics altered by the impact.

This type of contact is detrimental to the comparison process because the information pertinent to performing the comparison can be lost. However, in the instances of scuff marks from impact with a hard surface, only a portion of the bullet may be affected (Fig. 9.7). Also, if the bullet fragments due to an orthogonal strike, it is likely that the bullet jacket will contain much of the rifling, albeit in a flattened condition rather than cylindrical.

The individual characteristics on fired bullets encompass the entire circumference of the bullet; therefore, to conclude an identification of an evidence bullet to test-fired bullets, it is not necessary to have a fully intact bullet. Depending on the quality of the marks present, a bullet jacket fragment with as little as one bullet groove may be sufficient for the identification of a suspect bullet to a firearm. As with every aspect of forensic firearm examination, there are very few absolutes and any statement warrants a cautionary note that there is always the potential for a factor that could have an effect on the results. Therefore just because there is only one groove exhibiting individual characteristics, it should not be dismissed as not of value.

The process of forensic firearm examination is different than other areas of forensics in that the findings of the analyst are based on the observation of the correspondence of the evidence bullet or cartridge case with those which were test fired from a suspect source. In the cases where no suspect firearm was recovered the firearm examiner will be asked to determine if the evidence was from one firearm or multiple firearms. Conversely, when evaluating drug or DNA evidence, little discretion is left to the examiner due to the instrumentation and resulting data reported by the instrument.

Instead, forensic firearm examination relies on the examiner's ability to observe both the class and individual characteristics resulting from the manufacturing process that was imparted on the surfaces of the workpiece. To perform this a comparison microscope is used, allowing for the viewing of both the evidence item and the item from the known source. The evaluation of either bullets or cartridge cases is based on the education, training, and experience of the examiner.

The elements of education, training, and experience in the firearm examiner's decision-making process are crucial because they are the foundation when concluding an identification, inconclusive, or elimination. The science of the individuality and randomness of marks produced on workpieces has been demonstrated not only in the forensic firearm community but also for decades among researchers in the field of machining, metallurgy, tribology, and tool manufacturers. Therefore the ultimate contribution to the field of forensic firearm examination relies on the examiner and his observations.

The nature of both the class and individual characteristics are topographical irregularities on the surface of the workpiece created by the tool, in this case, the firearm. These irregularities can be thought of as a topographical map where there are different peaks and valleys on the surface of the bullet or cartridge case. The three-dimensional attributes of the surface allow for much more detail than in other areas of forensic science that are observational based, such as fingerprint and shoe wear analysis. The relative topographical and three-dimensional alignment allows for smaller relative areas with more detail to establish a correlation between items being examined. Because of this, there is no set "number" for traditional pattern matching of the evidence to the known standard.

The lack of a set number of points for identification is beneficial; in that, the examiners have the ability to take into consideration the areas of absence of marks in both samples as being a characteristic in itself that is specific to that firearm. Situations like this can be further validated by taking subsequent test fires with ammunition to demonstrate the reproducibility of an area that fails to demonstrate individual characteristics.

In addition to the marks left by the passage of a bullet through a barrel, other areas of the firearm may come in contact with the bullet resulting in marks that may be identifiable. One example of this is the feed ramp of the firearm. The feed ramp is the area preceding the barrel that guides the cartridge into the chamber. Feed ramps are machined parts, which have individual characteristics. If a bullet comes in aggressive contact with the feed ramp upon being forced into the chamber by the slide, the feed ramp may deposit marks on those bullets. This occurrence was documented and further researched in an article by Hartman (2014).

Individual characteristics resulting from alteration

The typical sources of individual characteristics arise from the manufacturing process. However, the alteration of a firearm can result in the deposition of individual characteristics on components fired from that firearm. When discussing projectiles, barrels that have been altered are a likely source of individual characteristics. This is because the barrel is altered at the muzzle of the firearm if it is cut to a shorter length. An amateur barrel shortening modification will result in rough burrs along the perimeter of the barrel (Fig. 9.8).

Figure 9.8 Barrel shortened by hacksaw cut.

For shotguns, a shortened barrel can leave individual marks on the wads which pass through the muzzle of the barrel (Wright, 2003). As discussed in Chapter 3, the wad may not always extend to surround the shot. This is generally the case with larger sized shot. As with the wad interaction when passing across the burrs of an altered barrel, large shot pellets are susceptible to incurring the individual characteristics of the barrel modification. These individual characteristics can in turn be used to identify the fired pellets as having come from that barrel (Pendleton et al., 2011).

The result of these imperfections at the muzzle of the barrel provides a wealth of information due to the potential relative roughness. As demonstrated in the articles by Wright and Pendleton, identifications can be made on evidence which, if fired from an unaltered barrel, would be impossible. Therefore evaluating the wad, sabot, or shot is an important step when examining shotgun-related evidence.

The occurrence of burrs from barrel modification can also be demonstrated in rifles where the barrel has been modified without subsequent finishing processes typically performed in the traditional manufacturing process, such as crowning, where the muzzle of the firearm is slightly recessed at an angle.

Alternative comparisons involving bullets

Most comparisons performed by forensic firearm examiners involve comparing evidence bullets and/or cartridge cases to test-fired bullets and/or cartridge cases to determine if they are from the same source. However, there may be instances where it is of value to determine if two pieces of ammunition components were at one time from the same source. In an article by Clow, both a copper bullet jacket and a lead core were recovered separately at a crime scene. Upon examination of the bullet core, it was observed that there were striated marks near the base of the core. Clow made test marks using the copper jacket to abrade the base of the jacket against lead. This resulted in marks that could be compared to the bullet core. Based on the comparison of the marks on the bullet core with the test marks, it was determined that the core was at one time part of the bullet jacket (Clow, 2011a). This can be beneficial in providing information to investigators as to the number of bullets recovered.

CHAPTER 10

Documentation, notes, and reports

The cumulation of the work and analysis of the evidence will result in a written report that will be provided to the parties involved in the case. There are many steps in the analysis process that will contribute to the final report that may ultimately be used in court testimony.

Documentation

Documentation is an essential part of the analysis process. Documentation through notes provides the analyst and reviewers details of the evidence, an indication of which tests were performed, how the tests were performed, and the results of the tests. The time that can lapse between the testing process and trial can be years. In the interim, the analyst may have worked hundreds of other cases, which would make recollection of that case a difficult task. For the sake of analyst's recollection, as well as transparency for all parties involved, it is vital to take contemporaneous and complete notes.

Casework notes can include any or all of the following: written descriptions, sketches, diagrams, measurements, photographs, videos, and reference materials. The type of notes will be dictated by the kind of evidence present in the case. While thorough documentation is mandatory, there is currently no standard documentation format for all crime laboratories.

Advancements in digital photography have made it an easy and accurate method to document items such as bullets, cartridge cases, and clothing. Photographs depict the condition of the evidence, and measurements and annotations indicating any anomalies can supplement the photographs. Anomalies might include trace evidence, such as wood fibers, paint transfer, abrasions from impact, drywall, hairs, and fibers. Collection of physical evidence should be considered for evaluation by other sections of the crime laboratory.

To assist in the documentation of evidence, analysts may opt to use worksheets. Worksheets are beneficial in that they provide designated areas for data such as weights, measurements, and component design. Examples of worksheets that could be used for firearm, bullet, and cartridge case evidence are provided in Figs. 10.1–10.3.

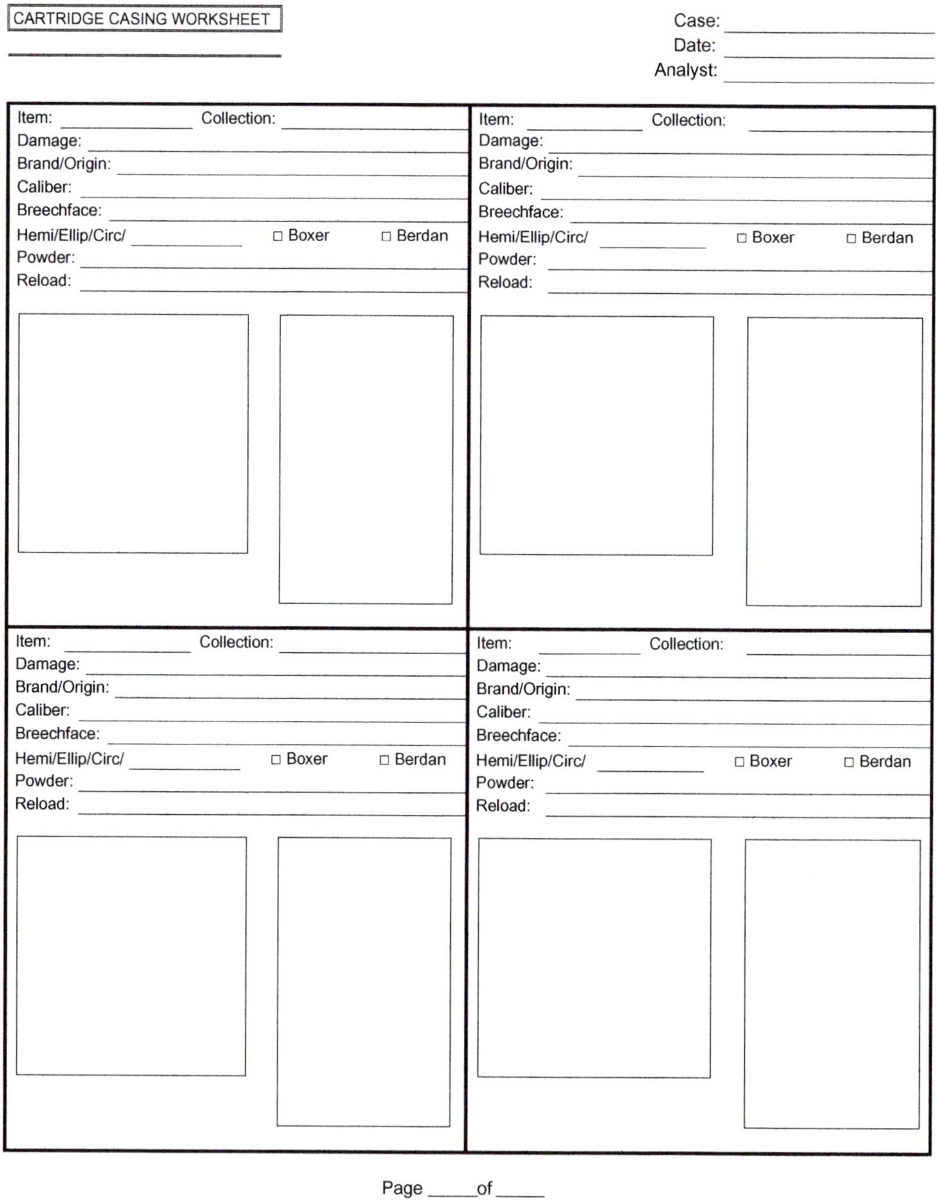

CARTRIDGE CASING WORKSHEET

Case: ____________
Date: ____________
Analyst: ____________

Item: ______ Collection: ______
Damage: ______
Brand/Origin: ______
Caliber: ______
Breechface: ______
Hemi/Ellip/Circ/ ______ □ Boxer □ Berdan
Powder: ______
Reload: ______

Item: ______ Collection: ______
Damage: ______
Brand/Origin: ______
Caliber: ______
Breechface: ______
Hemi/Ellip/Circ/ ______ □ Boxer □ Berdan
Powder: ______
Reload: ______

Item: ______ Collection: ______
Damage: ______
Brand/Origin: ______
Caliber: ______
Breechface: ______
Hemi/Ellip/Circ/ ______ □ Boxer □ Berdan
Powder: ______
Reload: ______

Item: ______ Collection: ______
Damage: ______
Brand/Origin: ______
Caliber: ______
Breechface: ______
Hemi/Ellip/Circ/ ______ □ Boxer □ Berdan
Powder: ______
Reload: ______

Page _____of _____

Figure 10.1 Cartridge case worksheet.

Marking evidence

Marking of evidence is important both in the analysis and court presentation of evidence. A good practice is to immediately photograph and then mark the evidence upon removing it from the external packaging. Photographing and marking evidence

FIREARM WORKSHEET

Analyst: ____________________
Case: ____________________
Date: ____________________

Item: ___________ Collection ____________________
Damage: ☐ None ____________________
Trace/Location: ☐ None ☐ Evid ____________________
Metallic Residues: ☐ Cu + Pb @ Muzzle ____________________
Patch Fouled: ☐ Yes ☐ No ☐ Evid ____________________
Powder Residues/Location: ☐ None w/Morph ☐ None ____________________

Make/Origin: ____________________ Model: ____________________ Caliber: ____________________
Serial Number: ____________________ Locations: ____________________

Operating System:
☐ Blowback
☐ Delayed Blowback
☐ Recoil
☐ Gas
☐ Bolt
☐ Pump
☐ Lever
☐ ________

Cycle:
☐ Semiautomatic
☐ Full Auto
☐ Manual
☐ ________

Operability:
Inherent Safety: ☐ OK ☐ N/A ☐ See Notes
Disconnector: ☐ OK ☐ N/A ☐ ________
Shock Test: ☐ OK ☐ N/A ☐ ________
Lock Open On Empty: ☐ Y ☐ N ☐ No Mag ☐ N/A
Manual Safety: ☐ OK ☐ N/A ☐ See Notes
Push Off: ☐ OK ☐ N/A ☐ ________
Malfunctions: ☐ N ☐ N/A ☐ Y/See Notes

Action:
☐ Single
☐ Double
☐ Double Only
☐ ________

Inherent Safety:
☐ None
☐ F/P Block
☐ Trigger
☐ Grip
☐ Magazine
☐ Inertial F/P
☐ Rebound Hammer
☐ ________

Manual Safety:
☐ None
☐ Lever
☐ Rotating
☐ Cross Bolt
☐ Sliding
☐ Quarter Cock
☐ Half Cock
☐ Decocker
☐ ________

Properties/Class Characteristics
L/G: ☐ 5 ☐ 6 ☐ 8 ☐ ________
L/G Ratio: ______ Direction: ______
Rifling Type: ________
Firing Pin: ☐ Hemi ☐ Ellip ☐ ____
Position: ☐ C/F ☐ ________
Extractor: ________
Ejector: ________
OA Length (in): ________
Barrel Length (in): ________
Magazine: ☐ Y Cap: ____ ☐ N ☐ N/A
☐ Removable Box ☐ Tubular
☐ Detachable Box ☐ Drum/Rot.
☐ Internal Box

Firing Mechanism
☐ Hammer
☐ Int. ☐ Ext.
☐ Striker
☐ ________

Trigger:
S/A: ________
D/A: ________

Cocked Ind. ________ **Chamber Ind.:** ________

TF Ammo: ____________________
≈Times Fired: ____________________
TF Intercomparisons: ____________________

Notes: ____________________

Page____of_____

Figure 10.2 Firearm worksheet.

during each unpackaging step also serves to protect the analyst: sometimes, what is described on the packaging is not what is inside. Firearm-related evidence can range from a single item, such as a fired bullet or cartridge case, to hundreds of pieces of evidence depending on the incident. As evidence is being removed from the exterior packaging, it is essential to properly mark and document it to prevent misidentification. Because of the type and amount of evidence received in cases, the

PROJECTILE WORKSHEET

Analyst: ____________
Case: ____________
Date: ____________

Item: ______ Collection: ______
Description ______
Damage ______
Trace ______
Type/Design ______
Base: ______ Cannelures: ______
Wt. (gr): ______ Dia (in): ______
Brand: ______ Bullet Style: ______
Caliber: ______ Twist: [R] [L] ______
L&G: ______ Ratio: ______
Cleaned: ______

Item: ______ Collection: ______
Description ______
Damage ______
Trace ______
Type/Design ______
Base: ______ Cannelures: ______
Wt. (gr): ______ Dia (in): ______
Brand: ______ Bullet Style ______
Caliber: ______ Twist: [R] [L] ______
L&G: ______ Ratio: ______
Cleaned: ______

Item: ______ Collection: ______
Description: ______
Damage: ______
Trace: ______
Type/Design: ______
Base: ______ Cannelures: ______
Wt. (gr): ______ Dia. (in): ______
Brand: ______ Bullet Style ______
Caliber: ______ Twist: [R] [L] ______
L&G: ______ Ratio: ______
Cleaned: ______

Item: ______ Collection: ______
Description: ______
Damage: ______
Trace: ______
Type/Design: ______
Base: ______ Cannelures: ______
Wt. (gr): ______ Dia. (in): ______
Brand: ______ Bullet Style: ______
Caliber: ______ Twist: [R] [L] ______
L&G: ______ Ratio: ______
Cleaned: ______

Figure 10.3 Projectile worksheet.

documentation process is commonly done in a different location than where the actual analysis is performed. Most of the evidence received in the forensic firearm section will require analysis using the comparison microscope. However, the unpackaging and documentation will take place on a table with ample space for the evidence, a computer or notepad, and photography equipment. Ensuring evidence is properly marked as it comes out of its packaging aids in the documentation of the items and dramatically reduces the chance of mixing up samples during an examination, especially when moving between workbenches and comparison stations. In addition to documentation purposes, proper marking of the evidence is essential in future identification of the evidence in court.

Report writing

The report is the product of the analysis and is intended to clearly and succinctly convey results to the agency or parties requesting the analysis. In addition, the report will ultimately be provided to both the judge and jury for consideration. There is no standard in the forensic community as to what information is provided to the requesting agency or individual in the final report. As a result, the information provided by forensic laboratories may vary from extensive to basic. An extensive report might include the weight of the bullet, the number of lands and grooves, and diameter in the description of the bullet. In contrast, a basic report may simply include "one fired bullet" in the description of the evidence. Reports should include, at a minimum, the date of the report, a brief description of the evidence packaging, the evidence examined, the tests that were performed, the results of the tests, and the signature of the analyst authoring the report.

CHAPTER 11

The expert witness

Bias

Bias was defined by Haber and Haber as, "a mindset in which a person expects or believes something without examining the underpinnings of the belief" (Haber and Haber, 2013). There are several types of potential biases to which the expert witness may be subjected, including motivational and cognitive. Additionally, there are two types of cognitive bias that are commonly present in evidence examined by forensic firearm examiners: contextual and confirmation biases. Prior to analysis, it is important that the expert be aware of potential biases. The most commonly encountered types of biases in the forensic sciences are contextual and confirmation.

Contextual bias

In forensic science, contextual bias occurs when an examiner uses information included with the case to form an assessment of the expected results prior to examining the evidence. The concept of contextual effects on forensic science is not a new one. A paper written by William Hagan, when discussing handwriting analysis, stated, "There must be no hypothesis at the commencement, and the examiner must depend wholly on what is seen, leaving out of consideration all suggestions or hints from interested parties...Where the expert has no knowledge of the moral evidence or aspect of the case ... there is nothing to mislead him" (Kassin et al. 2013).

According to Stoel et al., there are four levels in order of their proximity to the item that is provided. Level 1 is the item itself. In the area of firearm identification, the item that constitutes the first level would be the firearm associated with the case. Level 2 are the items associated with the level 1 item in the case, in this instance the reference bullets and cartridge cases produced by the firearm. Level 3 is the portion of the case that includes case information in any form. This can comprise both oral and written communication from any source associated with the case, including police officers, attorneys, and other analysts. Level 4 is information that is organization or discipline specific. An example of this is knowledge of the outcome of a previous case. With respect to firearm identification, knowing that the suspect had previously been convicted of a shooting would be a level 4 (Stoel et al., 2014).

One method of eliminating contextual bias is described by Koppl and Krane in their chapter in a book titled "Blinding as a Solution to Bias Strenthening Biomedical

Science, Forensic Science, and Law." There, it is suggested that information regarding the client and any related information that could lead an examiner to a preconceived finding be removed from accompanying documentation. In this book, they state the following:

> *Sequential unmasking is far from the only masking measure available in forensic science. With sequential unmasking, the individual examiner does not know potentially biasing information until such information is required to make a scientific decision. But the lab (in the person of the case manager) does know this information, including what answer the "customer" desires, which may create a risk of bias. One approach that could counter this risk in part would be measures meant to mask from the lab the identity of the party requesting forensic science service. By obscuring the "right" answer from the examiner, sequential unmasking does help alleviate the problem. But if the monopsony structure is retained, then it may provide only a partial solution. Creating a substantive defense right to forensic expertise would help to make both the police and the accused "customers" of the lab. When the lab is unsure from whom a request for service originates, it cannot know what answer is preferred by the "customer." Such an arrangement would itself be a blinding measure.*
>
> **Koppl and Krane (2016)**

Removing the background information included with the case is one method to reduce the potential of contextual bias, which may affect an analyst with respect to preconceived results. With that removal, there is still another potential source that is present in most laboratories. The verification process, where firearm examiners have their results observed and confirmed by a second examiner, can be subjected to contextual bias. In these instances, there are two methods of verification.

The quickest method would be to have the second examiner observe the comparison immediately after the primary examiner has made what they perceive as an elimination, identification, or inconclusive result. This is the most efficient method due to the nature of forensic firearm identification, which relies on the positioning of the cartridge case or bullet on the comparison microscope and the lighting associated with it. An additional contributor to contextual bias would be for the primary examiner to state something to the effect of, "Do you agree this is an identification?" or "I was able to identify these five samples to the test-fired bullets/cartridge cases." These statements would obviously indicate to the second examiner that they should expect to identify the bullets/cartridge cases to the test-fired samples.

Another method of verification that is effective in removing the potential of contextual bias is an independent examination of the evidence with independent results, which is compared after the second examiner has completed the comparison and documented their results. This process would remove any chance of preconceived conclusions; however, it would essentially double the time required for analysis.

Both methods of verification have benefits and drawbacks. An optimal situation would have a totally independent analysis of the evidence. This would give a truly independent verification of the findings and be a consensus, in a sense. However, most of the forensic analyses are performed in government-funded laboratories. The lack of unlimited funding of government laboratories results in minimum staffing to complete the tasks presented for analysis. A fully independent evaluation of an analysis would significantly increase the use of resources of the laboratory. This, in turn, would reduce the capacity of case output.

The verification of evidence, where the evidence has been previously aligned under the comparison microscope, is a much more efficient method. The time to find corresponding areas of identification, if that is the final determination, has been arranged. This is indeed a time saver, yet it could easily provide the second examiner with a preconceived impression of what to expect. However, this does not necessarily require a transition to an independent review. As discussed further in this chapter, an awareness of this potential bias and correct mindset would minimize, if not eliminate it. This can only be accomplished with the correct mindset.

The total removal of case information can be detrimental to the findings or opinion of the forensic firearm examiner. There are circumstances that can influence the evidence. For example, firearms that have been subjected to water may rust and, in doing so, alter the individual characteristics within the barrel on the breech face, firing pin, extractor, and ejector. If the evidence bullet or cartridge case had been fired through the firearm prior to exposure to water, the individual characteristics may appear different than those that have been fired through a barrel with rust. The change in individual characteristics will depend on the amount of rust on the surface of the firearm in contact with the cartridge component. While this information will not allow an examiner to change their findings from inconclusive to an identification, it will assist them in being able to articulate to the attorneys and jurors what factors could have come into play in the altering of individual characteristics.

Confirmation bias

Confirmation bias is present if the examiner, for example, produces a hypothesis that the bullet was fired from a specific firearm. Then, when evaluating the evidence, the examiner lends more weight to any markings on the bullet agreeing with test-fired bullets from that firearm and selectively ignores significantly differing marks indicating an identification may not be present. According to Charman in his article titled, "The forensic confirmation bias: A problem of integration, not just evidence evaluation," it is stated, "A cognitive coherence approach has at least two stages. First, it emphasizes the interplay not just between a preexisting belief and the subsequent evaluation of evidence, but also between the evaluation of evidence and the emerging conclusion that is being formed (e.g., whether the suspect is guilty or not guilty). Second, it emphasizes the bidirectionality of effects: Not only does the evaluation of a piece of evidence affect the emerging conclusion, but the emerging conclusion feeds back to affect the evaluation of other evidence" (Charman, 2013).

When evaluating firearm-related evidence, frequently both fired bullets and fired cartridge cases are submitted for evaluation. If the examiner were to first examine the fired cartridge cases and determined that they had characteristics of having been fired from the same firearm, then the firearm examiner may have a preconceived conformational bias that the associated bullets in the case are automatically from the same firearm as well. That preconceived notion, if kept unchecked, could easily lead to an incorrect identification.

However, this potential bias can be overcome and eliminated from the decision-making process of the analyst if the proper approach to evidence is taken. Along with the research on causes of confirmation bias, Charman describes countermeasures that reduce and eliminate the occurrence of bias. He states, "And we may be given hints how to eliminate, or at least reduce, this bias. For instance, if coherence effects occur due to the constraints imposed by the emerging conclusion on the evaluation of a piece of evidence, then manipulations that delay the formation of an emerging conclusion should mitigate subsequent tendencies toward coherence. Although some attempts to do just this via an explicit instruction to delay one's conclusion have failed to eliminate coherence effects, there are other avenues to be explored. For instance, the belief perseverance literature has shown that having people think of reasons why a 'fact' might be wrong at the time they receive it tends to reduce people's tendency to stubbornly persist in that belief despite it later being discredited" (Charman, 2013).

Ethics and court testimony
Ethics

During both the examination of evidence and the testimony relating to the evidence, not only forensic firearm examiners, but all analysts performing forensic testing are expected to maintain ethical standards. A strong ethical commitment is essential in the area of forensics, and if not followed, brings about both moral and legal ramifications. Intentional misrepresentation of findings can result in criminal charges.

The expected minimal ethical behavior by a forensic firearm and toolmark examiner is outlined in the Preamble of the Code of Ethics as defined by the Association of Firearm and Toolmark Examiners:

As a member of the Association of Firearm and Toolmark Examiners, I pledge myself to make a full and fair investigation of both the relevant facts and physical evidence under examination, to render an opinion strictly in accordance with the information obtained from my examination of the relevant facts and physical evidence, and only to the extent justified by such information, to render an opinion only within my field of competence, to maintain an attitude of independence, impartiality, and calm objectivity, in order to avow personal or professional involvement in the proceedings, to constantly seek to improve my professional capability by experimentation and study and to improve standards and techniques in the field by making available the benefits of my professional attainments.

Association of Firearm and Tool Mark Examiners (2018)

The line between ethical analysis and testimony, and the attempt to provide the expected result to the agency or person providing the request for analysis is one that must always be in the mind of the examiner. While it is important that they do their best to analyze the evidence, to provide an identification if one is indeed present, the observation, documentation, and discussion of inconsistencies should have equal weight if questioned about in the courtroom.

Court testimony

Forensic firearm examiners are commonly called to testify with respect to their findings on the evidence they analyzed. They are notified of their requirement to appear in court by means of a subpoena. A subpoena is a court document issued by an attorney, requiring the appearance of an individual for providing testimony. Either counsel, prosecution or defense, can issue a subpoena. If the results of the report strengthen the case of either attorney, it is likely the side for which the findings best assist will issue a subpoena.

The end result of the documentation, analysis, and report produced regarding the evidence analyzed is the presentation of the results in a courtroom. There are many steps involved in the trial process. This includes pretrial meetings, qualifying as an expert, voir dire, direct examination, and cross-examination.

Prior to court, analysts, who are considered witnesses, may attend a pretrial conference with the attorneys representing either or both sides of the case. This is a somewhat informal meeting where the witness is not under oath, and the purpose is to discuss any information relating to the evidence and the findings with respect to the analysis. The area of forensic firearm examination is a specialized one and like other disciplines of forensic science, analysts may have years or even decades of training and experience. Because of this, people with minimal exposure to firearms and firearm evidence may ask for elaboration on the theory, process, and results of the analysis. This will assist them in understanding and attributing the proper weight to the findings of the evidence.

An example of this would be a report with finding where a bullet was found to have the same class characteristics as the firearm in question. It is important that it is clearly understood that while the bullet cannot be excluded from that firearm, it could potentially have come from any other firearm produced with those same class characteristics. If the report were to be read quickly and not thoroughly understood, it could be confused with individual characteristics, which would contribute significantly more weight to evidence.

When an analyst appears in court to present their findings, they must first qualify as an expert. The attorney who calls the expert as a witness, is responsible for qualifying the witness as an expert. To qualify as an expert, the attorney will ask the witness to describe their education, training, work history, and past qualifications. If the opposing attorney concedes to the qualifications of the witness, the witness will be accepted as an expert.

If there is concern regarding the competency of the witness, the opposing attorney may choose to voir dire the witness. Voir dire is a legal term, which in this instance is the opportunity for the opposing attorney to question specific details of the witness' qualifications and their ability to accurately assess the evidence. Depending on the witness' qualifications, they may or may not be qualified to offer an opinion on the evidence. The use of voir dire is most commonly utilized on witnesses who have minimal qualifications or are extending a particular knowledge base into another field. In the area of forensic firearm examination, witnesses such as gun shop owners, gunsmiths, and those with firearm handling expertise, such as range officers, are sometimes approached for opinions on forensic topics. While these witnesses may be experts in their respective fields, providing testimony on specific forensic topics is most likely beyond the scope of their training and experience. In these instances, voir dire is essential in preventing potentially misleading testimony.

During the aforementioned voir dire and future testimony, it is critical that the expert witness provides quality, professional testimony. There are many aspects to the delivery of testimony that conveys the information in the most effective method. The first impression of the expert to the jury will be in their appearance as they enter the court. The most commonly worn outfit for men is a suit and tie. Women are expected to wear a business-appropriate attire. In addition, hair and grooming should be kept neat for both sexes.

Once on the stand and after being sworn in, the questioning will begin. While seated, posture is an easily overlooked component of speaking that can be detrimental to the effectiveness of the testimony. Slouching, leaning on the edge of the stand, or swiveling in the chair are all subconscious positions/movements that an inexperienced examiner may display and will detract the jury from the information being given.

In addition to body posture, facial expressions and verbal tone are important considerations for providing testimony. Making eye contact with both the individual posing the question and the jury or judge when responding is essential when testifying. When explaining something in detail, it is good to turn towards the jury and make eye contact with them in order to establish a connection. But, if the answer is a simple yes or no, it is not necessary. The body language of indirect eye contact can imply a sense of uncertainty of the answer provided. If there were any uncertainty in the finding, it should be clearly conveyed, and if the finding is presented by the analyst, they are confident. Eye contact is critical in these instances.

After the forensic firearm examiner has been established as an expert, the next step in the process is to provide testimony regarding the evidence as it was received and its subsequent analysis. Based on challenges raised in the legal system, it is important that the analyst preface their testimony with the fundamental basis on the source of individual and/or class characteristics depending on which are included in the results. If they are not discussed in direct testimony, the addressing of these characteristics should be expected.

Testimony regarding the evidence and its associated findings is the purpose for the expert witness. When discussing the evidence and the results of analysis, it is essential that the analyst remain focused on their contribution to the analytical findings. One danger that analysts should be aware of is the leading by attorneys into areas beyond their expertise. If the analyst has specialized training exclusively in forensic firearm examination and only that field, any questions regarding topics such as fingerprint analysis or fingerprint processing should be avoided or answered with a simple, "that is beyond my area of expertise." Any attempt to answer such questions will lead to further questions which will eventually lead to the analyst being dismissed and all associated testimony disqualified.

Another pitfall that can be encountered during testimony is the over embellishment of analysis. The purpose of the expert witness is to provide facts to the court with respect to their findings. Testifying to such events as a bullet having been fired from one particular firearm "to the exclusion of all other firearms" is an example of this. This could be perceived as the examiner indicating that they have physically compared the evidence to literally every other firearm ever produced. Obviously, this is not the case. However, based on the source of individual characteristics as discussed in Chapter 5, Firearm manufacturing techniques, the comparison is within the realm of a practical exclusion.

In addition to the overextension of certainty in observed results, another caution to the expert is in the testimony in which they have not done testing or have firsthand knowledge with respect to the expected results. An example of this is a report issued by an "expert" observed by the author regarding the ejection of a cartridge case from a Glock semiautomatic pistol without a magazine. The claims of the expert were that the cartridge case from a Glock without a magazine would extract and eject in the same manner as a Glock with a magazine. When in actual testing, a Glock fired without a magazine will primarily eject the cartridge case through the magazine well, instead of through the ejection port as demonstrated in actual testing and further documented in an article by Kerkhoff et al. (2017). Clearly, issuing a report on what one thinks would happen without performing scientific testing would provide a disservice to the criminal justice system.

After the analyst has presented the direct examination, the opposing side in the case will have the opportunity to ask questions regarding the evidence, analysis, testing, and results. Other questions may also be raised that may not have been addressed during direct testimony. At this time, the opposing side may either intentionally or unintentionally ask questions that go beyond the scope of the examination performed by the analyst. It is human nature to try to be helpful and assist in explaining the evidence. However, caution must be exercised in overextending opinions beyond the scope of expertise of the analyst.

The analyst, while subpoenaed by one attorney should not present a bias in their testimony, demeanor, or tone when being questioned by the opposing party. Lending more weight by means of longer, more elaborate answers to questions posed by either party could easily be perceived as a biased testimony. The function of the expert witness is to testify as to the evidence examined and the related findings. If the attorney elaborates on specific questions, it is proper to answer them. However, unsolicited elaboration on a particular finding would be an example of bias to a particular party on the part of the witness.

While it may seem apparent that excessive testimony in response to question is an obvious bias, there are also unintentional biases that may occur. If the witness is more comfortable with one attorney, they may unintentionally answer a question with more than the required "yes" or "no." Providing more information to one attorney over the other is both inappropriate and a clear example of lending more weight to the evidence if a simple reply would suffice. However, some questions cannot be answered without elaboration. In those instances, turning to the judge and asking permission to elaborate or prefacing the answer with a response affirming that qualification is necessary to provide an appropriate answer is the proper way to reply.

Depending on the extent of the analyst's involvement with the evidence and the types of training they have, limited testimony should be provided. For example, questions may be asked regarding the collection process or where the evidence was recovered. Unless the witness was directly involved with the collection of the evidence, their testimony should be limited to the information provided to them and prefaced with verbiage such as, "it is described on the packaging as having been collected from the master bedroom of 123 North Main Street." Another route of questioning that can lead an analyst beyond their area of expertise is questions delving into other areas of forensic examination. If a forensic firearm examiner's exclusive area of analysis in a laboratory is firearm examination and comparison, questions regarding fingerprint analysis or DNA analysis should be answered with only the most basic of answers of which the analyst is confident and has training or knowledge to affirm their opinion. Also, limiting the answers to those opinions and ceasing further questions which may lead to more detailed discussion is an important aspect of testifying. While the analyst may have limited education on fingerprinting and conductive surfaces for recovering fingerprints, elaborating on details such as the percentage of time fingerprints are recovered from a firearm would be beyond the scope of a majority of forensic firearm examiners.

CHAPTER 12

Subclass characteristics in firearm examination

Subclass characteristics

The Association of Firearm and Toolmark Examiners Glossary defines subclass characteristics as, "features that may be produced during manufacture that are consistent among items fabricated by the same tool in the same approximate state of wear. These features are not determined prior to manufacture and are more restrictive than class characteristics." (AFTE Glossary, 2013). As discussed in Chapter 5, Firearm manufacturing techniques, and Chapter 6, Barrel manufacturing and rifling, class characteristics are measurable features of a specimen which indicate a restricted group source and result from design factors and are determined prior to manufacture (AFTE Glossary, 2013). In the course of the manufacturing process, factors contributing to subclass characteristics may occur. Those factors include the general profile of the tool being used, damage to the tool, feed and speed rate of the tool, and manufacturing process.

Subclass due to tool manufacture

Tools that mechanically cut a workpiece do so by using an edge that was sharpened by the grinding process. As discussed in Chapter 3, Ammunition, the grinding wheel will leave microscopic irregularities on the surface of the cutting tool. For example, a mandrel, even when new from the factory, will have defects from the grinding process. These irregularities will be transferred onto the workpiece in the form of striated marks. Because every cutting tool is produced with the final step incorporating the grinding method, mandrels are not the only tool to exhibit these surface irregularities. Rifling buttons, broaches, drill bits, and endmills will also demonstrate these features.

Cutting tools are made from a harder grade of steel than the workpiece they are cutting. Some metals can be further hardened by heat treatment. Because of the hardness, use of coolant, and specialized coatings, the wear on the tool is relatively minimal on any type of workpiece. If the tool was to wear appreciably, in just a few interactions with workpieces, the tool would be constantly changed, and production would be inefficient and not profitable. The limited change in the tool surface in its interaction will result in similarity with the manufactured marks on the workpiece (Fig. 12.1).

Figure 12.1 Grinding wheel marks on mandrel groove.

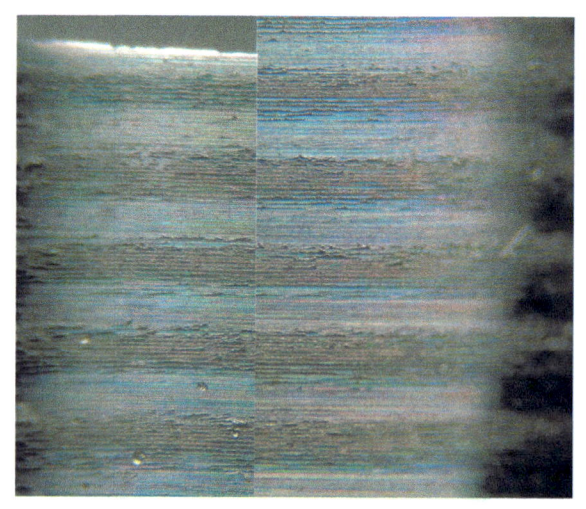

Figure 12.2 Lathe-turned samples turned at the same feed and speed.

Subclass due to tool use

The use of the tool can also cause subclass characteristics. This can arise in many forms. A single-point cutting tool, like a lathe, will demonstrate evenly spaced longitudinal marks that are prevalent in the manufacturing of firing pins produced on a screw machine. The reason for the evenly spaced marks is due to the speed of the rotating spindle holding the workpiece (firing pin) and the feed rate at which the tool is fed into the workpiece. Current manufacturing processes utilize CNC

Figure 12.3 Plunge endmilled marks.

(computer numerically controlled) machines which perform all the functions at the same feed rate and speed for each part produced. The result of the controlled speed and feed is consistent with the spacing of inclusions from the cutting tool (Fig. 12.2).

Another commonly encountered occurrence of tool use leading to subclass characteristics is the use of plunge endmilling in the production process. Plunge endmilling is most commonly done using a four-flute endmill to plunge directly into the surface of the workpiece to produce a flat-based circular recessed area. The rotation of the endmill will produce concentric marks and any irregularities in the surface of the tool will be imparted onto the surface of the workpiece (Fig. 12.3).

The use of an endmill to bring the surface to the final tolerances by running the face of the endmill across the surface is called face milling. The resulting marks from face milling are arched marks with evenly spaced defects. The spacing of the arch defects is dependent on the speed at which the endmill is rotating and the speed at which it is traveling. As the endmill moves faster at a constant rotational speed, the distance between the resulting marks will increase. If the rotational speed is increased as the lateral movement is kept constant, the resulting marks will have a shorter distance between them (Figs. 12.4 and 12.5).

As with any tool, broaches are also susceptible to wear from use. Broaches are not typically used to produce precision tolerance pieces; therefore they may be used for longer periods of production without replacing. Any inclusions in the broach teeth have the potential to reproduce gross marks on subsequent workpieces (Fig. 12.6).

Figure 12.4 Face milled marks.

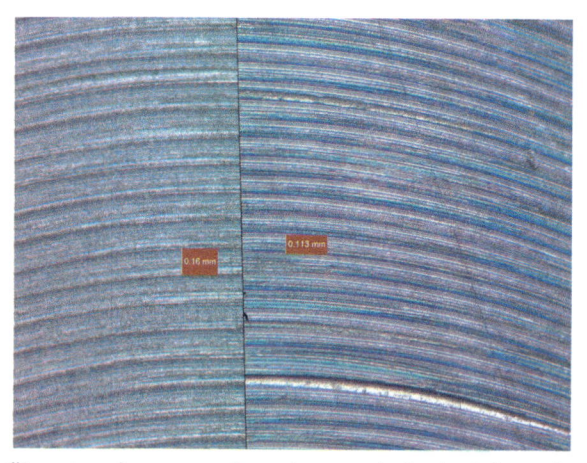

Figure 12.5 Face milling at a slower speed on the sample in the left resulting in more distance between repeating marks than the sample in the right which was face milled at a faster rotational speed.

Examples of tool use causing subclass characteristics
Subclass marks on firing pins

The Smith & Wesson model M&P 22-15 is an example of a firearm that has exhibited significant subclass characteristics on the surface of the firing pin (Lee et al., 2016). The Smith & Wesson M&P 15-22 is a .22 LR version of the AR-15 rifle. As it is a .22 rimfire, the cartridge is struck along the outer side of the rim to ignite the cartridge. In this study, which began in 2014, Lee observed similarities between fired cartridge cases from two different M&P 22-15 firearms. To further his research, Lee obtained 19 Smith & Wesson M&P 22-15 rifles from the Michigan State Police

Figure 12.6 Broach with damage from use.

Figure 12.7 Subclass characteristics demonstrated on some Smith & Wesson M&P 22-15 cartridge cases.

Training Academy. Test fires were made with the rifles, and of the 19 samples, 13 rifles were able to be placed into two groups. Each of those groups exhibited significant subclass carryover, indicating they were made by the same tool (Fig. 12.7).

The question may be posed: Why didn't all the 19 have the same subclass carryover? This is due to the manufacturing process. Firing pins are made in bulk production runs. Based on the observable machine marks on the firing pin faces, it is most likely that the firing pins are placed in a fixture then run across the mill or grinder for profiling. Any time the fixture is moved, the feed or speed rate is changed, or a new tool is used, there will be a different area of the tool contacting the firing pin face. This will result in a different set of characteristics. Because firing pins are made in bulk and undergo further finishing such as heat treatment, tumbling, and surface coating, they are placed in a bin after machining. The result is a mixed bin, full of firing pins containing marks from their run.

To observe these subclass characteristics first hand, the author purchased 70 M&P 22-15 firing pins from Smith & Wesson in 2017. The class characteristics of these firing pin faces were arched machine marks rather than the parallel marks observed by Lee. This demonstrates that Smith & Wesson changed its manufacturing method and, more importantly, emphasizes that just because a firearm may have a certain class characteristics, it may change if the manufacturer finds a faster or less expensive method.

The arched marks on the firing pins obtained by the author appear to have been made by a turning process such as that on a screw machine. It appears that the mill profiling step has been eliminated. However, the arched marks did show some gross signs of subclass characteristics (Fig. 12.8).

The occurrence of subclass in firing pins has also been observed as a result of the metal injection molding (MIM) manufacturing process (Kramer, 2012; Hunsinger, 2013). This manufacturing method is commonly used in the production of firearm parts due to low economic cost and the fact that the part is produced to the correct specifications without additional machining time or costs. The process of MIM is discussed in length in Chapter 5, Firearm manufacturing techniques.

Both Kramer and Hunsinger observed characteristics on firing pin impressions on Smith & Wesson Sigma series firing pins that had significant correspondence. Because the MIM process incorporates dies which are separated after production, there is a

Figure 12.8 Arched marks on two different Smith & Wesson M&P 22-15 firing pins.

break line in the middle of the mold. This break line can be reproduced onto subsequent firing pin molds. This, in turn, results in firing pin impressions with similar appearances. Once again, this could lead to a misidentification if the firearm examiner were to rely solely on the firing pin impression as a source of identification. Therefore, it is essential to consider all characteristics on the cartridge case when performing comparisons of evidence.

Subclass marks on breech faces

There have been several occurrences of subclass carryover on breech faces of firearms produced during the manufacturing process. One example that has been documented on more than one occasion is on the breech face of the Smith & Wesson Sigma (Rivera, 2007; Lightstone, 2010). The Smith & Wesson Sigma series of firearms are manufactured using a broach to cut the area for the breech face. This is one of the most common methods for machining this area of the firearm if the slide has an open design with clearance above and below for the passage of the broach. Both authors observed some degree of correspondence in the breech face area.

Lightstone further studied the correspondence of subclass carryover in the Smith & Wesson Sigma series firearms by touring the factory and subsequently obtaining 10 consecutively manufactured slides. As with firing pins, the slides are manufactured in large batches and are not kept sequential during production and assembly. Therefore, firearms with consecutive serial numbers will most likely not have barrels or other parts manufactured in consecutive order.

The 10 slides examined by Lightstone were first cast to allow observation of breech face marks using a comparison microscope. In comparing the 10 castings to each other, there were significant marks to determine that the same broach in the same state of wear had contacted the breech faces. However, it was also noted that there were individual inconsistencies within the marks from the broach. It was determined that additional finishing processes (abrasive blasting) had affected the breech face. This random distribution of grit from the abrasive process provided for individuality within the subclass broach marks.

The next step in documenting the potential for subclass and its effect on evidence is to test fire the slides to obtain samples of cartridge cases. The casts previously observed are an excellent way to view the machine marks because they are exact reverse replicas of the breech face. However, in practical application, the cartridge case does not record 100% of the breech face. Variables such as pressure generated by the ignition of the gunpowder, hardness of the primer, thickness of the primer, and contact zones of the primer are among the factors that affect the reproducibility of the breech face marks onto the primer and cartridge case.

The intercomparing of cartridge cases by Lightstone revealed that while there were some gross marks that carried over throughout the breech faces of the 10 slides, there were sufficient differences in individual characteristics to associate the fired cartridge case with its respective slide. The fired cartridge cases from the firearms observed by Rivera, in contrast, had a large amount of gross carryover to the point that, without a thorough examination, a false identification could conceivably be concluded. The breech face marks observed by Rivera and Lightstone had significantly different amounts and severity of subclass carryovers. This difference is clearly a result in the amount of wear on the broach at the time of manufacture. Those produced during the run in the article by Rivera had been produced by a broach in a considerable state of wear. Factors such as evaluating areas other than only the breech face would preclude the chance of this type of error.

Breech face marks that are concentric due to a plunge milling manufacturing process may also exhibit subclass characteristics (Lopez and Grew, 2000). If the endmill has a defect in one of the cutting edges, it will be transferred onto the workpiece. Without having access to breech faces produced prior to and after the one being examined, subclass influences should be considered a potential source of the concentricity of the marks. The evaluation of starting and stopping points within the concentric marks should be used to demonstrate marks as individual and a result of the imperfections from the machining process discussed in Chapter 5, Firearm manufacturing techniques.

Another potential source of subclass characteristics can be contributed to the casting process. Casting is done by injecting molten metal into a die in a shape close to the final product. Due to the relatively low melting temperature, one of the most commonly used metals for firearm production is a zinc alloy. Zinc is a softer metal and, if used for items such as firearm slides, reinforcement will be necessary in areas subjected to high pressures. To increase the lifespan of the firearm, manufacturers will use steel inserts and mold the slide around the reinforcement insert.

This is the case of the Jimenez Arms model JA Nine, which was the topic of research performed by Welch (2013). In this situation, it was observed that cartridge cases from different firearms had characteristics that carried over between the two different firearms. In an effort to understand the source of these marks, a tour of the manufacturing facility along with the procurement of 10 consecutively manufactured breech face inserts was obtained. It was expected that the source of the subclass would have been from the inserts, which were produced on a screw machine. The automated and preprogrammed nature of the screw machine would be a likely source for subclass marks. However, through research and observation of the manufacturing process, it was demonstrated that the repeating marks on the breech face were, in fact, from the casting process.

The dies for the casts are machined from large pieces of steel. Therefore, any tooling marks on the dies will be transferred onto items cast in that die. In the case researched by Welch, the marks on the breech faces were a result of marks from the die. As with the other instances of subclass in a particular area, other areas exhibited differences which would preclude an identification.

The use of MIM is typically reserved for parts that do not encounter a significant amount of stress such as firing pins, extractors, ejectors, and safeties. This is because severe pressure in those areas would potentially crack components manufactured by MIM. However, with the Jimenez Arms JA Nine, other manufacturers have elected to use inserts for the breech area. One firearm that has taken this approach and incorporated a metal-injected molded breech face insert is manufactured by Taurus, the model Protector Poly (Thompson, 2015). This firearm has a polymer frame with an MIM insert for added reinforcement. However, in the research performed by Thompson, it was discovered that postmanufacturing finishing processes, which include abrasive bead blasting, impart individual characteristics to significantly differentiate the MIM inserts and any carryover from the manufacturing process which could potentially lend to subclass characteristics misidentification. This is important to note because future productions from Taurus and other manufacturers may use MIM breech face inserts and not include postproduction steps to alter the carryover.

Subclass in barrels

The hammer forging process of barrel manufacturing is a method that has demonstrated subclass marks on the resulting barrel surface (Scala, 2006). As discussed in Chapter 6, Barrel manufacturing and rifling, the hammer forging process involves a mandrel, typically made of carbide, and machining with the profile of the reverse image of the barrel. The mandrel is placed inside the barrel, and the exterior of the barrel is rapidly hammered in all directions by tons of pressure forming the barrel around the mandrel. Any imperfections on the mandrel will be imparted onto the surface of the barrel interior. The mandrel is made from a carbide rod with the grooves cut in by a fine grinding wheel. Any imperfections in the grinding wheel will be imparted onto the surface of the subsequent grooves until the grinding wheel changes through use. The hammer forging process is a cold working process, meaning no material is removed by the tool, the mandrel. Because there is no cutting performed by the mandrel, it is subjected to minimal wear and minimal change from barrel to barrel. Therefore, there is a high likelihood of carryover of these marks from barrel to barrel (Fig. 12.9).

That being said, it is incorrect to say that hammer-forged barrels cannot be identified by individual characteristics back to a particular firearm. One of the initial stages

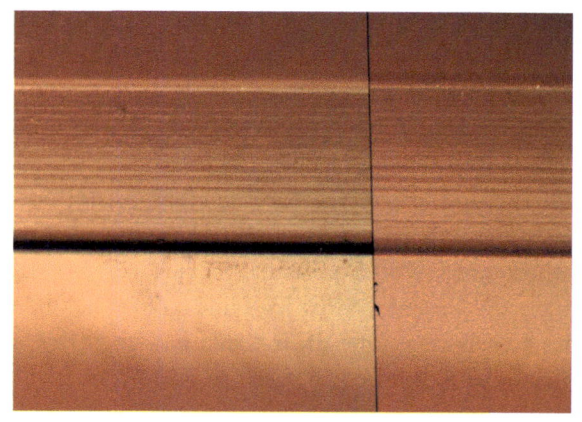

Figure 12.9 Corresponding subclass on two different grooves of a mandrel.

of the manufacturing process of hammer-forged barrels is the drilling of the barrel with a gun drill. This process creates concentric marks inside the gun barrel, which will be individual in nature. The step after drilling is reaming, which is another cutting process with more precise tolerances. Reaming brings the barrel to its final diameter. Again, concentric marks will be imparted during this process.

Broach cut rifling also has the potential to create subclass characteristics in barrels. As with the broaching of breech faces, any damage to the broaching teeth, especially the final teeth contacting the workpiece surface, will result in those gross marks being imparted to the barrel. This was observed in several studies where broached barrels exhibited subclass during examination of both the barrel castings and fired bullets. In research by Miller (2000), the barrel casts produced very prevalent subclass marks; however, when bullets were pushed through the barrels, the subclass failed to reproduce. In contrast, Lomoro (1977) observed a high degree of correspondence when comparing bullets from two different F.I.E Titanic .32 caliber revolvers. In this case the broach left very gross marks as it cut the rifling.

Summary of subclass in rifled barrels

While all methods of rifling that employed the physical impartation lands and grooves have demonstrated the potential to leave subclass marks in the barrel as cited in the previous studies, it is important to note that a majority of the subclass that was observed in the barrel castings failed to reproduce in actual test firing of bullets through those barrels (Miller, 2000). In this chapter, Lomoro describes that the persistent carryover from the broached rifling was only present in the barrel groove (bullet land). The bullet grooves did not exhibit any correspondence. This is important to note because firearm examiners do not typically rely solely on the bullet lands in forming an opinion with respect to agreement. The button rifling that demonstrated agreement was primarily gross marks, which were not supported by other individual characteristics (Hall, 1983).

The one exception to the lack of production of any significance on the fired bullets occurred most prominently in barrels that were hammer-forged and produced by Ruger (Scala, 2006). Although there was a noticeable correlation in subclass carryover, it should be noted that there were sufficient individual characteristics to correctly identify fired bullets to the particular firearm that fired them.

Subclass due to damage and wear

Another situation where subclass will be exhibited is in the case of damage to the cutting tool surface. Along with the hardness of carbide comes a tendency to be brittle. If, throughout the cutting process, the tool fractures due to excessive strain, the result is a chip in the cutting edge. The workpiece will reflect that damage by repeating gross marks. Depending on the amount of damage to the tool, manufacturers may choose to replace the tool or continue to use it. If the final workpiece is within the specifications of the product, the tool will continue to be used.

Every cutting tool is susceptible to damage during the machining process, including broaches, endmills, lathe cutting tools, drills, and saw blades. In the event that a broach is damaged, it may only be one tooth of the broach or multiple teeth. Regardless of the number of teeth damaged, the result will be the same—an area on the workpiece with noticeable deviation from the rest of the surface. If the overall dimensions of the workpiece are within the manufacturer's dimensional specifications, production will continue. All subsequent items produced by the broach in this condition will exhibit similar gross characteristics in the same area of contact. The two most commonly broached areas of a firearm that contact a bullet or cartridge case are barrels and breech faces.

As with the broach, endmills are susceptible to breakage. Endmills are typically made from carbide, which is very hard and brittle. If the endmill chips in an area where the dimensional tolerances are still maintained on the final product, the damage may not be noticeable to the machine operator. However, microscopically, a repeating pattern in the workpiece will be observable. In addition to chipping, any aggressive damage to the endmill from tool interaction with the workpiece, as discussed in Chapter 5, Firearm manufacturing techniques, can cause significant changes to the endmill as to production of gross marks, which would be considered subclass and carryover from workpiece to workpiece. When it contacts the workpiece, the endmill is rotating. At the same time, the workpiece is in either the X, Y, or Z axis, or any combination of those axes. The damaged portion of the endmill will leave an irregular mark during its rotation, the workpiece will move, then the damaged area will again leave an irregular mark at a short distance from the previous mark. Modern milling machines used for production purposes are CNC and will run the workpiece at the same feed rate and the endmill at the same rotational speed for every part produced. The resulting occurrence of irregular marks will produce a pattern on the workpiece that has very consistent distances between markings (Figs. 12.10 and 12.11).

Figure 12.10 Endmill with a chipped edge from use.

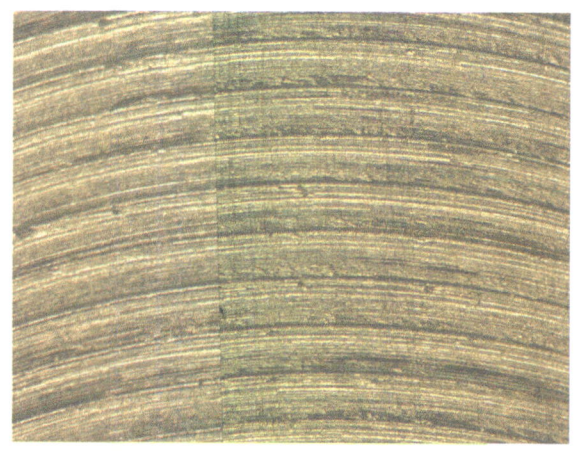

Figure 12.11 Repeating pattern on two different workpieces due to damage to endmill.

In the same fashion as endmills, lathe tools are typically made from carbide. The benefit to carbide is extended tool life, which means longer production runs with minimal downtime for changing out tooling. If a lathe tool is subjected to a large chip on the tip, the parts will most likely fall out of specifications and the tool will be replaced. However, small chips or chips in a secondary contact surface would not significantly change the tolerances of the workpiece but would have a large effect on the surface roughness and result in subclass carryover. Additionally, gross wear from factors discussed in Chapter 5, Firearm manufacturing techniques, will result in subclass characteristics. The lathe functions differently from the milling machine in that the tool remains fixed with respect to the orientation of the cutting surface. It most commonly moves in the X and Y axes to produce the desired profile. During the lathe operation, the workpiece rotates to facilitate cutting by the single point of the tool. Again, like modern milling machines, lathes are CNC and the rotational speed of the workpiece and movement of the cutting tool is electronically controlled and will have consistent spatial arrangement of imperfections from a damaged or severely worn tool.

Subclass due to manufacturing method

There are times when a manufacturer may impart subclass characteristics on a part in the process of performing a step of manufacturing the item. An example of this was observed by the author when evaluating consecutively broach-rifled aftermarket, and Glock barrels for the presence of subclass carryover from the broaching process. As part of the examination, the barrels were cast with Accu-Trans casting material to examine any broach marks that may have persisted throughout the entire length of the barrel. While looking at the casts under magnification, a gross linear mark was observed that carried through both the lands and grooves of the barrel. The presence of the mark on top of both the areas indicated that it was made after the broaching process. Had the mark been made prior to broaching, it would have been obscured by the broach teeth (Fig. 12.12).

The manufacturer was contacted to determine the source of the marks inside the barrel. During a detailed discussion of the manufacturing and finishing process of the barrel, it was learned that the final stage of finishing the outside of the barrel involves placing the barrel on a fixture on a lathe to rotate the outside of the barrel against fine sandpaper to remove any blemishes and machine marks on the outside of the barrel. The fixture on which the barrel is placed is a metal rod that inserts into the barrel for alignment. During the placing of the barrel onto the rod, the rod contacts the barrels in the same orientation and at the same angle. If the barrel is not perfectly straight when the operator places it on the rod, the barrel will be marked by the rod (Figs. 12.13 and 12.14).

Figure 12.12 Toolmark on two different barrels caused by the manufacturing process.

Figure 12.13 Metal mount for further barrel processing as a source for potential subclass.

Figure 12.14 Barrel mounted on rod for exterior finishing.

Ways to avoid subclass misidentification

Subclass observed on a surface can be in the form of fine striated marks from a machining process or gross marks from a molding process. As manufacturing processes evolve, there will always be a potential for subclass characteristics. This has been demonstrated by the prolific incorporation of CNC machines and MIM in the manufacturing industry. It is important to understand that this does not mean that items that exhibit subclass cannot be individualized back to a specific surface. However, caution should be taken, and additional examinations may be necessary.

A method for dealing with suspected subclass characteristics on cartridge cases would be to evaluate multiple areas to form a conclusion for an identification. In addition to breech face marks or firing pin impressions, other areas that contact the firearm should be considered. Marks on the side walls of the cartridge case caused by the swelling of the cartridge case in the chamber, extractor, ejector, and aperture shear should be considered in the identification of evidence with suspected subclass characteristics. Manufacturers change their manufacturing processes as new equipment is purchased or time consuming steps can be eliminated. Because of this potential for manufacturing deviations from previous methods, the assumption of absence of potential subclass due to manufacturer should be avoided, and multiple areas of correspondence should be considered prior to determining agreement of fired components.

As discussed previously, during the manufacturing of firearms, the parts are produced in batches and placed into bins. The assembly of the parts from the production is random. The likelihood of all of the parts having been metal-injected molded for that firearm from the same mold is so infinitesimal as it is a practical impossibility. Therefore, using multiple areas for examination can ensure against a misidentification based on subclass characteristics.

When evaluating parallel breech face marks on cartridge cases for subclass characteristics, any gross imperfections from the broaching process that will carry on from slide to slide will also continue across the entire length of the breech face. Therefore, if a mark continues across the entire length of the marks on the breech face of the cartridge case, it is a good indication that subclass may be a contributor to the marks. If continual parallel marks are present, then special attention should be focused on the random machining marks caused by the tool interaction as discussed in Chapter 5, Firearm manufacturing techniques, which include built-up edge, plowing, sideflow, and chatter. These marks should be considered as part of the comparison process for the same reasons as provided above with respect to the potential for subclass as a result of manufacturing change.

Breech face marks with concentric marks can easily be evaluated for subclass characteristics by casting the breech face with Accu-Trans or similar casting material and examining the impressions of the castings. Using a comparison microscope, the breech face castings can be rotated 180 degrees in orientation. Concentric marks that are in agreement in the rotated position may be characteristics that are subclass. As with other breech face marks, marks produced by the manufacturing process should be considered for the individuality of the toolmarks.

Subclass can also be observed in the comparison of fired bullets. The most common subclass on fired bullets will be in the form of gross marks caused by a damaged or worn tool. When examining broached barrels, a chip or defect in the final teeth in contact with the rifling can deposit these types of marks. A rifling button with damage will have the same effect with respect to a coarse mark traversing throughout the barrel. Rifling produced by hammer forging using a mandrel is subjected to less wear in the traditional fashion than tools which have cutting edges contacting steel surfaces. Therefore, any change is less pronounced. Change that does occur is due to the forces imparted by the hammering action of the forging process. The marks that are present on mandrels are caused by the manufacturing process. Because mandrels are made from carbide, the most effective way to machine them is with a grinding wheel. The random interaction of the grit will leave longitudinal marks along the surface of the mandrel. These marks will, in turn, be impressed into the surface of the barrel interior. As discussed previously, the carbide will not change appreciably through limited runs of barrel production. Therefore there is a strong possibility of these marks continuing on multiple barrels.

In the event that there are gross marks present, they can be valuable as a method for indexing the bullets for further comparison. Once bullets have been aligned under the comparison microscope, the evaluation of individual marks from the hammer forging process can be explored. These marks will be more subtle, as they are from previous and subsequent manufacturing processes. Prior to being forged, the barrels have their initial bore created by drilling and reaming. These processes may leave marks which are faint yet contributors to individual characteristics. Barrels may also be lapped, which is a process to further smooth the inside of the barrel. This is done with a very fine abrasive. Again, while faint, there may be marks left by this process. In the continuum of manufacturing methods, barrels produced by hammer forging are the most challenging in the field of forensic firearm examination.

CHAPTER 13

Pitfalls and challenging comparisons

Preexisting marks

As discussed previously, the manufacturing of ammunition may leave tool marks on the cartridge. At the time of a forensic firearm examination, these marks would be considered preexisting and may be difficult to differentiate from tool marks left from the firearm. This situation has been reported in many instances from a variety of manufacturers (Yborra and McClary, 2004; Flater, 2002; Tam, 2001; Dyvesveen, 2000; Patty, 2000; Kennington, 1999; Klees, 1997; Robinson, 1996; Maruoka and Ball, 1995; Maruoka, 1994; Reitz, 1975; Warner, 1971).

The presence of preexisting marks on cartridge case head is a result of the manufacturing processes of cartridges contacting machinery during production. The most commonly encountered types of marks left on a cartridge case observed by forensic firearm examiners are striated marks imparted on the cartridge case head or primer as it slides through the loading machinery (Fig. 13.1).

Not only can the production process of loading the cartridge leave marks, but the production of the primer is also a source of potential preexisting marks. Primers are made from thin sheets of brass with the primer cup formed by the stamping process. During production, the sheets of brass may encounter irregularities or rough surfaces of the material-handling equipment resulting in striated marks (Fig. 13.2). These marks will, in turn, become incorporated in the cartridge. This can be problematic for multiple reasons. First, they may hinder and mask the deposition of characteristics from contact with the firearm breech face. In addition, if the firearm has a breech face lacking in individual characteristics, such as those with a cast slide and heavy chrome plating, the chrome plating produces a smooth finish minimizing the manufacturing characteristics. When cartridge cases with preexisting marks are fired from firearms with few manufacturing characteristics, the preexisting marks on the cartridge cases could be confused for characteristics left by contact with the firearm. Differentiating marks on primers from the manufacturing process from marks imparted by the breech face of a firearm can be achieved by evaluating the curved surfaces of the primer. If the primer was prestriated, the striations will carry through into the impact of the firing pin and where the primer tapers downward into the cartridge case (Fig. 13.3).

Figure 13.1 Different cartridge cases exhibiting marks prior to firing from the manufacturing process.

Figure 13.2 Primer with striated marks produced during the manufacturing of the primer.

Figure 13.3 Prestriated primer with striations continuing into firing pin mark.

There are instances where manufacturers intentionally mark their primers either for brand identification, designating a specific characteristic, or as a means for documenting a certain lot of production. These markings are most easily accomplished by impressing numbers, letters, or symbols into the primer. Forensically, the information on these primers can assist a firearm examiner in determining if the ammunition is factory loaded, has been reloaded, or contains the features designated by the manufacturer.

An example of primer markings for lot identification is demonstrated by Cascade Cartridges, Incorporated. In September of 2001, they changed their primer-production process and removed the thin foil between the primer mix and anvil. Because of this change, some problems were encountered, and the design was abandoned in March of 2002. To differentiate the new production returning to the use of the foil, subsequent primers were identified with the addition of an "A" on the primer (Skoglund, 2008). The use of the "A" designation on the primer continued until 2005 (Braswell, 2008). At the time of this writing, current primers do not contain additional characters for lot designation (Fig. 13.4).

One manufacturer that uses primer markings for the purpose of authenticity is Companhia Brasileira de Cartuchos (CBC) which works in conjunction with Magtech. CBC supplies Magtech with ammunition and as an assurance that the ammunition is indeed produced by CBC, a "V" impression is stamped on the primer (Eastham, 2010).

Some manufacturers use primers with specific properties and choose to designate them by stamping identifiers on them. An example of this is the Leadless .38 Special by Remington. This cartridge utilizes an encapsulated bullet in conjunction with a primer that does not use lead as part of the priming compound. To easily identify these primers, they are stamped with the letters "LF" that signify "lead free" (Fig. 13.5).

Figure 13.4 Primers marked by the manufacturer with the letter "A."

Figure 13.5 Primer marked by the manufacturer with the letters "LF." *LF*, Lead free.

Figure 13.6 Primer marked by the manufacturer with the letters "HF." *HF*, Heavy metal free.

Another type of primer offered by Remington that have a distinguishing mark are those with an "HF" impressed on it. It is speculated that the "HF" designates heavy metal free, whereas previous primers were only LF. Due to health concerns associated with various heavy metals other than lead, such as antimony, which can contribute to illness with long-term exposure, this primer was developed. This primer can be distinguished by the letters "HF" stamped on top of each other on the primer (Fig. 13.6).

Other stamped indicators have been placed on primers as a means for identification by manufacturers; however, they are not commonly encountered in forensic laboratories. An example of this is markings placed on primers and cartridges loaded by Norma brand cartridges (Fig. 13.7). Norma is known for their hunting and target rifle caliber ammunition which is not typically used in crime. However, at times, firearms are used as a weapon of opportunity and, therefore, knowledge of these types of primers is warranted.

Figure 13.7 Primer marked by the manufacturer with the letters "NP." *NP*, Norma Precision.

Reloading and associated marks

Reloading is the practice of using a fired cartridge case to produce a complete cartridge capable of being fired again. This is done by both hobbyists and manufacturing companies using fired brass cartridge cases as the starting point. The fired cartridge case is cleaned in a vibrating tumbler with a polishing media, typically ground up corn cob or walnut shells. A polishing compound is added to improve the cleaning and removal of tarnish and discoloration due to firing.

A reloading press is machine-designed for the cartridge reloading process. The press uses caliber-specific dies that are specifically made to address the various stages of reloading. Some dies complete two operations in one step to increase productivity. For example, the first die used in reloading will deprime the cartridge case and resize it to factory specifications. Depriming is the removal of the fired primer to allow for a new, unused primer to be inserted. The depriming step is essentially a metal rod that passes through the flash hole of the cartridge and pushes out the old primer. Due to the design of the priming system, boxer-style primers that use one centrally located hole for passage of the ignition spark are the most commonly reloaded type of cartridge.

After the primer has been removed and the cartridge case resized, the downward stroke of the reloading press will seat a new primer. The next stage of the process is to deposit a predetermined amount of gunpowder and slightly open the mouth of the cartridge case to accept the new bullet. The final stage of reloading a complete cartridge is placing a new bullet in the cartridge and seating it. The die will press the bullet into the cartridge and the final contact of the die will press the cartridge case tightly against the bullet ensuring that it is held firmly in position. Some reloaders or manufacturers will perform an additional step and crimp the cartridge. This is a step that places additional pressure on the cartridge case to hold the bullet in place. The entire time the cartridge is in the reloading press, it is being contained by the shell holder that grips the cartridge case by the rim.

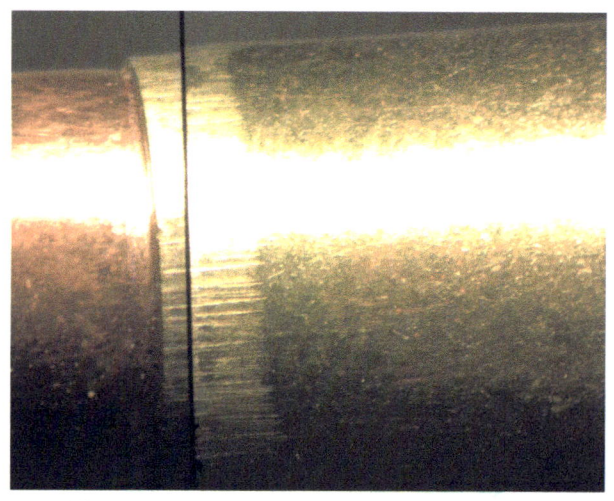

Figure 13.8 Marks caused by the reloading die near the mouth of the cartridge.

The reloading process encompasses many steps that are important to understand for a multitude of reasons. Reloaded ammunition is commercially available as a cost-effective alternative to factory new ammunition; therefore it is popular and not uncommon to encounter in casework. Also, reloaded ammunition will contain marks from both the previous firearm and the reloading process, which could be confused as marks from the firearm that fired it. The dies that contact the cartridge case can leave longitudinal marks along the sidewall that could appear similar to chamber marks produced during the discharge of a cartridge (McCombs and Hamman, 2016) (Fig. 13.8).

Marks on the cartridge case from previous interaction with a firearm will also likely be present. Common marks such as extractor, ejector, some breech face, and associated marks from the extraction and ejection process may all be present. The primer on reloaded cartridges is new; therefore it will not have preexisting marks from prior contact. When evaluating marks for comparison purposes, the primer should be an area of focus and be considered when establishing an association of the cartridge cases. In addition, because of the random orientation of the cartridges when chambered in the firearm, the spatial alignment of firing pin drag, aperture shear, extractor, and ejector marks should be taken into consideration. For example, if an extractor mark is in the same location as an ejector mark, it would be an indication that one of them was from a previous event. It is worth noting that manually cycling cartridges though a firearm may result in both ejector and extractor marks being deposited on a cartridge case. However, the violent interaction of the discharge of a cartridge will generally leave deeper and more aggressive marks than those by hand cycling. Some cycling marks simply cannot be reproduced by hand cycling such as those commonly left by Glock firearms (Bruce, 2014).

Marks from previous interaction

In addition to marks produced by previous firing and subsequent reloading, the cartridge case may have marks imparted on it from simply cycling, and not firing, through a firearm (Clow, 2011b). Regardless of firing or cycling, the cartridge case comes in contact with the breech face of the firearm. During the firing process, due to the ignition of the cartridge, the impact of the cartridge case is much more forceful than simply pulling the slide to the rear by hand. However, the act of hand cycling an unfired cartridge also has the potential to deposit marks from the breech face onto the cartridge. The amount of breech face marks from firing will be significantly more than those caused by hand cycling due to the higher pressures from firing. Caution should be exercised in the use of small areas of breech face impressions for identification purposes. In instances where there are few breech face areas reproducing for comparison, additional areas of the cartridge case should be considered. An example of a cartridge case with breech face marks imparted by hand cycling, then subsequently being fired from a different firearm, is demonstrated in Fig. 13.9A and B. In this instance, the cartridge was cycled through a Hi-Point 9 mm then fired through a Lorcin 9 mm pistol.

The primer of the cartridge may also have firing pin marks from previous interactions. As discussed in Chapter 8, Comparison of cartridge cases, some firearms utilize the firing pin as an ejector. The impact of the firing pin can leave impressions that are not of sufficient depth to ignite the cartridge; however, they may have sufficient characteristics for comparison purposes. These lighter impact marks should be avoided in the use of identifying the cartridge case as having been fired through a specific firearm.

Figure 13.9 (A) Unfired cartridge cycled through a Hi-Point pistol with both breech face marks (in the 10:00 position) and firing pin marks; (B) Same cartridge fired in a Lorcin pistol with breech face marks and firing pin mark carry over from previous interaction.

Differences in ammunition

When a firearm discharges, the firing pin contacts the primer with force significant enough to dent the primer, thus causing the internal components of the primer to ignite. The primer is a cup with an anvil inside. The contact with the primer cup, which has a shock-sensitive explosive, with the anvil results in sparks that travel to the gunpowder in the cartridge case. The ignition of the gunpowder produces an abundance of gas that pushes the bullet out of the gun barrel. In turn the reciprocal energy from that discharge results in pressure of the cartridge case against the breech face of the firearm. This produces an impressed image of the harder breech face of the firearm onto the softer material of the cartridge case.

While the breech face of the firearm contains an entire surface of random imperfections from the machining process, the degree and clarity of the marks from the breech face that are imparted onto the cartridge case can be affected by a variety of contributing factors. Because the breech face is hardened steel, the amount of change due to impact during contact with cartridge cases is not significant enough to affect change to the breech face.

In contrast to the breech face the cartridge cases, and more specifically, primers, are commonly made of thin brass. These primers are inherently soft and susceptible to accepting marks from the impact of the discharge of a cartridge. While primers may generally be made from the brass, there can be significant differences between primers, even from the same manufacturer. These attributes include thickness, hardness, coating, and depth of seating. An additional factor that can contribute to the marks produced during the firing process, is the pressure at which the cartridge impacts the firearm.

Primers begin as sheets of brass that are stamped into their final shape, as discussed in Chapter 3, Ammunition. While the brass is fairly uniform in thickness, there can be deviations within a few thousandths of an inch. Thicker brass will be less susceptible to receiving impressed marks due to the resistance of movement associated with a thicker, thus stronger, surface.

Brass is an alloy composed of copper and zinc. The suppliers of brass to manufacturers are required to produce brass with specified compositions, but there can be minor variations. These variations will change the resulting hardness characteristics of that batch of brass. The change to the hardness of the brass will result in a resistance to accepting breech face marks relative to softer brass even of the same thickness.

Primers may be plated with nickel for both corrosion resistance and appearance. The nickel is electrically plated, and the thickness of the plating is determined by the manufacturer. As with the thickness of the brass, there can be deviations in the thickness of the nickel plating. As with the increased thickness of the brass, a primer with thicker nickel plating will be more resistant to impressed marks.

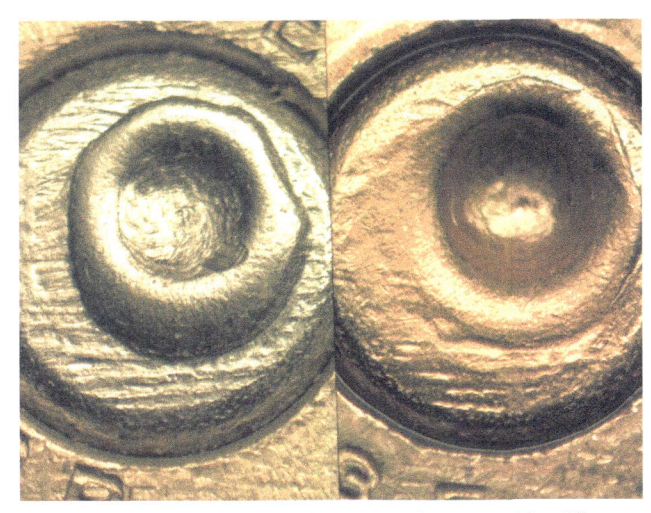

Figure 13.10 Breech face marks made by the same firearm with different reproductions of characteristics.

The body of the primer is called the primer cup. The primer cup height, in conjunction with the primer seating tool, controls the depth at which the primer will be set in the cartridge case. The depth of the primer in the cartridge can affect the amount of interface of the firearm seating.

The hardness, thickness, and additional coatings of the primer along with the depth of the seating of the primer can all have an effect on the interaction of the breech face and firing pin in the course of discharging the cartridge. The effect of primer hardness on receiving marks from the breech face was further demonstrated by Justine Davis in an article which tested the hardness of various primers. It was found that when testing six different cartridge manufacturers with both brass and nickel-plated primers, the hardness of the various primers ranged from 84 to 124 on the Vickers hardness scale (Davis, 2010). The large variation of hardness demonstrates just one of the obstacles in the comparison of cartridge cases from different manufacturers (Fig. 13.10).

Bullet seating marks

Bullets are examined under magnification using the comparison microscope to attempt to associate or disassociate test-fired bullets as being the source of the bullets recovered at autopsy or the crime scene. In the absence of a suspect firearm, it would be of interest to the investigating party to know if only one firearm or multiple firearms were used.

Figure 13.11 Bullet seating marks caused by interaction with the cartridge case mouth.

One source of marks that can interfere with rifling or be improperly interpreted as rifling are marks produced by the passage of the bullet out of the cartridge case. When ammunition is loaded, the cartridge case is pressed tightly against the bullet to securely hold it in place. The mouth of the cartridge case contains burrs and other imperfections from the manufacturing process which are in turn pressed into the side of the bullet. As the bullet exits the cartridge case during the course of firing, these burrs will produce marks on the bullet that are not attributed to the firearm. However, since these marks are not a result of the rifling, they will not display the marks traditionally imparted by rifling. Rifling marks are angled to the left or right depending on the direction of twist of the rifling. Marks from the exit of the bullet from the cartridge case have not yet encountered rifling within the barrel and, therefore, exit in a straight movement. When this happens, the marks on the bullet will be perpendicular to the base of the bullet rather than angled (Fig. 13.11).

The perpendicular marks on bullets, if observed, should be noted as bullet seating marks. Perpendicular marks, when in the presence of angled rifling marks, should not be used for comparison or identification purposes when comparing the bullets to each other.

However, depending on the condition of the bullets and amount of rifling contact, it may be possible to associate the fired bullet with a specific cartridge case. In an article by Clow, bullet seating marks were used to identify the bullet to a cartridge case. The research performed in this article was done with a Glock firearm that has a barrel with polygonal rifling. Because heavy rifling marks can obscure bullet seating marks, this type of examination lends itself to firearms with polygonal rifling or those with poor rifling engagement. To obtain test marks from the rim of the fired cartridge case, Clow used a new, unloaded bullet and drove it into the empty cartridge case. As the bullet was placed into the empty cartridge case, marks from the mouth of the cartridge case were imparted onto the bullet. The marks on the test bullet were then compared to the marks on the fired bullet. The agreement of the individual marks from the cartridge case mouth between the evidence bullet and the test bullet was sufficient to determine that the bullet had been in contact with that cartridge case prior to having been fired (Clow, 2008b).

Incorrect ammunition usage

Firearms are required to have the ammunition designed for them indicated somewhere on the firearm. This does not preclude users, especially casual or inexperienced people, from using a cartridge that will fit in a firearm although it is not the intended caliber. One of the most frequently incorrect firearm/ammunition combinations encountered in crime laboratories is the use of .380 Auto ammunition in a firearm chambered for the 9 mm Makarov firearm (Anderson, 1984). The .380 Auto cartridge contains a bullet that is .356 in. in diameter and is slightly smaller than the diameter of the 9 mm Makarov which is .365 in. The overall length of the .380 Auto is also slightly shorter at .910 in., whereas the 9 mm Makarov has an overall length of .974 in. (Sporting Arms and Ammunition Manufacturers' Institute, Inc., 2018).

The introduction of a cartridge that is smaller in diameter than the intended chamber will result in a fired cartridge case that takes on the characteristics of the firearm chamber. In the instance of .380 Auto cartridges in a 9 mm Makarov, the .380 Auto cartridge case will swell to form the larger interior diameter of the 9 mm Makarov chamber. This will be easily observable in the belled shape of the .380 Auto cartridge case (Fig. 13.12). In addition to having an effect on the cartridge case, the fired bullet will have noticeable characteristics of having been fired from an incorrectly sized barrel. The undersized bullet of the .380 Auto will not consistently engage the rifling of an oversized barrel. The resulting rifling on the bullet produced from firing will have inconsistent and sporadic rifling present (Fig. 13.13). It is important to recognize these signs of incorrect coupling by observing the characteristics of the cartridge that deviate from what is expected from those fired from the correct caliber/cartridge combination. Failing to recognize this could lead an examiner to provide an incorrect lead to those investigating the crime.

Figure 13.12 .380 Auto cartridge fired in a .380 Auto on the left, .380 Auto fired from a 9 mm Makarov on the right.

Figure 13.13 .380 Auto bullet fired from a 9 mm Makarov.

Aperture shear presence and absence

Aperture shear, as discussed in Chapter 8, Comparison of cartridge cases, is a very valuable resource in performing cartridge case comparisons. This is because the aperture shear is typically very pronounced when present and useful for aiding in identification and to index the cartridge cases in corresponding agreement for further comparison. However, aperture shear is a result of many factors. The lack of any of the contributing influences can result in the absence of reproduction of aperture shear. These concepts were previously discussed but bear emphasis as an example of the variation in which cartridge cases mark when fired from the same firearm (Fig. 13.14).

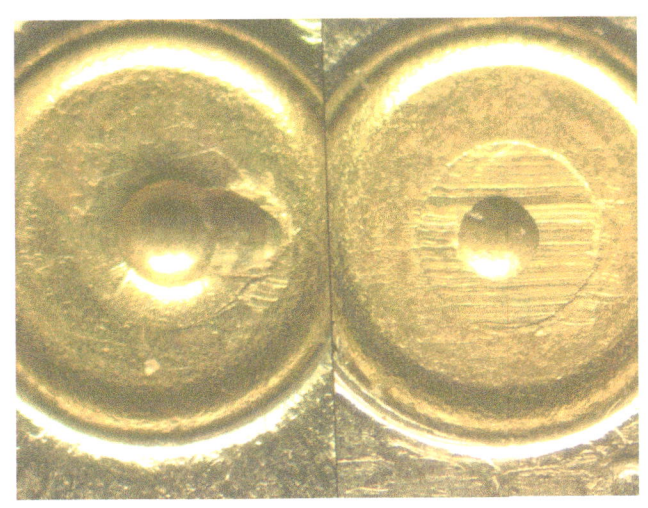

Figure 13.14 Same firearm, no aperture shear on left, aperture shear on right.

Ported barrels

Some firearms include porting in the barrels. Porting is the addition of holes or slots in the top and toward the end of the muzzle of the firearm. The purpose of porting a barrel is to redirect the gases released by the discharge of a cartridge. The release of gases upward assists in counteracting the rise of the barrel by pushing the barrel downward. In the course of machining these ports, burrs from the machining process may be left on the interior of the barrel. These burrs will abrade the bullet upon passage through the barrel and could be confused for lands or grooves.

Porting can be distinguished from land or groove markings by examining the bullet in its entirety. The pattern of land and groove orientation will be consistent and evenly spaced; the addition of an area of abrasion will disrupt the pattern and may be an indication that the bullet was fired from a ported barrel. In addition, there are different types of porting schemes used by manufacturers. The most common are a series of ports in a line at the top of the barrel and two rows of ports placed slightly offset from the centerline of the top of the barrel. In the second example the spacing of two abraded areas of the bullet is a very strong indication of a ported barrel as having been used to produce the recovered bullet (Fig. 13.15). This can be a valuable piece of information when predicting the type of firearm for investigative purposes as the number of firearms with ported barrels is a very small percentage.

Replacement barrels

The use of aftermarket components is not uncommon in the firearm industry. One commonly substituted firearm part, when upgrading a firearm, is a replacement barrel.

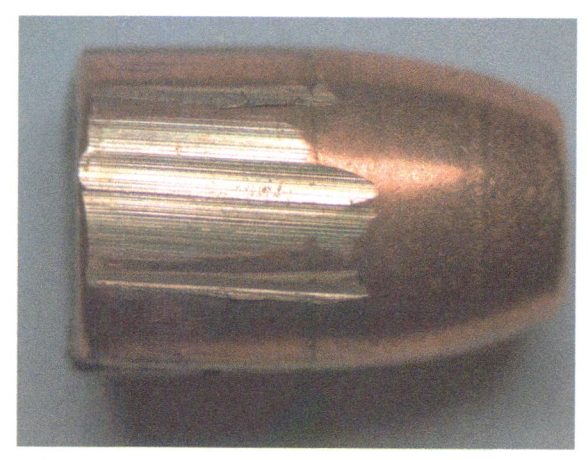

Figure 13.15 Deep mark produced by a ported barrel.

There are companies that specialize in only producing aftermarket barrels for firearms marketing them as an improvement in accuracy. These barrels will most likely have different rifling characteristics than the factory barrel. This could cause confusion when encountering evidence from a scene that includes both bullets and cartridge cases. If the cartridge cases were all to be identified to each other and have characteristics of a Glock type firing pin and aperture, it may be assumed by the examiner that the bullets would be expected to exhibit polygonal rifling. However, if the bullets associated with the incident were to have cut rifling, an examiner may instinctively automatically assume that there were two firearms present at the time of the shooting—a Glock that produced the cartridge cases, and a second firearm that produced the bullets. An awareness of other possibilities is important in having a broad understanding of the significance of evidence.

Convex and blown out primer

The interaction of the cartridge with the breech face and aperture hole can influence the resulting shape of the primer. A larger aperture hole, in conjunction with pressure and a thinner primer cup, can result in the firing pin and surrounding area protruding outward rather than inward. The outward movement of the metal distorts the characteristics originally present on the primer (Fig. 13.16).

Another factor that can affect the comparison of cartridge cases is pierced primers. When a primer is pierced, there is a void in the primer where the firing pin hit. Obviously, with that void, there are no marks from the firing pin impression for comparison purposes. The most frequent cause of this is the firing of a cartridge that is shorter than the chamber from which it was fired. The movement

Figure 13.16 Convex primer.

Figure 13.17 Pierced primer.

of the cartridge case within the chamber allows it to move into the firing pin further than it normally would if an appropriately sized cartridge case were used (Fig. 13.17).

Cartridges made from different calibers

Some cartridges are designed to be utilized in existing firearms, but modified to perform a specific function. An example of this is the .300 AAC (Advanced Armament Corporation) Blackout. This cartridge is based on the basic design of the 5.56 × 45 mm NATO cartridge. However, the cartridge was modified to utilize a larger diameter and heavier bullet. The overall length of the cartridge remained consistent with the parent cartridge, which allows for use in firearms and magazines already chambered for that ammunition. The difference in bullet diameter and cartridge case profile requires only the changing of a barrel to facilitate use. The use of a larger, heavier bullet in this application allows manufacturers to load the cartridges to subsonic velocities, while providing a projectile with sufficient energy to perform on targets. The advantage to subsonic flight of a bullet is reduced sound when fired in conjunction with a sound suppressor.

The use of a parent cartridge to develop a new cartridge is not a new concept as discussed in Chapter 3, Ammunition. However, most wildcat cartridges are used by avid target shooters and hunters and used in firearms that have dedicated barrels not easily changed. In contrast, the .300 AAC Blackout has gained a large following due to its versatility for target shooting, sport shooting, and hunting. The popularity of the cartridge has caused a demand for low-priced ammunition options. To accommodate this, manufacturers of reloaded ammunition and home reloaders have incorporated the use of fired 5.56 × 45 mm cartridge cases as a source for the .300 AAC Blackout. The observation of a converted 5.56 × 45 mm cartridge case would readily demonstrate the cartridge case is not typical of a standard of what one would expect due to the noticeably larger case mouth. In addition, the cartridge specifications on the headstamp would differ from actual caliber of the cartridge (Fig. 13.18).

Some cartridges are intended to be used with firearms manufactured to specifications, which are different than those designated for the firearm. The two most prevalent examples of that are the use of .38 Special ammunition in a .357 Magnum and firing a .44 Special in a .44 Magnum. The .38 Special has a bullet diameter of .357 in.; however, the length of the .357 Magnum is longer than the .38 Special. The additional length allows for increased gunpowder which, in turn, increases the pressure resulting in higher velocities. Firearms designed to chamber the .357 Magnum cartridge are manufactured with higher strength steel or thicker components to contain the pressure. The additional length of the .357 Magnum

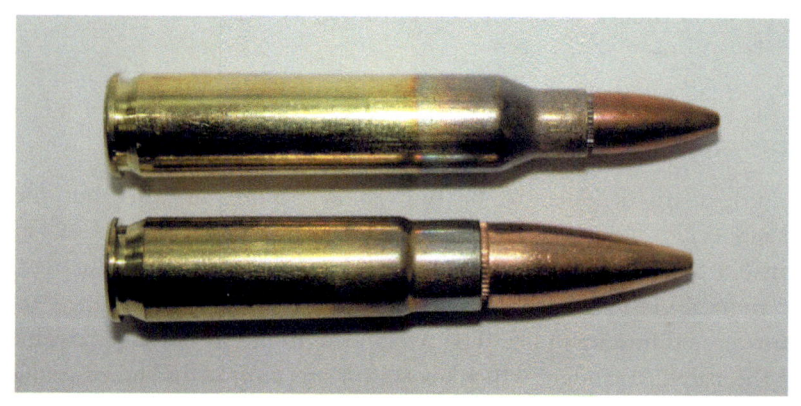

Figure 13.18 5.56 × 45 mm cartridge on top, .300 AAC Blackout on bottom. *AAC*, Advanced Armament Corporation.

cartridge precludes the use of this cartridge in firearms chambered for the .38 Special. This is also a safety measure to prevent the use of .357 Magnum cartridges in .38 Special firearms that would not safely contain the higher pressures. The use of .38 Specials in .357 Magnum revolvers is not an uncommon occurrence. Many target and sport shooters will use the .38 Special cartridges due to their lower price of .38 Special ammunition.

Another commonly interchanged cartridge is the use of .44 Special cartridges in firearms chambered for the .44 Magnum firearms. As with .38 Special and .357 Magnums, the .44 Special is a cartridge loaded with lower pressure and is slightly shorter than the .44 Magnum. Again, firearms designed to facilitate the .44 Magnum are manufactured to safely withstand the pressure created by the ignition of this cartridge. As with the .357 Magnum, the .44 Magnum is longer and cannot be chambered in firearms designed to chamber the .44 Special.

Manufacturers may also design a multicaliber firearm intended to fire a variety of cartridges. One fairly popular example of this is "The Judge" made by Taurus International (Fig. 13.19). This revolver is chambered for both .45 Colt and the .410 gauge shotshell. This is possible because the chamber dimensions with respect to the diameter of the .45 Colt and .410 gauge shotshell are similar enough to be interchangeable. Also, the firearm is designed to withstand the relative pressures. The major difference between the two cartridges is the length. This obstacle is addressed by chambering the cylinder of the revolver to a suitable length to accommodate the longer of the two cartridges, which is the .410 gauge shotshell. Therefore, the shorter .45 Colt will easily fit. The purpose of this type of firearm is to give users options with respect to ammunition depending on the situation they may encounter. For example,

Figure 13.19 Taurus Judge.

Figure 13.20 Revolver "moon clip".

if the user was planning to take "The Judge" as a defensive firearm while hiking in the desert, a .410 gauge shotshell with shot would be ideal to protect against snakes, whereas, if used for home defense, a .410 shotshell with buckshot or .45 Colt would be a better option.

Smith & Wesson followed in the development of a multicaliber firearm by introducing the Governor model. This firearm is designed to fire not only the .45 Colt and .410 gauge shotshell, but also the .45 ACP (Auto Colt Pistol). The .45 ACP cartridge does not have a rim to engage the cylinder of the revolver. Therefore when using .45 ACP ammunition, they must be placed in "moon clips." Moon clips are specially designed metal clips that hold cartridges in place to prevent them from sinking too far into the cylinder (Fig. 13.20).

It should be noted that both firearms have rifled barrels. The rifling in the barrel is imparted onto the bullet as with traditional firearms. However, when shooting .410 gauge shotshells, the shot does not directly contact the barrel, rather the wad that encapsulates the shot will contact the rifling. Depending on the amount of engagement between the wad and rifling, identification with the firearm is possible.

Subcaliber devices

Subcaliber devices are accessories used in firearms to allow for multiple calibers to be fired from one firearm (Thompson, 1988). This is accomplished by using a piece of steel that is machined into the profile of the cartridge designed for the firearm. The interior of the insert is machined to accommodate the smaller caliber cartridge (Fig. 13.21A and B).

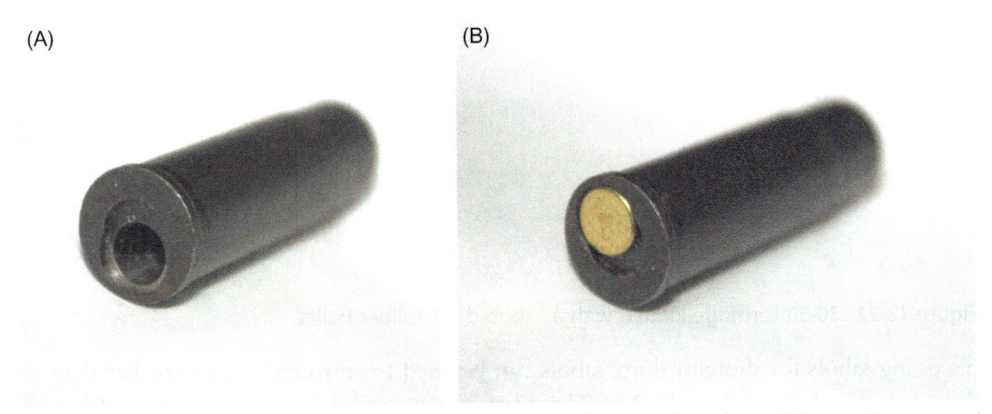

Figure 13.21 (A) Unloaded subcaliber device; (B) subcaliber device with .22 Long Rifle cartridge inserted.

The most common subcaliber devices are used in shotguns and rifles. The primary purpose is for hunting and target shooting. When used for hunting, there are instances where a hunter has wounded an animal, but it has not died. It may be necessary to dispatch the animal in a humane fashion. A smaller, well-placed caliber selection accomplishes this. With respect to target shooting, subcaliber devices allow for target shooters to practice with less expensive ammunition options than the caliber for which the firearm was originally designed.

Along with the chamber for the alternate cartridge size, subcaliber devices incorporate a short section of a rifled barrel. Due to the inherently small size of the subcaliber device, relative to a traditional firearm barrel, the bullets that pass through the device will have the same characteristics as those through traditional barrels. Some subcaliber devices utilize the rifling of the original rifle, by combining a subcaliber cartridge of the same caliber as the host rifle. An example of this would be a .22 Long Rifle (LR) conversion for the 5.56×45 mm firearm. The 5.56 mm conversion to imperial is .223 in. Therefore, the similarity of the caliber is close enough to allow the .22 LR to engage the rifling of the 5.56 mm (.223) barrel.

Forensically, subcaliber devices present a challenge in that the ones that have incorporated rifling will have different rifling characteristics than the firearm in which they were fired. This would potentially lead to an incorrect firearm prediction, if not taken into account. Fortunately, fired components commonly encountered in forensic laboratories, are not typically fired from firearms equipped with subcaliber devices. However, it is important to understand the potential for this option as a contributing source.

Sabot cartridges

An alternate approach to incorporating a caliber different than originally designed for the firearm is the use of a saboted bullet. As defined in Chapter 3, Ammunition, when

Figure 13.22 .30-30 cartridge loaded with a saboted .22 caliber bullet.

discussing sabots for shotgun slugs, sabots can be used to surround bullets smaller than the intended chambering (Fig. 13.22). The plastic that surrounds the bullet provides a seal between the bullet and barrel while engaging the rifling of the barrel providing gyroscopic stability as the bullet exits the barrel. As with the shotgun sabot, the plastic sleeve is designed to disengage from the projectile as it exits the barrel. The resulting bullet will be absent of rifling as it did not come in direct contact with the barrel (Hart, 1977).

Manufacturers produce these types of cartridges to offer users a means to dramatically increase the velocity of the bullet being fired. The sabot allows for the loading of a considerably lighter bullet; thus the increased amount of gunpowder used to propel the bullet relative to the traditional smaller cartridge will yield higher velocities. This concept is similar to those of wildcat cartridges discussed in Chapter 3, Ammunition. However, the firearm does not require any permanent change to allow for smaller projectiles to be fired when using saboted cartridges.

Copper plated bullets

Another challenging situation that has arisen as a result of technology and economics is the use of copper plated bullets in the production of ammunition. Traditionally, bullets were manufactured with a copper jacket that was progressively stamped from a thin sheet of copper to form the outer covering. The lead core was then pressed into the copper jacket. This provided a fairly thick copper jacket which engaged the rifling.

The evolution of copper plating technologies and the desire to reduce the amount of copper used to minimize costs has resulted in the production of cartridges with extremely thin copper plating. These projectiles meet the technical definition of "copper plated" for the purpose of reducing barrel fouling, which is the reason for jacketing bullets. However, due to the minimal amount of copper and the aggressive interaction of the barrel rifling with the bullet as it travels down the barrel, the copper plating tends to be stripped from the lead core (Fig. 13.23).

The removal of the copper plating is especially problematic because the area stripped away engages the rifling, thus removing the area containing the individual characteristics from the barrel (Fig. 13.24).

Figure 13.23 Copper-plated bullet top, copper jacketed bullet bottom.

Figure 13.24 Copper plated bullet stripped after having been fired.

Multiple loads in a single cartridge

The concept of using multiple-sized projectiles within a single load is not a new one. In the second edition of the US Ordnance Department printed in 1850, the use of "ball and buck" loads was discussed. The ball and buck loading consisted of a round ball, on top of it the diameter of the bore and additional buckshot placed.

Some manufacturers of shotshells will incorporate multiple types of shot in the shotshells to improve performance for a specified purpose. The most common reason for using multiple pellets or a variety of types of loads is for hunting and self-defense. Due to the volume necessary to accommodate a multitude of loads, the most commonly adapted cartridge for this purpose, is the shotshell. The awareness of these types of cartridges is important in recognizing that the presence of a different shot from one scene may not necessarily mean two firearms were involved.

Federal offers a few varieties of multiload shotshells for hunting. One shotshell that is designed to provide the maximum performance at various distances is sold under the name "3rd Degree." These shotshells comprise three different types of shot. They include a nontoxic pellet, copper-plated lead pellet, and Flitestopper lead pellet. The Flitestopper has a different profile than traditional pellets to improve the spread of the pellets and potential to wound (Fig. 13.25).

An additional shotshell design offered by Federal is branded as the Black Cloud line of shotshells. These shotshells are designed for waterfowl hunting, and as such, utilize nontoxic shot. The dual load of these cartridges includes both steel and tungsten shot pellets. In addition to a different composition, the tungsten pellets have an unconventional shape, incorporating a raised band around the spherical pellet (Fig. 13.26).

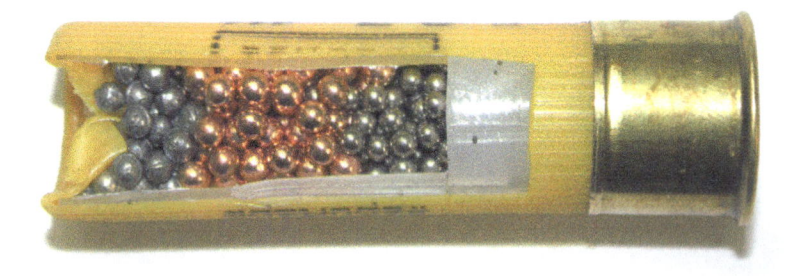

Figure 13.25 Federal Third Degree shotshell.

Figure 13.26 Federal Black Cloud shotshell.

Another company that has been prolific in producing multiload shotshells is Herter's. These shotshells are designed for the self-defense market. Herter's produces a double round 12-gauge shotshell that incorporates two .65-in. diameter lead balls stacked on top of each other. This load effectively provides double the performance of a single shotgun slug. In addition to the double ball shotshell, Herter's produces a "multidefense shotshell." This shotshell utilizes a .65-in. round lead ball coupled with six No. 1 buckshot pellets. In addition to varying the load, Herter's produces a mini shotshell. In contrast to the typical 2.75-in. shotshell, these are 2-in. in length. The diminished length allows for additional shotshells to be loaded in a tubular magazine of a shotgun. In addition to being shorter, they also contain fewer pellets. The Herter's mini shotshell contains six 00 sized pellets. This contrasts with traditional 2.75-in. buckshot loadings that have nine 00 pellets. Due to the unconventional loading of these shotshells, again, caution must be exercised when presented with recovered projectiles before making assumptions (Figs. 13.27 and 13.28).

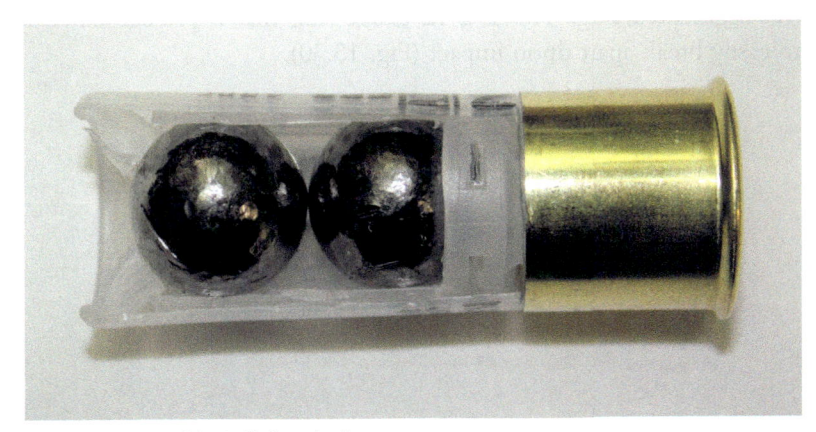

Figure 13.27 Herter's Double Ball shotshell.

Figure 13.28 Herter's Multidefense shotshell.

Winchester has also been active in producing self-defense specific shotshells that contain a variety of projectiles. As with other manufacturers, Winchester uses a combination of larger and smaller projectiles in their shotshells. The primary purpose of shotshells with a multiload is for self-defense. The .410 PDX1 shotshell produced by Winchester combines flattened disks in conjunction with BB pellets. The number of disks and pellets varies based on the length of the shotshell. In the shorter 2.75-in. .410 shotshells, there are three plated disks and 12 BBs, both of which are copper plated. The longer 3-in. .410 gauge shotshell contains four disks and 16 BBs which are also copper plated. Having knowledge of the various loadings and how they differentiate can be very beneficial in providing investigators with leads for their investigation (Fig. 13.29).

Winchester also manufactures a 12-gauge version of their PDX1 ammunition. In these shotshells, Winchester couples a 1-oz rifled slug with three additional 00 buckshot pellets. As with other defense loads, they are designed to provide more projectiles to produce a damaging effect. Along this venture, another product from Winchester is their PDX1 segmented slug. This is a 12-gauge slug that is presegmented into three sections to easily break apart upon impact (Fig. 13.30).

Figure 13.29 Winchester PDX1 .410 gauge shotshell.

Figure 13.30 Winchester PDX1 12 gauge shotshell.

Figure 13.31 Hornady Triple Threat shotshell.

Aguila ammunition is manufactured in Mexico and has developed a variety of specialty ammunition. In the area of shotshells, they first introduced the mini shotshell, with a length of only 1.75 in. Due to the diminished length of the shotshell, the loading consists of seven 4B pellets and four 1B pellets.

The multiload shotshell offered by Hornady is marketed to the owners of the Taurus Judge, which is a revolver that will fire both traditional centerfire handgun ammunition and .410 gauge shotshell ammunition. This shotshell, known as the Triple Threat, incorporates a .41 caliber projectile at the front of the cartridge and it is followed by two .35 caliber round balls (Fig. 13.31).

Frangible ammunition

Frangible ammunition is a valuable ammunition design for its intended purpose. The minimization of ricochets when training at close ranges is invaluable to law enforcement and civilians who shoot steel targets during these exercises. However, from a forensic perspective, frangible projectiles can present some degree of difficulty in the comparison process. The frangibility of the bullet is generally not as much of an issue when receiving bullets recovered from soft tissue because the human body is not sufficiently hard enough to cause the pulverization of the bullet. However, the inherent nature of the production process of powdered metal products results in contact surfaces which are marginal at best for the impartation of individual characteristics from the interior contact with the firearm barrel (Raines, 2015; Kim, 2006; Pilcher, 2004). The surface of the fired projectile from powdered metal bullets is prone to more disruption from the bullet composition than interaction with the barrel. This is demonstrated in Fig. 13.32. These types of bullets from crime scenes that encounter solid objects will most likely perform as designed and disintegrate into a pile of dark brown powder.

Some manufacturers produce variations of the sintered bullet which utilizes a copper jacket that encapsulates the sintered bullet. One manufacturer to take this

Figure 13.32 Rifling impressed on a frangible bullet.

approach is Dynamic Research Technologies. The purpose of the additional jacket component is to keep the bullet intact when traveling through certain barriers (Ainsworth, 2017). The use of copper jackets allows for direct contact of the firearm barrel with a surface that is conducive to the deposition of individual characteristics from the barrel. Therefore, traditional comparison techniques can be performed on these projectile jackets (Mikko and Miller, 2008).

Manufacturer coatings

Some manufacturers use coatings on their bullets for a variety of reasons. For example, hunting cartridges may have a coating of molybdenum disulfide (moly). This is a chemical composition that is lightly applied to the outside of the bullet to provide lubricity to the bullet for higher velocities. The moly coating is basically powdered coating that is applied to the surface through a tumbling process. The ability to compare bullets fired utilizing molybdenum disulfide appears to have mixed results. In cases where larger quantities of moly-coated bullets are fired in the barrel, the deposition of the fine lubricant may fill in the voids of the individual characteristics (Rayer, 2007). While in other instances, where fewer moly-coated bullets were fired through the barrel, identifications were unaffected (Wall, 1997).

Another bullet type that is encountered is lead bullets with a polymer coating. This coating, when used as an alternative to a traditional copper jacket, is intended

Figure 13.33 Rifling impression on a Federal Syntech bullet.

Figure 13.34 Rifling impression on a Federal Nyclad bullet.

to reduce airborne lead and barrel fouling. Additionally, it increases velocity due to the lubricating properties of the bullet. These bullets are sold both as loaded cartridges (Federal Syntech, Smith & Wesson NYCLAD, and Federal Nyclad) and individual components for reloading. The polymer coatings are applied significantly thicker relative to the moly coating. The result of the polymer coating combined with the heat of friction and the heat generated from the ignition of the cartridge makes for a poor surface for the deposition of individual characteristics (Figs. 13.33 and 13.34).

The appearance of these bullets is somewhat uncommon at the time of this writing; however, with the increasing price of metals and competition in the marketplace for reasonably priced target shooting ammunition, the appearance of polymer-coated ammunition could conceivably be a regular appearance in forensic laboratories.

Manufacturer primer sealant

Some manufacturers use a sealant as a means to protect their primer from contamination from the environment. This is typically in the form of a lacquer that is placed around the primer interface with the cartridge case; however, the lacquer may be deposited in a fashion that covers the entire primer, resulting in the primer being coated with a soft plasticized material (Fig. 13.35).

The primer sealant can serve to capture the breech face marks or can hinder the marks. There are instances where the lacquer captures the breech face marks and are essential to the comparison of evidence bullets with test-fired bullets. Conversely, there are times when the breech face marks penetrate the sealant and may not be visible without the removal of the lacquer (Fig. 13.36).

When performing comparisons where lacquer is present, it is important to examine and document the cartridge case with both the lacquer present in the original condition. If no class or individual characteristics are observed, the lacquer should be removed for further observation. As with any alteration of the evidence, the condition of the evidence prior to and after being altered should be thoroughly documented for further reference.

Figure 13.35 Lacquer covering primer.

Figure 13.36 Primer with lacquer removed (left) and lacquer present (right).

An additional effect lacquer can have on cartridge case comparison can occur when numerous cartridge cases containing lacquer have been fired and transfer the lacquer to the breech face of the firearm. In these instances, the class and/or individual characteristics may be obscured and not transposed onto the fired cartridge case.

CHAPTER 14

Legal challenges to the science of forensic firearm examination*

Ronald Nichols
Nichols Forensic Science Consulting, Antioch, CA, United States

Forensic science is rather unique among the various scientific endeavors because the findings of a forensic scientist often find their way into court proceedings designed to determine the guilt or innocence of an individual accused of a crime. Interestingly, what is often missed is that the findings of a forensic scientist can also cause investigations to steer in a different direction, resulting in the release of a person or interest, or in findings that are of no investigative value. Critics of the firearm and toolmark discipline often point to various court decisions challenging the legitimacy of the common source conclusions but what is missed are the many more cases in which common source determinations were not made. But it is the courtroom where we find the debate occurring as to whether firearm and toolmark identification is sufficiently reliable for it to be considered by a court or jury in determining the guilt of innocence of an accused.

The *Daubert* decision is the context for many of the challenges that the firearm and toolmark identification discipline has faced (*Daubert v. Merrell Dow Pharm., Inc.*, 1993). This decision highlighted four conditions for the trial judge, referred to as "gate-keepers," to evaluate when considering the reliability of expert witness testimony that was to be offered. The first was that the theory or technique in question has been tested according to the precepts of the scientific method. It is important to understand and recognize that the *Daubert* decision did not require that the theory or technique be a science, just that it has been tested according to the precepts of the scientific methods. This is an important distinction because the discussion of whether or not firearm and toolmark identification is a science is not particularly relevant for the court; simply that the theory or technique in question has been tested in accordance with the scientific method. The second deals with the issue of publication and peer review and an evaluation of whether there has been research, publication, and an opportunity for criticism by peers. The third deals with issues of quality—not only standards of control but also what is the error rate, or, at the very least, a potential

*Contributor—Ronald Nichols.

error rate. The fourth deals with general acceptance by the relevant community in which the theory or technique in question operates. If one evaluates this decision in its simplest pieces, what the court wants to see is whether or not the expert witness can articulate what was done, why was it done, what safeguards are in place, and how do we know that it works.

Throughout the 21st century, there have been a number of decisions rendered by courts in *Daubert* or *Daubert*-type hearings involving firearm and toolmark-related evidence. Several things seem to be common to most of these decisions. The first is a recognition that acceptance of this type of testimony since the early 20th century has established a very significant precedent with which the court must be concerned and acknowledged. This certainly does not compel a court to follow precedent blindly, but it generally causes the court to issue a decision that is more focused on the case at the bar as opposed to a negative judgment of the entire discipline. One example of this was in a federal case heard in Massachusetts (*U.S. v. Monteiro*, 2006). This case involved testimony by two different experts on behalf of the prosecution. One of them offered testimony upon the current state of the art and practice in the discipline which the judge in the case recognized as demonstrating that firearm and toolmark identification was reliable. With respect to the issue of reliability, the court offered, "The government has met its burden with regard to demonstrating that the underlying scientific principle that firearms leave unique marks on ammunition is reliable under Rule 702 [Federal Rules of Evidence]." The other individual testified as to the work that he performed in the case and it was that work, as well as the qualifications of the individual, with which the judge had significant enough concerns to exclude the testimony related to that particular work unless certain conditions were met. Those conditions were subsequently met, allowing for the admission of the evidence. However, it was clear that the court knew two things had to be addressed—the overall reliability of the discipline itself and the manner in which those principles were applied in the case before the bar.

Another common thread is that, in general, the courts appear to have a sufficient understanding of the firearm and toolmark discipline apart from the precedent that has been set. They appear to recognize the general approach and subjectivity that underlies the common source identifications that are made. Most are confident that sufficient work has been performed and published and that the underlying theory and techniques are reliable such that the evidence can be of value in helping the trier of fact reach a verdict. There have been exceptions but, in general, the courts have overwhelmingly been supportive and accepting of testimony related to firearm and toolmark identification. This support and acceptance has come in the face of several reports that have called into question the foundations and reliability of firearm and toolmark identification (National Research Council, 2008, 2009; PCAST, 2016). A critical review of these reports with respect to firearm and toolmark identification was done by a number of groups, many responding in a way that highlighted legitimate concerns but also pointed out some of the shortcomings in the findings that were made in these reports. That is not to say that the reports did not have value, because they did. One item of great importance was that it helped to spur examiner to have a better understanding of the scientific foundations of the discipline and how to articulate them.

At the same time, even with the overwhelming support that the courts have afforded the firearm and toolmark identification discipline, there are a few areas with which they struggle. These issues have arisen in various forms, but they tend to boil down to one overarching concern. The courts seem to be content with the reliability of the work but are having a large amount of difficulty in dealing with the certainty with which examiners express their common source identifications. It is this particular issue that will serve as the framework for the rest of the discussion with respect to firearm and toolmark identification in the courts.

The range of court opinion with respect to certainty of identification is large, extending from no restriction on an examiner's testimony with respect to certainty of a common source opinion to a complete exclusion of the testimony. In between are various decisions that clearly demonstrate that the courts are struggling with what certainty a common source determination can be expressed. Looking at the various court decisions, this struggle can be conceptualized into six different groups of thought.

The first group of thought is that there should be no restriction at all; that the examiner is free to testify that in his or her opinion, the identification to a particular tool means that no other tool would have been responsible. Or, that the issue is one for cross-examination and the defense is free to question such an absolute stance but the court would not prohibit that examiner from offering such a stance because it was, in the end, an expert opinion. Based on testimony provided in Wren (*State of Alaska v. Wren*, 2009) and Turner (*Turner v. State of Indiana*, 2011), the courts were satisfied that a common source identification to the exclusion of all other tools was appropriate. In *Wren* the court wrote, "The Court first notes that these decisions [decisions offered by the defense in support of their argument to limit testimony – *U.S. v. Green, U.S. v. Monteiro, U.S. v. Diaz*] represent an extreme minority of cases. The vast majority of courts have not limited firearm toolmark examiner testimony. Second, the Court found in the first section of this order that the theory and techniques underlying firearm toolmark identification is a sufficiently reliable subject for expert scientific testimony. For the reasons set forth below, the Court will not then limit that expert's opinion testimony of his conclusions premised on that subject and based upon his specialized training and experience in the field." In *Turner*, the court determined, "Having considered the motions, the evidence, arguments from counsel, and expert testimony, the court concludes that the firearm toolmark identification is reliable for expert testimony. Moreover, expert witnesses may testify that the shell casings match the relevant firearm to the point of exclusion of all other firearms."

In two separate cases in California Superior Courts the courts made the determination that no restriction on certainty would be forthcoming that it was an issue to be approached with a rigorous cross-examination (*State of California v. Carter*, 2009; *State of California v. Blacknell*, 2012). In *Carter* the court issued a bench ruling in which was stated, "However, the final request was for me to limit the testimony to something other than to state that, in his [the examiner] opinion, the firearm matched the shell casings or to use the word 'match' in some context. I'm going to reject that ... The test to me is cross-examination and the adversary system... So the request to prevent the testimony all together is denied. The request to limit the testimony is denied." The Court in Blacknell stated something very similar when it replied to the defense asking if the court would limit the testimony of the expert by saying, "I'm not going to limit his expert opinion as to how accurate or absolute the shell casing comparison is. However, he will be subject, I'm sure, to careful cross-examination, and the jury will have an opportunity to hear what the basis is for his opinion and whether or not they consider it in any way will be up to them."

The second group of thought consists of decisions in which the judge believed that absolute certainty was not appropriate yet, recognized that based on the work done in the field, there is a high level of certainty that needs to find expression in some form. The judge in Monteiro coined the phrase, "reasonable degree of ballistic certainty," when it was believed that, "there is no reliable statistical or scientific methodology which will currently permit the expert to testify that it is a 'match' to an absolute certainty, or to an arbitrary degree of statistical certainty" (*U.S. v. Monteiro*, 2006). In this case the judge did not have concern with respect to the reliability of the discipline but had serious reservations with respect to the practice of the discipline by the examiner in this particular case. Therefore the court granted the defendant's motion to exclude the firearm evidence but allowed the examiner time to rectify the identified issues with respect to the case.

One year later, a judge used the same phrase because he was of the opinion that, "The record, however, does not support the conclusion that identifications can be made to the exclusion of all other firearms in the world" (*U.S. v. Diaz*, 2007). The judge was confident that there is a "method and science behind firearm and toolmark identification" and that all the prongs of *Daubert* were adequately satisfied. In the Superior Court of Washington, the judge opined that, "There is insufficient database for the firearm expert to testify all other pistols are excluded. The expert cannot advise of any statistical evidence or present probabilities of a match" (*Washington v. Berg and Reed*, 2010). Therefore the judge ruled that, "evidence of firearm identification shall be limited to the expert testifying as to his opinion based on a reasonable degree of certainty in the ballistic field." In a 2011 ruling, the judge would permit testimony to this same standard provided that there was sufficient documentation to assist the trier of fact and that the expert was capable of explaining the theory behind his or her opinion (*Commonwealth of Massachusetts v. Heang*, 2011).

In the first *Daubert* case after having been a Frye state the court ruled that the analyst could not testify to the significance of the identification with an exact statistical certainty but only to this same "reasonable degree of ballistic certainty" (*Florida v. Richardson*, 2013). In a case out of New Mexico, the defendant claimed that firearm and toolmark identification is a "pseudoscience" (*U.S. v. McCluskey*, 2013) using two reports of the National Research Council for support (National Research Council, 2008, 2009). In this decision the court made a point that it was not making a determination of whether or not firearm identification is a science or not but, that such testimony, "is admissible under Rule 702 and *Daubert*." In this particular case the court heard testimony from a firearm and toolmark identification expert that the term "reasonable degree of ballistic certainty" is "undefined" and therefore the examiner in the case at the bar could testify that, "she has reached her conclusions to a 'practical certainty,' or to a 'practical impossibility' of dissimilar origin, and nothing more." In a case out of California, the court did not see any significant distinction between practically impossible, which is a term associated with the Association of Firearm and Toolmark Examiners (AFTE) Theory of Identification (AFTE Criteria for Identification Committee, 1992; AFTE Committee for the Advancement of the Science of Firearm and Toolmark Identification, 2011), or reasonable degree of ballistic certainty (*California v. Miller*, 2012). The court wrote, "In this Court's view, as long as the expert does not mislead the jury into believing that a match is a 100% certainty, whether other firearms are excluded to a 'practical impossibility' or to a 'reasonable degree of certainty in the ballistics field,' will have no practical meaning to the average lay juror."

The issue in these cases has to do with the definition of "reasonable degree of certainty within the ballistic field" along with its various corollaries. This is strictly a legal term and has no definition within the community of firearm and toolmark examiners to which it has been applied. The term used by examiners within the field, as expressed in the AFTE Theory of Identifications, is that of a practical certainty (AFTE Criteria for Identification Committee, 1992; AFTE Committee for the Advancement of the Science of Firearm and Toolmark Identification, 2011). But, it is that term with which the courts have had a challenge and, instead, many have adopted their own term, a term which has no substantive definition. Of that, a group of examiners have written, "Practical certainty should not be allowed to be seen as an enemy of justice. Firearm and toolmark examiners have struggled with how to accurately express the certainty of opinions as related to the uniqueness of the evidence with which they are confronted. But then others have struggled as well with the concept of uniqueness—philosophers, Boolean algebra mathematicians, and rare stamp dealers. Ultimately, we all must make peace with this elusive concept. In addressing this criticism, one is left to wonder why it is that the legal academics who have been vocal on this issue seem to have no problem with the 'reasonable doubt' concept, yet are mystified and/or outraged at the collateral 'reasonable (practical) certainty concept'" (Murdock et al., 2017).

The third group of thought was that the testimony did not support a certainty of anything higher than a more likely than not scenario. There were different reasons the courts gave for this opinion including concerns with the underlying science, documentation, or potential confusion with other forensic disciplines they felt had a greater level of scientific foundation. In the Southern District of New York the court was of the opinion that while there appeared to be some substance to the reliability of firearm and toolmark identification, it was believed that "it could not be fairly called 'science'" (*U.S. v. Glynn*, 2008). A significant issue in this particular case is that the government did not contest the pleas of the defense nor the court's conclusions, including "the methodology was too subjective to permit opinions to be stated to 'a reasonable degree of ballistic certainty.'" By permitting the examiner to testify to a significance of "more likely than not," the court was satisfying Rule 401 [Test for Relevant Evidence (and its Limits)] of the Federal Rules of Evidence without overstating the significance. It should be noted that had the examiner not ultimately produced photographs of the work, testimony would have not been permitted at any level. This theme of poor documentation was key in a case out of Ohio (*State of Ohio v. Anderson*, 2009). The court expressly stated that had there been documentation beyond what was presented, "the Court may have been warranted in permitting [examiner] to testify to a reasonable degree of scientific certainty." Instead, the court directed that the examiner would "be able to testify that the firearm's match was more likely than not that the projectile was fired by the firearm that was tested."

In the US District Court out of Maryland the court was mindful of the role that case precedence can have when it warned that "courts should guard against complacency in admitting it [toolmark identification evidence] just because, to date, no federal court has failed to do" (*U.S. v. Mouzone*, 2009). In its review of the case circumstances, the US Magistrate Judge recommended to the local court that no statement of certainty with respect to the identification be permitted. However, if one had to be given then "more likely than not" would be the preferred testimony, and if that was to low then to a reasonable degree of ballistic certainty. Further, he stated that testimony indicating a practical impossibility should not be permitted.

After hearing testimony from witnesses including an examiner from the Federal Bureau of Investigation and two experts called by the defense, a court out of Georgia was not comfortable that there was sufficient scientific support to state that fired ammunition components were fired from a particular firearm (*U.S. v. Jackson and Durham*, 2012). The court ruled that "the opinion that I think is defensible that doesn't violate what I have my own concerns about as far as the exactness is that... the comparison results in similarities that are consistent with the fragments or the casings having been fired from or in the same weapon." The concern with this ruling is that much like "reasonable ballistic certainty," there is no clarification as to what "consistent with" means.

In 2014 a court was concerned that the use of the terms "virtual certainty or practical certainty" would create confusion with DNA evidence which was believed to be on stronger scientific footing than firearm and toolmark identification (*TX v. Harper*, 2014). The court did decide that it would "allow the witness to talk in terms of high degree of confidence, which I think is really what I heard from the witness's mouth when she was talking." The concern in all these cases in which the decision amounted to the expert being allowed to testify to a confidence level of more likely than not is that it understates the value of firearm and toolmark identification. "More likely than not" is not practically defined by any of the courts and to different jurors could mean as little as 51% certainty, which seems to be at odds with the undefined "high degree of confidence" specified in *Harper*.

This was recognized by courts that comprise the fourth group of thought which is that the "more likely than not" was too low but, they did not have a good sense as to the maximum level of certainty that could be expressed, with some falling back on the certainty within the ballistic field. As an example, Circuit Court in Maryland stated, "I believe, and *clearly* I believe [emphasis added], that more likely than not is way too low of a standard. But I also believe that, to the exclusion of all other firearms, is not the proper standard either" (*Maryland v. Wittingham*, 2009). In this particular case the court looked to *Monteiro* and *Diaz* when it specified that the allowable certainty would be "to a reasonable degree of *practical* certainty in the field of ballistics" [emphasis added]. Note the qualification of practical certainty in this particular instance. In the case *U.S. v. Cerna* the court declared that "more likely than not" was "not appropriate as it suggests the expert is no more than 51% sure that there was a 'match.' Likewise, the proposed 'practical certainty' standard, as articulated at the hearing, is not preferable to the *Diaz* 'reasonable degree of certainty in the ballistics field' standard" (*U.S. v. Cerna*, 2010).

In a similar vein the US District Court of the District of Columbia believed that the standard of "more likely than not" was too low (*U.S. v. Anderson*, 2010). The court was emphatic when it stated that such a standard, "sharply understates the reliability that has been demonstrated to underpin the AFTE methodology itself — despite the as yet unripe efforts at quantification and application of statistical probabilities to identifications." Like *Whittingham* and *Anderson* the court did permit certainty to a "reasonable degree of certainty in the field of firearms and toolmark identification." The court was clear that the examiner could not testify to a scientific certainty, seemingly separating firearm and toolmark identification from the realm of science either intentionally or unintentionally. The court also would not permit testimony reflecting that the potential of another firearm was practically impossible because that would be too easily confused with absolute certainty.

The fifth group of thought was that the issue should be avoided all together indicating that no statement with regard to certainty should be expressed. In a *Daubert* hearing held in a US District Court out of New Mexico, the court ruled favorably on all aspects of the *Daubert* criteria (*U.S. v. Taylor*, 2009). In his ruling, the judge called into question the "scholastic integrity" of the defense expert who testified in the hearing and excluded that expert from testifying at trial. The examiner would be permitted to testify to a "match" but would not be permitted to testify to a scientific certainty or to the exclusion of all other firearms, whether that was an absolute or practical certainty. The court ruled that the expert "may only testify that, in his opinion, the bullet came from the suspect rifle to within a reasonable degree of certainty in the firearms examination field."

In a US District Court out of Ohio the court declared that the examiner "may not testify as to her opinion on whether the casings are attributable to a single firearm to the exclusion of all other firearms. Such testimony would be misleading and prejudicial given the inherent subjectivity in Firearm and Toolmark Identification" (*U.S. v. Alls*, 2009). A US District Court out of Tennessee made a similar ruling, declaring that the examiner could not testify to an absolute or practical certainty (*U.S. v. Love*, 2011). In each case the court did not state what level of certainty could be applied or that the examiner would be able to state; just what they *were not* permitted to state.

In a case out of the Southern District of New York the court did not believe that the people adequately established firearm identification as a science, saying that they failed to show that the underlying theory was empirically proven (*U.S. v. Dore and Bennett*, 2013). The court was critical of the examiner and his inability to articulate several key concepts that the court deemed important including a definition of sufficient agreement and how proficiency tests distributed by Collaborative Testing Services are administered. Even with these reservations, the court ruled that the examiner could testify to his results but only state that it was his opinion that the fired cartridge cases were fired in the same firearm. However, this was not the opinion of other courts that had concerns with respect to the reliability of the firearm and toolmark identification discipline. This leads to a discussion of the final, sixth group of thought.

The sixth group of thought was that at some level, the discipline was insufficiently reliable and excluded or severely limited the testimony of the examiner. In one of the first cases that severely limited the testimony of the examiner the court had contemplated not permitting the testimony at all (*U.S. v. Green*, 2005). The court wrote, "...notwithstanding my serious reservations, I feel compelled to allow [EXAMINER NAME REDACTED] to testify about his observations... I will not allow him to conclude that the shell casings come from a specific Hi Point pistol 'to the exclusion of every other firearm in the world'... I reluctantly come to the above conclusion because of my confidence that any other decision will be rejected by appellate courts, in light of precedents across the country, regardless of the findings I have made." The examiner was permitted to testify as to his observations only.

In a case heard before a magistrate of the US Army the defense contended for a dismissal of the firearm evidence on a number of grounds to include the subjective nature of the examination that error rates had not been established, that there was no peer review in the discipline, and that the principle of uniqueness had not been tested. Supporting their claims, the defense used a report of the National Research Council (2009) and a defense expert (*US Army v. St. Gerard*, 2010). While impressed with the examiner's qualifications, a recognition that there was sufficient basis for the testimony and that the subject of the testimony was within the realm of the examiner's qualifications, the court did restrict the testimony. The court wrote, "Considering the Daubert factors in light of [EXAMINER NAME REDACTED] anticipated testimony, the Court finds that any testimony indicating that the shell casing *must have* [emphasis added] come from the AK-47 would be unreliable... Accordingly, the defense motion to exclude the testimony of [EXAMINER NAME REDACTED] that it would be a practical impossibility for the cartridge case to have been fired by any other weapon other than the seized AK-47 is GRANTED. This ruling is *limited solely* [emphasis added] to testimony concerning the level of certainty of the origin of the marks."

Unlike the Green and St. Gerard cases in which the examiner was ultimately permitted to testify with respect to firearm-related evidence (albeit with restrictions) a Court in Kentucky excluded toolmark evidence all together involving marks produced by a knife (*U.S. v. Smallwood*, 2010). In this particular case, the court did not consider "precedent in firearm identification is applicable to toolmark identification" and "given the subjective nature of firearm and toolmark identification, the relative frequency of firearm cases compared to toolmark cases—and knife cases in particular—necessarily makes a toolmark identification less reliable than a firearm identification." The court was careful to say, "This is not to say that a toolmark identification could never be admissible. Given an appropriate amount of expertise in marks by a particular tool, an examiner may very well be able to make an identification with the amount of reliability required for a court of law." In the case at the bar the motion to exclude the testimony was granted because in the court's opinion the examiner did not have the skills and experience with knife marks in particular to reliably form the required subjective opinion with respect to whether or not the toolmarks were made by the knife in question. This particular case highlights a misunderstanding on the part of the court that should have been avoided given proper preparation and presentation by the prosecution. Firearms are a specialized form of tool, and the principles that guide firearm identification are the very same principles that guide toolmark identification. It is not the specific tool in question but rather the manufacturing process that created the working surface of the tool in question. In the case of knives, the final manufacturing process will more likely than not be grinding, the very same process by which breechfaces may be finished in a number of firearms. Had this been appropriately presented and clarified by the prosecution, it is quite possible that the court in this case would have reached a decision similar to other courts in which nonfirearm toolmark testimony was permitted.

When looking at court decisions that have limited the testimony related to firearm and toolmark evidence, one of the more common themes is centered on the examiner in the case at hand before the court. Whether it was the supposed lack of training, or qualifications, or the work performed by the examiner in the case, or some combination, the primary reason for the courts to limit the offered testimony was not because the courts had concerns with the reliability of the discipline but rather some aspect of the examiner or his/her handling of the case or testimony.

It is also significant that these cases took place early on in the period in which firearm and toolmark testimony was being more actively challenged. Prior to the 21st century, such testimony had routinely either faced minimal or little challenge. As a result, there was a complacency with which some examiners and laboratories would not only conduct their work but also in the testimony that they provided. This complacency was exposed with the earlier challenges and, as a result, some courts were more restrictive than others depending on the quality of the work and presentation of that work at hand before those specific courts. As the years have progressed, the findings of the courts have been more routinely favorable as this complacency now seems to be something of the past. There are continued challenges as there should be. As the Court in California so aptly pointed out, "The test to me is cross-examination and the adversary system" (*State of California v. Carter*, 2009).

CHAPTER 15

Emerging technology in comparisons*

T.V. Vorburger[1], J. Song[1], N. Petraco[2] and R. Lilien[3]
[1]National Institute of Standards and Technology (NIST), Gaithersburg, MD, United States
[2]John Jay College and The Graduate Center, City University of New York, New York, NY, United States
[3]Cadre Research Labs, Chicago, IL, United States

Introduction

This chapter is designed to introduce the reader to emerging technologies relating to 3D surface topography measurement and comparative analysis. While the chapter includes several technical terms and a few equations, effort has been made to omit content that only would be of interest to a metrologist. We encourage readers to push through the entire chapter. Technology is developing quickly, and we hope that the content will provide a roadmap and some important waypoints to this emerging discipline. Note that this chapter has been adapted from a longer and slightly more technical paper. The interested reader is pointed toward the original content (Vorburger et al., 2016).

This review describes some of the methods practiced and results accomplished thus far in the field. Gerules et al. (2013) published a broad review of methods for firearms analysis. The current review focuses on topography methods with some illustrative examples and on recent work. The remainder of the "Introduction" section provides a short history of ballistics identification systems. The "Topography measurement" section describes surface topography measurement, and the "Analysis and parameters" section describes analysis procedures and parameters, especially those to quantify similarity between surface topography images. The "Statistical error rate estimation" section discusses all the important issues of error rate estimation. The "Standards, traceability, and uncertainty for topography measurements" section describes standards, notably physical standards and the concept of traceability. Information on the transition of these technologies into the crime lab, including interoperability, the X3P file format, and virtual comparison microscopy (VCM), is given in the "Ballistics identification systems in the crime lab" section. The "Ongoing issues and opportunities" section highlights a few ongoing issues and opportunities.

---

* Certain commercial equipment, instruments, or materials are identified in this paper to specify adequately the experimental procedure. Such identification does not imply recommendation or endorsement by the National Institute of Standards and Technology, nor does it imply that the materials or equipment identified are necessarily the best available for the purpose.

Since the early 1990s, commercial automated ballistics identification systems, such as the Drugfire (Roach, 1997) and the Integrated Ballistics Identification System (IBIS) (Braga and Pierce, 2004), have been developed, producing a revolution in the speed at which microscope inspections can proceed. These early systems served to partially replace physical open case files for database search and were not intended to be used for the reaching of conclusions regarding common origin. These systems typically include a digitized optical microscope to acquire 2D images of bullets and cartridge case surfaces, a signature analysis station, correlation software, and access to a large database where accumulated images reside. With such a system, a large number of comparisons can be performed automatically. When a suspect image is input into the database, it is correlated with the images in the database, and a list of possible leading matches is output for further analysis by firearms examiners. These initial systems utilized 2D images, and therefore confirmation of an identified hit required examination of the original materials under a traditional comparison microscope.

Most of these original systems were based on comparisons of the optical intensity images acquired by the microscope. The quality of these 2D optical images is largely affected by lighting conditions, such as the type of light source, lighting direction, intensity, color and reflectivity of the material, and the image contrast. Since each of the images is acquired alone and not in a comparison microscope, the systems are more susceptible to slight variations in the alignment and lighting conditions. The significant effect of lighting conditions on the optical image has been discussed by Song et al. (2012) and Chu et al. (2014).

Accurate identification also depends on the capability of the correlation software to identify the related correlation regions and to eliminate the unrelated regions from correlation. Most commercial systems use proprietary correlation parameters and algorithms to quantify image similarity. These proprietary correlation methods often lack objective open tests of their parameters and algorithms. This may pose difficulty for laboratory assessments and intercomparisons among different systems.

It was stated in the *Theory of Identification* issued by the Association of Firearm and Tool mark Examiners (AFTE) that "...the comparison of tool marks..." are to be made on the "...unique surface contours..." and "surface contour patterns comprised of individual peaks, ridges and furrows. Specially, the relative height or depth, width, curvature..." (SWGGUN, 2005; Hamby, 1999). Because ballistics signatures are geometrical microtopographies by nature, direct measurement and correlation of the 3D surface topographies have been proposed for ballistic identification (DeKinder and Bonfanti, 1999; Weller et al., 2015; Song and Vorburger, 2006; Vorburger et al., 2007). Such methods can avoid the confusing effects of variable lighting conditions and shadowing and should likely improve correlation accuracy of automated systems. Several different types of optical instruments have been developed, which are capable of precise measurement of 3D surface topography. These methods will be discussed in the "Topography measurement" section. They are making it possible to use quantitative topography measurements for firearm evidence identifications, in addition to traditional methods based on conventional image comparisons. Development of ballistics identifications is therefore facing a likely evolution from qualitative image comparisons to quantitative topography measurements. Not all modern ballistic identification systems are making the transition to quantitative 3D measurements. Some systems are shifting their role from laboratory instruments to investigative tools for generating leads. These systems appear to be shifting away from quantitative 3D measurements. The reader is advised to evaluate each system for its intended use.

Topography measurement

A number of different methods have been developed to measure surface topography. They may first be classified into three categories—line-profiling, area-integrating, and areal-topography—as described in an ISO standard (ISO 25178-6, 2010). In this review, we will emphasize areal topography, as it is the technology employed in all current ballistics identification systems. The surface topography features of cartridge cases and bullets, which are of interest to firearms experts, are generally in the micrometer-to-millimeter lateral range with heights in the submicrometer-to-hundred-micrometer range. Even in this relatively narrow range, there are at least four different methods, most of them optical, which are useful and available as commercial instruments. Most of these methods are the subject of international documentary standards that outline the key properties and describe influence factors that are potential sources of uncertainty and error. Calibration procedures are currently the subject of further standardization efforts. In the following subsections, each method is presented with a bit of technical detail and references from which significantly more information can be obtained. If the reader skips these sections, note that there are multiple different methods for obtaining 3D surface topographies that different ballistic identification systems utilize different methods, and that not every ballistics identification system utilizing the same method will obtain the same quality scans.

The first two described methods, confocal microscopy and coherence scanning interferometry (CSI), are capable of collecting scans at high resolution, perhaps higher than is required for firearm and toolmark examination. They also require long scan acquisition times. Therefore while they may have been used by academic research groups in the transition to 3D scanning technology, they may not end up in the crime laboratory.

Confocal microscopy

Confocal microscopy (Hamilton and Wilson, 1982) is widely used, not only for fluorescence microscopy and 3D sectioning of transparent materials, but for the measurement of surface topography when used in reflection mode. A standards document, which describes confocal microscopy and its influence quantities, has recently completed an ISO ballot as a final draft international standard (ISO FDIS 25178-607, 2018). A schematic diagram of a typical confocal microscope is shown in Fig. 15.1 (ASME B46-2009, 2010; Weller et al., 2012). Most examples of this method rely on the use of pinholes for height discrimination. Incident light is focused through a pinhole, refocused onto the surface and reflected from it, then refocused through a conjugate pinhole placed before the detector. A strong signal through the pinhole will be detected only when the surface point is at the focusing height. This discrimination enables the tool to detect variations in surface height and topography when the surface is vertically scanned (Fig. 15.1) along the optical axis of the microscope. Variations in the method include laser scanning confocal microscopy, disk scanning confocal microscopy (DSCM), and programmable array microscopy (ISO FDIS 25178-607, 2018).

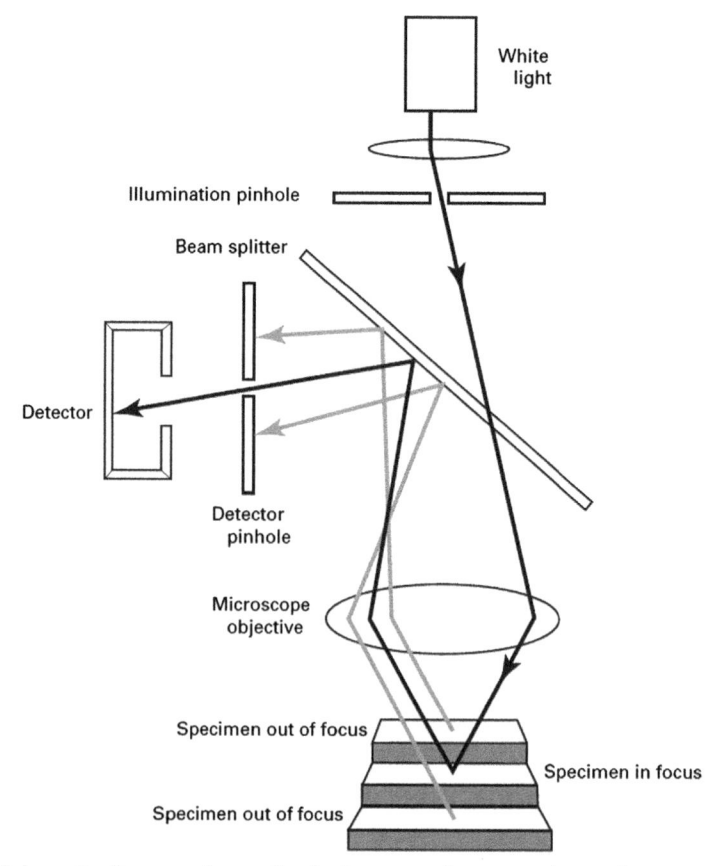

Figure 15.1 Schematic diagram of a confocal microscope for measuring surface topography (ASME B46-2009, 2010; Weller et al., 2012).

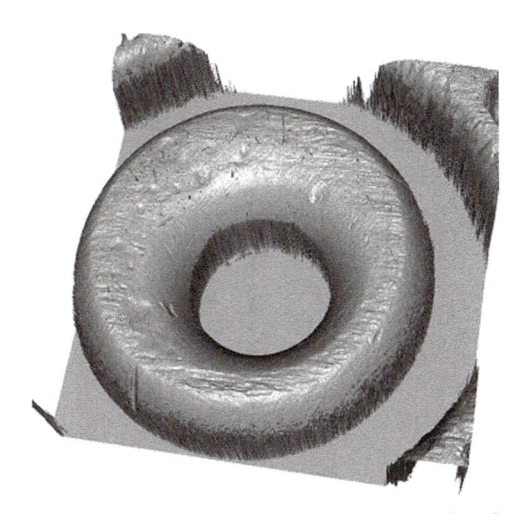

Figure 15.2 Topography image of the breech face impression of a fired 9 mm cartridge case obtained with disk scanning confocal microscopy (Vorburger et al., 2007). The field of view is roughly 4 mm on a side.

Different confocal microscopes have been used in a number of firearms and toolmark research studies (Vorburger et al., 2007; Petraco et al., 2013; Brinck, 2008; Bachrach et al., 2010). The vertical noise resolution and lateral resolution improve with the numerical aperture (NA) of the microscope. With a $50\times$ objective, having a NA of 0.5, the vertical resolution can reach a few nanometers, and the lateral resolution is on the order of a micrometer or less. A topography image of a fired cartridge case obtained with confocal microscopy is shown in Fig. 15.2 (Vorburger et al., 2007).

Coherence scanning interferometry

CSI relies on interference between a beam of light reflected from the surface under study and a beam of light reflected from a reference surface. This method is the subject of a published standard (ISO 25178-604, 2013) and other reviews (DeGroot, 2011). A schematic diagram is shown in Fig. 15.3 (Bennett, 1985). When the optical paths reflected from the reference surface and the test surface are equal, an interference pattern of bright and dark fringes is formed on the camera detector, but as either optical path is changed by distances larger than the coherence length of the light, the fringe contrast disappears. One can move the surface or the microscope vertically to observe a maximum in the signal modulation in order to locate the height of a surface point relative to its neighboring points. This depth localization process is repeated for all surface points. The vertical noise resolution is routinely a few nanometers but under some conditions can be as small as about 0.1 nm. The lateral resolution scales with the NA of the microscope in a manner similar to the confocal method.

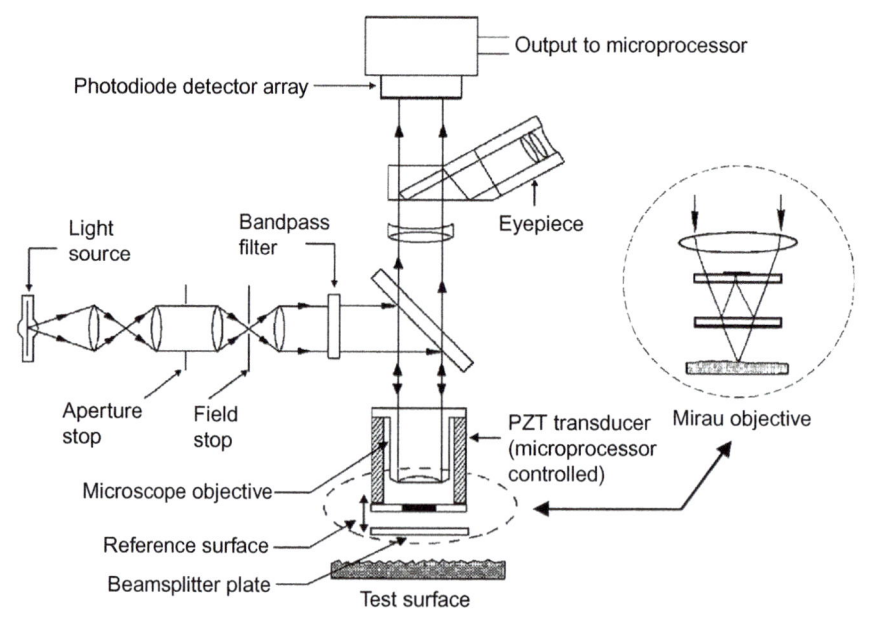

Figure 15.3 Schematic diagram of a coherence scanning interferometric microscope in the Mirau configuration. *Reprinted with permission Bennett (1985).*

Focus variation

Both confocal and CSI methods involve some manipulation of the light traveling through a microscope, either with pinholes or beam splitters. This leads to a cost in signal-to-noise. Focus variation (Fig. 15.4) is conceptually simpler (Helmli, 2011). The height sensing function derives from locating the surface at its sharpest, best focus position in the microscope. The peaks and valleys of the surface are focused at different positions as the surface scans vertically with respect to the microscope, a mode of operation similar to those of confocal and CSI. Focus variation is the subject of an international standard (ISO 25178-606, 2015). The method is capable of measuring steeply sloped surfaces, up to nearly 90 degrees (Helmli, 2011). Because the method relies on contrast in images resulting from peaks and valleys of surface features, averaging of individual pixels is required to provide the height sensitivity, which involves a collective response from neighboring pixels as illustrated in Fig. 15.5 (ISO 25178-606, 2015). This implies that both the lateral resolution and vertical resolution of the focus variation method may be more limited than those for confocal or coherence scanning. Focus variation has been favorably reviewed by Bolton-King et al. (2010).

Photometric stereo

Photometric stereo, also called shape from shading, involves the decoding of illumination patterns on surfaces cast by multiple light sources to produce a surface topography

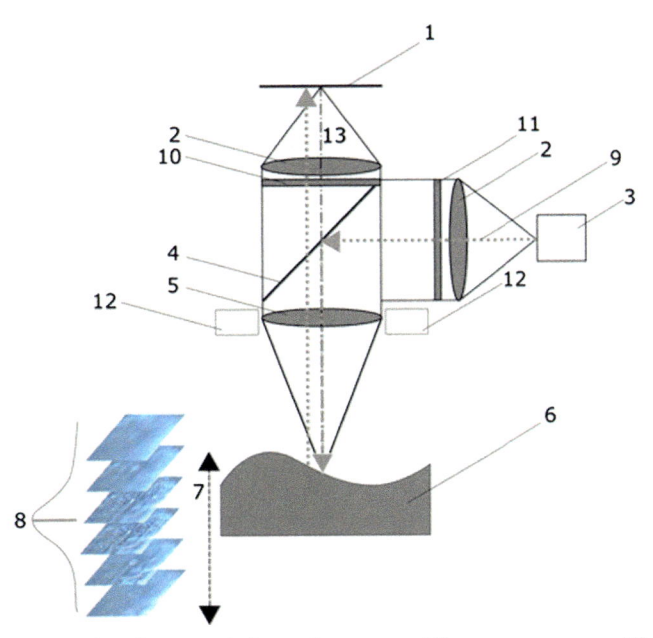

Figure 15.4 Schematic of a focus variation microscope: (1) camera sensor, (2) lenses, (3) light source, (4) semitransparent mirror, (5) objective lens with limited depth of field, (6) sample, (7) vertical movement with drive unit, (8) contrast curve calculated from the local window, (9) light rays from the white light source, (10) analyzer, (11) polarizer, (12) ring light. Items 10–12 are optional. © ISO. This material is reproduced from ISO 25178-606: 2015 with permission of the American National Standards Institute (ANSI) on behalf of ISO. All rights reserved.

measurement. Depending on the number and directions of the light sources, this method can have different manifestations (Johnson, 2011; Sakarya et al., 2008). One of these is shown in Fig. 15.6 (Johnson, 2011). Six light sources evenly spaced azimuthally illuminate the surface in turn at a grazing angle. The illumination patterns are analyzed, and a surface topography image was produced. The method illustrated here includes an additional technique, called GelSight, to reduce the sensitivity to variations in surface optical properties and to emphasize the surface topography. Integral to the setup is a soft, transparent gel with a pigmented film that directly contacts the surface. The film has uniform optical properties and a small grain size, which helps to minimize the effects of nonuniform surface reflectance properties (e.g., specularities). The microscope above the gel observes the illumination of the gel surface, which is itself reproducing the underlying surface topography. A topography image of the breech face impression of a unit of National Institute of Standards and Technology (NIST) Standard Reference Material (SRM) 2461 (Vorburger et al., 2014) obtained with GelSight photometric stereo is shown in Fig. 15.7 (Weller et al., 2015; Lilien, 2016).

Scan position	Surface image	Standard deviation
Out of focus		10
Almost in focus		20
In focus		50

1   Point of interest for which the focus information is calculated
2   5×5 neighborhood of points used to calculate the focus information (standard deviation)

Figure 15.5 Calculation of focus information at a position of interest (1) using the contrast from a neighborhood of points (2). The contrast may be quantified by the standard deviation of the intensities of the neighboring points. © ISO. This material is reproduced from ISO 25178-606: 2015 with permission of the American National Standards Institute (ANSI) on behalf of ISO. All rights reserved.

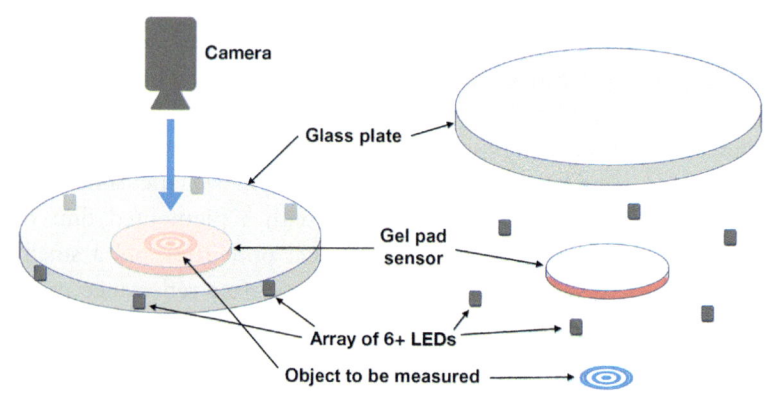

Figure 15.6 Schematic detail of a photometric stereo tool for measuring surface topography [assembled (left), separated (right)] (Weller et al., 2015; Johnson et al., 2011; Lilien, 2016). Six or more LED light sources illuminate the rough surface of the object in turn at near grazing incidence angle. The gel pad sensor is a soft material with uniform optical properties that replicates the rough surface topography of the object when pressed down against it. The microscope between the glass plate and the camera is not shown.

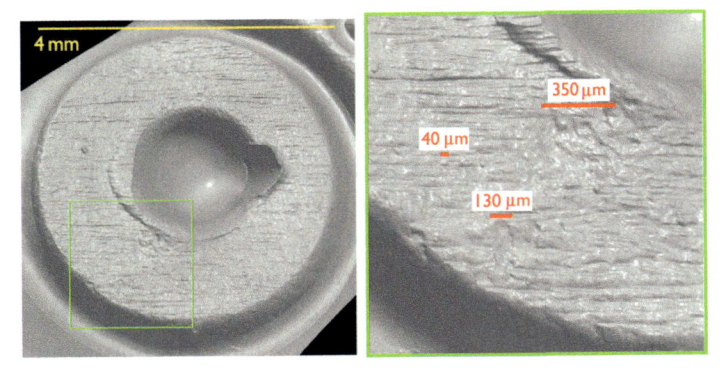

Figure 15.7 Topography image of the breech face impression of a unit of Standard Reference Material (SRM) 2461 Cartridge Case obtained with a photometric stereo tool (Lilien, 2015a).

Analysis and parameters
The importance of similarity as a surface property in this field

The function of establishing whether or not two bullets or cartridge cases were fired through the same firearm depends on obtaining some assessment of similarity between them. More specifically, we want to derive a quantitative measure of geometric similarity that will lead to identification or exclusion of them as being fired by the same firearm. To accomplish this task, the firearms examiner applies his/her expert judgment in a way that is difficult to quantify. An automated system, by contrast, must be programmed to produce a quantitative measurand for similarity, which the expert can use. Hence, much research in firearms identification is concentrated on finding algorithms and parameters that emphasize the individualized characteristics of surfaces and their similarity to those of other surfaces. The two most common ways of accomplishing this are to match a large section of one surface to that of the other or to identify individual features on one member of a pair and look for similar features on the other (Zitova and Glusser, 2003). This section presents a vast simplification of each described analytic method. Analytic methods are rapidly evolving, and the methods described below are continually being improved. Textbooks have been written on the component parts of each method described later. Additional details can be found in the provided references. This chapter is by no means a complete list of analytic methods. The intent of this chapter is not to make the reader an expert in comparison algorithms but rather to provide an overview of the types of methods currently in development.

Scoring functions can be developed to address two main comparison tasks: (1) a sorting function which accepts a single reference surface and a set of candidate surfaces and which sorts the candidate set to rank the surface scans from most to least similar as compared to the reference, and (2) a scoring function that, given two surfaces, computes a statistically meaningful quantified measure of comparison. The quantified statistical comparison can take the form of a likelihood, an odds ratio, or an absolute probability, not merely a ranking. However, each of these statistical measures presents their own challenges.

In the "Preprocessing" section, we describe an important required step prior to surface comparison. In the "Basic similarity parameters for topography measurements" section, we introduce the basic cross-correlation function (CCF). In the "Advanced similarity methods" and "Statistical error rate estimation" sections, we move onto more sophisticated comparison approaches. While these methods continue to evolve, the presentation in this section should provide a framework onto which other, new, methods can be understood.

Preprocessing

Preprocessing is an important part of any surface measurement and analysis methodology. The details of each preprocessing step involve significant math and are beyond the scope of this chapter. Preprocessing may include the following steps. Decimation (or downsampling) may be performed to reduce the number of data points, for example, to reduce file size and to speed potential calculations. Bad data in the form of dropouts (i.e., unmeasured points) and outliers (i.e., mismeasured points) must be recognized and ignored or repaired. Filtering is the process of removing select structures (e.g., mismeasured baseline drift) and is often performed to emphasize individual characteristics. Two common filters typically operate to remove very coarse or very fine features. These coarse and fine features are often referred to as low and high spatial frequencies, respectively. Any preprocessing utilized by a scanning system should be done in a way that it does not affect the useful information within the measured surface. In other words, preprocessing should not change the underlying toolmark information content and should not push the toolmarks into erroneous identification or elimination. It is important that practitioners utilize established preprocessing techniques supported by the literature. The rest of this section describes several details of the filtering process (Fig. 15.8).

One of the most common filtering approaches is the digital Gaussian filter (ASME B46-2009, 2010; ISO 11562, 1996). The Gaussian filter is a kind of moving-average, smoothing filter, where the moving-average window uses a Gaussian weighting function. The smoothed profile that results can be subtracted from the original profile to produce a profile where the long wavelength features are diminished. The scale of features that are diminished or eliminated is given by the long cutoff wavelength (ISO 25178-2, 2012). Conversely, if one wants to remove short-wavelength (high-frequency) noise, the Gaussian smoothing filter may be applied with a short cutoff wavelength. Combining these two processes gives us a desired Gaussian bandpass filter

Emerging technology in comparisons 285

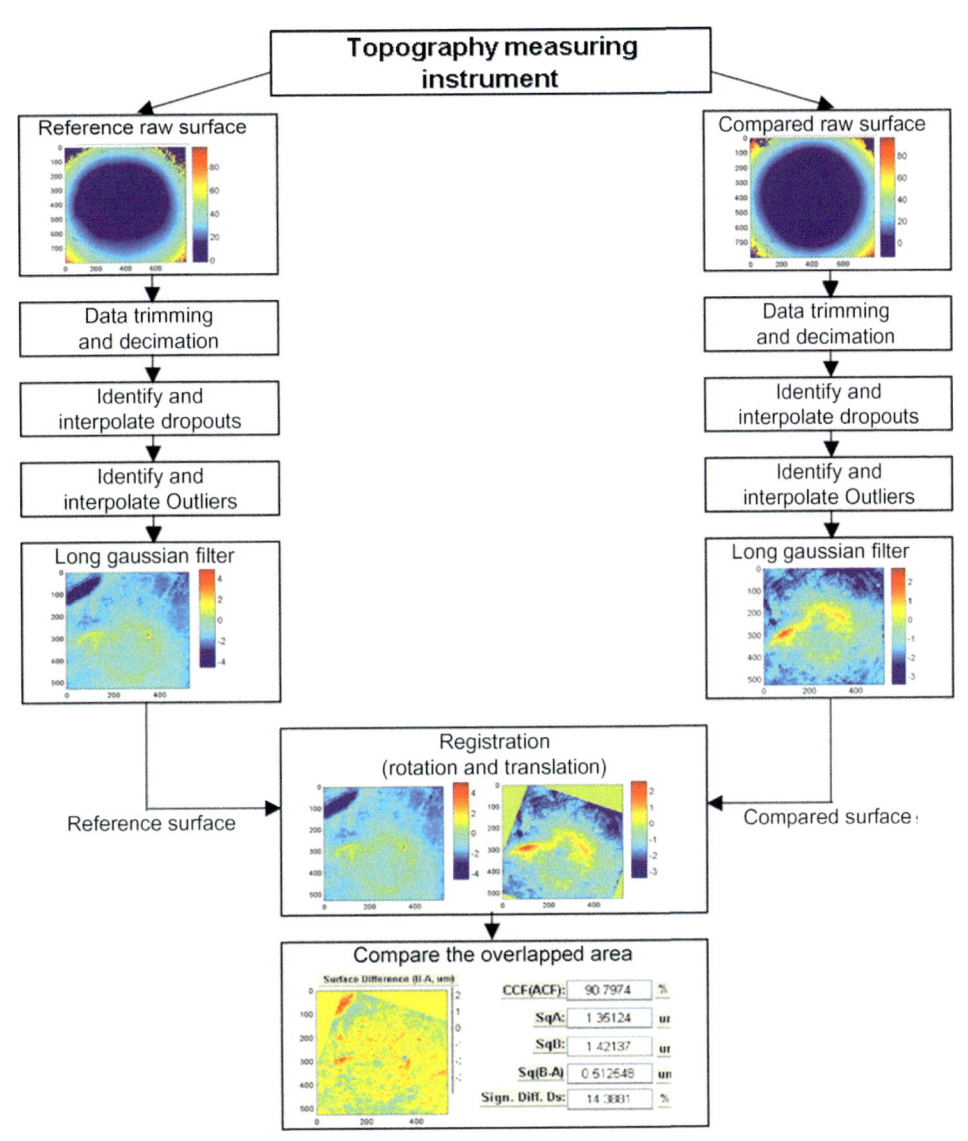

Figure 15.8 Illustration of a procedure for assessing the similarity of two topography images: dropout and outlier detection, filtering, registration, analysis, and parameters. In addition to the long-scale filtering operation (shown), a short-scale or smoothing filter may also be applied (not shown) (Vorburger et al., 2007).

defined by long and short cutoffs. Fig. 15.9 illustrates how a filtered profile might appear. Fig. 15.9A shows a segment of a longer profile containing the sum of three sinusoidal components: a waviness component with a wavelength of 1000 μm, a roughness component with a wavelength of 100 μm, and a noise component with a

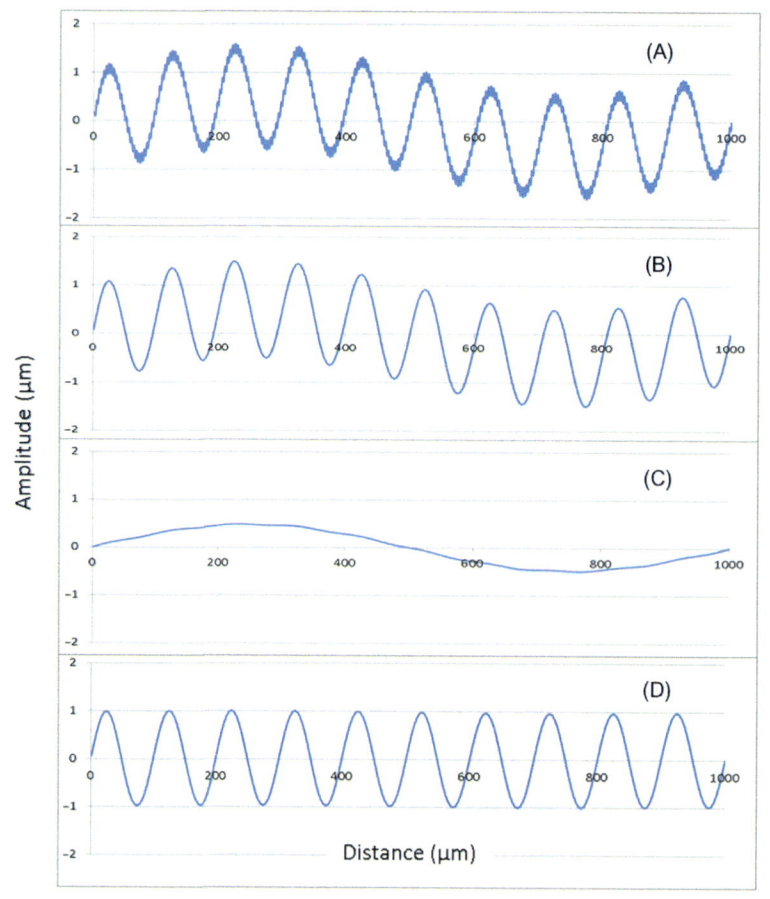

Figure 15.9 Illustration of a bandpass Gaussian filter; (A) segment of original profile with three sinusoidal components; (B) 25 μm short-wavelength filter attenuates the noise component; (C) 250 μm short-wavelength filter attenuates the roughness component; (D) subtracting (C) from (B) emphasizes the roughness component and attenuates the waviness component.

wavelength of 4 μm. We wish to emphasize the 100 μm roughness component and attenuate the other two. Applying a Gaussian filter with a short-wavelength cutoff of 25 μm attenuates the noise component by about 94%, while leaving the roughness and waviness components attenuated by less than 0.5% (Fig. 15.9B). Applying a second Gaussian filter with a short-wavelength cutoff of 250 μm attenuates the roughness component by about 98.7% but attenuates the waviness component by only 4.2% (Fig. 15.9C). Subtracting Fig. 15.9C from Fig. 15.9B yields a relatively unattenuated roughness component while severely attenuating the waviness component (Fig. 15.9D). It is of course important to not "throw out the baby with the bathwater" when filtering. Filters must preserve structural elements relevant to identification.

An important limitation of the basic Gaussian filter is the sensitivity of the filtered result to peaks and valleys in the data, which may not be of interest to the user (Blunt and Jiang, 2003). For these and other reasons, a wide number of other filtering methods have been developed and defined in documentary standards.

Both impressed and striated marks can be preprocessed using filtering. In addition, striation patterns are often summarized by mean profiles, which are often averaged along the surface in the direction of tool travel (Bachrach et al., 2010; Faden et al., 2007; Chumbley et al., 2010; Chu et al., 2010; Bachrach, 2002). These mean profiles represent the cross-sectional linear profile of the striated mark.

Basic similarity parameters for topography measurements

One of the oldest and most common similarity measures is the CCF and the areal CCF (ACCF). The CCF can be used when comparing linear striated profiles (e.g., a bullet's land area), and the ACCF can be used when comparing areal impressed toolmarks (e.g., a cartridge cases' breech face impression). Unless specified, when we mention the CCF, we are referring to both the CCF and ACCF. The basic idea of these methods is to identify the best alignment between two surfaces and to quantify the degree of corresponding pixel-to-pixel similarity at that orientation. For a given alignment of two surfaces, the CCF compares each corresponding (overlapping) pixel. If the surfaces are the same (e.g., identical), we would expect the same values at each corresponding pixel. That is, where one surface has a height of 3.2 µm, the second surface should also have a height of 3.2 µm, and where one surface has a height of 1.2 µm, the second surface should have a height of 1.2 µm. Mathematically, the equations below measure this similarity. A maximum CCF score occurs where each corresponding pixel has the same value. The use of averages (e.g., means) and variances simply ensures that the maximum value of CCF for perfectly correlated surfaces be 1, and the maximum value of CCF for similar, but not identical surfaces, should be near 1. Dissimilar surfaces have a CCF value near 0. During the development of NIST's SRM bullets (NIST, 2013), Song et al. used the CCF to quantify the similarity of bullet signatures (Ma et al., 2004; Song et al., 2004). The CCF between two surface profiles $z_A(x)$ and $z_B(x)$ may be calculated by

$$\mathrm{CCF}\,(A,B,\tau) = \lim_{L \to \infty} \frac{\left((1/L)\ \int_{-L/2}^{L/2} z_A(x)\ z_B(x+\tau)\,dx\right)}{R_q\,(A)\ R_q\,(B)}, \tag{15.1}$$

where τ is a shift distance between the profiles, and $R_q(A)$ and $R_q(B)$ are the root mean squared (rms) roughness values of the two profiles in the region of overlap. The CCF for areal topographies may be calculated by

$$\text{ACCF} = \frac{\sum_m \sum_n (\mathbf{A}_{mn} - \overline{\mathbf{A}})(\mathbf{B}_{mn} - \overline{\mathbf{B}})}{\left[\left(\sum_m \sum_n (\mathbf{A}_{mn} - \overline{\mathbf{A}})^2\right)\left(\sum_m \sum_n (\mathbf{B}_{mn} - \overline{\mathbf{B}})^2\right)\right]^{1/2}}, \quad (15.2)$$

where the two arrays $\mathbf{A}_{mn}$ and $\mathbf{B}_{mn}$ here are the digitized surface topography images $z_A(m,n)$ and $z_B(m,n)$, and m and n represent indices in the x and y directions. Eq. (15.2) is the discrete form of Eq. (15.1) extended to three dimensions. The CCF is computed as a function of displacement of two profiles, and the ACCF is computed as a function of alignment (displacement or rotation or both) of two surfaces. A curve is often generated to show the ACCF or CCF score as a function of alignment position, such as the relative displacement between two striation profiles. The terms, CCF_{max} and ACCF_{max}, are used to represent the largest correlation achievable for any alignment of the profiles or surfaces.

The CCF parameter is not a unique parameter for topography comparison because CCF is not sensitive to vertical scale differences. If two profile signatures A and B have exactly the same shape but different vertical scales, their CCF_{max} is still 1. A parameter, called the signature difference, D_s, is useful for quantifying both scale and shape differences between profile or topography signatures A and B. It may be calculated as the normalized rms amplitude of the difference profile or difference topography image. For example,

$$D_s = \frac{R_q^2(B-A)}{R_q^2(A)}, \quad (15.3)$$

where $R_q^2(A)$ is the mean square roughness of the reference signature $z_A(x)$, used here as a comparison reference. When two compared profile signatures are exactly the same, $D_s = 0$. In this way, D_s is a complementary parameter to CCF.

Weller et al. used the CCF_{max} parameter to compare topography images to identify spent cartridge cases from the same firearm slides (Weller et al., 2012). They started with ten 9 mm Luger caliber slides that were consecutively manufactured and that revealed both subclass characteristics and individual characteristics. This set of slides should be especially difficult to distinguish one from another. They obtained nine test fires from each slide, measured the topography of the breech face impression of all 90 cartridge cases and performed cross-correlation calculations for the 8010 combinations of pairs. There were 7290 nonmatching pairs, that is, fired from different guns and 720 matching pairs. A graph of their results is shown in Fig. 15.10. Although this set of consecutively manufactured slides potentially contains subclass characteristics, which could persist from one firearm to another, there is good separation between the cross-correlation values for the matching pairs and the nonmatching pairs.

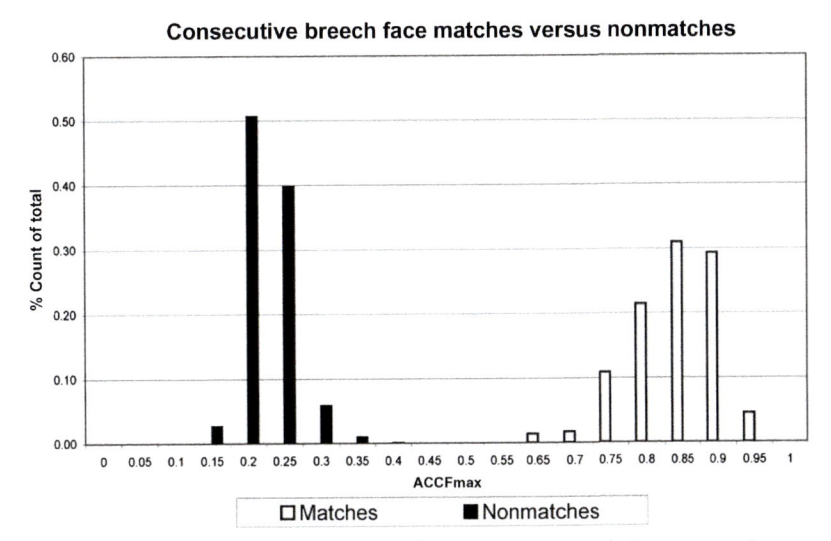

Consecutive breech face matches versus nonmatches

Figure 15.10 Data from Weller et al. (2012) showing cross-correlation comparisons using the CCF_{max} parameter among 90 test fires from 10 consecutively manufactured breech faces. No overlap of data was observed between matching (same breech face) and nonmatching (different breech face) comparisons. © 2012 American Academy of Forensic Sciences, reproduced with permission of John Wiley and Sons.

Several additional comparison methods have been developed, many of which involve sophisticated mathematics and computational algorithms. One method, closely related to CCF_{max}, which has been proposed for quantitative comparison is Chumbley et al.'s "T1" statistic (Chumbley et al., 2010). Their method takes pairs of striated toolmark profiles and searches for a region of best agreement (as measured by a correlation coefficient) within a user-defined window.

Methods like the CCF and the difference profile which rely on comparison of the entire surface may work well when the entire surface is reliably reproduced from test fire to test fire. However, when reliable individual marks only appear on a portion of the measured surfaces, these methods may have difficulty identifying this similarity. That is, if only a small portion of two surfaces are similar, then a score dependent on the entire surface will be lower than desired.

Advanced similarity methods
Congruent matching cells

Song has developed an analytical method that seems to improve on the basic approach of correlating entire images (Song, 2013). The method systematically divides measured 3D forensic images into "correlation cells" and uses cell correlation instead of correlation of the entire images. This is done because a firearm often produces characteristic marks, or individual characteristics, on only a portion of the surface. If a quantitative measure of correlation is obtained from the entire areas of a pair of images, the correlation accuracy may be relatively low because some *invalid regions* may be included in the correlation (Chu et al., 2010, 2013). If, instead, the correlation areas are divided into cells, the *valid regions* can be identified and the invalid regions can be eliminated. The use of a sufficiently large number of cells may provide a statistical foundation for estimating error rates from a well-characterized population. Typically, there may be 7×7 cells in an image of a breech face impression and on the order of 10,000 pixels in a cell.

The congruent matching cell (CMC) method works as follows. If topographies A and B originating from the same firearm are registered at their position of maximum correlation (Fig. 15.11), the registered cell pairs located in their common valid correlation regions, as shown by the solid cell pairs located in (A_1, B_1), (A_2, B_2), and (A_3, B_3), are characterized by

1. high pairwise topography similarity as quantified by a high value of the CCF maximum CCF_{max};
2. similar registration angles θ; and
3. similar $x-y$ spatial distribution patterns.

On the other hand, if the registered cell pairs are located in the invalid correlation regions of A and B, such as the dotted cells (a', a'', a''') and (b', b'', b''') in Fig. 15.11, or if they originate from different firearms, their maximum cross-correlation value CCF_{max} would be relatively low, and their cell arrays would show significant differences in $x-y$ distribution patterns and registration angles θ.

CMC pairs are therefore determined by four criteria, which must be satisfied simultaneously. The correlation value CCF_{max} must be larger than a chosen threshold T_{CCF}, and the registration angle θ and x, y registration positions are within the chosen threshold limits T_θ, T_x, and T_y, respectively.

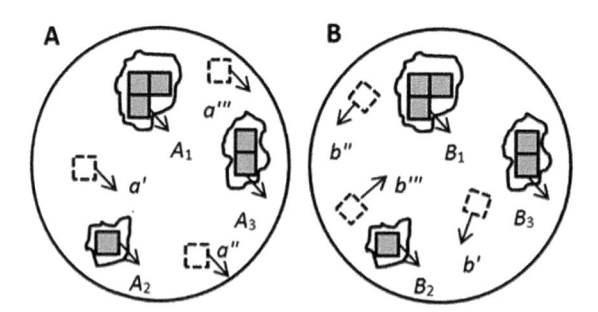

Figure 15.11 Schematic diagram of topographies *A* and *B* originating from the same firearm and registered at the position of maximum correlation. The six solid cell pairs are located in three valid correlated regions (A_1, B_1), (A_2, B_2), and (A_3, B_3). The three dotted cell pairs (a', b'), (a'', b''), and (a''', b''') are located in the invalid correlation region.

A fifth criterion is the number of matching cell pairs required to satisfy the above criteria in order to decide that two images are truly matching overall. Chu et al.'s (2013) initial results for a set of breech face impressions suggested that a pattern of six matching cells was a sufficient identification criterion for pairing up the breech face impressions that were studied. Thus when the number of CMC pairs of the correlated topographies A and B is equal to or greater than 6, A and B are concluded to be a match. Significant work has gone into developing a family of methods based on the CMC method. These approaches all utilize the same idea of identifying small patches of similarity, comparing them using a cross-correlation, and then quantifying the number of sufficiently similar regions.

Principal component analysis

An example of an alternative to the cross-correlation approach is the multivariate *machine learning* scheme discussed by Petraco (2011, 2012, 2013). A toolmark surface contains a tremendous amount of information. Most of the information is lost in summarizing the surface with a single number (i.e., a single univariate similarity metric). Instead, the machine learning approach derives a set of values to characterize surfaces. These vectors of *features* can be standard surface parameters or any other numerical or categorical values that potentially discriminate one surface from another, assuming that the surfaces are generated from different sources (ASME B46-2009, 2010; ISO 4287, 1997).

For the system constructed by Petraco et al., preprocessing first involves dropout/outlier interpolation. The surfaces are filtered into roughness and waviness components via the methods and standards outlined in the "Preprocessing" section. Registration with a quick cross-correlation between pairs of profiles is performed to find translations that yielded maximum, though not necessarily high, similarity (areas of overhang are padded with zeros) (Petraco et al., 2012, 2013; Gambino et al., 2011). Next, feature extraction is performed to produce feature vectors of the surfaces. Petraco then automatically extracts a set of features by applying principal component analysis (PCA) to a set of mean profiles. PCA is a mathematical method for analyzing points to identify ways in which they covary. It is often used to reduce the spatial dimensionality of points while maintaining desired mathematical properties. Intuitively, PCA transforms mathematical representations of the surface features to simplify their representation and to make these representations amenable to further analysis.

Once a feature set is chosen, the data are split randomly into training and testing sets. Machine learning algorithms are "trained" to recognize toolmarks in the training set with a high probability. The training is essentially a model fitting procedure with many methodologies to choose from. When a machine learning scheme is selected and fit, the discrimination functions are applied on the test set in order to estimate an overall error rate.

Choices must be made concerning the discrimination algorithm to be used and the method to assess intermediate error during the training/fitting process. Petraco et al. have found that the support vector machine (SVM) discrimination algorithm combined with PCA and hold-one-out cross-validation is a balanced machine learning scheme for forensic toolmark discrimination (Petraco et al., 2012, 2013; Petraco, 2011; Gambino et al., 2011). An SVM is a mathematical method for determining efficient decision rules in the absence of any knowledge of probability densities (Vapnik, 2013). Two surfaces can be compared using these rules to reach a "decision" regarding common origin. This procedure produces linear decision-making rules for identification, while minimizing the risk of error.

Feature-based methods

Recently, Lilien completed a development study of a commercial firearms identification system comprised of (1) a photometric stereo system with GelSight imprinting for measuring the surface topography of breech face impressions and (2) a feature-based system for characterizing the surface signatures and identifying matches (Weller et al., 2015; Johnson et al., 2011; Lilien, 2016). The basis of the comparison algorithm is the automated identification of 3D geometric features on each cartridge case surface. These features range in size from a few micrometers to hundreds of micrometers in diameter. When comparing the measured 3D surfaces of two cartridge cases, the algorithm looks for similar arrangements of similar features. The system was tested in cooperation with the Oakland and San Francisco police departments. One of the tests involved 47 firearms of the 9 mm Luger type and three test fires for each firearm. A round-robin comparison of all test fires should produce 141 different matches among more than 19,000 possible combinations. Lilien's software found 111 correct matches at the number one ranked position and with the criterion that the match score be greater than a certain threshold (i.e., that the algorithm should be confident). Notably, there were no false positives among the chosen matches. Lilien also developed a procedure to calculate a confidence level for these matches and claimed confidence levels of 99.99% or higher for 102 of the matches found. Fig. 15.12 shows a "confusion matrix" that plots the match scores as shades of gray for all comparisons. The overall array shows 141 × 141 comparisons. Cartridge cases fired by the same gun form close-knit 3-by-3 arrays straddling the central diagonal. Roughly 23 firearms stand out as highly identifiable, such as the one indicated by the blue arrow. Roughly nine firearms are much more difficult to identify, such as the one indicated by the red arrow, where the comparison of different cartridge cases from the same gun appears to give results that are indistinguishable from nonmatches in this chart. Entries exactly along the diagonal are trivial cases where a single image is compared with itself.

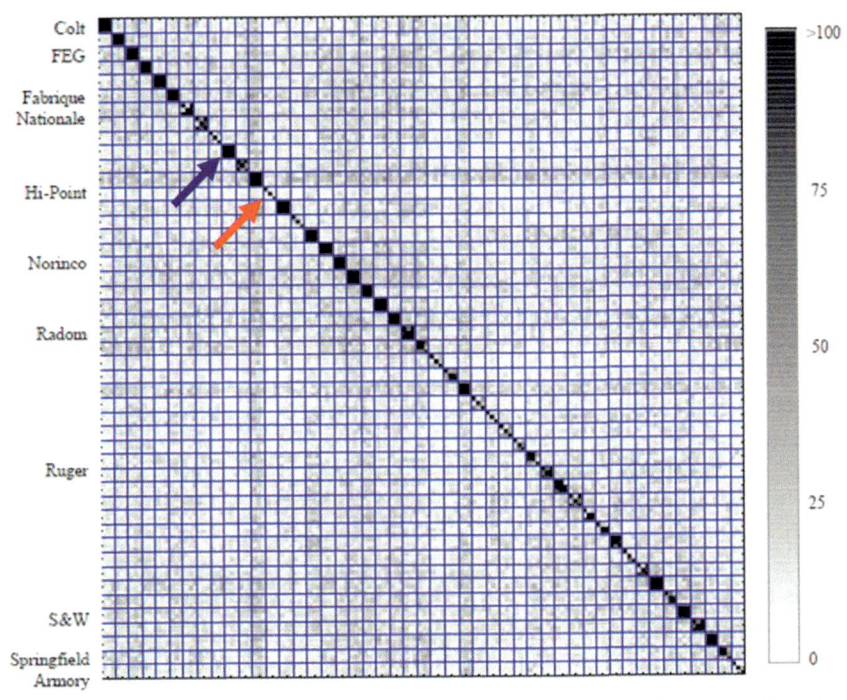

Figure 15.12 Results by Lilien of 19,981 comparisons among 141 cartridge cases (3 each from 47 firearms). "Each cell in the matrix corresponds to the match score between two casings (specified by the involved row and column)." The firearms are separated in the matrix by *blue lines*. All cartridge cases fired by the same firearm are grouped into 3 × 3 cells along the main diagonal. The *blue arrow* indicates an example where the separation of matches is well differentiated from nonmatches. The *red arrow* indicates an example where very little differentiation of matches from nonmatches is occurring (originally published by the National Institute of Justice, US Department of Justice) (Lilien, 2015a).

Statistical error rate estimation

Reporting an error rate for firearm identification—that is, the probability that an identification is actually a false positive or the probability that an exclusion is actually a false negative—has been singled out as a fundamental challenge in forensic science [National Research Council, 2008; National Research Council, 2009; President's Council of Advisors on Science and Technology (PCAST), 2016]. Coincidentally, there is much debate in the community about the desired output of a comparison algorithm. For example, there is growing consensus that a comparison algorithm should output a statistical measure quantifying the support for common origin and not a discrete conclusion of identification, inconclusive, or elimination. In this scenario the algorithm would report a likelihood ratio, probability, or coincidental match rate.

Central to any statistical model is the assembly and analysis of toolmark surfaces from a complete range of toolmark types. In other words, it is important to study and quantify the degree of geometric similarity and difference seen among known matches and known nonmatches for different firearm makes/models, calibers, manufacturing methods (e.g., granular, milled, broached, filed), ammunition type, ammunition material, and ammunition condition. Assembling such data is not an easy challenge. It is estimated that test fires from more than 10,000 firearms would need to be examined to establish this information. Work toward this critical research goal is underway.

Bayesian statistics

Bayesian statistics are based on Bayes' rule that defines the probability of a hypothesis in the presence of observed data.

$$p(H|D) = p(D|H) \times \frac{p(H)}{p(D)}$$

where H is the hypothesis, and D is the data. $p(H)$ is the probability of the hypothesis being true in the absence of any data, $p(D)$ is the probability of observed the data under any condition, $p(D|H)$ is the probability of observing the data given that the hypothesis is true, and $p(H|D)$ is the probability of the hypothesis being true given the observed data. We note that Bayes' rule is a mathematical truth and is not up for debate. However, what is unsettled is the numerical value of each term in the context of firearm forensics. Let us describe each of the four terms in additional detail. Consider that H is the hypothesis that two test fires were fired through the same firearm and that D is the computed (algorithm) match score between the two 3D topographies of these test fires.

- $p(H)$ is also known as the "prior" probability and represents the probability (between 0% and 100%) that the test fires came from the same firearm before you have even looked at the scans and before we know the similarity score D.
- $p(D)$ represents the probability (between 0% and 100%) that any pair of cartridge cases have a similarity score of D regardless of whether the two test fires came from the same or different firearms.
- $p(D|H)$ is also known as the "likelihood" and represents the probability (between 0% and 100%) that a pair of cartridge cases fired through the same firearm obtain a similarity score of D. It is called the likelihood because it measures how likely one is to see the data D given hypothesis H.
- $p(H|D)$ is also known as the "posterior" probability and represents the final desired probability (between 0% and 100%) that the two test fires came from the same firearm after (e.g., posterior) you have observed (e.g., computed) the similarity score of D.

Of these four terms, we want to get values for the three on the right side of the equation, so that we can compute the value $p(H|D)$ on the left. Unfortunately, it is very difficult to compute some of these terms. For example, $p(D|H)$ is computable that is given a large population of firearms. We would simply assemble an extensive set of firearms, collect pairs of test fires from each firearm, and compute the distribution of similarities we observe. We can then see how often a score of D arises. Unfortunately, it is not so easy to estimate $p(D)$ and $p(H)$. Remember that $p(H)$ represents the probability that the two test fires came from the same firearm before you've looked at the evidence. If the total population of firearms of the target class is say 50 million, is $p(H)$ simply 1 in 50,000,000? This may provide a lower bound; but in reality, not all 50 million firearms were in the same city where the crime took place, so $p(H)$ is probably a bit higher than that. Similarly, $p(D)$ depends on the number of firearms of the target class.

Despite the difficulty of estimating these terms, all is not lost. Conservative estimates can be made for each term, which provides a lower estimate (a lower bound) on the desired $p(H|D)$. Another approach is to compute a likelihood ratio which represents the ratio of probabilities between the two competing alternatives. In our example, the two alternatives are (H) that the two test fires came from the same firearm and (not H) that the two test fires came from different firearms. The likelihood ratio is thus $P(D|H)/P(D|\text{not } H)$. In other words the probability of observing similarity score D given that the two test fires were fired through the same firearm divided by the probability of observing similarity score D given that the two test fires were fired through different firearms. Recall that both these likelihoods can be estimated using a sufficiently large sample set of test fires.

The use and implications of Bayesian probabilities and likelihood ratios goes beyond the scope of this book. Because they can be estimated with less difficulty, these quantities are generally used instead of $p(H|D)$ to quantify the degree of evidence and support for a hypothesis, but both require careful application and appropriate data estimation to be utilized correctly. We expect that researchers will build these models into software that can be used by the firearms examiner. The models should be supported by large peer-reviewed studies capable of validating their accuracy. In the future, it is possible that an examiner will compare two pieces of evidence, reach their conclusion, and then submit the scans to an automated scoring function to provide a quantified degree of statistical confidence which can be included in their final report.

Standards, traceability, and uncertainty for topography measurements

Instrument calibration and measurement traceability is important when performing comparisons of surface topography, especially if the topography images to be compared are generated by different instruments. For example, the CMC method, which divides images into small cells and uses pairwise cell correlations, quantifies both the topography similarity of the correlated cell pairs and their pattern congruency. Both metrics are based on geometrical topography measurement with traceability to the SI unit of length.

According to the *International Vocabulary of Metrology* (VIM), metrological traceability is defined as "property of a measurement result whereby the result can be related to a reference through a documented unbroken chain of calibrations, each contributing to the measurement uncertainty" (BIPM 2012) (see also ASCLD/LAB, 2013).

In light of the earlier definition, three key steps for establishing metrological traceability and quality assurance for the topography measurements and imaging correlations of ballistics signatures have been proposed (Song et al., 2010):
- the establishment of reference standards for topography measurements;
- a chain of comparisons relating topography measurements of the reference standards to topography measurements of bullets, cartridge cases, and toolmarks; and
- the estimation of uncertainty in the measured quantities and/or the estimation of error rates in classifications and firearms identifications based on topography measurements.

We confine the discussion of these issues primarily to topography profiles and images.

Physical standards

Physical and documentary standards are critical for maintaining control in surface topography measurements.

Over the years, crime laboratories have implemented quality control (QC) bullets and cartridge cases for testing the accuracy and reproducibility of their surface imaging systems. These are bullets and cartridge cases fired from a single firearm, which is kept in the central laboratory as a reference and which may be typical of firearms recovered during investigations. This firearm could be used successively over time to provide artifacts (QC bullets) for different laboratories or at different times. However, the QC bullets could have problems with uniformity and traceability. In the late 1990s the ATF expressed the need for physical standards that would be more stable over time and more reproducible. In response, NIST developed SRM bullets and cartridge cases, SRMs 2460 and 2461 (NIST, 2013), respectively (Fig. 15.13). These highly reproducible standards enable users of optical imaging and topography measuring systems to test the quality and stability of their systems from time to time and from one place to another.

For topography measuring systems, master profiles and topography images of the standard bullets and cartridge cases, respectively, are available online for downloading

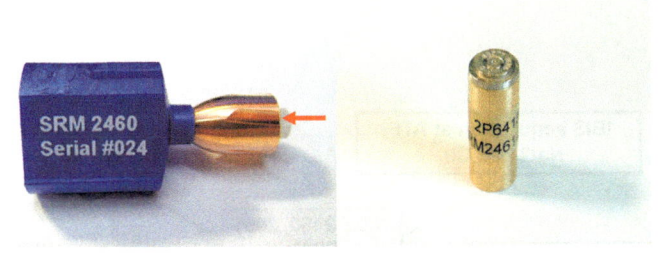

Figure 15.13 An Standard Reference Material (SRM) 2460 standard bullet (left) and a SRM 2461 standard cartridge case (right). The *red arrow* indicates one of six land engraved areas around the periphery of the standard bullet.

and correlation with users' own topography measurements (Bui and Vorburger, 2007). For crime labs participating in the ATF's NIBIN with IBIS optical imaging systems (Ultra Electronics, accessed 2019), the ATF maintains *Golden Images* of bullets and cartridge cases, acquired with IBIS workstations, to which NIBIN users can correlate their own acquired images (Song et al., 2012; Vorburger et al., 2014). Users with other types of optical systems may develop their own Golden Images using the SRMs as well.

A chain of comparisons

An example flow diagram for the establishment of a Traceability and Quality System using the SRM materials is shown in Fig. 15.14 (Vorburger et al., 2014). For topography profiles and images, we emphasize the right side of the chart. The topographies of the SRM bullets are nearly identical to one another as are the topographies of the SRM cartridge cases. These similarities are quantified by the cross-correlation maximum and the fractional difference parameters quoted on the SRM certificates of calibration. Most of the units of the SRMs are made available to industry, and a few are held at NIST as check standards for NIST's own topography measurement QC. Since 2003, one of them, SRM 2460, Serial No. 001, land engraved area (LEA) 1, has been routinely measured and correlated with a NIST master topography image more than 35 times and has demonstrated high measurement reproducibility: all the correlation values CCF_{max} are higher than 99% (Song et al., 2012).

Topography images of the master surfaces are available online and may be downloaded for correlation. These include the profiles of all six LEAs of SRM 2460 Standard Bullet masters and master topography images of the breech face impression, firing pin impression, and ejector mark of the SRM 2461 Standard Cartridge Case. By correlating measurements of the user's own SRM with the master profiles or images, the user can provide evidence that his/her topography measurements are accurate and that the user's system can measure bullet and cartridge case surfaces similar to those of

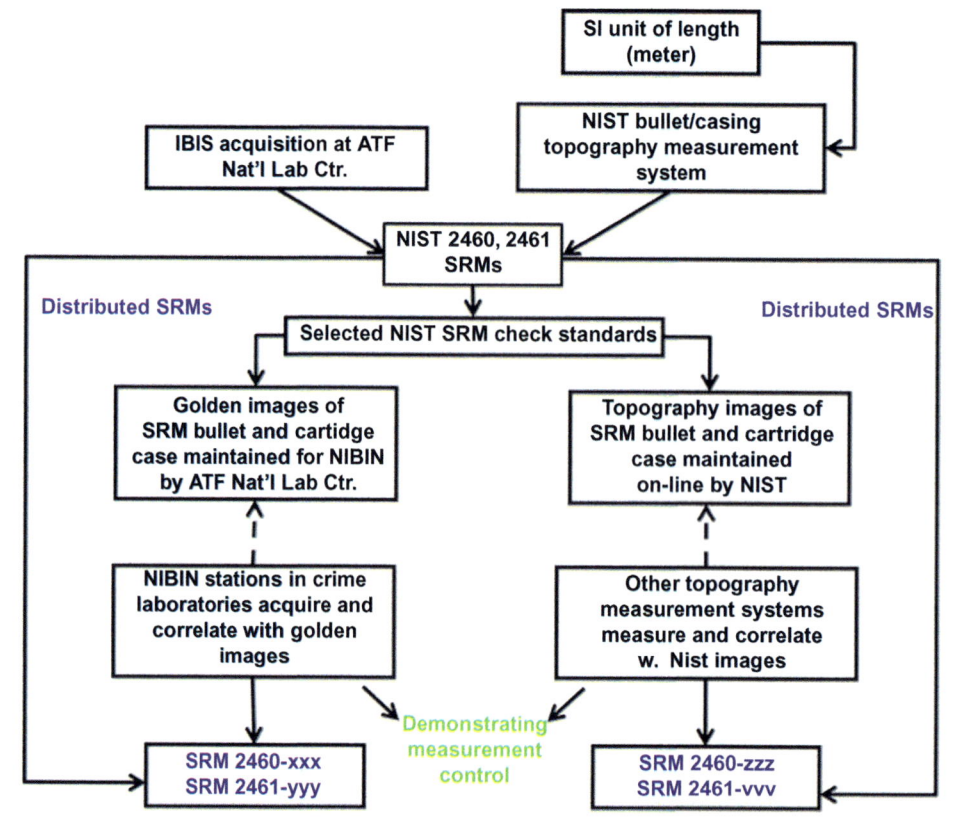

Figure 15.14 Establishment of a traceability and quality system for NIBIN acquisitions and correlations.

the SRM standard. Control charts can be used to further demonstrate that the system is stable over time (Song et al., 2012; Vorburger et al., 2014).

Uncertainty and error rate

The issue of uncertainty in topography measurements of bullets and cartridge cases largely amounts to the specific task of calculating an error rate for making identifications and exclusions, about whether there is a common origin for a pair of surfaces, using topography data and software analysis. The usual approaches to calculating uncertainties in the measured properties of a single object do not apply when two surfaces are compared for their similarity. Quantifiers of similarity between them need to be established as well as uncertainties in those quantifiers. For conventional, open parameters of similarity, such as cross-correlation and relative difference, the results are unitless, and traceability to SI units is not relevant (Ma et al., 2004). Calculation of uncertainty and error rate for ballistic evaluations is still an evolving research issue.

We make the following observations about uncertainty using cross-correlation as an example of a similarity metric. Sources of measurement error are likely to reduce the calculated cross-correlation between two measured topography images, not to increase it. If two topographies are measured by the same instrument, systematic sources of error are likely to cancel out. If so, they would not change the accuracy of the result. If they do not cancel out, the resulting errors in a series of correlations are likely to lead to variations in the results that can be recognized as statistical uncertainty. If two topographies are measured by different instruments and even more so by different methods, errors in either measurement lead again to reduced correlation values. Since errors of measurement generally lead to reduced correlation, we do not expect these errors to cause a decision error when a *positive identification* between two surfaces is made based on correlation results. However, if the correlation results suggest a choice of *exclusion* or *inconclusiveness*, the probability of error should be estimated.

Ballistics identification systems in the crime lab

Virtual comparison microscopy

The analysis of the microscopic features of a measured 3D surface topography on the computer and without physical access to the original specimen is referred to as VCM or virtual microscopy (VM) (Senin et al., 2006). A full discussion of VCM is beyond the scope of this chapter; however, we will point out a few advantages and novel uses of VCM as compared to traditional light comparison microscopy (LCM).

First, VCM allows instant access to remote or historic data without the need to requisition or physically transfer the items to your possession. This is a significant advantage when casework requires the analysis of specimens from a different physical location (e.g., requesting a specimen from a different laboratory within the same state system). All that is required for comparison is the digital data file that can be transferred without the risk of damage to the original specimen.

Second, VCM offers advantages for training, proficiency testing, and validation studies. It allows for training examples to be shared worldwide, providing trainees at any location the opportunity to see the most useful examples of specific or rare phenomena. Proficiency tests and validation studies can be conducted using a core set of scanned samples, thereby eliminating test set to test-set variability that is inherent to physical tests and studies. In addition, tests can be more easily "injected" into an examiner's digital casework thereby eliminating the potential effects of knowing that one is being tested.

Third, VCM can improve lab efficiency of verifications and blind verifications. Using VCM, verifications can be conducted remotely by examiners at another location. VCM verification can be truly blind in that all information from the first examiner's analysis can be hidden from the verifier.

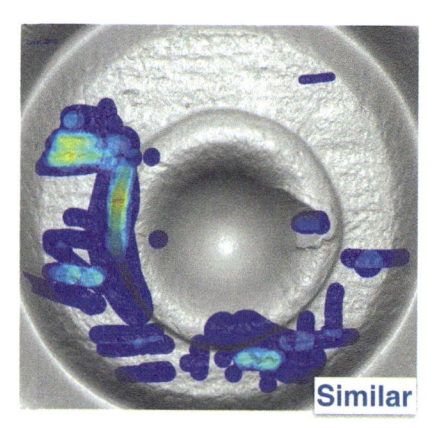

Figure 15.15 Similarity annotation map from the study of Duez et al. Regions in dark blue were marked as similar individual characteristics by a small number of participants. Regions in yellow and red were marked by almost all participants. Images like this can provide insight into the examiner's decision-making process and can serve as teaching points if mistakes are made.

Current studies are validating the use of VCM for firearm and toolmark analysis. Duez et al. conducted a study with 46 qualified firearms examiners and 3D surface topographies collected on a Cadre TopMatch 3D scanning system (Duez et al., 2018). The study design included two test sets each with three knowns and four unknowns. Participants were asked to complete a comparison worksheet and to annotate the surfaces of provided topographies to indicate regions of similarity and difference (Fig. 15.15). This annotation map highlights the regions of the surface that were marked as similar while making an identification. The reported conclusions of all 46 firearms examiners (368 of 368 conclusions) were correct.

Data exchange

In theory, any system that measures surface topographies in standard units should be able to exchange data with any other system, which does the same. In 2014 the Open Forensic Metrology Consortium (OpenFMC), a group of academic, government, and industry researchers agreed to support the use of the X3P file format for the exchange of 3D surface topography data in firearm and toolmark analysis. The X3P data file is an ISO standard (ISO 25178-72:2017) that can be implemented by any vendor, researcher, government agency, or interested party. X3P is simply a container for the efficient and accurate transfer of 3D surface topographies. It has been used to exchange data between measurement systems within multiple disciplines (including firearm and toolmark analysis). X3P is intended to be extended for application-specific use. OpenFMC has created a firearm specific data record that allows an X3P file to contain firearm specific metadata, such as firearm make/model, imaged region of interest, caliber, cartridge case material, primer material, bullet diameter, and bullet weight.

While it is not required to use this firearm specific data record, it is OpenFMC's hope that vendors and labs will adopt it for data exchange. Vendors participating in OpenFMC have expressed this intent. Virtually all vendors making equipment for 3D imaging within firearm forensics are part of the OpenFMC group.

Algorithm requirements

Comparison algorithms should meet three criteria to be used within a crime lab. First, the score should be statistically grounded in that numbers should be consistent where a score of k in two different runs should provide the same amount of confidence and support. Algorithms that are consistent in this way can form the basis of a statistical model. Second, the algorithm should be explainable in that a firearms examiner should be able to describe in a few sentences the basic principles on which it works. This explanation should not include PhD-level scientific detail nor should it include equations. Finally, the algorithm should be interpretable in that the algorithm should be able to explain, typically through visual representation, evidence to support the reported score. For example, algorithms have recently been developed for visually representing regions of geometric similarity through colored shading (Fig. 15.16) (Lilien, 2015b; Ott et al., 2017).

Standards and guidelines

In 2014 NIST and the Department of Justice formed the Organization of Scientific Area Committees (OSAC) for the establishment of standards and guidelines for forensic science. The Firearms and Toolmarks Subcommittee organized within the Physics and Pattern Interpretation Committee is creating standards to ensure accurate and high-quality results for 3D topographic analysis including VCM. When these standards

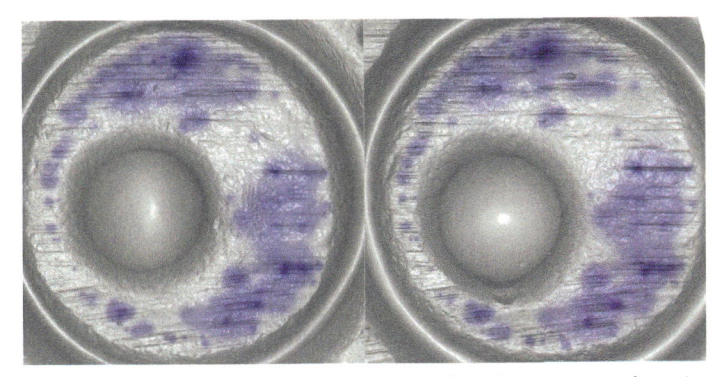

Figure 15.16 Heatmap visualization. The comparison algorithm can produce images like that shown here where the identified geometric similarity between two cartridge cases is highlighted in blue. Darker blue indicates more geometric similarity, and unshaded regions indicate that the algorithm did not find similarity (Lilien, 2015b).

are published, they will provide excellent guidance to those interested in utilizing this new technology. It will be highly recommended that labs comply with the approved standards.

Shift from the lab

There is a recent shift where some systems are moving their focus from the crime laboratory to early analysis within police departments. That is, the vendor is shifting the use of the ballistics identification system from a high-end laboratory instrument to a rapid investigative tool. We advise readers which are part of crime labs to keep an eye on this transition and to consider 3D measurement systems, which calibrate against known reference standards, comply with OSAC and AFTE standards, and support the X3P file format. Through the use of these standards, one can guarantee the quality and accuracy of the measured 3D surface topography.

Ongoing issues and opportunities

This review has been largely concentrated on the emerging field of surface topography measurements and analysis for ballistic surfaces and toolmarks and aimed to provide useful information to surface metrologists and ballistics examiners in their common field of interest. Whether VCM methods come to rival or outstrip, the usefulness of conventional optical microscopy will likely depend on the following several factors:

Outliers and dropouts

Methods for measuring 3D surface topographies often produce dropouts (or nonmeasured points) and outliers. These erroneous point measurements must be identified as such by the measurement system software. A number of statistical methods have been used to discern and minimize the effect of these erroneous data points in the stored data. However, a standard approach for fired ballistics and toolmarks may need to be defined in order to promote interoperability among topography images obtained with different optical methods.

Speed

Many of the optical topography methods discussed here require the collection of lots of images, perhaps 1000, as the surface is scanned through different heights relative to the microscope housing. Some of these systems therefore require significant time to measure an entire surface. One should inquire about and be aware of the imaging times of various systems.

Expense

Currently, most topography measuring systems cost significantly more than conventional microscopes—roughly speaking, the one costs more than $100,000 and the other, less than $100,000.

Measurement accuracy and resolution

As described earlier, not all 3D measurement systems collect data at the same sampling resolution, and pixel size is not always representative of the size of features, which can be resolved. That is, not all 3 μm/pixel sampling scanners are the same. In addition, some systems may display a higher resolution 2D image on top of a 3D surface measured with lower resolution, providing the illusion of a 3D surface measured at higher resolution than is actually the case. Measuring the surface against known microscale references is one way to assess the resolution of these systems.

As of this writing, it is not yet known what measurement resolution is required for accurate human and algorithm—based comparisons. As the topographic resolution decreases, the surface loses fine features that may be critical for analysis. For example, at lower resolution fine striated marks such as those on a bullet land or a cartridge case aperture shear may be lost. In place of fine striations, one may only see a blurred region. Topographies should be captured at a resolution that allows human and algorithm—based comparison at a level comparable to or better than traditional LCM.

Uncertainty

Topography methods coupled with advanced statistical analyses have finally provided an opportunity to address the question of uncertainty in firearm and toolmark identifications. Several case studies are beginning to calculate an error rate for identification and exclusion of matching surfaces. In some cases, those error rates have been impressively small even for consecutively produced barrels or slides or tools. However, the most advanced work has so far been performed on small databases or on small collections of firearms or other materials. Scaling up the models to large databases, such as the NIBIN, and adjusting the statistical model to produce believable error rates for real criminal cases are a major challenge and a major opportunity for researchers. Once accomplished, such a development will pave the way to calculating error rates for firearms identification for real court cases, first as an independent approach to support conclusions drawn by firearms experts using comparison microscopes, and possibly afterward, to stand on its own as admissible evidence in court in a manner similar to DNA evidence.

Conclusions

This chapter provided a high-level introduction to the emerging field of 3D topographic imaging and analysis within the firearm and toolmark discipline. Although the focus of this chapter was not on vendor-specific ballistic identification systems, to the best of our knowledge, all systems currently on the market utilize one or more of the described scan acquisition and analysis methods. Rather than attempting to drill down into too many specific studies, which will likely be replaced by newer results by the time you read this chapter, we attempted to provide the framework for the technology that is less likely to change.

Labs will soon transition to the use of VCM. The first step of this is already underway, and crime labs are beginning to validate 3D VM for use by qualified firearms examiners. In some cases, if a conclusion can be reached from the 3D topography, then it is not necessary to go back to examine the physical evidence. The second step will be the development of statistical functions capable of providing an examiner a quantitative statistical measure to support reported conclusions. We do not see the role of the firearms examiner going away anytime soon as a human still needs to lead the analysis, perform the comparison, and reach a conclusion. The computational algorithm will support the examiner's report with a quantified number.

It is important that any 3D system utilized in forensic work conducts a series of performance checks designed to assess its accuracy both before and during active use. That is, all systems should be calibrated against known microscale reference standards as described in the previous section to ensure the accuracy of the measurement system.

To ensure interoperability and data exchange between labs, it is critical that all systems and all labs support the ISO standard X3P file format for the exchange of surface topography data when it has been collected in standard units.

Acknowledgments

The authors are grateful to B. Muralikrishnan, J.H. Yen, and M.E. Nadal for their careful review of the manuscript and to X.A. Zheng (Fig. 15.1), F. Helmli (Figs. 15.4 and 15.5), and T.J. Weller (Fig. 15.10) for use of their illustrations. The work was supported in part by the NIST Special Programs Office.

References

AFTE Committee for the Advancement of the Science of Firearm and Toolmark Identification, 2011. Theory of identification as it relates to toolmarks: revised. AFTE J. 43 (4), 287.

AFTE Criteria for Identification Committee, 1992. Theory of identification, range of striae comparison reports and modified glossary definitions. AFTE J. 24 (3), 336–340.

Ainsworth, K., 2017. The benefit of frangible bullets. Shooting illustrated (on-line). Available from: <https://www.shootingillustrated.com/articles/2017/1/30/the-benefits-of-frangible-bullets/> (accessed 03.11.18.).

Altintas, Y., Chan, P., 1992. In-process detection and suppression of chatter in milling. Int. J. Mach. Tools Manuf. 32 (3), 329–347.

Altintas, Y., Weck, M., 2004. Chatter stability of metal cutting and grinding. CIRP Ann. 53 (2), 619–642.

American Society of Crime Laboratory Directors. Measurement Traceability Policy. Laboratory Accreditation Board. <http://www.ascld-lab.org>.

Anderson, E., 1984. Makarov pistol. AFTE J. 16 (4), 70–74.

Association of Firearm and Tool Mark Examiners, 2018. AFTE Bylaws (On-Line). Available from: <https://afte.org/about-us/bylaws> (accessed 02.11.18.).

Association of Firearm and Tool Mark Examiners, 2013. Association of Firearm and Tool Mark Examiners Glossary, sixth ed.

Barnes, F., Woodard, W., 2016a. Cartridges of the World: A Complete and Illustrated Reference for More Than 1500 Cartridges. Krause Publications, p. 218.

Barnes, F., Woodard, W., 2016b. Cartridges of the World: A Complete and Illustrated Reference for More Than 1500 Cartridges. Krause Publications, p. 368.

Begic-Hajdarevic, D., et al., 2014. Experimental study on the highspeed machining of hardened steel. Procedia Eng. 69, 291–295.

Binder, M., et al., 2017. Abrasive wear behavior under metal cutting conditions. Wear 376–377, 165–171.

Bolton-King, R., 2017. Rifling methods of factory fitted 9 mm Luger (9 × 19 mm) pistol barrels: a reference resource. AFTE J. 49 (4), 225–238.

Braswell, C., 2008. "A" on primers. In: On-line AFTE Forums. AFTE Message Board. Available from: <http://forum.afte.org/index.php?topic = 4903.msg26009#msg26009> (accessed 02.11.18.).

Bruce, I., 2014. Previous cycling/firing marks, reloading marks and primer marks on winchester 9 × 19 mm remanufactured ammunition. AFTE J. 46 (2), 152–156.

Bussard, M., et al., 2017a. Ammo Encyclopedia: For All Rimfire and Centerfire Cartridges, plus Shotshells. Blue Book Publications, Minneapolis, MN, p. 140.

Bussard, M., et al., 2017b. Ammo Encyclopedia: For All Rimfire and Centerfire Cartridges, plus Shotshells. Blue Book Publications, Minneapolis, MN, p. 152.

Carter, A., 2013. Mastery of Metals: Federal HST and Guard Dog Loads. American Rifleman. On-line. Available from: <https://www.americanrifleman.org/articles/2013/12/23/mastery-of-metals-federal-hst-and-guard-dog-loads/> (accessed 03.11.18.).

Chang, H., Wang, J., 2008. A stochastic grinding force model considering random grit distribution. Int. J. Mach. Tools Manuf. 48 (12–13), 1335–1344.

Charman, S., 2013. The forensic confirmation bias: a problem of evidence integration, not just evidence evaluation. J. Appl. Res. Mem. Cogn. 2 (1), 56–58.

Clow, C., 2008a. Bullets and cartridge cases identified to a single unknown firearm using magazine marks. AFTE J. 40 (3), 309–311.

Clow, C., 2008b. A method for the production of test specimens for the comparison of bullet seating marks. AFTE J. 40 (3), 296–299.

Clow, C., 2011a. Identification of a bullet jacket to a lead core. AFTE J. 43 (3), 267–268.

Clow, C., 2011b. Breechface impressions produced on unfired cartridges by Hi-Point firearms. AFTE J. 43 (4), 342–344.

Commonwealth of Massachusetts v. Heang, 2011. Case No. SJC-10376 (Appellate Court of Massachusetts, 2011).

Conrad, W.E., 1979. Comparisons of nyclad ammunition. AFTE J. 11 (4), 116–117.

D'Acunto, M., 2003. Wear and diffusive processes. Tribol. Int. 36 (7), 553–558.

Daubert v. Merrell Dow Pharm., Inc., 509 U.S. 579, 593-94 (1993).

Davis, J., 2010. Primer cup properties and how they affect identification. AFTE J. 42 (1), 3–22.

DeFrance, C., VanArsdale, M., 2003. Validation study of electrochemical rifling. AFTE J. 35 (1), 35–37.

Dillon, J.H., 1991. The manufacture of conventional smokeless powder. AFTE J. 23 (2), 682–688.

Dutton, G., 2002. Firearms identification, comparison microscopes and the spencer lens company. AFTE J. 34 (2), 186–198.

Dyvesveen, G., 2000. Identification of tool marks from a priming tool in reloaded ammunition. AFTE J. 32 (2), 54–55.

Eastham, G., 2010. CBC primer stamp 2010. In: Online AFTE Forums. AFTE Message Board. Available from: <http://forum.afte.org/index.php?topic = 6504.msg3470#msg34704> (accessed 03.11.18.).

Fadul Jr., T.G., et al., 2013. An empirical study to improve the scientific foundation of forensic firearm and tool mark identification utilizing 10 consecutively manufactured slides. AFTE J. 45 (4), 376–393.

Fang, N., Dewhurst, P., 2005. Slip-Line modeling of built-up edge formation in machining. Int. J. Mech. Sci. 47 (7), 1079–1098.

Fang, X.D., Jawahir, I.S., 1992. The effects of progressive tool wear and tool restricted contact on chip breakability in machining. Wear 160, 243–252.

Federal Ammunition, 2018. Personal Defense Hydra-Shok Low Recoil. On-line. Available from: <https://www.federalpremium.com/products/handgun/premium-personal-defense/personal-defense-hydrashok-low-recoil/pd380hs1-h> (accessed 04.11.18.).

Finklestein, N., et al., 2005. Ejection port marks on cartridge cases discharged from glock pistols. AFTE J. 37 (4), 346–351.

Flater, J., 2002. Manufacturing marks on Winchester USA brand 9mm Luger primers. AFTE J. 34 (3), 315.

Fukuda, K., Morita, T., 2017. Physical model of adhesive wear in early stage of sliding. Wear 376–377, 1528–1533.

Haber, R.N., Haber, L., 2013. The culture of science: bias and forensic evidence. J. Appl. Res. Mem. Cogn. 2 (1), 65–67.

Hall, E., 1983. F.I.E. Titanic up-date. AFTE J. 15 (1), 33–53.

Hall, A.L., Fairhaven, N.Y., 1900. The missile and the weapon. Buffalo Med. J. LV–XXXIX, 727–736.

Hambli, R., 2001. Blanking tool wear modeling using the finite element method. Int. J. Mach. Tools Manuf. 41 (12), 1815–1829.

Hamby, J.E., Thorpe, J.W., 1999. The history of firearm and tool mark identification. AFTE J. 31 (3), 266–284.

Hart, R., 1977. An unrifled bullet at 4000 FPS. AFTE J. 9 (1), 55–56.

Hartman, S., 2014. Feed ramp marks produced from a ruger model LCP. AFTE J. 46 (1), 59–66.

Hernández, J., et al., 2006. Modelling and experimental analysis of the effects of tool wear on form errors in stainless steel blanking. J. Mater. Process. Technol. 180 (1–3), 143–150.

Higley, J., Briggs, V., 2007. Notes on Hammer Forged Barrels (On-Line). Available from: <http://biblioteka.mycity-military.com/biblioteka/Diemaco/NotesOnHammerForgedBarrels.pdf> (accessed 03.11.18.).

Hou, Z., Komanduri, R., 2003. On the mechanics of the grinding process, Part I—Stochastic nature of the grinding process. Int. J. Mach. Tools Manuf. 43 (15), 1579–1593.

Hou, Z., Komanduri, R., 2004. On the mechanics of the grinding process, Part III—Thermal analysis of the abrasive cut-off operation. Int. J. Mach. Tools Manuf. 44 (2–3), 271–289.

Hunsinger, M., 2013. Metal injection molded strikers and extractors in a Smith & Wesson Model M&P pistol. AFTE J. 45 (1), 21–29.

Izwan, N., et al., 2016. Prediction of material removal rate in die-sinking electrical discharge machining. Procedia Manuf. 5, 658–668.
Kassin, S., et al., 2013. The forensic confirmation bias: problems, perspectives, and proposed solutions. J. Appl. Res. Mem. Cogn. 2 (1), 42–52.
Kennington, R.H., 1999. Identification of cartridge cases fired in different firearms: pre-Identified cartridges. AFTE J. 31 (1), 15–19.
Kerkhoff, W., Alberink, I., Mattijssen, E., 2017. Magazine influence on cartridge case ejection patterns with glock pistols. J. Forensic. Sci. 63 (1), 239–243.
Kibbe, R., Neely, J., Meyer, R., White, Warren, 1999a. Machine Tool Practices, sixth ed. Prentice Hall, Columbus, OH, p. 631.
Kibbe, R., Neely, J., Meyer, R., White, Warren, 1999b. Machine Tool Practices, sixth ed. Prentice Hall, Columbus, OH, p. 516.
Kim, D., 2006. Identification of frangible bullets in case work. AFTE J. 38 (3), 239–241.
Klees, G., 1997. Aberrant manufacturing marks on federal ammunition. AFTE J. 29 (1), 21–23.
Ko, D., Kim, B., 2000. Development of an analytical scheme to predict the need for tool regrinding in shearing processes. Int. J. Mach. Tools Manuf. 40 (9), 1329–1349.
Koppl, R., Krane, D., 2016. Minimizing and leveraging bias in forensic science. In: Kesselheim, A., Robertson, C. (Eds.), Blinding as a Solution to Bias Strengthening Biomedical Science, Forensic Science, and Law. Academic Press.
Kramer, S., 2012. Subclass characteristics on firing pins manufactured by 'metal injection molding'. AFTE J. 44 (4), 364–366.
Laakso, V.A., et al., 2018. The mystery of missing feed force—the effect of friction models, flank wear and ploughing on feed force in metal cutting simulations. J. Manuf. Processes 33, 268–277.
Lamraoui, M., et al., 2014. Indicators for monitoring chatter in milling based on instantaneous angular speeds. Mech. Syst. Sig. Process. 44 (1–2), 72–85.
Lee, M., et al., 2016. Subclass carryover in Smith & Wesson M&P 15-22 rifle firing pins. AFTE J. 48 (1), 27–32.
Lightstone, L., 2010. The potential for and persistence of subclass characteristics on the breech faces of SW40VE Smith & Wesson Sigma pistols. AFTE J. 42 (4), 308–322.
Liu, R., et al., 2017. An investigation of side flow during chip formation in orthogonal cutting. Procedia Manuf. 10, 568–577.
Lomoro, V.J., 1977. F.I.E. Titanic up-date. AFTE J. 9 (2), 64–75.
Lopez, L., Grew, S., 2000. Consecutively machined Ruger bolt faces. AFTE J. 32 (1), 19–24.
Maddox, Z., 2017. STI Warranty Dept. E-mail.
Malkin, S., 2008a. Grinding Technology: Theory and Application of Machining withAbrasives, second ed. Industrial Press, p. 122.
Malkin, S., 2008b. Grinding Technology: Theory and Application of Machining withAbrasives, second ed. Industrial Press, p. 112.
Marks, L.S., 1916. Mechanical Engineers' Handbook, first ed. McGraw-Hill Company, New York, p. 1449.
Martini Research Group, 2018. Introduction to Tribology. On-line. Available from: <http://faculty1.ucmerced.edu/amartini/tribology.shtml> (accessed 03.11.18.).
Maruoka, R., 1994. Guilty before the crime?—the potential for a possible misidentification or elimination. AFTE J. 26 (3), 206–213.
Maruoka, R., Ball, P., 1995. Guilty before the crime II? AFTE J. 27 (1), 20–21.
McCarthy, W.J., Smith, R.E., 1968. Machine Tool Technology, third ed. McKnight & McKnight Publishing Company, Bloomington, IL, p. 501.
McCombs, N., 2001. Case report: ejection port marks: a signature of Beretta. AFTE J. 33 (3), 251–252.
McCombs, N., Hamman, J., 2016. Recognizing reloaded ammunition: an examination and evaluation of reloading marks. AFTE J. 48 (4), 215–222.
McConaghy, J.L., 1999. Federal's new frangible ammunition. AFTE J. 31 (1), 53–54.
Mechanical Engineers' Handbook. McGraw-Hill, 1916.
Mikko, D., Miller, J., 2008. Frangible bullets, dynamic research technologies. AFTE J. 40 (1), 91–95.

Miller, J., 2000. An examination of two consecutively rifles barrels and a review of the literature. AFTE J. 32 (3), 259–270.
Molans, P., 2018. Primers With Manufactured Marks on Them. E-mail.
Munoa, J., et al., 2016. Chatter suppression techniques in metal cutting. CIRP Ann. 65 (2), 785–808.
Muñoz-Escalona, P., Cassier, Z., 1998. Influence of the critical cutting speed on the surface finish of turned steel. Wear 218 (1), 103–109.
Murdock, J., Petraco, N.D.K., Thornton, J., Neel, M., Weller, T., Thompson, R., et al., 2017. The development and application of random match probabilities to firearm and toolmark identification. J. Forensic. Sci. 62 (3), 619–625.
National Research Council, 2008. Ballistic Imaging. National Academies Press, Washington, DC, pp. 3, 20, 82.
National Research Council, 2009. Strengthening Forensic Science in the United States—A Path Forward. National Academies Press, Washington, D.C., pp. 5–20, 6–2.
Patty, B., 2000. Manufacturing marks on primers. AFTE J. 32 (3), 300–301.
Pendleton, D., et al., 2011. Identification of three 000 buck pellets fired from a sawed-off .410 bore shotgun. AFTE J. 43 (2), 176–178.
Pilcher, L.C., 2004. Lead free frangible ammunition: a closer look. AFTE J. 36 (4), 281–285.
President's Council of Advisors on Science and Technology (PCAST), 2016. Forensic Science in Criminal Courts: Ensuring the Scientific Validity of Feature-Comparison Methods.
Price, J., et al., 2008. Investment casting in barrel manufacture of the thunder five. AFTE J. 40 (3), 303–308.
Qi, H.S., et al., 1997. Experimental investigation of contact behaviour in grinding. Tribol. Int. 30 (4), 283–294.
Quereau, A., 2018. Another (new!) elliptical FPI: Sarlsimaz. In: On-line AFTE Forums. AFTE Message Board. Available from: <http://forum.afte.org/index.php?topic = 13148.msg70807;topicseen#new> (accessed 02.11.18.).
Raines, M., 2015. The effects of frangible ammunition on the structure of striae created by a rifled barrel and the value of frangible ammunition for examination. AFTE J. 47 (1), 4–14.
Ramasawmy, H., Blunt, L., 2004. Effect of EDM process parameters on 3D surface topography. J. Mater. Process. Technol. 148 (2), 155–164.
Rayer, R.J., 2007. Molybdenum disulfide (MoS_2) influence on fired bullets. AFTE J. 39 (3), 199–204.
Reitz, J., 1975. Unfired cartridge phenomenon. AFTE J. 7 (2), 103–104.
Rivera, G.C., 2007. Subclass characteristics in Smith & Wesson SW40VE sigma pistols. AFTE J. 39 (3), 247–253.
Robinson, M.K., 1996. Another manufactured tool mark. AFTE J. 28 (3), 164–165.
Rosatti, C.J., 2000. Examination of four consecutively manufactured bunter tools. AFTE J. 32 (1), 49–50.
Scala, G., 2006. Subclass characteristics of ruger firearms. In: 2006 Annual Training Conference. Association of Firearm and Tool Mark Examiners, Springfield, MA.
Shem, R.J., 1993. Cartridge caliber conversions. AFTE J. 25 (3), 209–213.
Shaw, M.C., 2005a. Metal Cutting Principles, second ed. Oxford University Press, New York, p. 157.
Shaw, M.C., 2005b. Metal Cutting Principles, second ed. Oxford University Press, New York, p. 438.
Shaw, M.C., 2005c. Metal Cutting Principles, second ed. Oxford University Press, New York, p. 156.
Shaw, M.C., 2005d. Metal Cutting Principles, second ed. Oxford University Press, New York, pp. 445–446.
Shaw, M.C., 2005e. Metal Cutting Principles, second ed. Oxford University Press, New York, pp. 171–178.
Shaw, M.C., 2005f. Metal Cutting Principles, second ed. Oxford University Press, New York, p. 157.
Shaw, M.C., 2005g. Metal Cutting Principles, second ed. Oxford University Press, New York, p. 397.
Siddhpura, M., Paurobally, R., 2012. A review of chatter vibration research in turning. Int. J. Mach. Tools Manuf. 61, 27–47.
Skoglund, L., 2008. "A" on primers. In: On-line AFTE Forums. AFTE Message Board. Available from: <http://forum.afte.org/index.php?topic = 4903.msg26009#msg26009> (accessed 02.11.18.).

Smith, G.T., 2010. Cutting Tool Technology: Industrial Handbook. Springer, p. 88.

Sporting Arms and Ammunition Manufacturers' Institute, Inc., 2018. Cartridge and Chamber Drawings. Available from: <https://saami.org/wp-content/uploads/2018/01/Z299-3_ANSI-SAAMI_CFPandR.pdf#page = 10> (accessed 11.11.18).

State of Alaska v. Wren, 2009. No. 3AN-03-10649CR (Superior Court for the State of Alaska, Third Judicial District at Anchorage, 2009).

State of California v. Blacknell, 2012. No. 5-110816-6 (Superior Court of California for the County of Contra Costa, 2012).

State of California v. Carter, 2009. No. 157693 (Superior Court of California for the County of Alameda, 2009).

State of Ohio v. Anderson, 2009. No. CR 509503 (Court of Common Pleas, Cuyahoga County, 2009).

Stoel, R., et al., 2014. Minimizing contextual bias in forensic casework. Forensic Science and the Administration of Justice: Critical Issues and Directions. SAGE Publications, Inc, pp. 67–86.

Szabo, P., 2010. Winchester silvertip update. AFTE J. 42 (1), 81.

Tam, C., 2001. Overview of manufacturing marks on center fire cartridges. AFTE J. 33 (2), 112–115.

Tay, F., et al., 2002. Topography of the flank wear surface. J. Mater. Process. Technol. 120 (1–3), 243–248.

Taylor, F., 1907. On the Art of Cutting Metals. The American Society of Mechanical Engineers, New York, p. 148.

Thompson, E., 1988. National cartridge 'Rifled' sub-caliber adapters. AFTE J. 20 (4), 463–464.

Thompson, E., 2015. Metal injection molded breech face of a Taurus revolver. AFTE J. 47 (4), 230–231.

Turner v. State of Indiana, 2011. No. 49S00-0912-CR-565 (Indiana Supreme Court, 2011).

Uhlmann, E., et al., 2016. Modelling and simulation of grinding processes with mounted points: Part I of II – Grinding tool surface characterization. Procedia CIRP 46, 599–602.

United States War Department, 1907. Brownsville Investigation. Washington, DC, pp. 35–36.

U.S. v. Alls, 2009. No. CR2-08-223(1) (District Court, Southern District of Ohio, 2009).

U.S. v. Anderson, 2010. No. 20009 CF1 20672 (Superior Court of the District of Columbia, 2010).

U.S. v. Cerna, 2010. No. CR-08-0730 WHA (Northern District Court of California, 2010).

U.S. v. Diaz, 2007. No. CR-05-0016-WHA (U.S. District Court for the Northern District of California, 2007).

U.S. v. Dore and Bennett, 2013. No. 12 Cr. 45 (RJS) (Southern District of New York, 2013).

U.S. v. Glynn, 2008. No 06 Cr. 580(JSR) (United States District Court from the Southern District of New York, 2008).

U.S. v. Green, 2005. No. 02-10301-NG (U.S. District Court of Massachusetts, 2005).

U.S. v. Jackson and Durham, 2012. No. 11-CR-411-WSD (Northern District of Georgia, 2012).

U.S. v. Love, 2011. No. 09-CR-20317-JPM (Western District Court of Tennessee, 2011).

U.S. v. Monteiro, 2006. 407 F. Supp. 2d 351 (2006).

U.S. v. Mouzone, 2009. No. WDQ-08-086 (U.S. District Court for the District of Maryland, 2009).

U.S. v. Smallwood, 2010. No. 08-CR-38-TBR (District Court, Western District of Kentucky, 2010).

U.S. v. Taylor, 2009. No. 07-CR-01244 WJ (District Court of New Mexico, 2009).

Waikar, R., Guo, Y., 2008. A comprehensive characterization of 3D surface topography induced by hard turning versus grinding. J. Mater. Process. Technol. 197 (1–3), 189–199.

Wall, J., 1997. Matching molycoated bullets. AFTE J. 29 (3), 357–358.

Wallace, E., 2000. MagSafe epoxy core bullets in .40 and .45 caliber. AFTE J. 32 (2), 168.

Wallace, E., Becker, J., 2000. New ammunition from Aguila. AFTE J. 32 (2), 167.

Warner, E., 1971. Misleading shotshells. AFTE J. 3 (13), 25.

Washington v Berg and Reed, 2010. No. 09-1-00761-6 and No. 09-1-00762-4 (Superior Court of the State of Washington in and for the County of Clark, 2010).

Welch, A., 2013. History and manufacturing process of the Jennings/Bryco/Jimenez arms pistols. AFTE J. 45 (3), 260–266.

Wright, D.C., 2003. Individuality and reproducibility of striae on plastic wad components fired from a sawed-off shotgun. AFTE J. 35 (2), 161–166.

Yborra, L., McClary, J., 2004. Tool marks on Remington 9mm Luger caliber ammunition. AFTE J. 36 (4), 308–310.
Zanger, F., et al., 2014. Surface quality after broaching with variable cutting thickness. Procedia CIRP 13, 114–119.

Further Reading

American Society of Mechanical Engineers, 2010. Surface Texture (Surface Roughness, Waviness and Lay), No. B46-2009.
Bachrach, B., 2002. Development of a 3D-Based automated firearms evidence comparison system. J. Forensic Sci. 47 (6), 1–12.
Bachrach, B., et al., 2010. A statistical validation of the individuality and repeatability of striated tool marks: screwdrivers and tongue and groove pliers. J. Forensic Sci. 55 (2), 348–357.
BIPM, IEC, IFCC, ILAC, ISO, IUPAC, IUPAP, and OIML, 2008. International Vocabulary of Metrology—Basic and General Concepts Associated Terms (VIM), JCGM 200. <http://www.bipm.org/en/publications/>.
Blunt, L., Jiang, X.Q., 2003. Advanced Techniques for the Assessment of Surface Topography. Kogan Page Science, London, England.
Bolton-King, R., et al., 2010. What are the prospects of 3D profiling systems applied to firearms and tool mark identification. AFTE J. 42 (1), 23–33.
Braga, A.A., Pierce, G.L., 2004. Linking crime guns: the impact of ballistics imaging technology on the productivity of the Boston Police Department's Ballistics Unit. J. Forensic Sci. 49 (4), 701–706.
Brinck, T.B., 2008. Comparing the performance of IBIS and bullet TRAX-3D technology using bullets fired through 10 consecutive rifled barrels. J. Forensic Sci. (53), 677–682.
Bui, S.H., Vorburger, T.V., 2007. NIST surface metrology algorithm testing system (SMATS). Precision Eng. 31, 218–225. Available from: http://pml.nist.gov/smats (Updated October 22, 2012).
Chu, W., et al., 2010. Pilot study of automated bullet signature identification based on topography measurements and correlations. J. Forensic Sci. 55 (2), 341–347.
Chu, W., et al., 2013. Validation tests for the congruent matching cells (CMC) method using cartridge cases fired with consecutively manufactured pistol slides. AFTE J. 45 (4), 361–366.
Chu, A., et al., 2014. A Computerized Database for Bullet Comparison by Consecutive Matching. National Institute of Justice, Washington, DCno. 247771. Available from: http://nij.gov/publications/Pages/publication-detail.aspx?ncjnumber=247771.
Chumbley, L.S., et al., 2010. Validation of tool mark comparisons obtained using a quantitative, statistical algorithm. J. Forensic Sci. 55 (4), 953–961.
DeGroot, P., 2011. Coherence Scanning Interferometry. Optical Measurement of Surface Topography, Chapter 9. Springer-Verlag, Berlin.
DeKinder, J., Bonfanti, M., 1999. Automated comparisons of bullet striations based on 3D topography. Forensic. Sci. Int. 101 (2), 85–93.
Duez, P., et al., 2018. Development and validation of a virtual examination tool for firearm forensics. J. Forensic. Sci. 63 (4), 1069–1084.
Gambino, C., et al., 2011. Forensic surface metrology: toolmark evidence. Scanning 33 (1–7), 272–278.
Gerules, G., et al., 2013. A survey of image processing techniques and statistics for ballistic specimens in forensic science. Sci. Justice 53 (2), 236–250.
Hamilton, D.K., Wilson, T., 1982. Three-dimensional surface measurement using the confocal scanning microscope. Appl. Phys. (27), 211–213.
Hannibal Carbide Tool Inc., 2018. Titanium Coatings TiN, TiCN, TiAlN, AlTiN. <https://www.hannibalcarbide.com/technical-support/titanium-coatings.php> (accessed 11.11.18.).
Helmli, F., 2011. Focus Variation Instruments. Optical Measurement of Surface Topography, Chapter 7. Springer-Verlag, Berlin.
International Organization for Standardization, 1996. Geometrical Product Specifications—Surface Texture: Profile Method—Metrological Characteristics of Phase Correct Filters, No. 11562.

International Organization for Standardization, 2010. Geometrical Product Specification—Surface Texture: Areal: Part 6—Classification of Methods for Measuring Surface Texture, No. 25178, p. 6.

International Organization for Standardization, 2013. Geometrical Product Specification—Surface Texture: Areal: Part 604—Nominal Characteristics of Noncontact (Coherence Scanning Interferometry) Instruments, No. 25178, p. 604.

International Organization for Standardization, 2015. Geometrical Product Specification—Surface Texture: Areal: Part 606—Nominal Characteristics of Non-Contact (Focus Variation) Instruments, No. 25178, p. 606.

International Organization for Standardization, 2018. Geometrical Product Specification —Surface Texture: Areal: Part 607—Nominal Characteristics of Non-contact (Confocal Microscopy) Instruments, No. 25178, p. 607.

Johnson, M.K., Cole, F., Raj, A., Adelson, E., 2011. Microgeometry capture using an elastomeric sensor. ACM Trans. Graph 30 (4), 8. Available from: https://doi.org/10.1145/1964921.1964941.

Lilien, R., 2016. Applied research and development of a three-dimensional topography system for firearm identification using GelSight. In: National Institute of Justice, Report No. 248639. National Institute of Justice, Washington, DC. <https://www.ncjrs.gov/pdffiles1/nij/grants/248639.pdf>.

Ma, L., et al., 2004. NIST bullet signature measurement system for RM 8240 standard bullets. J. Forensic Sci. 49 (4), 649–659.

Petraco, N., 2011. Color Atlas of Forensic Tool Mark Identification. CRC Press, Boca Raton, FL.

Petraco, N.D.K., et al., 2013. Estimates of striation pattern identification error rates by algorithmic methods. AFTE J. 45 (3), 235–244.

Ramirez v. State, 2001. 810 So.2d 836 (2001).

Roach, R., 1997. Drugfire and IBIS help Lawmen fight bad guys. Wash. Bus. J. Available from: http://www.bizjournals.com?washington/stories/1997/05/19/focus6.html?page = all.

Robertson, C., Kesselheim, A., 2016. Blinding as a Solution to Bias Strengthening Biomedical Science, Forensic Science, and Law. Elsevier, Academic Press.

Sakarya, U., et al., 2008. Three-dimensional surface reconstruction for cartridge cases using photometric stereo. Forensic Sci. Int. (175), 209–217.

Senin, N., et al., 2006. Three-dimensional surface topography acquisition and analysis for firearm identification. J. Forensic. Sci. 51 (2), 282–295.

Song, J., 2013. Proposed NIST ballistics identification system (NBIS) using 3D topography measurements on correlation cells. AFTE J. 45 (2), 184–189.

Song, J., Vorburger, T.V., 2006. Topography measurement and applications. Proc. SPIE 6280, 1T1–1T8.

Song, J., et al., 2004. SRM 2460/2461 standard bullets and cartridge cases project. J. Res. Nat. Instit. Stand. Technol. 109 (6), 533–542.

Song, J., et al., 2010. Three steps towards metrological traceability for ballistics signature measurements. Meas. Sci. Rev. 10 (1), 19–21. Available from: https://doi.org/10.2478/v10048-010-0004-8.

Song, J., et al., 2012. The national ballistics imaging comparison (NBIC) project. Forensic Sci. Int. 216, 168–182. Available from: https://doi.org/10.1016/j.forsciint.2011.09.016.

State of California v. Miller, 2012. Case No. 62-98243 (Superior Court of California for the County of Placer, 2012).

State of Florida v. Richardson, 2013. Case No. 11-1858CFA (18th Judicial Circuit for Seminole County, 2013).

State of Maryland v. Wittingham, 2009. No. 08-1682X (Circuit Court of Prince George's County, Maryland, 2009).

State of Texas v. Harper, 2014. No. 11DCR056513 (District Court of Bend County, 2014).

U.S. v. St. Gerard, 2010. No. APO AE 09107 (U.S. Army Judiciary Fifth Circuit, Germany, 2010).

Vapnik, V.N., 1998. Statistical Learning Theory. Wiley, New York.

Vorburger, T., et al., 2007. Surface Topography Analysis for a Feasibility Assessment of a National Ballistics Imaging Database. National Institute of Standards and Technology, no. 7362, Gaithersburg, MD.

Vorburger, T., et al., 2016. Topography measurements and applications in ballistic and tool mark identifications. Surf. Topogr.: Metrol. Prop. 4 (1).

Weller, T., et al., 2012. Confocal microscopy analysis of breech face marks on fired cartridge cases from 10 consecutively manufactured pistol slides. J. Forensic Sci. 57 (4), 912–917.

Weller, T., et al., 2015. Introduction and initial evaluation of a novel three-dimensional imaging and analysis system for firearm forensics. AFTE J. 47 (4), 198–208.

Zheng, X.A., 2008. Standard bullets and casings. <http://www.nist.gov/pml/div683/grp02/sbd.cfm> (updated 31.08.12.).

Zitova, B., Flusser, J., 2003. Image registration methods: a survey. Image Vision Comput. 21, 977–1000.

Index

Note: Page numbers followed by "*f*" and "*t*" refer to figures and tables, respectively.

A

"A" designation, 239
AAC. *See* Advanced Armament Corporation (AAC)
Abrasive blasting, 138–139
Abrasive grit, 139
Abrasive process, 225
Abrasive wear, 105
ACCF. *See* Areal CCF (ACCF)
Accu-Trans casting material, 232
ACP. *See* Auto Colt Pistol (ACP)
Adhesive wear, 105–106
Advanced Armament Corporation (AAC), 251–252
Advanced similarity methods
　congruent matching cells, 291–293
　feature-based methods, 294
　principal component analysis, 293–294
AFTE. *See* Association of Firearm and Tool Mark Examiners (AFTE)
AFTE Theory of Identification, 271
Aguila ammunition, 261
Aguila IQ bullet, 44–45, 46*f*, 56
　with production identifier in cavity, 58*f*
Aguila. 22 SSS cartridge, 45
AK-style rifle system, 172
Alternative shot compositions, 65–66
Aluminum, 115–116
　jackets, 39–40, 40*f*
Aluminum titanium nitride (AlTiN), 116–117
Ammunition, 21, 170–172, 189, 219, 255–256. *See also* Firearms
　Aguila, 44–45
　boattail bullet, 33, 34*f*
　browning jacketed hollow point, 46–49, 48*f*
　bullets, 25–26
　cannelures, 34–35, 35*f*
　copper-plated bullet, 29, 29*f*
　differences in, 244–245
　federal, 36–40

full metal jacket bullet, 27–28, 28*f*
gunpowders, 23–24
Hornady line of premium ammunition, 42–44
jacketed hollow point bullet, 30, 31*f*
jacketed soft point bullet, 29–30, 30*f*
lead round nose bullets, 33, 34*f*
primers, 21–23
Remington Black Belt cartridge, 41–42
semiwadcutter bullets, 31–33, 33*f*
solid copper hollow point bullet, 30–31, 32*f*
special purpose/premium, 35–36
Speer, 41
Spitzer bullet, 33
starfire bullet, 45–46, 47*f*
wadcutter bullets, 31, 32*f*
Analysis and parameters
　advanced similarity methods, 291–294
　basic similarity parameters for topography measurements, 289–291
　importance of similarity as surface property, 285–286, 287*f*
　preprocessing, 286–289
　statistical error rate estimation, 295–297
Annealing process, 58
Antimony, 240
Aperture shear, 74, 74*f*, 168–172, 171*f*
　from Beretta Storm with rotating barrel action, 173*f*
　firearm, cartridge case, 171*f*
　firearm with barrel in position prior to discharging cartridge, 170*f*
　presence and absence, 248
AR-15 barrels, 150
AR-15–style firearms, 178
Arched breech face marks, 76, 77*f*
Area-integrating, 279
Areal CCF (ACCF), 289–290
　ACCF$_{max}$, 289–290
Areal-topography, 279
ASI 52100 steel, 96

313

Associated marks, 241−242
Association of Firearm and Tool Mark Examiners (AFTE), 73, 168, 196−197, 219, 278−279
Auto ammunition in firearm, 247
Auto Colt Pistol (ACP), 37−38, 254

B

"Ball and buck" loads, 257
Ballistics identification systems in crime lab
  algorithm requirements, 303
  data exchange, 302−303
  shift from lab, 304
  standards and guidelines, 303−304
  virtual comparison microscopy, 301−302
Bandpass Gaussian filter, 286−288, 288f
Barrel condition, 199
Barrel drilling
  and reaming processes, 195
  and rifling processes, 198
Barrel fouling, 256
Barrel groove, 196−197
Barrel manufacturing
  barrel drilling and reaming, 143−144
  cast barrels, 154−155, 154f
  hammer forging, 148−150
  honing and lapping, 155
Barrel rifling, 129
  broach rifling, 145−148, 146f
  button rifling, 150−151
  electrochemical rifling, 152−154
  hook rifling method, 145
Barrels, 3, 151, 235
  shortened by hacksaw cut, 202, 202f
  subclass in, 227−228
    arched marks, 228f
    corresponding subclass on two different grooves of mandrel, 228f
  tilting, 12, 13f
Basic Gaussian filter, 289
Bayes' rule, 296−297
Bayesian statistics, 296−297
Belted base cartridges, 60, 61f
Berdan primer, 21, 22f
Beretta 92 series, 118
Beretta 92/96 series, 172
Beretta Storm 9 mm semiautomatic pistol, 172
Beretta/Taurus 92 models, 12−13
Bias, 211

biased testimony, 218
confirmation, 211, 213−214
Binders, 135
Biomedical science, 211−212
Black Talon line of ammunition, 40, 41f
Blank stamping, 134
Blanking method. See Stamping method
Blowback design, 12, 172
Blown out primer, 250−251
Boattail bullet, 33, 34f
Body posture facial expressions, 216
Bolt action rifle, 16−17, 17f
Boolean algebra mathematicians, 271−272
Bottleneck
  cartridges, 59, 60f
  rifle-type cartridge cases, 58
Boxer primer, 21, 22f
Brass, 244
  cartridge cases, 58, 163−166
Break-open action, 17, 18f
Breech faces, 3, 4f, 167
  design, 120
  impression, 279−281, 281f
    of unit of SRM 2461 Cartridge Case, 285f
  marks, 74, 167, 226, 245, 245f
  subclass marks on, 225−227
Broach, 129f, 221, 229−230
  cut rifling, 228
  with damage from use, 223f
  rifling technique, 145−148, 146f
    broached barrel, 147f
Broaching, 128−129
Browning jacketed hollow point, 46−49, 48f
Bryco, 178
Buckshot, 63, 65
Built-up edge (BUE), 98−100, 99f, 108−109
Bullet(s), 1, 25−26, 160, 163, 205. See also Firearms
  comparison, 195
    alternative comparisons involving bullets, 203
    bullet exhibiting poor rifling, 199f
    bullet groove produced by barrel land, 197f
    bullet land, 197f
    conventionally rifled bullet left, polygonal rifled bullet right, 200f
    firearm, flattened bullet groove on left, pristine bullet on right, 196f
    flattened bullet jacket, 200f

good correspondence of individual
characteristics, 198f
individual characteristics resulting from
alteration, 202–203
composition, 195, 198
engraving, 9
groove width, 90–91, 91f
jackets, 198
fragment, 201
land width, 90–91, 92f
recovery method, 157
seating marks, 245–247, 246f
Bunters, 58, 130
marks, 191–192, 193f
Button rifling method, 150–151
barrel groove reamer marks in button rifled
barrel, 152f
rifling button, 150f
sideflow in rifling from button rifling, 151f

C

Cadre TopMatch 3D scanning system, 302
Caliber, 57–58, 88–89
Calibration procedures, 279
California v. Miller (2012), 271
Calipers, 160
Cannelures, 34–35, 35f
Cartridge cases, 58–59, 75, 205, 298
class characteristics, 75–77
comparison, 163
aperture shear, 168–172
breech face marks with lighting in opposite
directions, 164f
bunter marks, 191–192
chamber marks, 187
ejection port marks, 187–189
ejector, 178–183
extractor, 183–186
firing pin, 175–176
gross and fine breech face characteristics,
167f
individual characteristic comparison,
193–194, 193f
magazine marks, 189–190
primer flowback, 168
slide drag, 190–191
evidence, 205
for evidentiary purposes, 1–2
head, 3

worksheet, 206f
Cartridges
component, 213
made from different calibres, 251–254
Casework notes, 205
Cast barrels, 154–155, 154f
Casting process, 154
Cathode, 130
CBC. *See* Companhia Brasileira de Cartuchos
(CBC)
CCF. *See* Cross-correlation function (CCF)
CCF_{max}, 289–291
CCI shot cartridges, 49–50, 49f
Cellulose, 23
Centerfire
primers, 21
rifle ammunition, 59
Chamber, 3, 4f
marks, 187
on cartridge case, 188f
from reaming process, 188f
reamer, 143–144, 144f
marks, 145f
walls, 8
Chatter, 103–104, 104f
Chip
with built-up edge, 98
chipped end mill tooth, 231f
in cutting edge, 229
formation, 98
Chisel edge, 126
Chokes
shotgun, 69
types, 69
Chrome plating technique, 140–141
chrome-plated firing pin, 142f
chromed breech face, 141f
Class characteristics
of cartridge cases, 75–77
of firearm barrel, 87–92
of firing pin, 78–79
of firing pin aperture, 83–87
Clockwise twist, 90
"Close Quarters Training" frangible
ammunition, 54
Clothing, 205
CMCs. *See* Congruent matching cells (CMCs)
CNC machining. *See* Computer numerically
controlled machining (CNC machining)
Cobra Enterprises, 178

Cobray (M-11) style firearms, 80, 81f, 82f
Cobray-style semiautomatic pistol, 181f
Cognitive bias, 211
Coherence effects, 214
Coherence scanning interferometry (CSI), 279, 281, 282f
Collaborative Testing Services, 274
Commercial automated ballistics identification systems, 278
Commonwealth of Massachusetts v. Heang (2011), 270−271
Companhia Brasileira de Cartuchos (CBC), 239
Comparison microscope, 157−159
Compressed metal bullets, 53−54
Compression marks, 73
Computer numerically controlled machining (CNC machining), 115, 123, 124f, 220−221
Concentric breech face marks, 76, 77f
Confirmation bias, 211, 213−214
Confocal microscopy, 279−281, 280f
Confusion matrix, 294
Congruent matching cells (CMCs), 291−293
Contextual bias, 211−213
Continuous chip, 98
Convex primer, 250−251, 251f
Copper bullet jacket, 203
Copper plated bullets, 256, 257f
Copper plating technologies, 256
Copper-plated bullet, 29, 29f
  copper jacketed bullet bottom, 256, 257f
Correlation cells, 291−292
Cost-effective method, 131
Cotton boxes, 157−158
Counterclockwise twist, 90
Countersinking, 124−125, 126f
Court decisions, 267, 269, 276
Court testimony, 215−218
Criminal justice system, 217
Critical Defense, 42−44
Critical Defense Lite, 42−44
Cross-correlation function (CCF), 286, 289−290, 291f
Crosshatched breech face marks, 76, 77f
CSI. *See* Coherence scanning interferometry (CSI)
Cutting process, 129−130, 150−151
Cutting tool edge, 133−134
Cylinder, 3
  choke, 69

D

Data exchange, 302−303
Daubert decision, 267−268
Daubert or *Daubert*-type hearings, 268
Daubert v. Merrell Dow Pharm., Inc., (1993), 267−268
Davis firearms, 178
Davis semiautomatic pistol, 12
Decimation, 286
Decision-making process, 201
Deep-hole drilling, 143
Delayed blowback firearms, 125−126
Depriming, 241
Derringers, 18−19, 19f, 20f
  extracting cartridge, 187f
Desert Eagle. 357 Magnum and larger caliber pistols, 14
Deterring recoil method, 168−169
Dial calipers, 161f
Die casting method, 137
Die sinking EDM, 130
Diffusive wear, 106
Digital Gaussian filter, 286−288
Digital measuring device (DMD-48), 161, 162f
Digital photography, 205
Discontinuous chip, 98
Disk powder, 24, 25f
Disk scanning confocal microscopy (DSCM), 279−281
DMD-48. *See* Digital measuring device (DMD-48)
DNA analysis, 218
Documentation, 205
  cartridge case worksheet, 206f
  projectile worksheet, 208f
Double action revolver, 14−16
Double-barrel derringer-designed firearms, 184
Drilling method, 124−127, 143
  countersinking, 126f
  drill bit diagram, 127f
Driving edge, 196−197
Dropouts, 304
Drugfire, 278
DSCM. *See* Disk scanning confocal microscopy (DSCM)
Dynamic Research Technologies, 261−262

E

ECM, 153–154
EDM. *See* Electrical discharge machining (EDM)
Ejection port, 3–5
    marks, 187–189, 189*f*
Ejector, 3, 178–183, 179*f*
    AR-15 ejector, 180*f*
    Cobray-style semiautomatic pistol, 181*f*
    with concentric marks, 181*f*
    mark, 242
    mark circled, 183*f*
    mark on fired cartridge cases with concentric marks, 182*f*
Electric primer, 22–23
Electrical discharge machining (EDM), 129–131
    granular marks on bunter from, 130*f*
    grinding marks from finishing process, 131*f*
Electrical spark, 130
Electrochemical rifling process, 152–154
    barrel produced by electrochemical machining, 153*f*
Elliptical firing pin impression, 79–80, 81*f*
Endmills, 104, 115–117, 116*f*, 120, 221, 229–230
    breech face plunge cut by, 120*f*
    with chipped edge from use, 230*f*
    cutting edge of, 118*f*
    flute, 117*f*
    repeating pattern on two different workpieces to damage to, 231*f*
    with replaceable inserts, 119*f*
Error rates, 267–268, 275
    for topography measurements, 300–301
Ethics, 214–215
Evidence, 205
    bullet, 195–196
    cartridge cases, 163, 205
    firearm-related, 206–209, 214
    marking, 205–209
    shotgun-related, 203
    trace, 205
Exclusion, 285, 295, 300–301
Expanded Hydra-Shok bullet, 37, 38*f*
Expense for topography measuring systems, 305
Expert witness, 211
    bias, 211
    confirmation bias, 213–214
    contextual bias, 211–213
    ethics and court testimony, 214–215

Extractor, 5, 5*f*, 183–186, 184*f*
    break-open shotgun prior to extraction, 185*f*
    derringer extracting cartridge, 187*f*
    grooves, 58
    mark, 242
    revolver with fired cartridge case in cylinder, 186*f*

F

Face milled marks, 222*f*
Face milling, 221
Feature-based methods, 294
Federal ammunition, 36–40
Federal Black Cloud shotshell, 258, 258*f*
Federal Bureau of Investigation, 272–273
Federal Guard Dog line of ammunition, 38
Federal Nyclad bullet, 262–263, 263*f*
Federal Syntech bullet, 262–263, 263*f*
Feed ramp, 202
Feedstock, 135
Filtering, 286–288
Fingerprint, 201
    analysis, 218
Firearms, 3, 11, 147, 151, 205, 213, 247. *See also* Ammunition; Forensic firearm examination equipment
    barrels, 3, 87–92, 195, 198
        caliber, 88–89
        direction of twist, 89–90
        lands and grooves, 90
        width of lands and grooves, 90–92
    bolt action rifle, 16–17
    break-open action, 17, 18*f*
    breech face, 3
    cartridge case head, 3
    chamber, 3
    cylinder, 3
    derringers, 18–19, 19*f*, 20*f*
    ejection port, 3–5
    ejector, 3
    extractor, 5
    finishing processes of firearm parts, 138
    firearm-related evidence, 206–209, 214
    firing pin, 5
        aperture, 5, 7*f*
    gas port, 5–6
    gas-operated semiautomatic firearms, 14
    hammer, 6

Firearms (*Continued*)
  lever action, 16
  magazine, 7
  mandrel, 7
  manufacturers, 153–154
  mechanism, 168–169
  muzzle, 8
  obturation, 8
  pistol, 8
  polygonal rifling, 8
  practical impossibility, 8–9
  primer, 9, 10*f*
  production, 226
  projectile, 9
  propellant, 9
  pump action rifle, 16
  revolvers, 14–16
  rifling
    marks, 9
    twist, 10
  safety mechanism, 10
  sear, 11
  semiautomatic, 11–14
  shotguns, 20
  striker, 11
  and toolmark
    discipline, 268–269
    examiners, 271–272
    identification, 267–269, 273–274
  trigger, 11
Firearms and Toolmarks Subcommittee, 303–304
Fired bullet, 163
Fired cartridge case, 163, 182*f*, 191–192
Fired plastic shotgun wad, 64, 64*f*
Firing pin(s), 5, 123–124, 125*f*, 141, 175–176, 220–221
  aperture, 5, 7*f*, 83–87
    rectangular firing pin apertures, 85–86
    round firing pin hole, 84, 84*f*
    square firing pin aperture, 87
  bounce, 176–177, 177*f*
  class characteristics of, 78–79
  concentric marks, 176*f*
  contact as result of cycling, 177, 178*f*
  drag, 172–173
    circled, 174*f*
    comparison, 174*f*
    as result of incidental interaction, 173–175

  impression, 168
  incorporated with hammer of revolver, 6*f*
  rectangular/elliptical, 79–82
  in semiautomatic pistol, 6*f*
  subclass marks on, 222–225
Firing process, 170–173, 187, 197
Flake powder, 24, 27*f*
Flank wear, 133–134
Flash deterrents, 24
Flash hole, 21
Flat-based firing pins, 82–83, 83*f*
Flattened ball powder, 24, 25*f*
Florida v. Richardson (2013), 271
Focus variation, 282, 283*f*
  calculation of focus information, 284*f*
Force gauge, 162
Forced vibration, 111
Forensic community, 209
Forensic firearm examination, 1–2, 73, 157, 201, 215
  challenges to, 267
  class characteristics
    of cartridge cases, 75–77
    of firearm barrel, 87–92
    of firing pin, 78–79
    of firing pin aperture, 83–87
  equipment
    balance, 160
    calipers, 160
    comparison microscope, 158–159
    force gauge, 162
    linear measuring device, 160–161
    stereo microscope, 160
  flat-based firing pins, 82–83, 83*f*
  impressed toolmarks, 73
  individual characteristics, 92–93
  marks for comparison purposes, 73
  rectangular/elliptical firing pins, 79–82
  striated toolmarks, 74–75
Forensic firearm examiners, 47–49, 215
Forensic firearm identification, 95
Forensic science, 211–212, 267
Forging process, 235
Four-flute end mill, 221
Frangibility of bullet, 261, 262*f*
Frangible ammunition, 53–54, 54*f*, 261–262
Full metal jacket bullet, 27–28, 28*f*

G

G2 Research cartridge, 52–53, 52f
Gas port, 5–6, 7f
Gas-operated semiautomatic firearms, 14
"Gatekeepers", 267–268
Gaussian smoothing filter, 286–288
Gaussian weighting function, 286–288
Gel surface, 282–283
GelSight, 282–283
General acceptance, 267–268
German Luger pistol, 59
Gesellschaft für Fertigungstechnik und Maschinenbau (GFM), 148
Glaser Safety Slugs, 50–51
Glock, 129
    aperture with squared edges and rounded corners, 85, 86f
    barrels, 232
    firearms, 187–188, 246–247
    firing pin, 79–80, 80f
    semiautomatic pistols, 79–80, 217
    type firing, 249–250
Gold Dot bullet, 41, 42f
Golden Saber Bonded line, 41–42, 43f
Grains, 25–26
Graphite cathode, 131
Grinding
    of metals, 111
    process, 108–114, 117, 219
        surface ground by 36 grit grinding wheel, 110f
        thirty-six grit grinding wheel surface, 109f
    wheel, 111
        marks on mandrel groove, 220f
Grinding Technology (Mailkin), 114
Grooves, 90, 91f, 195, 209
Gross marks, 167
Guard Dog bullet, 38, 39f, 55–56
Gun barrel, 227–228
Gun drill, 126–127, 143, 144f, 227–228
Gunpowders, 9, 23–24
    natural color, 24, 28f
    rifle calibre, 24

H

Hammer, 6, 8f
Hammer forging process, 148–150, 199, 227, 235
    bullet from hammer-forged barrel, 149f
    mandrel, 148, 148f
    polygonal hammer-forged barrel, 148–149, 149f
Heatmap visualization, 303, 303f
Heavy metal free (HF), 240
Heckler & Koch MP-5 series of firearms, 13–14
Hemispherical firing pin impression, 79, 79f, 81–82, 83f
Hemispherical with concentric marks, 79
Herter's double ball shotshell, 259, 259f
Herter's multidefense shotshell, 259, 259f
HF. *See* Heavy metal free (HF)
Hi-Point 9 mm pistol, 178, 243, 243f
    C9 9 mm pistol, 177
    semiautomatic pistol, 12, 173–175
High spatial frequencies, 286
Honing process, 155
Hook rifling method, 145
Horizontal milling machine, 114–115
Hornady 12 gauge slug, 67, 68f
Hornady line of premium ammunition, 42–44, 44f, 45f
Hornady triple threat shotshell, 261, 261f
Hydra-Shok bullet, 37, 37f
Hydraulic press, 151

I

IBIS. *See* Integrated Ballistics Identification System (IBIS)
Impressed toolmarks, 73
Incidental interaction, firing pin drag as result of, 173–175
Inconclusiveness, 301
Incorrect ammunition usage, 247
Individual characteristics, 92–93, 237
Integrated Ballistics Identification System (IBIS), 278
International Vocabulary of Metrology (VIM), 298
Interoperability, 277
Investment casting process, 138
ISO ballot, 279–281

J

Jacketed hollow point bullet, 30, 31f
Jacketed soft point bullet, 29–30, 30f
Jennings centerfire semiautomatic pistols, 178
Jimenez Arms JA Nine, 227
Jimenez model JA Nine, 226

K

Kel-Tec centerfire pistol calibers, 129
Kevlar fibers, 158
Kevlar traps, 158

L

Land engraved area (LEA), 299–300
Lands, 90, 91f
Lapping process, 155
Laser scanning confocal microscopy, 279–281
Lathe, 121–124, 220–221
 CNC lathes, 124f
 firing pin, 125f
 tool bits, 123f
 tool in relation to workpiece, 122f
LCM. See Light comparison microscopy (LCM)
LEA. See Land engraved area (LEA)
Lead, 53–54
 bullets with polymer coating, 262–263
 pellets, 61
 round nose bullets, 33, 34f
Lead free (LF), 239
Leading edge, 196–197
Left twist. See Counterclockwise twist
Lever action, 16
LF. See Lead free (LF)
Light comparison microscopy (LCM), 301
Likelihood ($p(D \mid H)$), 296
Line-profiling, 279
Linear measuring device, 160–161
Long Rifle (LR), 45
Lorcin 9 mm pistol, 243
Lorcin semiautomatic pistol, 12
Lost wax process. See Investment casting process
Low spatial frequencies, 286
LR. See Long Rifle (LR)
Lubricant utilization, 105
Luger cartridge, 9 mm, 88

M

70 M&P 22–15 firing pins, 224
"M" stamp on base of Barnes Magnum bullet, 56, 57f
Machining process, 95, 98, 103, 105, 137, 195
 in manufacturing of firearm parts
  abrasive blasting, 138–139
  broaching, 128–129
  chrome plating technique, 140–141
  die casting, 137
  drilling, 124–127
  EDM, 129–131
  finishing processes of firearm parts, 138
  investment casting, 138
  lathe, 121–124
  milling, 114–120
  MIM, 135–136
  parkerization, 141–142
  powdered metal process, 136–137
  reaming, 127–128
  stamping, 131–134
  tumbling, 139–140
 mechanics of, 95–96
 types, 108
Mag Safe, 51
Magazine, 7
 marks, 189–190, 190f
Magnum, 59
Mandrel, 7, 148, 148f
Manufacturer coatings, 262–264
Manufacturer identifiers on bullets, 55–56
Manufacturer primer sealant, 264–265
Manufacturing process, 163–166, 173, 234
 BUE, 98–100, 99f
 chatter, 103–104, 104f
 chip formation, 98
 grinding, 108–114
 machining methods of firearm parts, 114–129
 mechanics of machining, 95–96
 plowing, 100–101, 101f
 pressure welding, 108
 shearing, 102–103
 sideflow, 101–102, 102f
 subclass to, 232–233, 232f
  barrel mounted on rod for exterior finishing, 233f
  metal mount for further barrel processing, 233f
 surface roughness, 96–98
 tool wear, 105–107
 types of machining, 108
Marking evidence, 205–209
Marks
 for comparison purposes, 73
 from previous interaction, 243
Maryland v. Wittingham (2009), 273
Measurement accuracy and resolution, 305

Metal cutting process, 95–96
Metal injection molding (MIM), 135–136
　Hi-Point extractor, 135f
　manufacturing process, 224
　seam line on firing pin, 136f
Metal-cutting process, 145–146
Metal-injected molded breech face, 227
Microscope, 163, 213
MILI. *See* Munitions International Laboratories, Inc. (MILI)
Milling machine, 114–120
　beretta breech face with concentric marks, 119f
　concentric marks made from face milling operation, 116f
　endmill, 116f
　　breech face plunge cut by, 120f
　　cutting edge of, 118f
　　with replaceable inserts, 119f
　　flute endmills, 117f
　　Ruger AR-556 breech face, 121f
MIM. *See* Metal injection molding (MIM)
Mismeasured baseline drift, 286
Mismeasured points, 286
Mixed bin, 224
Modern comparison microscopes, 158, 159f
Modern lathes, 123
Modern machining process, 115
Modern milling machines, 229–230
Modern rimfire cartridges, 21–22
Molds, 137
Motivational bias, 211
Multiple slurry-covered wax molds, 138
Multivariate machine learning scheme, 293
Munitions International Laboratories, Inc. (MILI), 154
Muzzle, 8

N
NA. *See* Numerical aperture (NA)
National Institute of Standards and Technology (NIST), 282–283, 298
National Research Council, 271
Natural color gunpowder, 24, 28f
Necked down rimfire ammunition, 70–71
NIBIN, 305
　with IBIS optical imaging systems, 298–299, 300f
Nickel plating, 39–40, 40f

NIST. *See* National Institute of Standards and Technology (NIST)
Nitrocellulose, 23
Nominal caliber, 57–58
Non-expanding full metal jacket (Non-EFMJ), 37
Norma, 240
Numerical aperture (NA), 279–281
NYCLAD bullets, 36–37, 36f
Nylon polymer, 36–37

O
Obturation, 8
Open Forensic Metrology Consortium (OpenFMC), 302–303
Optical instruments, 278–279
Organization of Scientific Area Committees (OSAC), 303–304
Outliers, 304

P
Parabellum cartridge, 9 mm, 88
Parallel breech face marks, 76, 76f
　on fired cartridge case, 74–75, 75f
Parkerization, 141–142
Parting tool, 180
PCA. *See* Principal component analysis (PCA)
PDX1 line, 40
Peer review, 267–268, 275
Performance enhancing compounds, 24
Performing bullet comparisons, 195–197
Phoenix Arms model, 136–137
　HP25.25 ACP caliber semiautomatic pistol, 87, 87f
Photometric stereo, 282–284
　tool for measuring surface topography, 284f
Phthalates, 23–24
Physical standards for topography measurements, 298–299
Physics and Pattern Interpretation Committee, 303–304
Pierced primer, 250–251, 251f
Pistol, 8, 60
　caliber cartridge, 50
　Cobray-style semiautomatic pistol, 181f
　Davis semiautomatic pistol, 12
　German Luger pistol, 59
　Hi-Point 9 mm pistol, 178, 243, 243f
　Jennings centerfire semiautomatic pistols, 178

Pistol (*Continued*)
  Lorcin 9 mm pistol, 243
  Lorcin semiautomatic pistol, 12
  Raven semiautomatic pistol, 12
  SAR9 semiautomatic pistol, 79–80
  Semiautomatic pistol, 11–12
  Springfield XDs series semiautomatic pistols, 79–81, 82f
Plasticizers, 23–24
Plowing, 100–101, 101f, 108–109
Plunge end milling, 221
Plunge end-milled marks, 222f
Plunge milling manufacturing process, 226
.17 caliber bullet, 70–71
.17 HM2 cartridge, 70–71, 71f
.17 HMR cartridge, 70–71, 71f
.22 cartridge, 69, 70f
.22 Long Rifle (LR), 69–70, 70f, 71f, 255
.22 Magnum, 69, 71f
.22 rimfire, 70
.22 Short cartridge, 70
.25 ACP cartridge, 59
.30-06 cartridge, 59
.30-30 cartridge, 255–256, 256f
.38 Special cartridge, 59, 88, 252–253
.40 Smith & Wesson cartridge, 88
.44 Magnum, 252–253
.44 Special, 252–253
.45 ACP cartridge, 254
.45 Colt, 253–254
.45-70 caliber, 59
.250-3000 cartridge, 59
.300 AAC Blackout, 251–252, 252f
.300 Blackout cartridge, 88–89
.300 Winchester Short Magnum (WSM), 89
.357 Magnum, 88, 252–253
.357 Sig cartridge, 60
.380 Auto cartridges in 9 mm Makarov, 247, 248f
.410 gauge shotshell, 253–254
Polishing compound, 241
Polygonal hammer-forged barrel, 148–149, 149f
Polygonal rifling, 8
Ported barrels, 249, 250f
Porting, 249
Positive identification, 301
"Posterior" probability ($p(H \mid D)$), 296
Powdered metal
  bullets, 53–54
  process, 136–137
Practical impossibility, 8–9
Preexisting marks, 237–240
  on cartridge case heads, 237, 238f
Prefragmented ammunition, 52–53
Preprocessing, 286–289
Pressure welding, 108
Prestriated primer with striations continuing into firing pin mark, 237, 238f
Primer(s), 9, 10f, 21–23, 22f, 237, 244
  flowback, 168
    aperture with countersink relief, 168f
    heavy, 169f
  marked by manufacturer
    with letter "A", 239f
    with letters "HF", 240, 240f
    with letters "LF", 239–240, 240f
    with letters "NP", 240, 241f
  markings for lot identification, 239
  with striated marks, 237, 238f
Priming systems, 21
Principal component analysis (PCA), 293–294
"Prior" probability ($p(H)$), 296
Probability ($p(D)$), 296
Programmable array microscopy, 279–281
Progressive stamping, 134
Projectile, 9
Propellant, 9
Pseudoscience, 271
Pump action rifle, 16, 17f

Q

Quality control bullets (QC bullets), 298

R

Radial forgers, 148
Raven semiautomatic pistol, 12
Reamer, 143–144
Reaming process, 127–128, 128f, 144, 187, 188f
"Reasonable ballistic certainty", 272–273
"Reasonable degree of ballistic certainty", 270–271
"Reasonable degree of certainty within the ballistic field", 271–272
Recoil-operated firearm, 168–169, 172
Rectangular firing pin apertures, 85–86
Rectangular/elliptical firing pins, 79–82
Regenerative chatter, 103

Reliability, 267—270, 272—276
Reloading cartridges, 182
Reloading marks, 241—242
    caused by reloading die near mouth of cartridge, 242f
Remington 700 ETRONX, 22—23
Remington Black Belt cartridge, 41—42, 43f
"Remington" brand, 36
Replacement barrels, 249—250
Report writing, 209
Reproducibility, 161
Resharpening process, 146—147
Revolvers, 14—16
    clip, 254, 254f
    with cylinder opened and loaded with cartridges, 15f
    with empty cylinder opened, 15f
Rifles/rifling, 14, 89—90, 160—161, 195
    ammunition, 59—60
    broaches, 146, 146f
    button, 150, 150f
    calibre gunpowders, 24
    impression
        on Federal Nyclad bullet, 262—263, 263f
        on Federal Syntech bullet, 262—263, 263f
    marks, 9
    subclass in rifled barrels, 229
    twist, 10
Right twist. *See* Clockwise twist
Rimfire ammunition, 69—70
Rimfire primers, 21—22, 23f
Rod powder, 24, 24f
Round firing pin hole, 84, 84f
Ruger AR-556 breech face, 120, 121f
Rule 702 [Federal Rules of Evidence], 268

S
Sabots, 66—67
    cartridges, 255—256
Safety mechanism, 10
SAR9 semiautomatic pistol, 79—80
Scholastic integrity, 274
Scientific method, 267—268
Scoring functions, 285—286
Screw machine, 123—124, 175—176, 223—224
Sear, 11
Self-excited chatter, 111
    vibrations, 114

Semiautomatic firearm, 11—14
    gas-operated, 14
Semiautomatic pistol, 11—12
    firearm with barrel locked into position, 13f
    striker from, 11f
Semiwadcutter bullets, 31—33, 33f
Shape from shading. *See* Photometric stereo
Shearing, 102—103
Shim, 146—147
Shoe wear analysis, 201
Shot, 64—65
    cartridges, 49—50
Shotgun(s), 20, 160—161
    ammunition, 20, 61
    chokes, 69
    gauge, 61—62
    shortened barrel, 203
    shotgun-related evidence, 203
    slugs, 66—68
Shotshells, 61, 62f, 63f, 64, 65f, 66f
Sideflow, 101—102, 102f
Silencers. *See* Suppressors
Silvertip Hollow Point, 39—40, 40f
Similarity
    annotation map, 302, 302f
    importance as surface property, 285—286, 287f
    parameters for topography measurements, 289—291
Single action revolver, 14—16
Single cartridge, multiple loads in, 257—261
Single-fluted gun drill, 143—144
Single-shot break-open shotgun, 183—184
Sintered 12 ga slug with cardboard sleeve, 67, 68f
Sintered slugs, 67
Sintering, 136
Skeet choke, 69
Slide drag, 190—191, 191f
Slug, 61
Smith & Wesson M&P model
    firing pin aperture and impression, 84, 85f
    M&P 22—15 model, 222—223, 223f
Smith & Wesson NYCLAD, 262—263
Smith & Wesson Sigma polymer framed pistols, 79—80
Smooth breech face marks, 76, 78f
Solid copper bullets, 51—53, 51f
Solid copper hollow point bullet, 30—31, 32f, 53, 53f

Solid rubber slug, 67
Spacers, 63
Special purpose/premium ammunition, 35—36
Specialty ammunition by design, 49—50. *See also* Ammunition
  alternative shot compositions, 65—66
  belted base cartridges, 60, 61*f*
  caliber, 57—58
  cartridge case, 58—59
  frangible ammunition, 53—54
  Glaser Safety Slugs, 50—51
  grain full metal jacket bullet, 55*f*
  manufacturer identifiers on bullets, 55—56
  necked down rimfire ammunition, 70—71
  rifle ammunition, 59—60
  rimfire ammunition, 69—70
  shot, 64—65
    cartridges, 49—50
  shotgun
    ammunition, 61
    chokes, 69
    gauge, 61—62
    slugs, 66—68
  solid copper bullets, 51—53, 51*f*
  subsonic ammunition, 54—55
  types of chokes, 69
  wad, 62—64
  wildcat cartridges, 60—61
Specularities, 282—283
Speed, 304
Speer, 41
Spitzer bullet, 33
Spring-loaded extractor, 183—184
Springfield XDs series semiautomatic pistols, 79—81, 82*f*, 85, 86*f*
Square firing pin aperture, 87
SRM. *See* Standard Reference Material (SRM)
Stabilizers, 23—24
Stamping method, 131—134
  burred area of stamped workpiece, 134*f*
  punch and die set, 132*f*
  shear zone, 133*f*
  toolmarks imparted by die onto workpiece, 133*f*
Standard Reference Material (SRM), 282—283
  2460 standard bullet, 299*f*
  2461 cartridge case, 285*f*, 299*f*
Standards and guidelines in ballistics identification systems, 303—304

Starfire bullet, 45—46, 47*f*
State of Alaska v. Wren (2009), 269
State of California v. Blacknell (2012), 270
State of California v. Carter (2009), 270, 276
State of Ohio v. Anderson (2009), 272
Statistical error rate estimation, 295—297
  Bayesian statistics, 296—297
Steel grades, 96—97
Striated toolmarks, 74—75
Striker, 5, 11
  from semiautomatic pistol, 11*f*
Subcaliber devices, 254—255
Subclass characteristics, 219
  in barrels, 227—228
  to damage and wear, 229—232
  examples of tool use causing
    subclass marks on breech faces, 225—227
    subclass marks on firing pins, 222—225
  to manufacturing method, 232—233
  misidentification, 233—235
  in rifled barrels, 229
  to tool manufacture, 219
  to tool use, 220—221
Subclass marks
  on breech faces, 225—227
  on firing pins, 222—225
Subpoena, 215
Subsonic ammunition, 54—55
Sufficient agreement, 92
Support vector machine (SVM), 294
Suppressors, 54—55
Supreme Expansion Talon (SXT), 40, 41*f*
Surface roughness, 96—98
Surface topography, 279
  analysis and parameters, 285—297
  ballistics identification systems in crime lab, 301—304
  coherence scanning interferometry, 279, 281, 282*f*
  confocal microscopy, 279—281, 280*f*
  focus variation, 282, 283*f*
  issues and opportunities, 304—305
    expense, 305
    measurement accuracy and resolution, 305
    outliers and dropouts, 304
    speed, 304
    uncertainty, 305
  photometric stereo, 282—284

topography measurement, 279–284
    standards, traceability, and uncertainty for, 297–301
SVM. *See* Support vector machine (SVM)
Swarf, 98
SWD/Cobray/M-11 design, 180
Swiss-type machine, 79, 123–124
SXT. *See* Supreme Expansion Talon (SXT)
Syntech bullet, 38, 39f
Syntech cartridge, 38, 39f

T

"T" stamp on base of Federal Tactical bullets, 56, 57f
Taurus 92 series of firearms, 118
Taurus Judge, 253–254, 253f, 261
Taurus series, 172
Test-fired bullets/cartridge cases, 163, 190, 192, 195–196, 198, 212–214
Theory of identification, 92–93
Thermal analysis of grinding process, 112
"3rd Degree" shotshell, 258, 258f
Thunder Five, 154
Titanium aluminum nitride (TiAlN), 116–117
Titanium carbonitride (TiCN), 116–117
Titanium nitride (TiN), 116–117
Tool manufacture, subclass to, 219
    grinding wheel marks on mandrel groove, 220f
Tool wear, 105–107
    new lathe insertion, 107f
    worn lathe insertion, 107f
Toolmarks, 289–290
    analysis, 296
    examination, 279
    surface, 293, 296
    Toolmark information, 286
Topography measurement, 279–284
    chain of comparisons for, 299–300
    error rates for, 300–301
    physical standards for, 298–299
    similarity parameters for, 289–291
    uncertainty for, 300–301
Trace evidence, 205
Traceability and Quality System, 299
Traceability for topography measurements, 297–301
Traditional copper-jacketed lead bullets, 52
Trailing edge, 196–197

Tribology, 105
Trigger, 11, 162
"Trigger pull" of firearm, 162
True caliber of bullet, 57–58
Tumbling method, 139–140, 140f
Tungsten carbide, 148
    tools, 96–97
Tungsten pellets, 258
Turner v. State of Indiana (2011), 269
Twelve gauge
    cartridge loaded with sintered slug, 67, 68f
    rubber slug, 67, 68f
    saboted slug, 66, 67f
TX v. Harper (2014), 273

U

Uncertainty, 305
    for topography measurements, 300–301
Unfired cartridge case, 182f, 191–192
Unloaded subcaliber device, 254, 255f
Unmeasured points, 286
US Army v. St. Gerard (2010), 275
US District Court of District of Columbia, 273–274
US military. 45 caliber shot cartridge, 50, 50f
US Ordnance Department Ordnance Manual, 257
U.S. v. Alls (2009), 274
U.S. v. Anderson (2010), 273–274
U.S. v. Cerna (2010), 273
U.S. v. Diaz (2007), 269–271
U.S. v. Dore and Bennett (2013), 274
U.S. v. Green (2005), 269, 274–275
U.S. v. Glynn (2008), 272
U.S. v. Jackson and Durham (2012), 272–273
U.S. v. Love (2011), 274
U.S. v. McCluskey (2013), 271
U.S. v. Monteiro (2006), 268–270
U.S. v. Mouzone (2009), 272
U.S. v. Smallwood (2010), 275–276
U.S. v. Taylor (2009), 274

V

"V" impression, 239
Verbal tone (testimony), 216
Verification proces, 212
Vertical milling machine, 114–115
"Virtual certainty or practical certainty", 273

Virtual comparison microscopy (VCM), 277, 301–302
Virtual microscopy (VM), 301
Voir dire, 216

W
Wad, 61–64
Wadcutter bullets, 31, 32f
Washington v. Berg and Reed (2010), 270–271
Water, 157
Waterfowl hunting, 65
Width of lands and grooves, 90–92
Wildcat cartridges, 60–61
Winchester ammunition, 39–40
Winchester PDX1 12 gauge shotshell, 260, 260f
Winchester PDX1.410 gauge shotshell, 260, 260f
"Winchester" brand, 36
  Side shot pellets, 65, 66f

X
X3P file format, 277, 302–303

Z
Zinc, 226
  alloy, 137, 226
Zombie Max line of ammunition, 44

9780128145395